# Java Programming

## Introductory Concepts and Techniques

**Gary B. Shelly**

**Thomas J. Cashman**

**Joy L. Starks**

COURSE
TECHNOLOGY

**COURSE TECHNOLOGY**

**ONE MAIN STREET**

**CAMBRIDGE MA 02142**

Thomson Learning™

**SHELLY**
**CASHMAN**
**SERIES.**

Australia • Canada • Denmark • Japan • Mexico • New Zealand • Philippines
Puerto Rico • Singapore • South Africa • Spain • United Kingdom • United States

# Java Programming

**Introductory Concepts and Techniques**

# C O N T E N T S

## ● INTRODUCTION

### JAVA FIRST, AN INTRODUCTION TO JAVA PROGRAMMING

| | |
|---|---|
| **Objectives** | **J I.1** |
| **Introduction** | **J I.2** |
| **What Is Java?** | **J I.3** |
| History of Java | J I.3 |
| **Programming a Computer** | **J I.4** |
| **The Program Development Life Cycle** | **J I.5** |
| **Structured Programming** | **J I.6** |
| Algorithmic Thinking | J I.6 |
| **Control Structures** | **J I.8** |
| Sequence Control Structure | J I.8 |
| Selection Control Structure | J I.9 |
| Repetition Control Structure | J I.10 |
| Nesting | J I.10 |
| **The Object-Oriented Approach** | **J I.10** |
| Object-Speak | J I.12 |
| Nouns | J I.12 |
| Verbs | J I.13 |
| Adjectives | J I.14 |
| Object-Oriented Synonyms | J I.15 |
| **The Philosophy of Object-Oriented Programming (OOP)** | **J I.15** |
| **Encapsulation, Inheritance, and Polymorphism** | **J I.16** |
| Encapsulation | J I.16 |
| Inheritance | J I.16 |
| Polymorphism | J I.16 |
| **Rapid Application Development (RAD) and the Benefits of Object-Oriented Programming** | **J I.17** |
| **Summary** | **J I.18** |
| **Test Your Knowledge** | **J I.19** |
| **Apply Your Knowledge** | **J I.23** |

## ● PROJECT 1

### CREATING A JAVA PROGRAM

| | |
|---|---|
| **Objectives** | **J 1.3** |
| **Introduction** | **J 1.4** |
| **Project One — Anita's Antiques** | **J 1.5** |
| **Setting Up the Desktop** | **J 1.7** |
| Starting Notepad | J 1.7 |
| Opening the Command Prompt Window | J 1.9 |
| **Coding the Program** | **J 1.14** |
| Documentation | J 1.14 |

| | |
|---|---|
| The Access Modifier and Class Name | J 1.15 |
| Methods and the Method Header | J 1.16 |
| Code | J 1.17 |
| **Testing the Program** | **J 1.19** |
| Compiling the Source Code | J 1.19 |
| **Errors** | **J 1.22** |
| Syntax Errors | J 1.22 |
| Semantic Errors | J 1.23 |
| Run-time Errors | J 1.23 |
| Running the Program | J 1.24 |
| **Editing the Source Code and Recompiling** | **J 1.24** |
| Formatting Output Using Escape Characters | J 1.24 |
| Recompiling and Running the Program | J 1.27 |
| Printing the Source Code and Closing the Windows | J 1.28 |
| **Moving to the Web** | **J 1.30** |
| Opening Source Code Files | J 1.30 |
| Importing Packages | J 1.32 |
| Editing the Applet | J 1.34 |
| The Paint Method and DrawString Method | J 1.36 |
| Opening the MS-DOS Prompt Window and Compiling the Applet | J 1.38 |
| **HTML Host Documents** | **J 1.39** |
| HTML Tags | J 1.39 |
| Running an Applet Using Applet Viewer | J 1.41 |
| Closing the Open Applications | J 1.42 |
| **Summary** | **J 1.43** |
| **What You Should Know** | **J 1.43** |
| **Test Your Knowledge** | **J 1.44** |
| **Apply Your Knowledge** | **J 1.48** |
| **In the Lab** | **J 1.49** |
| **Cases and Places** | **J 1.52** |

## ● PROJECT 2

### MANIPULATING DATA USING METHODS

| | |
|---|---|
| **Objectives** | **J 2.3** |
| **Introduction** | **J 2.4** |
| **Project Two — Bert's Loan Kiosk** | **J 2.4** |
| **Starting a New Java Program** | **J 2.6** |
| Entering Beginning Code | J 2.7 |
| **Storing Data** | **J 2.8** |
| Java Data Types | J 2.9 |
| Variables and Identifiers | J 2.9 |
| Declaring Variables | J 2.10 |
| **Using Sample Data** | **J 2.12** |
| Writing Code with Sample Data | J 2.13 |

**Operators** — J 2.14
  Arithmetic Operators — J 2.14
  Comparison Operators — J 2.15
  Precedence — J 2.16
  Formulas — J 2.16
**Output** — J 2.18
  Using Variables in Output — J 2.19
  Using Methods in Output — J 2.19
**Saving, Compiling, and Executing** — J 2.23
  Saving the Source Code — J 2.23
  Compiling the Program — J 2.23
  Executing the Program — J 2.23
**User Input** — J 2.24
  Input from the Keyboard — J 2.25
  Streams and Constructors — J 2.25
  Instantiation and Constructors — J 2.26
  Modifying the Bert Program — J 2.27
  Data Handling — J 2.29
**Executing an Interactive Program** — J 2.35
  Saving and Compiling — J 2.35
  Running the Program — J 2.35
**Moving to the Web** — J 2.38
  Converting the Program to an Applet — J 2.38
  Label Components — J 2.41
  Text Field Components — J 2.41
  Button Components — J 2.41
  Programming Conventions — J 2.41
  The Init Method — J 2.44
  The ActionListener — J 2.46
  Saving And Compiling — J 2.50
**The HTML Host Document and Interactive Applets** — J 2.50
  Creating the Host Document — J 2.50
  Running an Interactive Applet Using Applet Viewer — J 2.51
**File Management** — J 2.53
**Project Summary** — J 2.54
**What You Should Know** — J 2.54
**Test Your Knowledge** — J 2.55
**Apply Your Knowledge** — J 2.58
**In the Lab** — J 2.61
**Cases and Places** — J 2.66

● **PROJECT 3**

**DECISION, REPETITION, AND COMPONENTS IN JAVA**

**Objectives** — J 3.3
**Introduction** — J 3.4
**Project Three — CandleLine Shipping Charges** — J 3.5
**Starting a New Java Program** — J 3.8
**User Input** — J 3.9
  Beginning Code — J 3.9
**Component Modularity** — J 3.11
  Saving, Compiling, and Executing the Program Stub — J 3.11
**Exception Handling** — J 3.12
  Try and Catch — J 3.13
**Testing Partial Programs** — J 3.18
  Testing for Exceptions — J 3.18
**The If Decision Structure** — J 3.21
  Reasonableness Check with the if Statement — J 3.24

**Creating Methods** — J 3.28
  Coding User-Defined Methods — J 3.28
  Coding the Output — J 3.32
  Testing the getCost Method — J 3.33
  The Case Structure — J 3.34
  The switch Statement — J 3.35
  Testing the switch Structure — J 3.36
**Repetition Structure** — J 3.37
  The while Statement — J 3.38
  Testing the while Structure — J 3.41
**Moving to the Web** — J 3.43
  Creating the Host Document — J 3.43
  Creating an Applet Stub — J 3.44
**Making Decisions in Applets** — J 3.46
  Constructing Check Boxes — J 3.46
  Adding Components, Color, and Focus to the Applet — J 3.49
  Decisions in the Applet — J 3.52
  Executing the Applet — J 3.53
**Project Summary** — J 3.56
**What You Should Know** — J 3.56
**Test Your Knowledge** — J 3.57
**Apply Your Knowledge** — J 3.59
**In the Lab** — J 3.61
**Cases and Places** — J 3.65

● **APPENDIX A**

**INSTALLING JAVA**

**Installling Java** — J A.1
  Downloading Java 2 SDK from the Sun Microsystems Web Site — J A.1
  Using the Java 2 SDK Documentation — J A.2
  Installing Inprise's JBuilder 3 Software — J A.2

● **APPENDIX B**

**RESERVED KEYWORDS** — J B.1

● **APPENDIX C**

**JAVA CERTIFICATION**

**What Is Certification?** — J C.1
**Why Should You Get Java Certified?** — J C.2
**How Can You Prepare for Java Certification Exams?** — J C.2
**Shelly Cashman Series Certification Web Page** — J C.3

● **APPENDIX D**

**OPTIONS AND EXCEPTIONS**

**Options and Exceptions** — J D.1
  Java Complier Options — J D.1
  Java Run-time Options — J D.2
  The java.io Exceptions — J D.2

**Index** — J I.1

# *Preface*

The Shelly Cashman Series® offers the finest textbooks in computer education. In our Java books, you will find an educationally sound and easy-to-follow pedagogy that combines a step-by-step approach with corresponding screens. An Introduction to Java Programming section at the beginning of the book emphasizes good programming practices and gives students the foundation to produce well-written applications and applets. The Other Ways and More About features offer in-depth knowledge of Java. The project openers provide a fascinating perspective on the subject covered in the project. The Shelly Cashman Series Java books will make your programming class exciting and dynamic and one that your students will remember as one of their better educational experiences.

## Objectives of This Textbook

*Java Programming: Introductory Concepts and Techniques* is intended for a one-credit course that includes a survey of Java programming. No experience with a computer is assumed, and no mathematics beyond the high school freshman level is required. The objectives of this book are:

- To teach the basic concepts and methods of object-oriented programming
- To teach the fundamentals of Java programming
- To use practical problems to illustrate application-building techniques
- To use applets for Web publishing and interactivity
- To encourage independent study and help those who are working alone in a distance education environment

When students complete the course using this textbook, they will have a firm knowledge and understanding of beginning Java and will be able to develop a wide variety of applications.

## Obtaining a Copy of Borland JBuilder 3.0 University Edition

A copy of Borland JBuilder 3.0 University Edition as well as a 60 day trial edition of the Borland JBuilder Enterprise Edition is included with this text free of charge, so your students will have their own copy of JBuilder University Edition. Bundling the textbook and software is ideal for those schools without an IDE version of Java or if you have students working at home at their own personal computers. Borland's JBuilder 3.0 University Edition does not contain all of the standard features of the Enterprise Edition, some projects in this book maybe limited depending on which version of Java you use.

## The Shelly Cashman Approach

Features of the Shelly Cashman Series Java books include:

- **Project Orientation:** Each project in the book builds a complete application using the three-step process: designing the application, writing structured code, and converting to an applet.

**Other Ways**

1. Right-click desktop, point to New, click Text Document, double-click the New Text Document icon that displays on the desktop

**More About**

**Applets**

An applet usually runs on the user's or client computer as opposed to running on the Web server. An applet is compiled, which means usually it runs faster than a script. Applets can add multimedia capability to a Web page, as well as facilitating information transfer from the client to the server.

- **Screen-by-Screen, Step-by-Step Instructions:** Each of the tasks required to complete a project is identified throughout the development of the project. Then, steps to accomplish the task are specified. The steps are accompanied by screens.

- **Thoroughly Tested Projects:** Every screen in the book is correct because it is produced by the author only after performing a step, resulting in unprecedented quality.

- **Other Ways Boxes for Reference:** When the Java environment provides a variety of ways to carry out a given task, the Other Ways boxes displayed at the end of many of the step-by-step sequences, specify the other ways to do the task completed in the steps. Thus, the steps and the Other Ways box make a comprehensive reference unit.

- **More About Features:** These marginal annotations provide background information to complement the topics covered, adding interest and depth to learning.

# Organization of This Textbook

*JavaProgramming: Introductory Concepts and Techniques* provides detailed instruction on how to use Java. The material is divided into an introductory section and three projects as follows:

**Introduction to Java Programming** This section provides an overview of Java, program development methodology, structured programming, control structures, and object-oriented programming.

**Project 1 – Creating a Java Program** Project 1 introduces students to the basic elements of Java. Students develop Anita's Antiques, the splash screen to an e-commerce Web site. The process of building the application consists of three steps: creating the interface, setting properties, and writing code. Topics include starting Note Pad; writing a simple Java output program; inserting block and line comments as documentation; compiling and executing a Java program; editing and saving source code; and converting the application to an applet.

**Project 2 – Manipulating Data Using Methods** Project 2 teaches students how to create a program that stores and retrieves data. Variables, operators, formulas and a variety of methods are used to create Bert's Loan Kiosk. Topics include entering sample data; using proper naming conventions; using constructors to add labels, text fields and buttons; adding interactive components into an applet; and identifying Java source code files and Java class files on a storage device.

**Project 3 – Decision, Repetition, and Componets in Java** Project 3 extends the basics of building applications. The CandleLine Shipping Charges application in this project consists of components and decision structures. Topics include coding structures and events; designing a program using components; writing decision structures; testing for exceptions; and using addItemListener to add components to an applet.

## Appendices

Appendix A describes how to download the Java 2 Standard Development Kit (SDK) from the Sun Microsystems Web site. Instructions for installing both the SDK and JBuilder 3.0 University Edition are also included. Appendix B provides a list of reserved keywords for Java programming. Appendix C describes all the types of certifications available for Java programmers; in addition, it also includes information on certification exams. Appendix D describes the compile and run-time options you may include at the command prompt and the java.io exceptions generated by input and output errors.

# End-of-Project Student Activities

A notable strength of the Shelly Cashman Series Java books is the extensive student activities at the end of each project. Well-structured student activities can make the difference between students merely participating in a class and students retaining the information they learn. The end-of-project activities in the Shelly Cashman Series Java books follow.

- **What You Should Know** A listing of the tasks completed within a project together with the pages where the step-by-step, screen-by-screen explanations appear. This section provides a perfect study review for students.
- **Test Your Knowledge** Four pencil-and-paper activities designed to determine the students' understanding of the material in the project. Included are true/false questions, multiple-choice questions, and two short-answer activities.

- **Apply Your Knowledge** This exercise requires students to open and manipulate a file on the Java Data Disk that accompanies the Java book. Students may obtain a copy of the Java Data Disk by following the instructions on the inside back cover of this book.
- **In the Lab** Three in-depth assignments per project require students to apply the knowledge gained in the project to solve problems on a computer.

- **Cases and Places** Six unique case studies require students to apply their knowledge to real-world situations.

# Shelly Cashman Series Teaching Tools

A comprehensive set of teaching tools accompanies this book in the form of a CD-ROM. The CD-ROM includes an electronic Instructor's Manual and teaching and testing aids. The CD-ROM (ISBN 0-7895-5967-6) is available through your Course Technology representative or by calling one of the following telephone numbers: Colleges and Universities, 1-800-648-7450; High Schools, 1-800-824-5179; and Career Colleges, 1-800-477-3692. The contents of the CD-ROM follow.

- **Instructor's Manual** The Instructor's Manual is made up of Microsoft Word files. The files include lecture notes, solutions to laboratory assignments, and a large test bank. The files allow you to modify the lecture notes or generate quizzes and exams from the test bank using your own word processor. Where appropriate, solutions to laboratory assignments are embedded as icons in the files.
- **Figures in the Book** Illustrations for most of the figures in the textbook are available. Use this ancillary to create a slide show from the illustrations for lecture or to print transparencies for use in lecture with an overhead projector.
- **Course Test Manager** Course Test Manager is a powerful testing and assessment package that enables instructors to create and print tests from the large test bank. Instructors with access to a networked computer lab (LAN) can administer, grade, and track tests online. Students also can take online practice tests, which generate customized study guides that indicate where in the textbook students can find more information for each question.
- **Lecture Success System** Lecture Success System files are for use with the application software, a personal computer, and projection device to explain and illustrate the step-by-step, screen-by-screen development of a project in the textbook without entering large amounts of data.
- **Instructor's Lab Solutions** Solutions and required files for all the In the Lab assignments at the end of each project are available.

- **Student Files** All the files that are required by the student to complete the Apply Your Knowledge exercises are included.

- **Interactive Labs** Eighteen hands-on interactive labs that take the student from ten to fifteen minutes each to step through help solidify and reinforce mouse and keyboard usage and computer concepts. Student assessment is available in each interactive lab by means of a Print button. The assessment requires students to answer questions.

# Java Data Disk

The Java Data Disk is required for some of the exercises and projects. Students can obtain a copy of the Java Data Disk by following the instructions on the inside back cover of this book. The Shelly Cashman Series Teaching Tools CD-ROM contains a copy of the files that comprise the Java Data Disk.

# Shelly Cashman Online

Shelly Cashman Online is a World Wide Web service available to instructors and students of computer education. Visit Shelly Cashman Online at www.scseries.com.

- **Series Information** Information on the Shelly Cashman Series products.

- **Teaching Resources** This area includes password-protected instructor materials.

- **Student Center** Dedicated to students learning about computers with Shelly Cashman Series textbooks and software. This area includes cool links, data that can be downloaded, and much more.

- **Community** Opportunities to discuss your course and your ideas with instructors in your field and with the Shelly Cashman Series team.

# Acknowledgments

The Shelly Cashman Series would not be the leading computer education series without the contributions of outstanding publishing professionals. First, and foremost, among them is Becky Herrington, director of production and designer. She is the heart and soul of the Shelly Cashman Series, and it is only through her leadership, dedication, and tireless efforts that superior products are made possible. Becky created and produced the award-winning Windows series of books.

Under Becky's direction, the following individuals made significant contributions to these books: Doug Cowley, production manager; Ginny Harvey, series specialist; Ken Russo, senior Web designer; Mike Bodnar, associate production manager; Mark Norton, Web designer; Meena Mohtadi, production editor; Hector Arvizu, cover design and graphic artist; Michelle French, and Christy Pardini, graphic artists; Jeanne Black and Betty Hopkins, Quark experts; Lyn Markowicz, copyeditor; Kim Kosmatka, proofreader; Cristina Haley, indexer; and Sarah Evertson of Image Quest, photo researcher.

Special thanks go to Richard Keaveny, managing editor; Lora Wade, product manager; Francis Schurgot, Web product manager, Erin Bennett, associate product manager; Marc Ouellette, associate Web product manager; Erin Runyon, editorial assistant; Rachel Lombardo, product manager; and Samantha Smith Cooper, developmental editor.

Gary B. Shelly
Thomas J. Cashman
Joy L. Starks

Java Programming

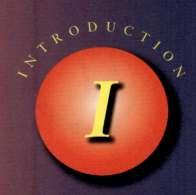

Java Programming

# Java First, an Introduction to Java Programming

You will have mastered the material in this project when you can:

**OBJECTIVES**

- Describe why Java is a good tool to learn computer programming
- Relate Java's history to the history of other programming languages
- Describe each of the steps in the program development life cycle
- Define structured programming
- Read and explain a flowchart
- Read and explain a hierarchical input process output (HIPO) chart
- Explain sequence, selection, and repetition control structures
- Describe object-oriented programming (OOP)
- Define the terms: objects, attributes, methods, and events
- Compare object-speak terminology to parts of speech
- Read, explain, and create a generalization hierarchy
- Read, explain, and create an object structure diagram
- Read, explain, and create an event diagram
- Define and explain encapsulation, inheritance, and polymorphism
- Describe rapid application development (RAD) and prototyping
- List the benefits of object-oriented programming (OOP)

Java Programming

# Java First, an Introduction to Java Programming

I N T R O D U C T I O N

**I**

Over the years, the Computer Technology Department at Central College has tried a variety of different programming languages in its Introduction to Programming Concepts course. The course attracts a wide array of students — both computer majors and minors, as well as students from other disciplines who know how vital computer skills have become. While many students have been successful in the course, instructors report that some students come to advanced courses focused on screens, graphics, and buttons of the user interface, but know little about the underlying structures of good programs.

The Computer Technology Department has asked students to enroll in a special trial section of this first programming course, taught with the Java programming language. The department hopes that the structure of Java, along with its object-oriented features and Web application, will facilitate the learning of programming constructs and help students to develop good beginning programming skills. If successful, next semester all sections of Introduction to Programming Concepts will use Java. You decide to enroll in the course.

## Introduction

Why Java? Why first?

- Beginning programmers need to learn the basic concepts of computer programming and the elementary structures that create good programs. *Java is a structured language.*
- Beginning programmers are more likely to improve when they see that their work is applicable to the real world. *Java is the language of choice for applications on the Web.*
- Beginning programmers who persevere tend to do so in direct relationship to accessibility to hardware and software. *Java is platform-independent.*
- Beginning programmers want to learn what is marketable. *Java is object-oriented.*

Java is a good general-purpose programming language. Schools, companies, and software houses are realizing that Java is extremely marketable, and that it provides the structured basis necessary to write good computer programs. Most industries that write computer programs also are coming to realize that object-oriented approaches create programs that are easier to develop, debug, and maintain. Beginning students, who are sometimes overwhelmed by the complexity of programming languages or those who become carried away with the bells and whistles of graphical user interfaces, need the structure — with the interactivity — of a language like Java to develop good programming habits.

# What Is Java?

**Java** is a computer programming language. Before a computer can start to produce desired results, it must have a step-by-step or systematic description of the task to be accomplished. A computer **program** is a set of instructions that tells a computer what to do. Java is a newcomer to the more than 2,000 programming languages and tools used to write computer programs. A **programming language** is a set of words, symbols, and codes used to create instructions a computer can understand or recognize. **High-level languages**, like Java, use commands and words instead of cryptic numeric codes or memory location addresses to process data into information. Each instruction in a high-level language corresponds to many instructions in the computer's machine language. The particular set of grammar or rules that specify how the instructions are to be written is called the **syntax** of the language.

## History of Java

Java was designed in the early 1990s by a team from Sun Microsystems lead by James Gosling. Java designers began with the basic syntax of languages like C, C++, and Smalltalk. The Java team wanted to develop a compact object-oriented language. Java first was used for information appliances such as cellular phones; however, within a few years, Sun Microsystems was using Java to provide animation and interactivity on the World Wide Web. IBM has adopted Java as its major application development language.

Web browsers have provided the opportunity to run Java **applets**, which are mini-programs that can be downloaded and executed as part of a displayed Web page. This has made Java the language of choice for applications on the Web. **JavaScript** is not the same as Java. It is a scripting tool created by Netscape and Sun to insert code statements directly into the **hypertext markup language (HTML)** of a Web page, adding functionality and improving the appearance of the Web page. Unlike a JavaScript statement, which is embedded in the HTML document, an applet is sent to the browser as a separate file alongside an HTML document. Examples of applets might include adding an interactive animation or game to a Web page.

Java is the fastest growing programming language in the world due in part to the design team's successful effort to make the language parsimonious, robust, secure, and portable. Computer professionals use the word **parsimonious** to mean that a language has a compact set of commands without numerous versions or adaptations of the same command. **Robust** means that Java supports the development of programs that do not accidentally overwrite memory and corrupt data, making Java suitable for network and distributed applications. Access to arrays of data, for example, is checked at run time to ensure that such access is within bounds. Java is a **strongly typed language**, which means that its compiler provides extensive compile-time checking for potential problems with data types — a big plus for beginning programmers. Java is **secure** because its programs are easy to protect from viruses and tampering.

**Portability** is attributed to a computer program if it can be used in an operating system other than the one in which it was created, without requiring major rework. Java is **platform-independent,** which means that it is architecturally neutral. You can use Java to write a program on any platform with any operating system, whether it is a PC, Macintosh, Unix, or mainframe machine. The Java **compiler,** which comes with Sun's Java Development Kit (JDK), converts the Java source code into computer-readable object code called **bytecode**. The same object bytecode can be run on any computer, as long as the computer has an **interpreter** to execute the Java byte-code. The interpreter for the Java programming language is called the **Java Virtual Machine (JVM)**. The JVM, which also comes with the JDK, contains the interpreter and the run-time system. The **run-time system** includes all the files and packages necessary to run Java programs. Other programming languages need system-specific interpreters and compilers.

In this text, the Java Development Kit will be used to develop **stand-alone** programs, which means that the programs can run independent of any other software. The programs will be executed by typing commands at the command prompt of the operating system, without an external user interface. Programs that run from the command line of an operating system are said to run in **console mode.** Many user interfaces and **Integrated Development Environments (IDEs)** have been developed to assist with the writing of Java programs. However, because schools and businesses may use a wide variety of different user interfaces and IDEs, running your programs in the console mode will make this text portable. It also will employ only true Java commands and classes, rather than those created by the interface. In each project, you will run your program in console mode and then you will modify the code to execute your program with the Java Applet Viewer. You also can run the modified version with a Web browser. You will learn more about Java's Web capabilities and IDEs as you progress through the projects.

Sun Microsystems released the Java 2 SDK Platform in 1999. The SDK includes the development tools such as the compiler, and the Java 2 Runtime Environment, Standard Edition, ver. 1.2. For more information on downloading the software from the Sun Microsystems Web site, see Appendix A. Inprise's J-Builder 3 University Edition, which may be included on a CD-ROM in the back of the book, also installs the Java 2 SDK.

# Programming a Computer

Most computer users do not write their own programs. Programs required for common business and personal applications such as word processing or spreadsheets can be purchased from software vendors or stores that sell computer products. These purchased programs are referred to as application software packages. **Applications** are programs that tell a computer how to accept instructions from the end user and how to produce information in response to those instructions.

Even though good application programs can be purchased inexpensively, people still need to learn programming. Learning a programming language improves logical and critical thinking skills for computer-related careers, and teaches why applications perform as they do. Large companies need industry-specific software not available in the retail market due to its limited use. Programs need constant maintenance and monitoring. Smaller companies want programs that can be adjusted and tailored to fit their needs. The software houses that produce application software always are looking for more programmers. As hardware, networking, and the Internet progress and change, people will be needed to meet the challenge of creating new applications. Programming, a combination of engineering and art, is a marketable skill.

# The Program Development Life Cycle

Programmers do not sit down and start writing code right away. Instead, they follow an organized plan, or **methodology**, that breaks the process into a series of tasks. Just as there are many programming languages, there are many application development methodologies. These different methodologies, however, tend to be variations of what is called the **program development life cycle (PDLC)**. The PDLC follows these six steps: (1) analyze the problem, (2) design the program, (3) code the program, (4) test the program, (5) formalize the solution, and (6) maintain the program. Table I-1 describes each step that a programmer goes through to arrive at a computer application. Figure I-1 portrays the PDLC as a continuing process or loop. When the maintenance phase identifies change, the cycle begins again.

| Table I-1 | Steps in the Program Development Life Cycle | |
|---|---|---|
| **STEP** | **PROCEDURE** | **DESCRIPTION** |
| 1 | Analyze the problem | Precisely define the problem to be solved, and write program specifications — descriptions of the program's inputs, processing, outputs, and user interface. |
| 2 | Design the program | Use algorithmic thinking to develop a detailed logic plan using tools such as pseudocode, flowcharts, object structure diagrams, or event diagrams to group the program's activities into modules; devise a method of solution or algorithm for each module; and test the solution algorithms. |
| 3 | Code the program | Translate the design into an application using a programming language or application development tool or IDE, by creating the user interface and writing code; including internal documentation (comments and remarks) within the code that explains the purpose of the code statements. |
| 4 | Test the program | Test the program, finding and correcting errors (debugging) until it is error-free and contains enough safeguards to ensure the desired results. |
| 5 | Formalize the solution | Review and, if necessary, revise internal documentation; formalize and complete end-user (external) documentation. Implement the solution at the user level. |
| 6 | Maintain the program | Provide education and support to end-users; correct any unanticipated errors that emerge and identify user-requested modifications (enhancements). |

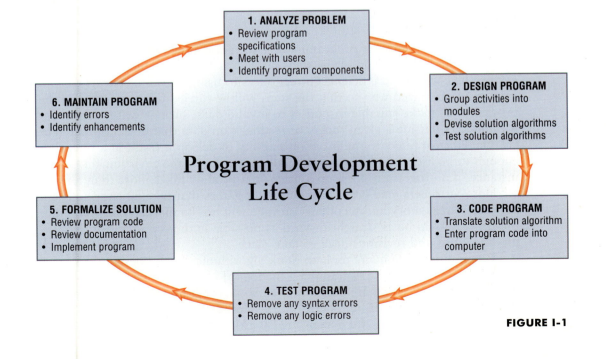

**Program Development Life Cycle**

**1. ANALYZE PROBLEM**
- Review program specifications
- Meet with users
- Identify program components

**2. DESIGN PROGRAM**
- Group activities into modules
- Devise solution algorithms
- Test solution algorithms

**3. CODE PROGRAM**
- Translate solution algorithm
- Enter program code into computer

**4. TEST PROGRAM**
- Remove any syntax errors
- Remove any logic errors

**5. FORMALIZE SOLUTION**
- Review program code
- Review documentation
- Implement program

**6. MAINTAIN PROGRAM**
- Identify errors
- Identify enhancements

**FIGURE I-1**

# Structured Programming

Java is a structured language. The concepts of a structured programming language are based on its ability to break down a large programming task into smaller, modular activities. Designing programs by following the steps of the PDLC, which is modular in nature, will lead to structured programs. Each phase of the PDLC will contain modules as well. For instance, in the design phase of the PDLC, the modular process of zooming in from the big picture to the lowest level of instruction is called top-down design. Figure I-2 illustrates a **hierarchy chart**, also called a **top-down chart** or **hierarchical input process output (HIPO) chart**. Java supports the modularity of taking the original set of program specifications and breaking it down into smaller, more manageable components, each of which is easier to solve than the original.

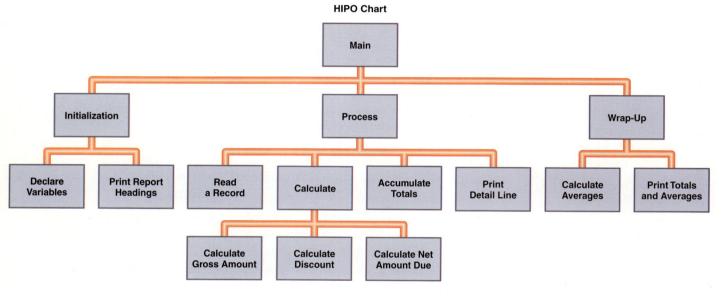

**FIGURE I-2**

## Algorithmic Thinking

The goal of computer programming is to create an **algorithm**, a clear and unambiguous specification of the steps needed to solve a problem. Algorithms also need to be correct and efficient. **Correct** refers to using logical constructs and valid data in an organized way so that the steps will be carried out correctly and the program will make suitable responses to invalid data, such as warning messages for numbers outside a given range, or feedback on data that does not match certain criteria. **Efficient** refers to the program's ability to deliver a result in a time short enough to be useful, and in a space small enough to fit the environment. For instance, if a program to look up a price on a product takes more than a few seconds, customers may be lost; or computer games that take an enormous amount of computer memory and secondary storage will not be marketable. Computer programs should be as straightforward as possible in the certain event that modifications and revisions need to take place.

Programmers use many tools to think algorithmically and design their programs correctly and efficiently. Diagramming the logical algorithm first leads to well-written programs and successful applications later. Some programmers use pseudocode to list the actions a computer should perform. **Pseudocode** (Figure I-3) expresses computer actions using keywords, and depicts logical groupings or structures using indentation.

Other programmers use a diagram or picture of the logic called a flowchart. A **flowchart** is a design tool used to graphically represent the logic in a solution algorithm. Table I-2 shows a standard set of symbols used to represent various operations in a program's logic. Figure I-10 on page J I-11 shows a complete flowchart.

When you draw a complete flowchart, you must begin with a terminal symbol connected by a flowline to the first logical step in solving the problem. Most of the time, each step in solving a problem is represented by a separate symbol. Most of the flowcharting symbols, except the decision diamond, have one entering flowline and one exiting flowline. Inside the symbol, you write words describing the logical step. Flowcharts typically do not display programming language commands. Rather, they state the concept in English, pseudocode, or mathematical notation. After the last step, you end a flowchart with a final flowline connected to another terminal symbol.

**Pseudocode**

```
MAIN MODULE:

        Call Initialization
        Call Process
        Call Output

END

PROCESS MODULE:
        Do While not End of File
                Read a record
                Call Calculate
                Call Accumulate
                Print detail line
        End Do

RETURN

CALCULATE MODULE:

        If Hours > 40 then
                Call Overtime
        Else
                Call Regular time
        End If

RETURN
```

**FIGURE I-3**

## Table I-2   Flowcharting Symbols and Their Meanings

| SYMBOL | NAME | MEANING |
|---|---|---|
|  ☐ | Process Symbol | Represents the process of executing a defined operation or group of operations that results in a change in value, form, or location of information. Also functions as the default symbol when no other symbol is available. |
|  ▱ | Input/Output (I/O) Symbol | Represents an I/O function, which makes data available for processing (input) or displaying (output) of processed information. |
| 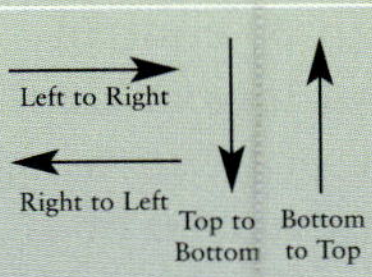 Left to Right / Right to Left / Top to Bottom / Bottom to Top | Flowline Symbol | Represents the sequence of available information and executable operations. The lines connect other symbols, and the arrowheads are mandatory only for right-to-left and bottom-to-top flow. |
| 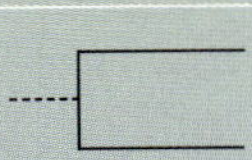 ⌐☐ | Annotation Symbol | Represents the addition of descriptive information, comments, or explanatory notes as clarification. The vertical line and the broken line may be placed on the left, as shown, or on the right. |
|  ◇ | Decision Symbol | Represents a decision that determines which of a number of alternative paths is to be followed. |
|  ▭ | Terminal Symbol | Represents the beginning, the end, or a point of interruption or delay in a program. |
| ○ | Connector Symbol | Represents any entry from, or exit to, another part of the flowchart. Also serves as an off-page connector. |
| ◫ | Predefined Process Symbol | Represents a named process consisting of one or more operations or program steps that are specified elsewhere. |

Because Java is used in designing Web pages and graphical user interfaces (GUIs), programmers may create a **storyboard** or hand-drawn sketch of how the screen will look and where the controls or objects will be placed on the screen. A storyboard also can serve as a reference for the logical names of these controls as you code your program (Figure I-4).

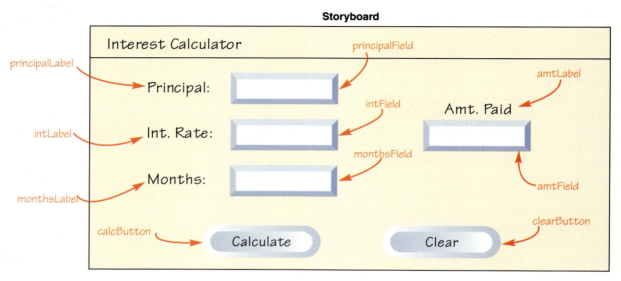

**FIGURE I-4**

Many programmers use combinations and variations of the algorithmic tools. Your instructor or supervisor may prefer one type of algorithmic tool to another, and you will probably find one or two more useful in your own programming style. As you will see later in this project, there are some additional types of diagrams to help you think logically about the objects that Java code will manipulate.

# Control Structures

No matter what **procedures,** or progression of logical actions, that you wish the computer to perform, all program logic can be broken down into one of three control structures or constructs. A **control structure** is a standard progression of logical steps to control the sequence of statement execution. The logic controls the order in which the program instructions are executed. The three basic control structures used in structured design are sequence, selection, and repetition. Each module in a program usually contains more than one control structure. Boxes, diamonds, and arrows are used to graphically depict or diagram the structures for design purposes. A rule of structures dictates that structures must demonstrate **single-entry, single-exit,** which means that a structure stays intact. You should not draw a line going into the middle of a structure; nor should you arbitrarily exit a control structure. Rather, the logic should flow into a structure at only one spot and out of the structure at only one spot.

## Sequence Control Structure

When a series of instructions is performed one after another, the logic order is called a **sequence control structure.** One action followed in order sequentially by another is executed as shown in Figure I-5. Actions can be inputs, processes, or outputs. For example, if you want the computer to retrieve a number, perform a calculation on that number, and then print the result exactly in that order, you would use a logical sequence of instructions. Flowcharting symbols representing the type of operation are used with flowlines connecting the sequential steps.

## Selection Control Structure

The **selection control structure** is used to tell the program which action to take based on a certain condition (Figure I-6). When the condition is evaluated, its result is either true or false — only these two choices are allowed. If the result of the condition is true, one action is performed; if the result is false, a different action is performed. The selection control structure is also called the **If...Then...Else structure**. For example, you decide that if a value is greater than zero, then you perform a calculation, otherwise you decide to print the value on an exception report. The computer has to evaluate the number to determine whether or not to perform the calculation. The action performed as a result of testing the condition may be a single instruction, or the action itself could be another control structure.

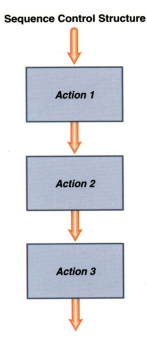

FIGURE I-5

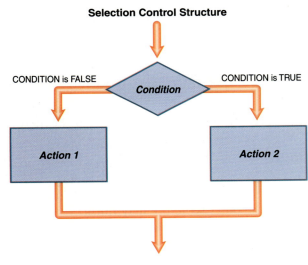

**FIGURE I-6**

The **case control structure** is a special kind of selection control structure that allows for more than two choices when the condition is evaluated (Figure I-7). For example, if a user can pick from several choices on a menu, the logic of the code behind that menu evaluates the choice. If a match is found, then the appropriate action is performed. Alternatively, if no match is found, the case control structure can provide that feedback to the user or store the result of no match for later use in the program.

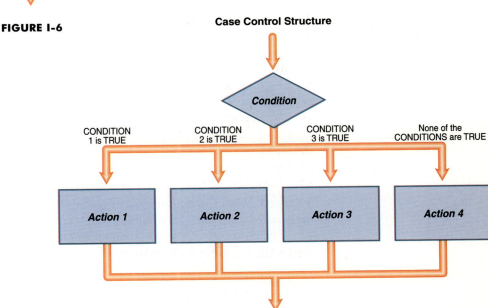

**FIGURE I-7**

## Repetition Control Structure

The **repetition control structure** is a logical way to write code that instructs the computer to perform a set of actions over and over again. This structure, sometimes called **looping** or **iteration**, is extremely useful in computer programming.

The key step of the repetition control structure is that a condition must be met to terminate the repetition. Two variations exist. The **Do...While loop** evaluates a condition and then repeats as long as a condition is true (Figure I-8). The **Do...Until loop** is similar, but it evaluates the condition at the end of the loop (Figure I-9). This means that the action(s) in the Do...Until loop always executes at least once, as opposed to the action in a Do...While loop, which may never execute if the condition is false.

A classic example of the repetition control structure involves data file processing. A condition says to continue executing commands while there are more records to process (or do the processing while the end-of-file marker is not hit). When the condition no longer is true, logic says to exit the structure (do no more processing on the data).

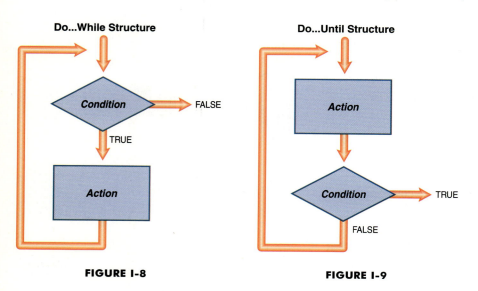

**FIGURE I-8**

**FIGURE I-9**

## Nesting

Procedures commonly contain more than one control structure. The action specified within a control structure may be a single instruction, multiple instructions, or the procedure may activate other procedures. **Nested** control structures are completely contained within other control structures. One rule of nesting logic is that a nested structure must finish before the outer structure may finish.

Figure I-10 shows a flowchart that illustrates the processing required to compute the average commission paid to a company's sales personnel and to determine the number of male and female salespeople. The flowchart contains sequence, selection, and repetition control structures. Notice that the selection control structure is nested entirely within the repetition control structure.

# The Object-Oriented Approach

Java is **object-oriented**, meaning that it packages the data and procedures together using elements called objects. Older programs that are not object-oriented are more linear in nature and must define precisely how the data will be used in each particular program. Traditionally, when the structure of the data changed, such as when a new field was added to a table in a database, the program had to be changed. With the dynamic nature of data in this information age, traditionally structured programs have limited use-time and high maintenance costs.

The concepts of **Object-Oriented Analysis and Design (OOAD)** and **Object-Oriented Programming (OOP)** represent a relatively recent methodology of application development. About 30 years ago, Dr. Kristen Nygaard of Norway and a design team had the task of using a computer to simulate boat movement through the fjords. When traditional programming became hopelessly bogged down due to the ever-changing data about speed, water displacement, fjord configuration, etc., Dr. Nygaard came up with the idea of keeping the boat (object) and the size, weight, and speed (data) packaged

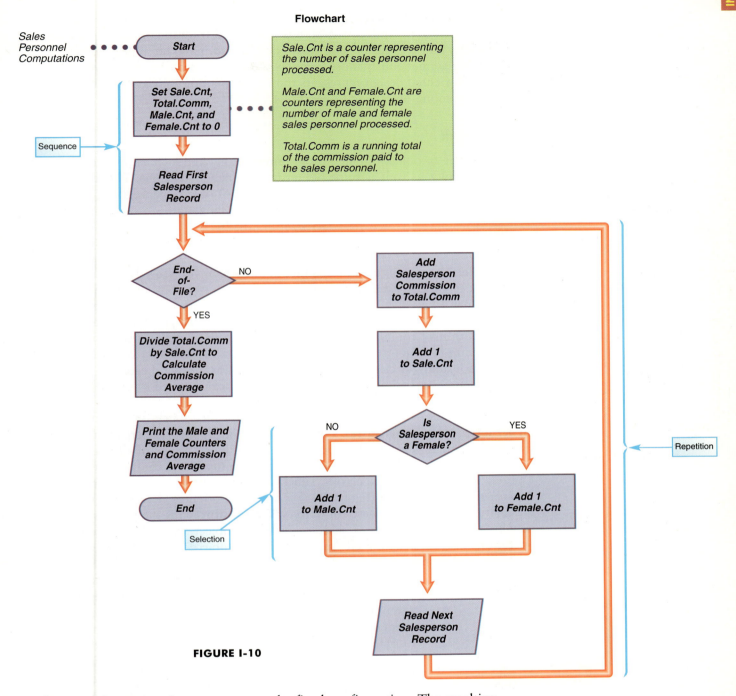

**Flowchart**

*Sales Personnel Computations*

Start

Set Sale.Cnt, Total.Comm, Male.Cnt, and Female.Cnt to 0

*Sale.Cnt is a counter representing the number of sales personnel processed.*

*Male.Cnt and Female.Cnt are counters representing the number of male and female sales personnel processed.*

*Total.Comm is a running total of the commission paid to the sales personnel.*

Sequence

Read First Salesperson Record

End-of-File?

NO → Add Salesperson Commission to Total.Comm

YES

Divide Total.Comm by Sale.Cnt to Calculate Commission Average

Add 1 to Sale.Cnt

Print the Male and Female Counters and Commission Average

Is Salesperson a Female?

NO ← / YES →

Add 1 to Male.Cnt

Add 1 to Female.Cnt

End

Selection

Repetition

Read Next Salesperson Record

**FIGURE I-10**

together to make appropriate responses to the fjord configuration. The resulting programming language, **Simula**, was the first language to use objects and methods.

OOP languages now are widely used in industry. Companies such as, General Motors, now program their assembly line cars (objects) to send messages to paint booths asking for an available slot and color (data).

However, even after 30 years, the object-oriented methodology still is not well-defined. Each book you read uses slightly different terminology. A number of Internet newsgroups exist in which the definitions, constructs, and implementations of OOP are debated hotly. Some managers still do not know how to parcel OOP modules to programmers in an efficient manner, nor do they estimate cost and time correctly. However, as the market requires these types of applications more and more, the concepts will become more stable.

Object-oriented programming has evolved as a better way to isolate logically related portions of an application than is possible in traditionally structured design. The benefit is that it is easier to develop, debug, and maintain applications that are becoming tremendously more complex than those created even a few years ago. Object-oriented design represents the logical plan of a program as a set of interactions among objects and operations.

## Object-Speak

The use of an object-oriented programming language such as Java requires some new terminology, as well as some old terms with new definitions. The following sections describe the nouns, verbs, and adjectives of object-speak, along with the grammatical rules or constructs of object-oriented languages.

## Nouns

An **object** is anything real or abstract about which you store both data and operations that manipulate the data. You can think of an object as any noun. Examples of objects are an invoice, a file or record, a computer screen used to interact with a computer program, or a check box. An object may be composed of other objects, which in turn may contain other objects. A **class** is an object or a set of objects that share a common structure and a common behavior. A class is created when objects are used repeatedly. A class also can be thought of as a general category of object types, sometimes called an implementation, which can be used to create multiple objects with the same attributes and behavior.

Each class may have one or more lower levels called **subclasses** or one or more higher levels called **superclasses**. For example, Java supports the creation of interactive toolbars in application development. A menu bar is a type of subclass of toolbar on a screen. On the other hand, the menu bar is a superclass to drop-down menus. The relationship among the classes, subclasses, and superclasses form a hierarchy. A **generalization hierarchy** (Figure I-11) is an object-oriented design tool used to show the relationships among classes of objects. **Data abstraction** is the process of creating new high-level data structures based on a defined object, through a set of interface operations instead of by directly manipulating the object. You will learn more about data abstraction in a later project.

A unique object or a specific occurrence of a class of objects is called an **instance**. Think of an instance as a proper noun. For example, options buttons are used on computer screens to allow users to choose from a list of options. Option buttons are a class of objects with the same attributes and the same method of displaying selected or not. The accompanying label, defining the purpose of the option button, has a unique value, signifying a particular instance. Specifically, an option button to set an electronic game for two players is a unique instance of the general class of option button objects. Each instance has a unique object name.

You can think of an object as a **black box** — a box that you cannot see inside. This is because an object is packaged with everything it needs to work in a computer program. The box receives and sends messages. The box also contains code and data. Users should never need to peek inside the box because the object package is self-sufficient. Programmers, however, need to know *how* the object works so they will be able to send messages to the object and use it effectively.

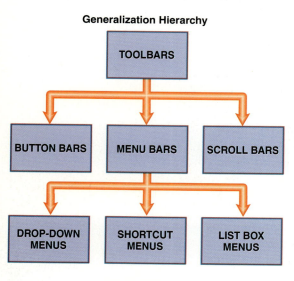

**Generalization Hierarchy**

TOOLBARS

BUTTON BARS   MENU BARS   SCROLL BARS

DROP-DOWN MENUS   SHORTCUT MENUS   LIST BOX MENUS

**FIGURE I-11**

## Verbs

An **operation,** or service, is an activity that reads or manipulates the data of an object. You can think of an operation as an active verb. Examples of operations include the standard mathematical, statistical, and logical operations as well as the input, output, and storage operations associated with computer data. A **method** is the code used to perform the operation or service.

For an object to do something, it must receive a message. The **message** defines the interaction of the object. Everything an object can do is represented by the message. The message has two parts — the name of the object to which the message is being sent, and the name of the method that will be performed. The impetus, or **trigger,** that causes the message to be sent may come from another object or an external user. The entire process of a trigger sending a message that causes an operation to occur is called an **event**. For example, if you click a button to save data, that action is the trigger. A message is sent to the disk to prepare for input. Writing the data to the disk is the operation. Saving is the event.

Programmers draw **event diagrams** to visually plan their programming of events and show relationships among events and operations. Event diagrams display the **trigger** as a shadowed button. When you draw an event diagram, you list the external trigger that causes this event to happen in the shadowed rectangle at the upper-left corner of the diagram (Figure I-12). Then you begin the next part of the diagram on an independent line, to show that the trigger is external.

On the independent line, you list the internal processing that describes the event. Many students find it helpful to describe what the computer senses at this point, or imagine themselves thinking from the CPU's point of view.

Operations are shown in rounded rectangles as results of the event. Here you should list any visual or procedural inputs and outputs. Some operations are an end to themselves. In contrast to flowcharts that must include terminal symbols, notice that these operations are dead ends because they cause no other events to occur. Other operations, however, may send additional messages or be triggers for other events. When possible, event diagrams are drawn left to right to represent what happens over time.

As shown in Figure I-12, nothing happens unless the trigger sends a message and causes the event to occur. At the conclusion of the operation, the system again will do nothing until another trigger causes an event to occur. This relationship is a key feature of OOP, and programs that are constructed in this way are said to be **event-driven.**

**Event Diagram**

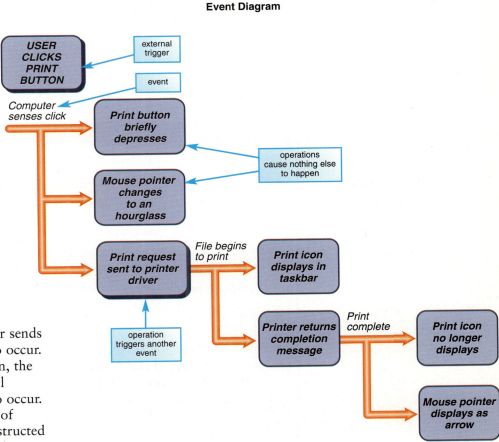

**FIGURE I-12**

## Adjectives

In object-oriented terminology, the data stored about an object is referenced by an attribute, or property. **Attributes** are identifying characteristics of individual objects such as name, size, or color. You can think of attributes as adjectives that describe an object. The attributes of a hyperlink on a Web page might include the font, the color, the font size, and the underline. Attributes should not be confused with the data itself. Color is an attribute; red is the data.

An **object structure diagram** provides a visual representation of an object, its attributes, and its methods (Figure I-13 and Figure I-14). The operations are described in terms of what they do, not how they do it.

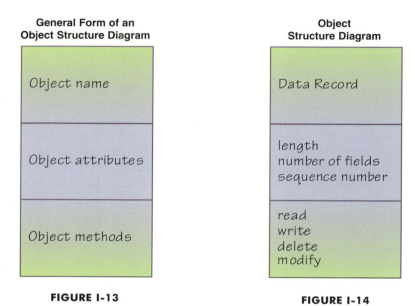

**General Form of an Object Structure Diagram**

Object name

Object attributes

Object methods

**FIGURE I-13**

**Object Structure Diagram**

Data Record

length
number of fields
sequence number

read
write
delete
modify

**FIGURE I-14**

Table I-3 lists the ten steps to object-speak in a quick reference format.

| Table I-3    Ten Steps to Object-Speak |
|---|
| 1. An **object** is the basic unit of organization, a combination of a data element and a set of procedures. |
| 2. A **method** is the code to perform a service or operation, including tasks such as performing calculations, storing values, and presenting results. |
| 3. A **class** is an object or a set of objects that share a common structure and a common behavior. A class is created when objects are used repeatedly. A specific occurrence of an object class is called an **instance**. |
| 4. A **subclass** is a lower-level category of a class with at least one unique attribute or method of its own, although it can make use of the same methods as its **superclass**. The resulting tree-like structure is called a **class hierarchy**. |
| 5. A subclass **inherits** the **attributes,** methods, and variables from its superclass. |
| 6. A **message** requests objects to perform their method. A message is comprised of the object name together with the method. |
| 7. An **event** occurs when a **trigger** causes an object to send a message. |
| 8. **Encapsulation** is the process of hiding the implementation details of an object from its user by combining attributes and methods. |
| 9. **Polymorphism** allows instructions to be given to an object in a generalized rather than specific detailed command. |
| 10. **Data abstraction** is the process of creating new high-level data structures based on a defined object. |

## Object-Oriented Synonyms

As the concepts of Object-Oriented Technology (OT), Object-Oriented Analysis and Design, and Object-Oriented Programming become more ingrained into computer curriculums and applications, the terminologies will solidify. Currently, many people use the terms class and object interchangeably. Table I-4 lists some of the synonyms used by different object-oriented philosophers, programmers, and reference books.

| Table I-4 Object-Oriented Terminology Synonyms | | |
|---|---|---|
| QT TERM | OAD TERM | OOP TERM |
| Object | Object Type | Class |
| | Object Class | Package |
| | | Module |
| Operation | Service | Method |
| Message | | Request |
| | | Event |
| Attribute | | Variable |

# The Philosophy of Object-Oriented Programming (OOP)

OOP is not just a different set of tools and methods from traditionally structured programming. It represents a different philosophy about the nature of computer programs and how they are assembled. The following case scenario about two students enrolled in the Java programming course is designed to help illustrate these differences and provide an analogy for discussing OOP constructs.

Paul Randall is a student of traditionally structured programming. He wants to create a work and study area in his room where he can write and draw and be able to store his work. He wants to sit at the work area, write, and then store his papers. Paul views the system as a set of functions — sitting, writing, and storing.

After a great deal of effort in drawing up blueprints, Paul has designed a one-piece, integrated study unit consisting of a writing surface with rolltop cover, a bench, and two drawers. By designing an integrated unit, the functions of sitting, writing, and storing will be compatible with each other and he will save on material costs and construction time. Paul travels to several lumber and hardware stores and purchases all the materials.

After considerable construction time, Paul is finished and satisfied with the result. He can work comfortably and does not need to reach too far to lift up the desktop or pull open the file drawers. Several weeks pass and Paul begins to think about making enhancements to his system. His bench is not as comfortable as he would like, his writing area feels cramped, and his two drawers are full. Paul decides to live with his system's shortcomings, however, because any change would require a substantial effort to dismantle and rebuild the entire system.

Mary Carter is a student of object-oriented programming. She would like to have a study area with the same functionality as Paul's study area. Mary, however, views the system as a set of objects — a sitting object, a writing surface object, and a storage object. Even though they are separate objects, Mary is confident she can make them interoperate with each other for an effective study area. Mary travels to a furniture factory warehouse and begins evaluating the hundreds of different chairs, desks, and file cabinets for their suitability to her needs and their compatibility with each other.

Mary returns to her room after purchasing a matching chair, two-drawer file cabinet, and rolltop desk. When the desk handle is pulled, it activates a hardware mechanism that raises the rolltop. With little effort, Mary's study area is complete.

Although Mary's furniture cost more than Paul's materials, the savings on her labor costs have more than made up for the difference. After several weeks, Mary's file cabinet is full. She returns to the furniture store, buys a three-drawer cabinet of the same style, and replaces the one in her study area.

# Encapsulation, Inheritance, and Polymorphism

Just as sequence, selection, and repetition are building constructs of logical procedural code, encapsulation, inheritance, and polymorphism are the conceptual building blocks of object-oriented design.

## Encapsulation

**Encapsulation** is the capability of an object to have data (properties) and functionality (methods) available to the user, without the user having to understand the implementation within the object. In other words, encapsulation implements data abstraction. Traditionally structured programming separates data from procedures. In the object-oriented world, an object contains functional methods as well as that method's associated data. Encapsulation is the process of hiding the implementation details of an object from its user, making those details transparent. **Transparent** refers to the ability to see through something that appears not to exist when in fact it really does. This process of making the implementation and programming details transparent to the user also is called **information hiding**. Providing access to an object only through its messages, while keeping the details private, is an example of information hiding. Users know what operations may be requested of an object, but do not know the specifics of how the operations are performed. Encapsulation allows objects to be modified without requiring the applications that use them also to be modified.

In the case scenarios, both Paul and Mary want drawers that cannot be pulled all the way out accidentally. In constructing his system, Paul had to attend to the details of how drawer stops work, which ones to use, and how to build them into the system. This is not to say that Paul understands his system better than Mary does. Mary, as an object-oriented programmer, does need to understand how her system is constructed. However, from a user's point of view, Mary did not need to concern herself with how the safety stops on her drawers work; only that they *do* work. For Mary, the safety stop functionality and behavior is encapsulated within the file cabinet object.

## Inheritance

**Inheritance** is the concept that a programmer can use a class, along with its functions and data, to create a descendent class or subclass — a capability of object-oriented programming that saves time and coding. A subclass usually differs from its superclass in at least one way, containing just the code or data necessary to explain the difference. Its status as a subclass is enough to give it access to all the superclass's functions and data. This is a very efficient way of reusing code. Also known as **subclassing**, this provides a way for programmers to define a class as an extension of another class, without copying the definition. If you let a class inherit from another class, it automatically will have all the data and methods of the parent class.

Mary's desk, chair, and cabinet all have similar wood grain, color, and style. If you think of the furniture as a superclass, then Mary's individual pieces are subclasses of that furniture line. Because they are subclasses of the same superclass, they *inherited* the same wood grain, color, and style attributes from the superclass.

## Polymorphism

**Polymorphism** allows an instruction to be given to an object using a generalized, rather than a specifically detailed, command. The same command will get different, but somewhat predictable, results depending on the object that receives the command. While the specific actions (internal to the object) are different, the results would be the same. In this way, one OOP function can replace several traditional procedures.

Paul must lift up his desktop when he wants to open it. You could say he must perform a lifting operation. To open his desk or file drawers, he must perform a pulling operation. Recall that Mary's rolltop desk has a pull handle with hardware encapsulated within the desk that translates the pull of the handle into the raising of the desktop. Mary's desk and file cabinet objects are polymorphic with respect to opening. Mary applies the same method, pulling, to open either object. She knows that the pull method will result in the object opening. As a user, how the object opens, or even that the object does open differently, is not a concern to Mary.

Many OOP languages, like Java, provide libraries, classes, and objects that already have been programmed to work in certain ways. Therefore, object-oriented programmers can employ these tools without knowing the intricacies of the programming behind them. From a programming point of view, you still need to understand how the drawer handle hardware is connected to the desk and what happens when you pull it.

# Rapid Application Development (RAD) and the Benefits of Object-Oriented Programming

**Rapid application development (RAD)** refers to the use of pre-built objects to make program development much faster. Using pre-built objects is faster because you use existing objects rather than writing everything yourself. The result is shorter development life cycles, easier maintenance, and the capability to reuse components in other projects. One of the major premises on which industry implementation of OOP is built is greater reusability of code.

Sun Microsystems uses an approach to RAD called the Java Factory. When a client company approaches Sun with a programming problem, Sun brings together Sun programmers, client programmers, and client users, for four to six weeks of intensive program development. The result is a **prototype,** or scaled-down working model, of a desired application. The client programmers return to their company understanding the classes, methods, and approach to the problem, and then are able to complete the full application in-house.

The adoption of object-orientation means that not all members of a development team need to be proficient in an object-oriented programming language such as Java. A practical and economical approach is to separate the task of creating objects from the task of assembling objects into applications. Some programmers, such as the client programmers that attend a Java Factory session, are called class providers.

**Class providers** can focus on creating classes and objects while other developers, called **class users,** leverage their knowledge of business processes to assemble applications using OOP methods and tools. An **end user** is the person who takes the Java program and executes it, either as an application or as an applet accessed over the Web. An end-user interacts with the program, and may be prompted to provide feedback or data.

Table I-5 summarizes the benefits of OOP.

| Table I-5 | The Benefits of Object-Oriented Programming |
|---|---|
| BENEFIT | EXPLANATION |
| Reusability | The classes are designed so they can be reused in many systems, or modified classes can be created using inheritance. |
| Stability | The classes are designed for repeated use and become stable over time. |
| Easier design | The designer looks at each object as a black box and is not as concerned with the detail inside. |
| Faster design | The applications can be created from existing components. |

# Summary

This introduction provided an overview of computer programming and the history of the Java programming language. The steps of the program development life cycle are essential to object-oriented programs as well as traditionally structured programs. Object-oriented programs use objects, methods, attributes, and events to package data and procedures together for rapid application development. Building block control structures, as well as the concepts of encapsulation, inheritance, and polymorphism, create reusable, stable programs that are easier and faster to design. This overview has provided a basic introduction to the concepts and technologies involved in the projects within this book. Java is a powerful and complex object-oriented programming language that is platform-independent, highly structured, and enormously marketable for applications on the Web.

# *Test Your Knowledge*

## *1* True/False

**Instructions:** Circle **T** if the statement is true or **F** is the statement is false.

T  F    1. The program development life cycle is an outline of steps used to build software applications.
T  F    2. The selection control structure also is called looping.
T  F    3. A flowchart is used to show the relationships among classes of objects.
T  F    4. In object-speak, when a trigger sends a message to an object, it is called an event.
T  F    5. Inheritance also is called information hiding.
T  F    6. Pseudocode is the object-oriented version of traditional code.
T  F    7. Event diagrams show the relationship among events and operations.
T  F    8. Do...While loops always are performed at least once.
T  F    9. A prototype is a scaled-down working model.
T  F   10. Data abstraction refers to reading data from a disk.

## *2* Multiple Choice

**Instructions:** Circle the correct response.

1. A method is another word for the code to perform a(n) _____ .
   a. service
   b. iteration
   c. event
   d. property change

2. Which of the following is a diagramming tool associated specifically with object-oriented concepts?
   a. flowchart
   b. event diagram
   c. HIPO chart
   d. pseudocode

3. A Java _____ is a mini-program that can be downloaded and executed as part of a displayed Web page.
   a. instance
   b. applet
   c. JavaScript
   d. method

4. The If...Then...Else structure is an example of _____ .
   a. sequence
   b. subclassing
   c. selection
   d. iteration

# Test Your Knowledge

5. _____ allows objects to be modified without requiring the applications that use them to be modified.
   a. Inheritance
   b. Polymorphism
   c. Encapsulation
   d. Data Abstraction

6. A(n) _____ is a unique occurrence of an object.
   a. instance
   b. attribute
   c. property
   d. event

7. Of the following, which is <u>not</u> a benefit of OOP?
   a. reusability
   b. disposability
   c. stability
   d. faster development

8. _____ refers to the use of pre-built objects to make application development faster.
   a. OOAD
   b. PDLC
   c. RAID
   d. RAD

9. Which of the following is <u>not</u> a reason to choose Java as a beginning programming language?
   a. Java is a structured language
   b. Java is used to develop applications on the Web
   c. Java is object-oriented
   d. Java is easier to learn than other programming languages

10. The compiled version of a Java program that can run on any platform is called _____ .
    a. J++
    b. JVM
    c. JDK
    d. bytecode

# Test Your Knowledge

## 3 Understanding Flowcharts

**Instructions:** A flowchart representation of part of a cardiovascular disease risk assessment is shown in Figure I-15. The higher the point total, the greater the risk. In the spaces provided, write the point total for the following persons.

1. A 33-year-old non-smoker with normal blood pressure who eats a low fat diet.

   _____

   _____

2. A 50-year-old non-smoker with high blood pressure who eats a high fat diet.

   _____

   _____

3. A 19-year-old non-smoker with high blood pressure who eats a high fat diet.

   _____

   _____

4. A 27-year-old smoker with high blood pressure who eats a low fat diet.

   _____

   _____

5. A 17-year-old non-smoker with normal blood pressure who eats a high fat diet.

   _____

   _____

6. A 43-year-old smoker with high blood pressure who eats a high fat diet.

   _____

   _____

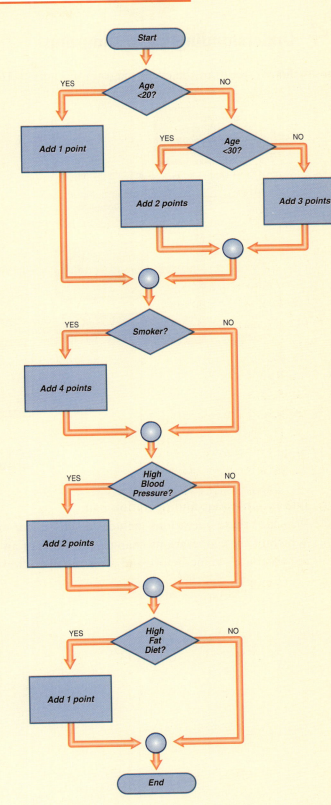

**FIGURE I-15**

# Test Your Knowledge

## 4 Understanding Event Diagrams

**Instructions:** Refer to the event diagram in Figure I-16 to answer the following questions:

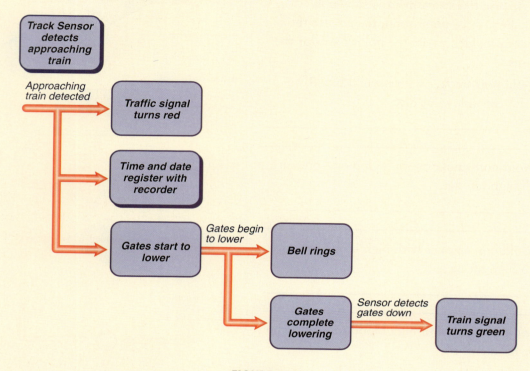

**FIGURE I-16**

1. List each message and operation pair.
2. Which of these operations includes a subsequent message? List any pairs of operations and their message.
3. Which of these operations changes the value of an attribute of an object? List the operation, attribute, and the attribute's value before and after the operation.

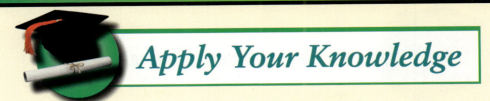

# Apply Your Knowledge

## 1 Creating a Generalization Hierarchy

**Instructions:** Pick any class of objects that interests you (for example, books, clothes, musical instruments, physical fitness equipment, etc.). Create a generalization hierarchy showing at least four levels of subclasses and superclasses. For each subclass, identify several attributes inherited from each of its superclasses.

## 2 Creating Object Structure Diagrams

**Instructions:** Draw an object structure diagram for each object in Figure I-16.

## 3 Creating an Event Diagram

**Instructions:** Using Figure I-16 as an example, draw an event diagram to raise the gates when the track sensor has detected the train is clear of the intersection. The trigger is the lack of weight on the tracks. The events that happen include the sensor detecting the loss of weight and the gates raising. Possible operations include traffic signal changing, time and date recording, and gate movement.

## 4 Thinking Algorithmically

**Instructions:** Take one of the following tasks and write a set of instructions, sufficiently complete so that another person could perform the task without asking questions. Test your solution by giving it to another class member and have him or her perform the steps. Notate selection structures with the words if, then, and else — if a step in your task is dependent upon two conditions. Notate repetition structures with the words do while, do until, or do a certain number of times.

1. light a candle
2. make a cup of tea
3. sharpen a pencil
4. walk from the classroom to the bookstore
5. logon to your school's network or intranet

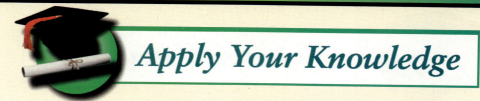

# Apply Your Knowledge

## 5 Understanding a Flowchart

**Instructions:** Using a drawing template or a drawing program on your computer system, re-create the flowchart shown in Figure I-17. Then, referring to the control structure examples and figures in the project, use colored pencils or markers to indicate the following on your flowchart. (Alternately, circle and label each structure or see your instructor about ways to turn in this assignment.)

1. Circle all selection structures in red.
2. Circle all repetition structures in green.
3. Highlight in yellow all flowlines indicating a sequential step.

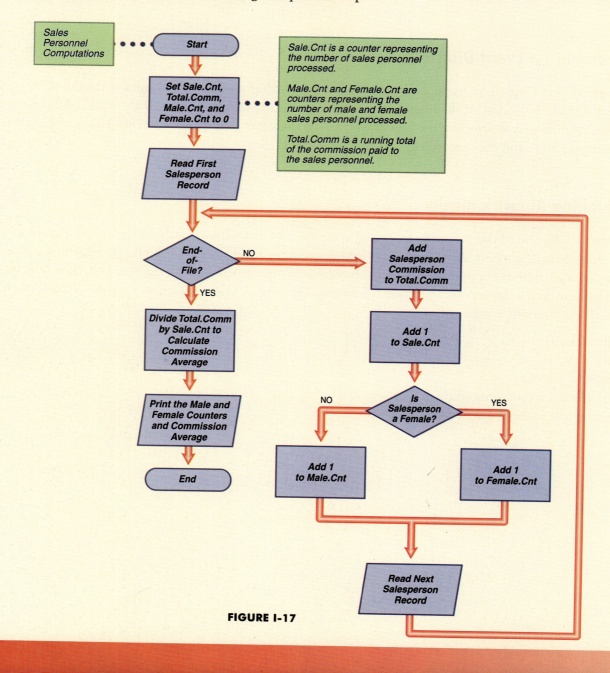

**FIGURE I-17**

**Java Programming**

Java Programming

# PROJECT

## 1

# Creating a Java Program

You will have mastered the material in this project when you can:

- Start Notepad to insert Java source code
- Open and format an MS-DOS Prompt window
- Arrange the desktop to facilitate Java program editing and compiling
- Define a Java program
- Write a simple Java output program
- Insert block and line comments as documentation
- Use proper naming conventions for classes and files
- Identify the parts of a method header
- Compile a Java program
- Execute a Java program
- Save Java source code
- Edit Java source code
- Differentiate between an application and an applet
- Create an applet from Java source code
- View an applet using Applet Viewer
- Create an HTML host document
- Use escape code sequences

**OBJECTIVES**

# The Network Is The Computer™

## Bright Days Ahead for Sun Microsystems

Imagine this job description: "Chat on the telephone, read lots of e-mail and trade rags, ride airplanes, and give speeches."

Sound like the ideal job? That is how Sun Microsystems' Scott McNealy describes his position as chairman and CEO. Despite these humble words, CBS-TV's 60 Minutes calls him "one of the most influential businessmen in America," and The New Yorker magazine says this amiable network industry leader is "one of the industry's budding celebrities."

From a meager beginning in 1982 with only four employees, McNealy has helped Sun Microsystems (www.sun.com) grow to a multi-billion dollar global entity with more than 29,000 employees in 150 countries.

McNealy graduated from Harvard University with a Bachelor of Arts degree in economics. He then earned a master's degree in business administration from Stanford, which he fondly describes as "the farm." Soon afterwards he co-founded SUN, an acronym for Stanford University Network, with Bill Joy.

Part of Sun's success is due to Java, the programming language and environment you will use throughout this book. Sun software engineers coined the name Java during a brainstorming session to "come up with a name that evoked the essence of the technology liveliness, animation, speed, inter-activity,

1982

2001

995

and more. The name is not an acronym, but rather a reminder of that hot, aromatic stuff that many programmers like to drink lots of."

The leader behind the Java technology development is James Gosling. On his home page (java.sun.com/people/jag/), he portrays himself as "do[ing] odd jobs like helping out with the system architecture and wandering around the country giving talks like why Java is the greatest thing since sliced bread."

When Java was introduced 1995, he described it as "A simple, object oriented, distributed, interpreted, robust, secure, architecture neutral, portable, high performance, multithreaded, dynamic language." Originally named Oak, Java's inception was part of Sun's Green project, which began in 1990 as part of the company's efforts to shape the "next wave" of

computing. The Java engineers disassembled and reassembled a variety of products with the goal of developing digitally controlled devices for consumers and computers that are simple to manufacture, easy to use, and communicate with each other irregardless of who built them. This platform took off when Java migrated to the World Wide Web and made Web pages come alive.

Sun's slogan, "The Network Is The Computer™," depicts the company's vision of connecting computers seamlessly in a wide variety of applications. Today more than 900,000 programmers are using this technology in a majority of the world's medium- to large-sized corporations.

For example, more than 120 Sun servers and 4.5 terabytes (trillion bytes) of storage were used to create Disney's Toy Story 2 at the Pixar Animation Studios. Sun's technology powers e-commerce systems at Egghead.com, CDNOW, and the GO Network, and it supports telecommunications giants AT&T and Ericsson Mobile Communications.

With this marketplace presence, certainly McNealy, Gosling, and the rest of the software engineers can chat on the phone and read their e-mail while enjoying a hot cup of java.

Java Programming

# Creating a Java Program

**CASE PERSPECTIVE**

Anita's Antiques is a small antique store in Albany, Missouri. The store sells antique craft creations including quilts, doilies, homemade toys, artwork, antique china, and collectibles.

Anita Louks, the owner, has asked you to help her get started with the Java programming language. She plans to set up a Web site to help sell her products. Anita recently downloaded the Java Development Kit from the Web and is ready to get started.

You both agree that creating a small program in Java to print the store's name and address on the screen will give you experience in programming and be something that the store can use in the future as it moves to e-commerce on the Web. Because you are studying the Java programming language, you volunteer to write the Java program.

# Introduction

The way in which you give instructions to a computer and receive feedback from the computer is called a **user interface**. Java's user interface may take on many forms. In its simplest state, the user interface is a command line that displays input and output on a blank screen, which is called **console mode** or **stand-alone mode**. Java programmers may view the output of applet programs using a Java tool called Applet Viewer. The **Applet Viewer**, which comes with the JDK and Java 2 platform, is like a mini-browser that can display the applet on the desktop. It loads and executes applets, but does not contain the menus and buttons that display in a full version of a browser. Recall that applets are mini-programs that may be executed as part of a displayed Web page.

In order for programmers to use Applet Viewer, or a browser to view their applets, they must create an accompanying **hypertext markup language** (**HTML**) program that directs the applet to the appropriate Java code. A growing number of third-party products, generally referred to as **Interface Development Environments** (**IDEs**), can be purchased and used to facilitate the creation of **graphical user interfaces** (**GUI**). IDEs, such as JBuilder and J++, provide programmers with a set of development tools which may include color coded editors, menus for compiling programs, and pre-written Java classes.

The first few projects in this text use the console mode and a text editor to write, compile, and execute Java programs. Even though communicating with a computer by typing at a command line may seem a tedious task in today's interactive, mouse-clicking world, typing commands is a common, easy place to start without having to purchase additional software. In this project, you will learn the basic parts of a Java program and the use of proper syntax. A programming language's **syntax** is the spelling of its commands, the order in which they are entered, and the required symbols that are a part of the language. After you analyze, design, and code the program, you will test for compile errors, and then run or execute the program. Finally, you will edit your program to make it run as an applet and create the HTML file to execute it.

In the Introduction Project, you learned that the **program development life cycle** (**PDLC**) is a good outline of steps to follow when creating a new computer program. The six steps are: (1) analyze the problem, (2) design the program, (3) code the program, (4) test the program, (5) formalize the solution, and (6) maintain the program.

# Project One — Anita's Antiques

**ANALYZING THE PROBLEM** A computer program that will display the name and address of Anita's Antiques on the screen is required as a first step in preparing an e-commerce Web site. It is a modest task, but it is a good starting point in creating a user interface. In this program, the user will read the name and address on the screen. You will use Java to create the user interface.

**DESIGNING THE PROGRAM** The structure of the program will be sequential in nature. The three lines will print one after another on the screen. Running the program from the command line of a computer, you will use code to send a message to an object — the default display device of your system (Figure 1-1a). You will add a line to display the company's e-mail address and then modify the program to run on the Web. The four lines will display in a window of their own (Figure 1-1b). The program should contain appropriate documentation and be saved for future use.

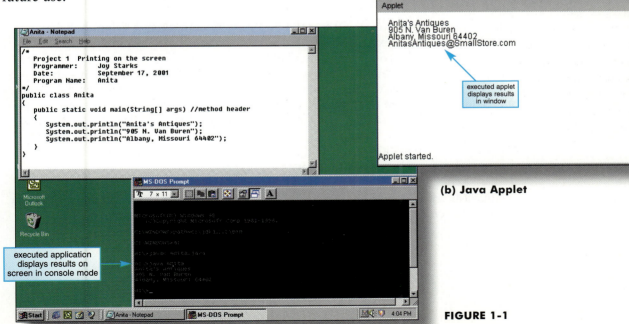

**(a) Java Application**

**(b) Java Applet**

**FIGURE 1-1**

Figure 1-2a displays a flowchart of the sequence of steps. Figure 1-2b displays an event diagram illustrating the execution of the program as a trigger to the display event.

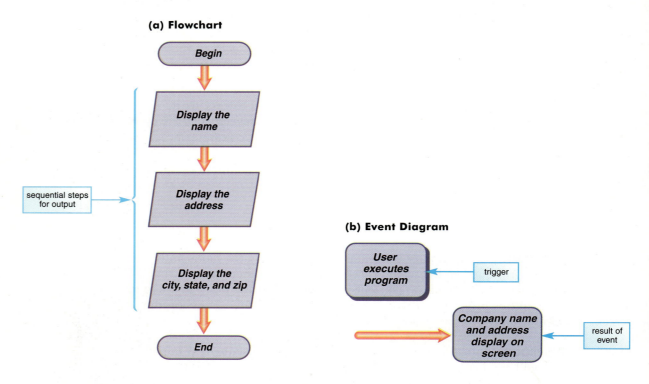

**FIGURE 1-2**

### More About

### Event Diagrams

Grady Booch, James Rumbaugh, and other noted object-oriented philosophers, have defined several kinds of event and state-event diagrams. For more information on event diagrams and philosophies, visit the Java Programming Web page (www.scsite.com/java/more.htm) and click Event Diagrams.

**CODING THE PROGRAM**   You will create Java source code using the syntax and commands of the Java programming language. This project presents a series of step-by-step instructions to write the code, explaining its parts.

**TESTING THE PROGRAM**   You will test the program by compiling it using the javac compiler and then by executing it in console mode using the Java interpreter. In the Introduction Project, you learned that compiling a Java program means using Sun's javac program to convert the Java source code into computer-readable bytecode — a necessary step in order to execute the program. The interpreter then runs the bytecode. You also will test the applet version of the program by viewing it, using Applet Viewer.

**FORMALIZING THE SOLUTION**   You will review the source code, use proper documentation, edit, recompile, and print a copy.

**MAINTAINING THE PROGRAM**   You will modify the program to move the output farther right on the screen and to include the e-mail address of the company.

# Setting Up the Desktop

Figure 1-3 shows a typical desktop with two open windows. In the upper-left portion of the screen, the Notepad application displays. You will use Notepad to edit Java source code. In the lower-right portion of the screen, the MS-DOS Prompt window displays. You will use the MS-DOS Prompt window to compile and execute your Java programs. Keeping both of these applications open on the desktop facilitates moving back and forth while editing and executing Java programs.

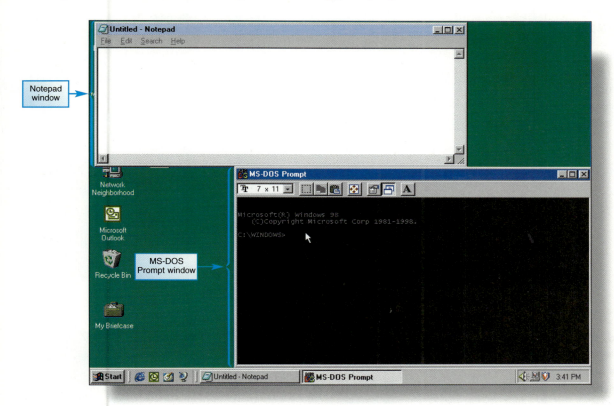

**FIGURE 1-3**

## Starting Notepad

Any text-editing program capable of creating a text file can be used to write Java programs. Text files are files without any special formatting. The examples in this book use Notepad, which is a common application on many desktop computers. You may use other programs to create text files, such as WordPad, Microsoft Works, WordPerfect, or Microsoft Word.

In order to start Notepad, Windows must be running. Perform the steps on the next page to start Notepad.

**To Start Notepad**

**1** **With the Windows desktop displayed, click the Start button on the taskbar and then point to Programs on the Start menu. Point to Accessories on the Programs submenu and then point to Notepad.**

The Programs submenu and Accessories submenu display (Figure 1-4). This desktop is Windows 98. Your system may have a different set of menus.

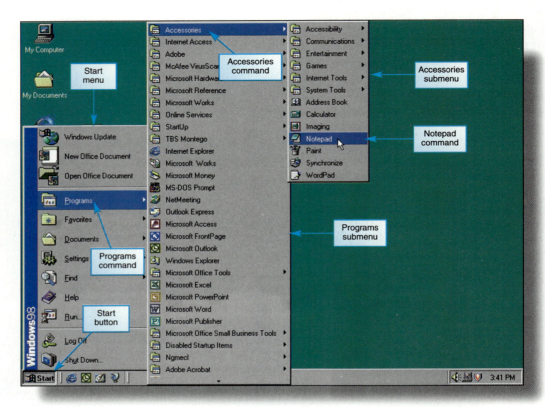

**FIGURE 1-4**

**2** **Click Notepad. When the Notepad window opens, drag the title bar to move the window to the upper-left corner of the desktop. Drag the lower-right corner to resize the window as shown in Figure 1-5.**

Notepad displays on approximately one-third of the desktop (Figure 1-5).

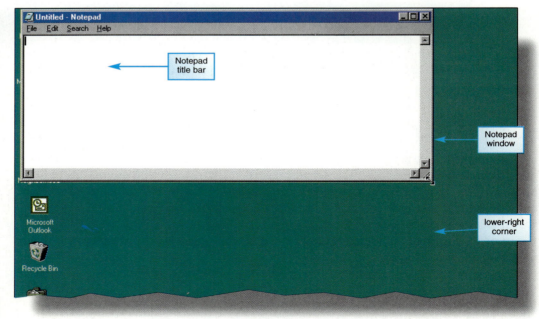

**FIGURE 1-5**

1. Right-click desktop, point to New, click Text Document, double-click the New Text Document icon that displays on the desktop

You will use this Notepad window to type and save lines of Java code that will occur during execution. Also referred to as a **list**, these lines of code will be entered and edited later in the project.

## Opening the Command Prompt Window

Accessing the command prompt allows you to **execute**, or **run**, Java programs that you have created. The **command prompt** is a way to communicate with the operating system without using any specific application. The command prompt normally displays as white text on a black screen. The Windows operating system displays the command prompt as a disk drive location, followed by a subdirectory location (if any), followed by a greater-than sign (>), and finally a flashing insertion point. You can access the command prompt by restarting the machine in its operating system mode, by temporarily exiting the Windows interface, or by opening a command prompt window on the desktop. However, opening a command prompt window on the desktop facilitates moving between editing the program and running it.

Perform the following steps to open and format the command prompt window.

### More About

### Running Java Programs

Java applications can be run using the Run command on the Start menu if your path is set automatically at start-up. Simply click the Start button, click Run, and then, in the Run dialog box, type java followed by the name of the compiled program.

## To Open and Format the Command Prompt Window

**1** **With the Notepad window still open, click the Start button on the taskbar. Point to Programs on the Start menu and then point to MS-DOS Prompt or Command Prompt for Windows NT on the Programs submenu.**

*The Programs submenu displays (Figure 1-6).*

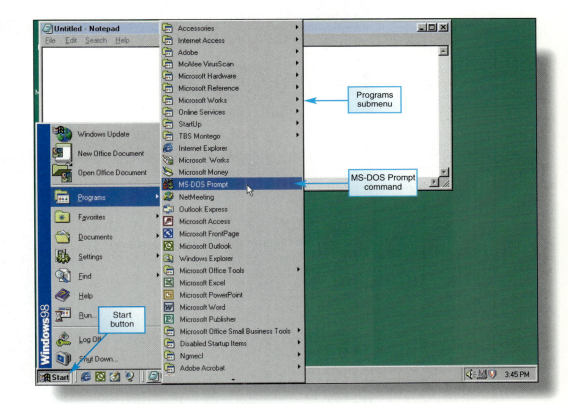

**FIGURE 1-6**

**Click MS-DOS Prompt.**

*If the MS-DOS Prompt window displays full screen, it will cover the entire desktop as shown in Figure 1-7a. Otherwise, it displays with a title bar as shown in Figure 1-7b.*

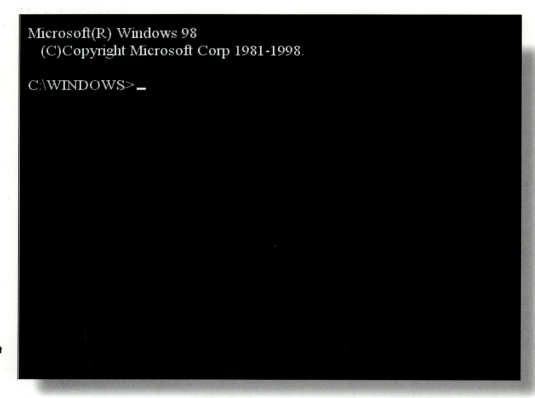

**(a) MS-DOS Prompt Window, Full Screen**

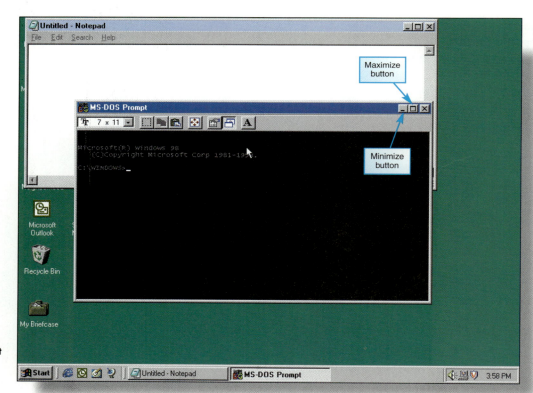

**(b) MS-DOS Prompt Window, Run On Desktop**

**FIGURE 1-7**

**3** If your system displays the MS-DOS Prompt window as a black, full screen, press and hold the ALT key while pressing the TAB key to minimize the window. Otherwise, minimize the MS-DOS Prompt window by clicking the Minimize button on the title bar. After minimizing, point to the MS-DOS Prompt button on the taskbar.

*The MS-DOS Prompt button displays on the taskbar (Figure 1-8).*

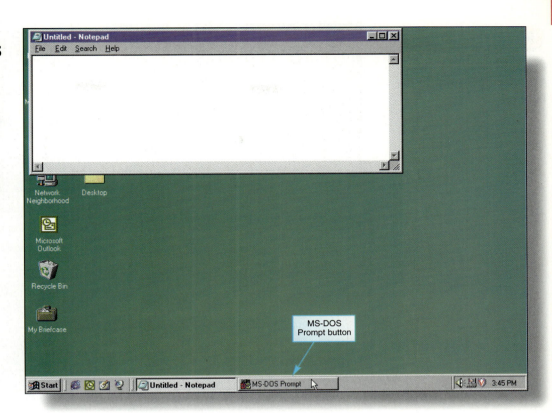

**FIGURE 1-8**

**4** Right-click the MS-DOS Prompt button and then point to Properties on the shortcut menu.

*The shortcut menu displays (Figure 1-9).*

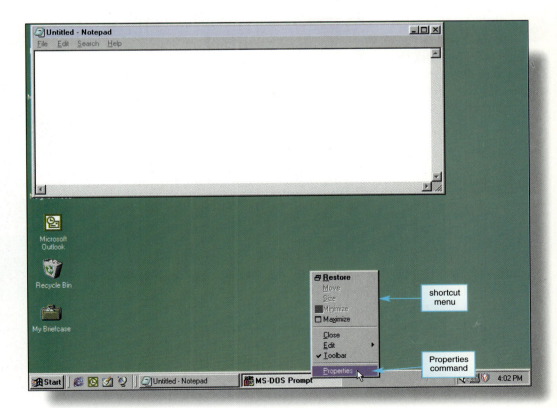

**FIGURE 1-9**

**5** **Click Properties. When the MS-DOS Prompt Properties dialog box displays, point to the Font tab.**

The MS-DOS Prompt Properties dialog box contains options to configure how the window will display (Figure 1-10). The options on your system may differ.

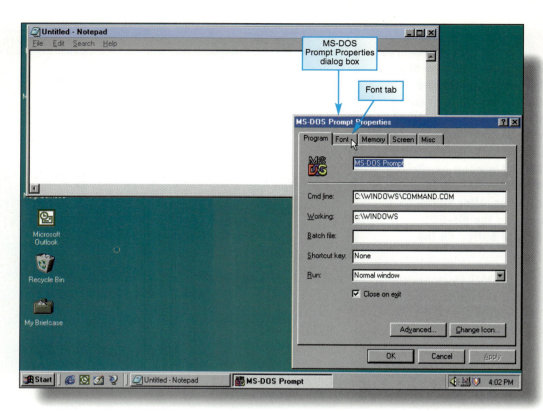

**FIGURE 1-10**

**6** **Click the Font tab. In the Font size box, scroll to and then click the 7 × 11 font size or a similar size font. Point to the Screen tab.**

The 7 × 11 font size is selected (Figure 1-11).ı

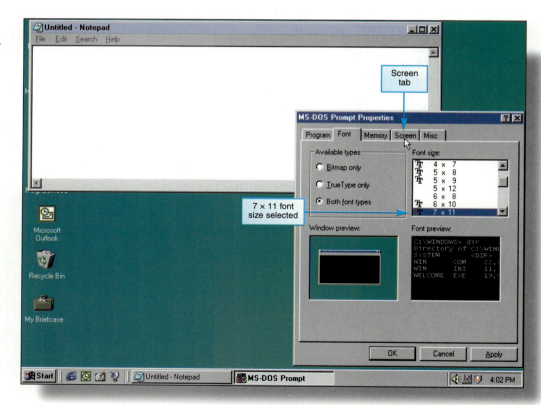

**FIGURE 1-11**

**7** Click the Screen tab. If necessary, click the Window option button in the Usage area to select it. If necessary, click the Display toolbar check box in the Window area so that it displays a check mark. All other settings should match those in Figure 1-12. Point to the OK button.

*The dialog box displays the selected options (Figure 1-12). The Window option button causes the MS-DOS Prompt window to display in a less than full screen view. The toolbar also will display. Windows NT may display these options on an Options tab.*

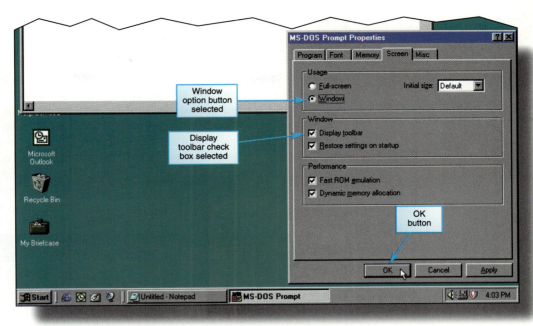

FIGURE 1-12

**8** Click the OK button. If necessary, click the MS-DOS Prompt button on the taskbar to display the MS-DOS Prompt window. When the MS-DOS Prompt window displays, drag its title bar so that the window displays in the lower-right corner of the screen as shown in Figure 1-13.

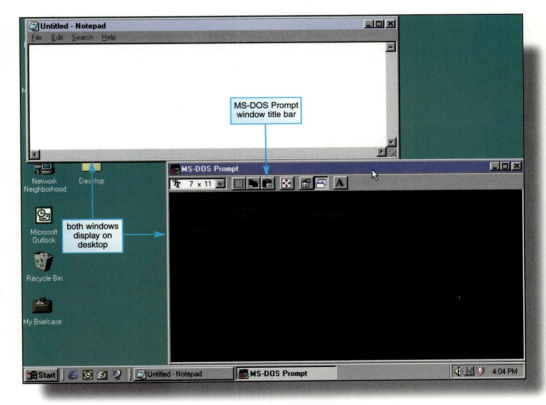

FIGURE 1-13

Java programmers set up their desktops in a variety of ways. Some like to maximize the Notepad window. Others use different text editors such as WordPad or Microsoft Word. Your instructor may suggest other ways to setup the desktop.

**Other Ways**

1. Click Start button, click Run, type `command.com`, click OK button

# Coding the Program

The third step of the PDLC is to code the program. A **program** is a set of detailed instructions to instruct the computer to perform a task. Figure 1-14 displays the lines of instructions, called **source code**, in the Java programming language to perform the given task. The task to be performed by the first program is to display the name and address of the company on the screen. Instructing the computer to save a set of instructions to perform the task, and then learning how to execute those instructions on any computer platform or the Web, is a stepping stone to creating larger, more intricate, and more useful programs. You may want to refer to Figure 1-14 as you read through the explanation of the code and commands on the following pages.

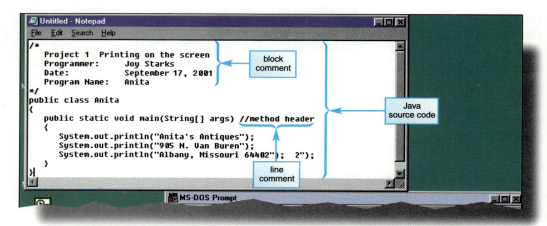

**FIGURE 1-14**

## Documentation

It is a good programming practice to include in Java programs remarks that are documentary in nature, providing comments about the program and programmer. Even though documentation sometimes is a means of formalizing the solution to a computer programming problem, including remark lines from the beginning is a good habit to form. When it is necessary to look at source code, comments placed at the beginning of the program provide an immediate description of what the program is going to do. Comments also help the programmer to think clearly about the purpose of the upcoming code.

The following lines of code are typical of documentation at the beginning of a Java program:

```
/*
    Project 1   Printing on the screen
    Programmer:    Joy Starks
    Date:          September 17, 2001
    Program Name: Anita
*/
```

These **comments** remind the programmer and other users of the purpose of the program, the name of the programmer, the date, and other pieces of important documentation. The comments are not executed when the program runs. Comment lines display in the coding itself and on printouts of the source code, but they do not cause the computer to perform any given task.

In Java, comments can take two different forms. A **block comment** begins with a forward slash followed by an asterisk (/*) and ends with the symbols reversed, an asterisk followed by a forward slash (*/). Block comments must stay together in a block; they cannot be interrupted or separated by commands or other lines of code. However, block comments can be placed before or after other lines of codes. Block comments may span as many lines as necessary within the beginning and ending marks. Typically, each line within a block comment is indented for ease in reading. Programmers may use a block comment at the beginning of a program to describe the entire program, or in the body of a program to describe the function of a specific method or routine.

A **line comment** is a comment that spans only a single line or part of a line. Sometimes called a traditional comment, a line comment commonly is used to describe the purpose of a single command and is placed at the end of the same line as that command. Line comments begin with two forward slashes (//). During execution, the two forward slashes cause the rest of that line to be ignored. Line comments have no ending symbol. A line comment is useful especially when describing the intended meaning of the current line of code, whereas the block comment generally is more useful in describing larger sections of code.

In Figure 1-14, the first six lines are a block comment. Line 9 contains a line comment describing that line.

## The Access Modifier and Class Name

After the comments, the first active line of code identifies how your code will be accessed and specifies the class name.

```
public class Anita
```

As you read in the Introduction Project, a class is an object or a set of objects that shares a common structure and a common behavior. The entire program in Java is considered a class. The keyword, public, is called an access modifier. Java code must begin with an **access modifier**, which specifies the circumstances in which the class can be accessed. In this program, public, indicates that this code can be accessed by all objects and can be extended, or used, as a basis for another class. If you omit the keyword, public, you limit the access to this class. Other access modifiers are discussed in a later project.

The access modifier is followed by the word, class, and the class name, which in this case is Anita. The **class name** or class identifier is assigned by you. It should be a user-friendly word that is not on the list of reserved words (see Appendix B). Java sets forth certain rules about class names; a class name may contain no spaces, and must not begin with a number. It is customary to begin a class name with a capital letter. Table 1-1 displays the naming rules and examples of legal class names as well as illegal names.

| Table 1-1   Java Class Naming Rules | | |
|---|---|---|
| **RULE** | *LEGAL EXAMPLES* | *ILLEGAL EXAMPLES* |
| Class names must begin with a letter (preferred because it is more user-friendly), an underscore, or a dollar sign. | Employee | 123Data |
| Class names may contain only letters (preferred), digits, underscores, or dollar signs. | Record<br>Record123 | Record#123<br>Record 123 |
| Class names may not use reserved words. Refer to Appendix B for a list of reserved words. | MyClass | Class |

When you save your file, the Java compiler expects the file name to match the same class name that you assigned at the beginning of your program. Java is **case-sensitive**, which means that if you use a class name beginning with a capital letter, you must name the file with a capital letter, too. The Java compiler considers uppercase and lowercase as two different characters. Conventionally, Java programmers use capital letters to distinguish words in the class names, such as MyAddressProgram or MarchPayroll.

Everything after the class name is considered the contents of the class and must be enclosed in **braces { }**.

### Object Oriented Terminology

For more information on instances, visit the Java Programming Web page (www.scsite.com/java/more.htm) and click OO Terminology.

```
public class Anita
{
    . . .
}
```

It does not matter if you place the first brace on the same line as the access modifier and class name or place it on the line below. Also, some Java programmers indent the braces; others do not. In any case, consistency makes for a more legible program, and each opening brace must be paired with a closing brace.

## Methods and the Method Header

The first line of code inside the class is the **method header**.

```
public static void main(String[ ] args)
```

As discussed in the Introductory Project, a method is the code to perform a service or operation, including tasks such as performing calculations, storing values, and presenting results. The **main method** is the usual starting point for all stand-alone Java applications.

In the above line of code, the word, public, is the access modifier. It declares or establishes the method as accessible to all classes. The word, static, is a method modifier. **Method modifiers** enable you to set properties for the method, such as where it will be visible and how subclasses of the current class will interact with the method. Static, as a modifier, means that this method is for a class, not an instance. An **instance** is a unique object or a specific occurrence of a class of objects or a method.

After the modifiers, a typical method has three parts: the return value, the method name, and the arguments list. In the program for this project, the method is written as follows:

```
void main(String[ ] args)
```

Void means that this method does not return a value when it is called. Methods can result in an **answer**, similar to the return value of a function in a spreadsheet application; or they can return nothing — as is the case in this method. The name of the method, main, comes next followed by parentheses. Inside the parentheses is any number of arguments. An **argument** is a piece of data, or a data location, sent along with the method to help it perform its operation. For example, a method to calculate sales tax would need to know the amount of the sale and the tax rate in order to return an answer. The sales amount and the tax rate would be arguments. In this example, args is an identifier for any string or character argument that the method, main, may need. An **identifier** is like a variable storage location to hold information.

Naming it args is traditional, but you can give it other names. The word, String, refers to a **data type**, or the type of data you expect the identifier to be. In this case, it must be capitalized.

Programmers and language documentation would say Java's main method accepts a String argument identified as args, and returns void.

## Code

You must enclose the lines of code, or **body**, of the method in pairs of braces just as you did with the class. The body of the method usually is indented to facilitate reading and editing. These lines of code in braces, following the main method header, actually perform the tasks.

```
{
    System.out.println("Anita's Antiques");
    System.out.println("905 N. Van Buren");
    System.out.println("Albany, Missouri 64402");
}
```

Classes, objects, methods, and arguments are used in this code. System is the name of the class. Out is the object that represents the default display, which is the monitor. Println is the name of a method that takes a string argument. Println returns its value to the System.out device. The method's argument, in this case, is a string of characters enclosed in quotation marks. The string of characters is called a **literal**, which means the data inside the quotes literally will display on the monitor.

These lines of code in Java must end with a semicolon (;). During execution, these command lines tell the default output device, the monitor, to print the literal text on the screen. Figure 1-14 on page J 1.14 displays the entire source code.

After entering the code, you will save the program. To prevent Notepad from assigning its standard .txt extension during the save process, you will enclose the file name in quotation marks.

Perform the following steps to enter the Java source code and save it on a floppy disk.

### More About

### System.out

The out object can accept methods related to things other than printing text. Methods such as writing data to a stream of characters, flushing data from that stream and checking for errors, and closing the stream each have their own method name and arguments.

### More About

### Displaying Blank Lines

If you want to display a blank line as part of your screen output, enter the Java statement, `System.out.println("")`, at the appropriate location in your code. The null string, "" will display nothing on the screen, but println will force a carriage return and line feed creating the blank line.

 ## To Enter and Save Java Source Code

 **Click the Notepad window.**

The insertion point displays in the Notepad window (Figure 1-15).

**FIGURE 1-15**

2 **Type the code as shown in Figure 1-16. Be sure to indent as shown using either the SPACEBAR key or the TAB key, and remember that Java is case-sensitive.**

The Notepad window displays the Java source code (Figure 1-16).

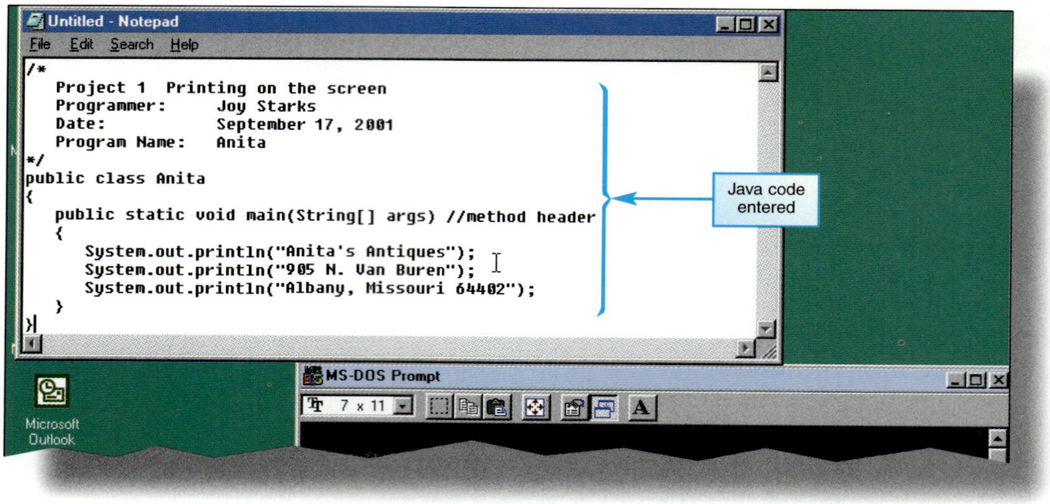

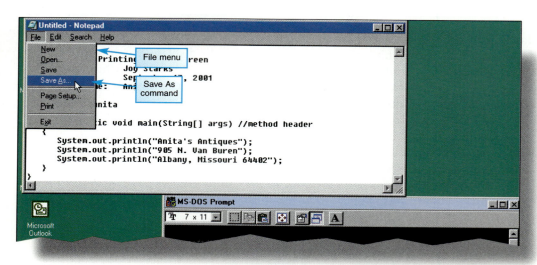

FIGURE 1-16

3 **With a floppy disk in drive A, click File on the menu bar, and then point to Save As.**

The File menu displays (Figure 1-17).

FIGURE 1-17

4 **Click Save As. When the Save As dialog box displays, type "Anita.java" in the File name text box. Point to the Save in box arrow.**

The Save As dialog box displays options for saving the code (Figure 1-18). Remember that Java is case-sensitive.

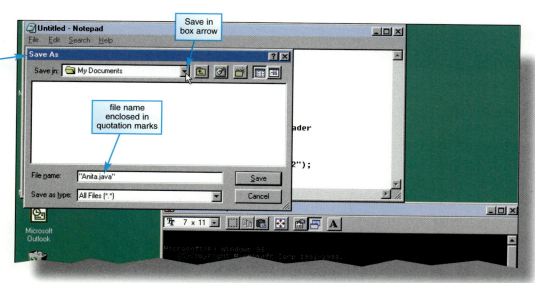

FIGURE 1-18

**5** Click the Save in box arrow and then click 3½ Floppy (A:) in the list. Point to the Save button.

*Drive A is selected (Figure 1-19).*

**6** Click the Save button.

*The file is saved on drive A.*

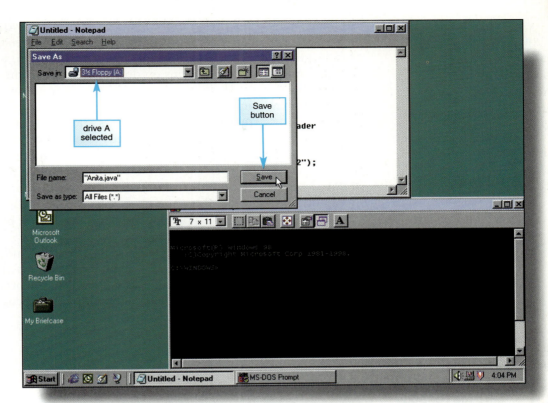

**FIGURE 1-19**

**Other Ways**

1. Type code, press ALT+F, press A

Notepad usually saves files with the extension .txt. Enclosing the file name in quotation marks in the File name text box forces Notepad to save the file as typed; that is, with the extension .java so that the compiler will recognize the file. If you decide to use another application to create the Java program, make sure you remember to save the file in a plain text format with the extension .java.

# Testing the Program

The fourth step of the PDLC is to test the program. Once you have written the program you must execute it in order to make sure it runs properly. In the Java programming language, executing the program is a two step process. First, you must compile the source code, and then you must run the resulting bytecode.

## Compiling the Source Code

Source code provides the keywords, commands, and language syntax that become the source the Java compiler can understand. Java source code must be compiled before it can be executed. A **compiler** is a programming language tool that translates source code that is closer to English, to executable code that is closer to machine language. Recall that Sun provides a Java compiler, javac, which translates the source code into bytecode. **Bytecode** is the code that can be interpreted on any machine. The name of the interpreter is called the Java Virtual Machine (JVM).

A Java programmer needs all of these tools in order to write, compile, interpret, and execute a Java program. The **Java 2 Software Development Kit (SDK)**, containing

## Setting the DOS Path

If you do a lot of programming in Java, you might want to consider changing the path statement in your autoexec.bat file which eliminates the need to set the path each time you open the MS-DOS Prompt window. For more information on adding the JDK path to your system, visit the Java Programming Web page (www.scsite.com/java/more.htm) and click Path Statements.

the JDK and accompanying tools, may be obtained in two different ways. First, programmers may download the SDK from the Web, free of charge. The second way is to install an IDE, such as Inprise's JBuilder 3 program, which includes the JDK. See Appendix A for instructions on downloading from the Sun Microsystems Web site or installing the JBuilder 3 CD-ROM that may accompany this text.

**Javac** is the command used to compile Java source code into bytecode. The compilation process creates a file for each class and saves it in the same directory as the source code file. The javac compiler needs to access certain files from the JDK. You must designate the location of these files by using an operating system path statement each time you open the MS-DOS Prompt window to compile a Java program. If you downloaded the JDK from the Sun Web site, your path will be c:\jdk1.2.2\bin. If you installed JBuilder 3, your path will be c:\jbuilder3\java\bin. Alternately, ask your instructor for ways to permanently add the correct path statement to your system's start up process.

In this project, however, you will use a path command at the command prompt to change the path for this session. The **path command** is an operating system command that sets the search path for executable files. Perform the following steps to designate the correct path and then compile the Anita program.

 ## To Set the Path and Compile the Program

 **1** **Click the MS-DOS Prompt window.**

*The insertion point displays in the MS-DOS Prompt window (Figure 1-20).*

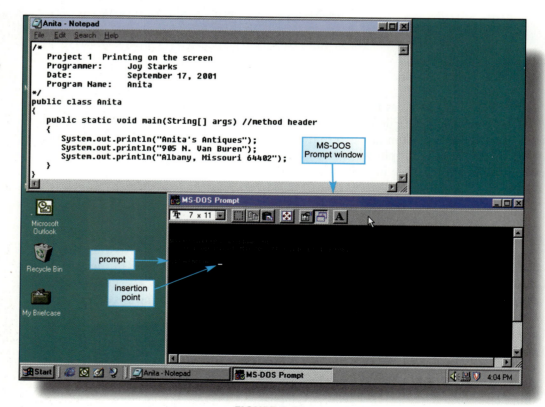

**FIGURE 1-20**

**2** **If you downloaded Java from the Sun Microsystems Web site, type** `path=c:\jdk1.2.2\bin` **at the prompt and then press the ENTER key. If you installed the Java compiler from the JBuilder 3 CD-ROM that may accompany this text, type** `path=c:\jbuilder3\java\bin` **and then press the ENTER key.**

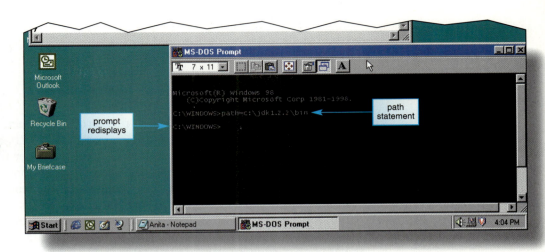

FIGURE 1-21

The command prompt redisplays (Figure 1-21). If no error messages display, the system accepted the command. See your instructor for the exact path of your JDK installation. The path statement is not case-sensitive.

**3** **Type** `a:` **and press the ENTER key to change to drive A.**

The command prompt now displays an A:\> indicating communication with drive A (Figure 1-22).

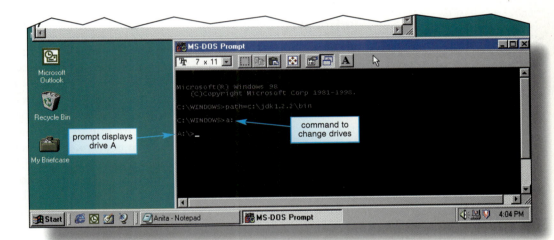

FIGURE 1-22

**4** **Type** `javac Anita.java` **at the prompt and then press the ENTER key.**

The system compiles the program on drive A (Figure 1-23). After a few moments, the command prompt redisplays on a new line. If no errors occur, only the command prompt will display.

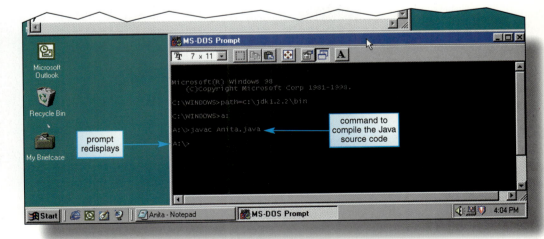

FIGURE 1-23

## Syntax Errors

Because so many typing errors can cause syntax errors when you try to compile, it is impossible to list them all. In general, however, beginning students usually have one of the following errors: a missing semicolon, a capitalization error, a missing brace, a missing parenthesis, incorrect programming punctuation, or a spelling error.

## Compile Errors

If you receive an error when you try to compile, such as "Bad command or file name" (Windows 9X or 2000) or "The name specified is not recognized as an internal or external command, operable program or batch file" (Windows NT), the operating system cannot find the Java compiler, javac. You might have forgotten to set the path, or your path might be incorrect. If you do not know where your system installation of JDK is located, click the Start button on the taskbar, click Find, click Files or Folders, type javac.exe in the Named text box, and then click the Find Now button in the Find: All Files window.

During compilation, javac adds a file to the disk called Anita.class, which is the actual bytecode.

# Errors

If the JDK is not properly installed or the path is incorrect, your program will not compile. The path command, as explained on page J 1.20, must direct the operating system to the location of the javac Java compiler in order for your program to compile. Additionally, you must reference the correct location, in this case on the floppy disk, by either changing to drive A or including an A: before the file name when compiling, as explained on page J 1.21. Javac also needs to find a valid Java file name, spelled correctly and with the correct capitalization.

If your program compiles but displays error messages, you may have a syntax, semantic, run-time, or other logic error.

The process of fixing errors is called **debugging**. Finding the bugs in your code and in your logic is a skill that will improve as you learn to program. It can be a time-consuming and frustrating process, which is why a thorough test of the code is done while formalizing the solution.

## Syntax Errors

**Syntax errors** usually are typing errors. Java attempts to isolate the error by displaying a line of code and pointing to the first incorrect character in that line. However, the problem may not be at that exact point. For instance, if you omit a necessary semicolon at the end of a line, you will see a message similar to Figure 1-24. The first error message says, Invalid type expression, and generates a second error, Invalid declaration. Both errors are due to the same missing semicolon and will not display once the syntax of the code is corrected. When the compiler cannot find the end of the first line, it generates a message with the file name, the line number, and suspected type of error. The compiler then tries to compile the two lines together, which results in a second error. A rule of thumb is to correct the first mistake in a long list. Doing so may reduce the total number of errors dramatically.

**FIGURE 1-24**

The most common mistakes are in capitalization, spelling, the use of incorrect special characters, and omission of correct punctuation. Table 1-2 lists some common syntactical errors, the messages you may see on the screen, and the method of correction.

## Semantic Errors

Whereas syntax refers to code structure or grammar, a **semantic error** is one dealing with the meaning of the code. These types of errors display themselves as unrecognizable code to the Java compiler. For example, if you misspell a method like println, the compiler will return an error that says the method was not found. If you use a variable name that has not been declared properly, the compiler will return an error that says the variable is undefined.

| TABLE 1-2  Typical Syntax Errors | | |
|---|---|---|
| SYNTAX ERROR | SAMPLE ERROR MESSAGE | METHOD OF CORRECTION |
| missing semicolon | invalid type expression<br>invalid declaration<br>';' expected | Add a semicolon at the end of the line |
| missing punctuation | ')' expected | Insert missing ) or } |
| incorrect file name | public class must be defined in a file | Make sure your class name and file name match exactly, both in spelling and capitalization |
| incorrect number of arguments | invalid argument | Add a comma between arguments in an argument list |
| incorrect use of mathematical operators | missing term | Correct operand error |

Most semantic errors can be fixed by correcting the spelling of the keyword or by properly defining the codes and methods you wish to use.

If errors occur when you try to compile your program, correct the errors in the Notepad window, save the file again, and then compile the program again using javac. If Java still displays error messages after correcting all typing errors, consult your instructor.

## Run-time Errors

**Run-time errors** will not display until you run or execute the program. Even programs that compile successfully may display wrong answers if the programmer has not thought through the logical processes and structures of the program. Your goal should be to have error-free programs, and by implementing the PDLC correctly, you will achieve that goal.

Occasionally, a logic error will surface during execution of the program because of an action the user performs, something that the programmer did not plan for ahead of time. During execution, users who input numbers outside of valid ranges, or those who enter the wrong types of data, can cause programs to stop executing. In future projects, you will learn how to look for data entry errors involving validity, range, and reasonableness. In this project, the user inputs no information, so you should not experience any abrupt termination of your program.

Other run-time errors may occur as you run a program. For instance, if you, as the programmer, entered the wrong address in a link or used an incorrect operator, the program still would compile and run correctly, but the wrong output would display. No run-time error message would occur. It is these kinds of errors that sometime appear in the final solutions to programs, even after the code has been released to the users.

A run-time error message also will display if you misspell the Java command, misspell the name of the bytecode file, or add an extension by mistake.

**More About**

## Run Errors

If you receive this error, "Exception in thread "main" java.lang.-NoClassDefFoundError:" Java cannot find your compiled bytecode file. One of the places in which Java tries to find your bytecode file is your current directory. If you do not store your files on drive A, you should change your current directory to that folder. Alternately, you can change the classpath permanently. For more information on changing the classpath, visit the Java Programming Web page (www.scsite.com/java/more.htm) and click Classpath Statements.

### Running the Program

Once the program is compiled, programmers use the Java interpreter to run the program. An **interpreter** executes instructions line by line. Once the program is compiled, you simply type the command, java, followed by the name of the program to begin execution, as shown in the following step.

## To Run the Java Program

**1** **If necessary, click the MS-DOS Prompt window and make sure drive A still is specified. At the A:\> prompt type** java Anita **and then press the ENTER key.**

*Java runs the program and displays the name and address of the company on the screen (Figure 1-25).*

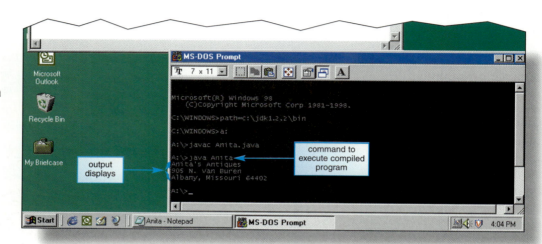

**FIGURE 1-25**

In addition to the println method, Java supports a method called print. The **print** method does not send a carriage return/line feed message to the monitor like println. The print method is useful when you want the insertion point to stay on the same line.

## Editing the Source Code and Recompiling

When you edit or modify the source code in any way, you must go through the steps of saving, compiling, and re-executing the program. Even something as simple as changing the spacing between characters necessitates these steps if you want the program to run properly.

### Formatting Output Using Escape Characters

In the Anita program, you will insert some special codes to move the output from the left side of the screen so it is positioned more toward the middle. Java uses **escape characters** inside the string arguments of the println method to move the insertion point, which thereby moves the text output. Escape characters, also called escape codes or escape sequences, are non-printing control codes. Table 1-3 displays some of the Java escape code characters related to the monitor.

| TABLE 1-3 | Java Escape Codes | |
| --- | --- | --- |
| CODE | CONCEPT | RESULT |
| \t | horizontal tab | moves insertion point eight spaces to the right |
| \b | Backspace | moves insertion point one space to the left |
| \n | new line | moves insertion point down one line and to the left margin |
| \r | carriage return | moves insertion point to the left margin |

In the following steps, you will edit the Anita program by adding escape characters to the string argument of the println method. You also will add an e-mail address to the output. Perform the following steps to edit the program.

 ## To Edit a Java Program and Save It with the Same File Name

**1** **Click the Notepad window, immediately to the left of the word, Anita's, on line 11.**

*The insertion point displays between the quotation mark and the A of Anita (Figure 1-26).*

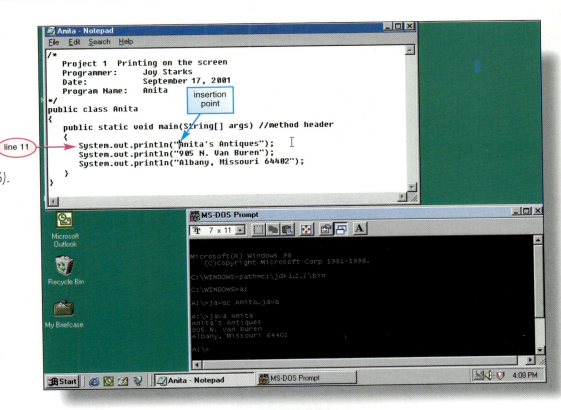

**FIGURE 1-26**

**2** **Type \t\t\t after the quotation mark in line 11.**

*The escape code characters display as part of the string argument (Figure 1-27). They will cause the insertion point to move 24 spaces to the right — eight spaces for each escape code — before printing the string on the monitor.*

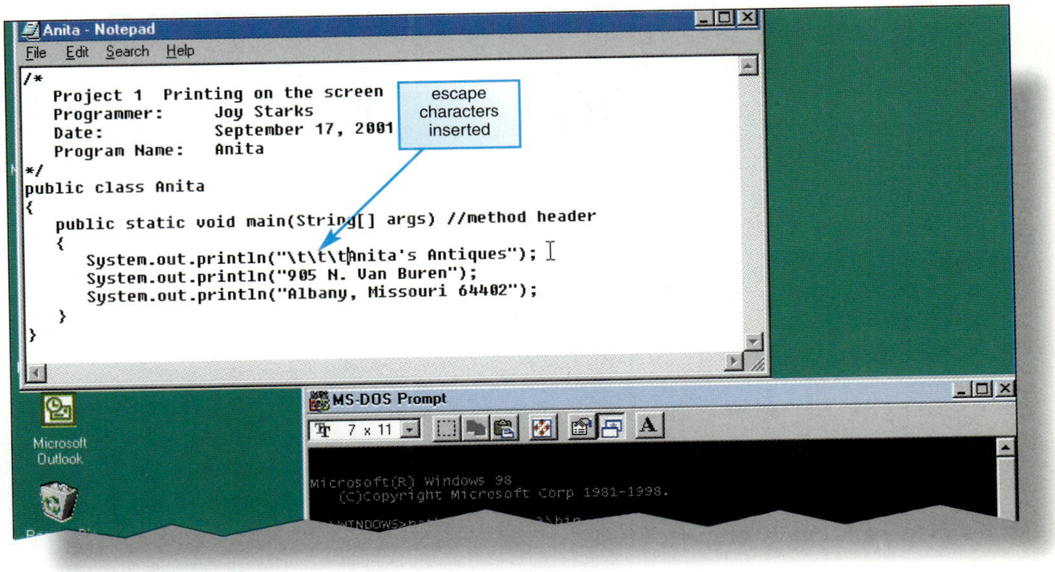

**FIGURE 1-27**

**3** **Repeat Step 2 for the address line, and the city/state/zip line of code, making certain you position the insertion point between the quotation mark and the first character.**

*The three println methods display escape code characters in their string arguments (Figure 1-28).*

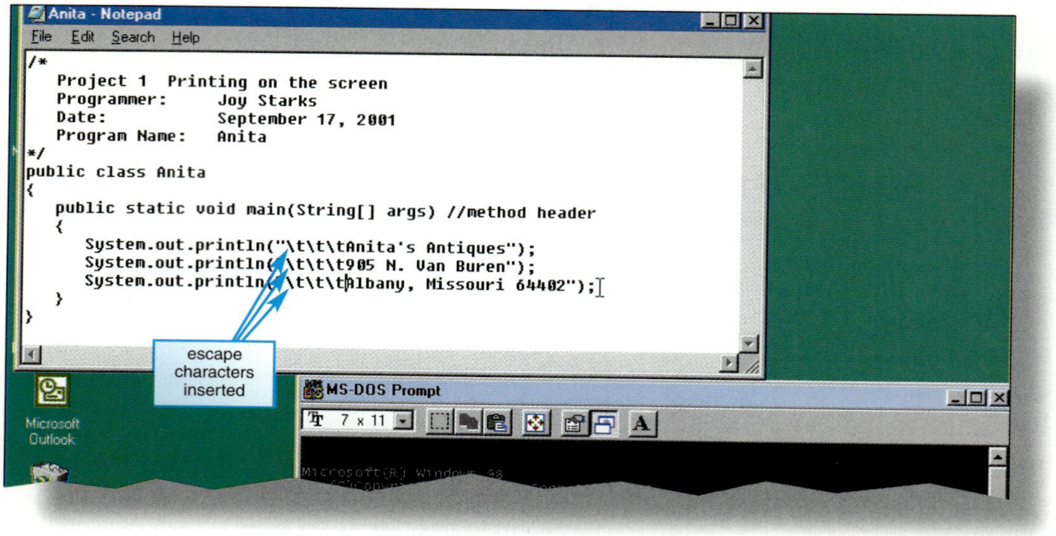

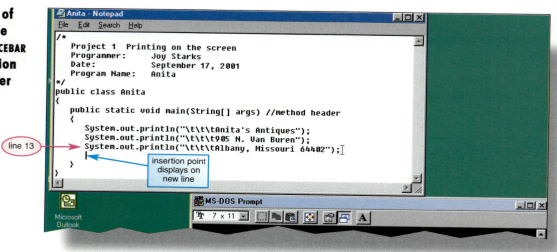

**FIGURE 1-28**

**4** **Click at the end of line 13. Press the ENTER key. Press the SPACEBAR or TAB key so the insertion point is positioned under the S in System on the previous line.**

*A new line displays with the flashing insertion point (Figure 1-29).*

**FIGURE 1-29**

**5** **Type System.out. println("\t\t\ tAnitasAntiques@Small Store.com"); to add an e-mail address line to the program.**

*The new line of code displays (Figure 1-30).*

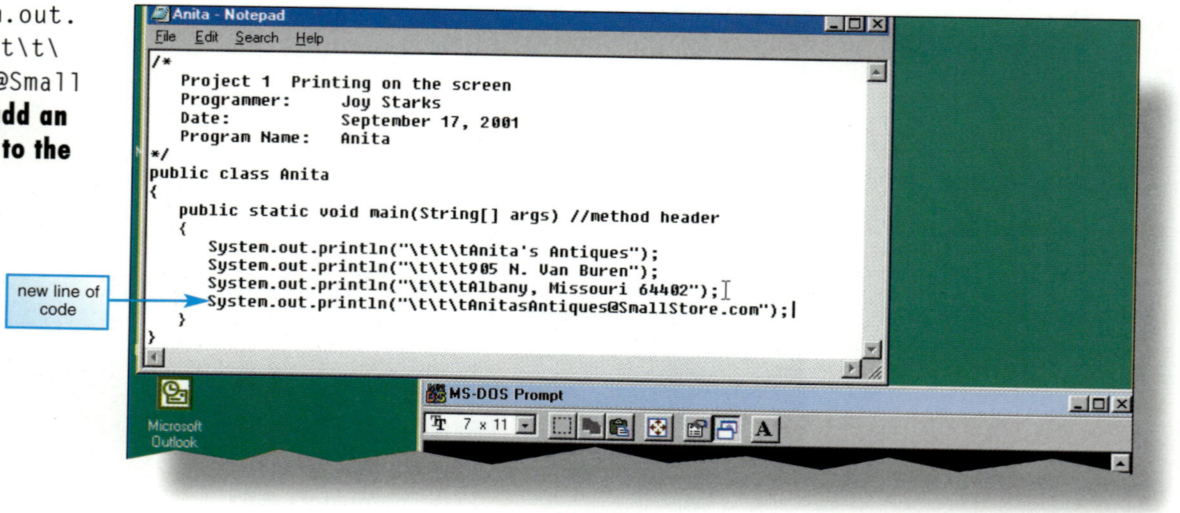

**FIGURE 1-30**

**6** Click File on the menu bar and then point to Save.

*The File menu displays (Figure 1-31).*

**7** Click Save.

*The file saves in the same location as specified in the previous Save As command, on drive A with the same file name, "Anita.java". The old version of the file is replaced with the new, edited file.*

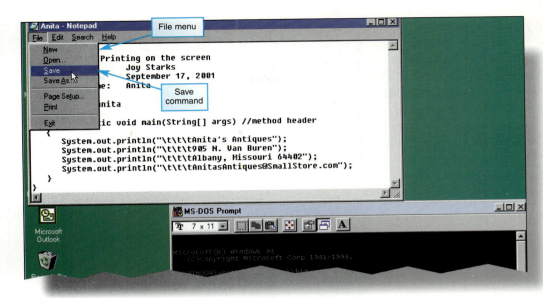

FIGURE 1-31

If you execute the program again, you will not see the newly formatted output. As you will see in the next series of steps, the program must be recompiled.

## Recompiling and Running the Program

As you may remember, after compiling, Java created the file Anita.class that contains the bytecode or object code from your program. It is this object code that actually executes when you type java and the file name. If you have not recompiled after editing, Java will execute the old bytecode and you will not see your updates. In order to run the most recent version of the program, you will compile Anita again and then run the new bytecode.

Follow these steps to recompile and run the program.

 **To Recompile and Run the Program**

**1** Click in the MS-DOS Prompt window or click the MS-DOS Prompt button on the taskbar to activate it. Type `javac Anita.java` and then press the ENTER key.

*The program compiles again (Figure 1-32).*

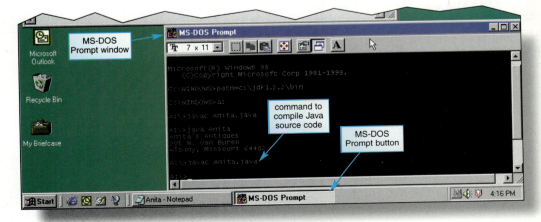

FIGURE 1-32

**2** If the compiler displays errors, locate and fix them in the Notepad window, save the file again, and then repeat Step 1. Once the program compiles successfully, run the program by typing `java Anita` at the command prompt and then press the ENTER key.

The program runs and the println methods send data to the monitor (Figure 1-33). The address lines display further to the right. The e-mail address also displays.

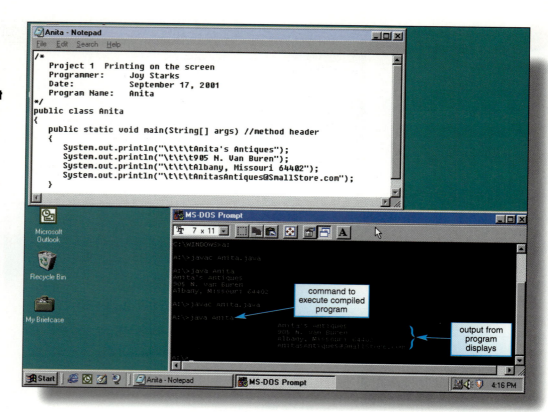

**FIGURE 1-33**

## Printing the Source Code and Closing the Windows

In the following steps, you will print a copy of the source code using the Print command on Notepad's File menu. You also will use the title bar's Close button in the following steps to close both the Notepad and MS-DOS Prompt windows.

 ## To Print the Source Code and Close the Windows

**1** Click File on Notepad's menu bar, and then point to Print.

The File menu displays (Figure 1-34).

**FIGURE 1-34**

**Click Print. Point to the Close button on the title bar of the Notepad window.**

*The source code for Anita.java prints on the system's default printer. The ScreenTip for the Close button displays (Figure 1-35).*

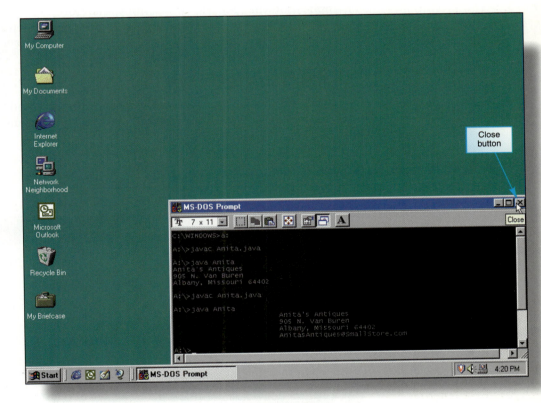

**FIGURE 1-35**

 **Click the Close button. Point to the Close button on the title bar of the MS-DOS Prompt window.**

*The Notepad window closes (Figure 1-36).*

 **Click the Close button.**

*The MS-DOS Prompt window closes and the desktop again is completely visible.*

**FIGURE 1-36**

Notepad reminds you if you have not saved since changing any data in the Notepad window. Notepad does not save any resizing you may have done to the window. When you start Notepad again, you may have to move its window and resize it to customize your desktop.

The MS-DOS Prompt window does not save the path settings or drive changes you made when you exit to the desktop. However, the property changes you made on pages J 1.10 through J 1.13 for the font and window size will stay in effect when you open the window again.

# Moving to the Web

### More About

## Applets

An applet usually runs on the user's or client computer as opposed to running on the Web server. An applet is compiled, which means usually it runs faster than a script. Applets can add multimedia capability to a Web page, as well as facilitating information transfer from the client to the server.

One of the features that makes Java so useful is its ability to program applications that are machine-independent. Much of Java's portability lies in the use of small application programs that can run on the Web. These extremely popular mini-applications, which run as a part of a Web page, are called **applets**. An applet actually is any program called from within another language. Prior to the Web, the built-in writing and drawing programs that came with Windows sometimes were called applets. Java applets can perform interactive animations, immediate calculations, or other simple tasks without having to access the computer that is hosting the Web page.

There are major differences between Java applications and Java applets. One difference is the mode in which they are run; applications run in stand-alone or console mode, while applets run in a browser or viewer. Another difference is in their scope for data handling. An applet cannot be used to modify files stored on a user's system; an application can. Security restrictions, therefore, have less impact on applications. Another difference is that applications do not need a memory intensive browser or viewer in order to execute.

## Opening Source Code Files

In the following steps, you will reopen the source code for the Anita program that was saved on your floppy disk. You then will edit and create an applet.

### Steps: To Start Notepad and Open a Java Source Code File

**1** **Click the Start button on the taskbar and then point to Programs on the Start menu. Point to Accessories on the Programs submenu, and then click Notepad. When the Notepad window opens, drag its title bar to the upper-left corner of the desktop.**

*The repositioned Notepad window displays (Figure 1-37).*

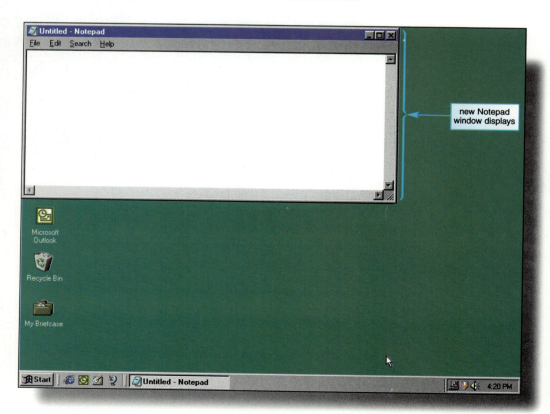

**FIGURE 1-37**

**2** Click File on the menu bar and then point to Open.

The File menu displays (Figure 1-38).

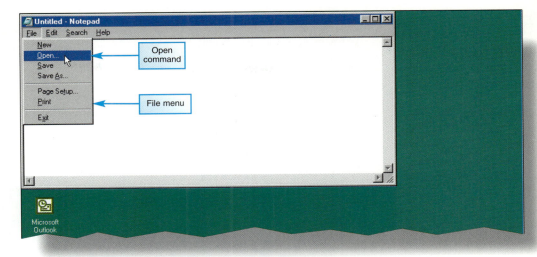

**FIGURE 1-38**

**3** Click Open. When the Open dialog box displays, point to the Files of type box arrow.

The Open dialog box displays choices for the location, name, and type of files for Notepad to open (Figure 1-39).

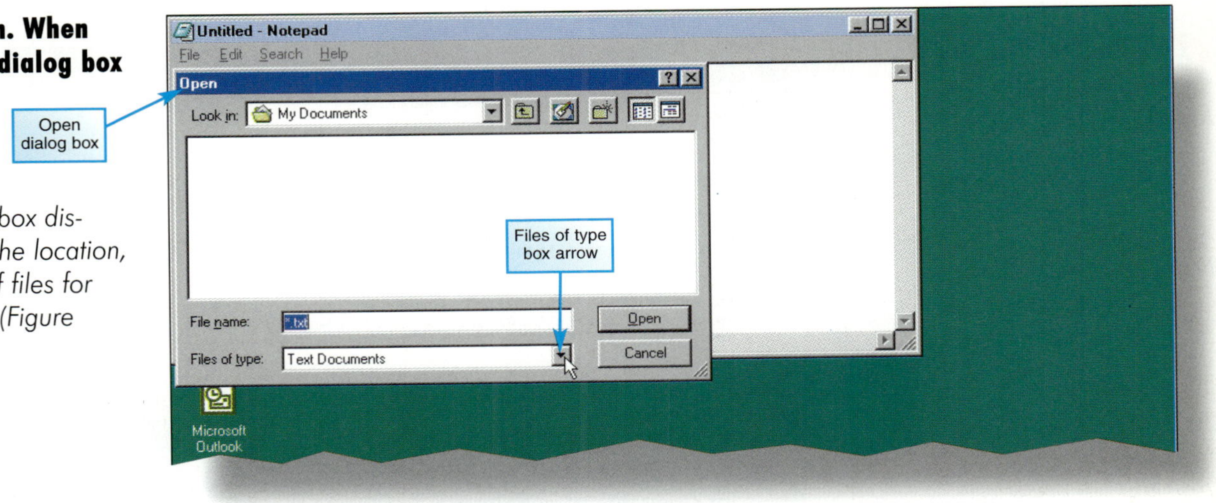

**FIGURE 1-39**

**4** Click the Files of type box arrow and then click All Files (*.*) in the list. Point to the Look in box arrow.

Notepad will display files of all types (Figure 1-40).

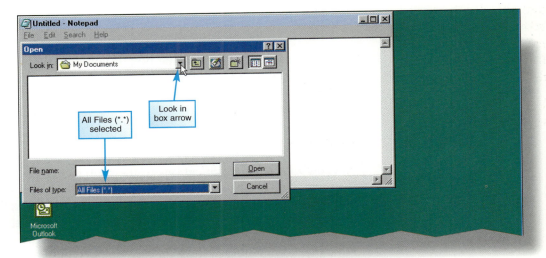

**FIGURE 1-40**

**5** Click the Look in box arrow and then click 3½ Floppy (A:) in the list. Point to the Java file named Anita.

*Files from the floppy disk display (Figure 1-41). Both the Java source code and the compiled bytecode are named Anita. The source code usually displays with a Notepad. Your icons may differ depending on your installation of the JDK or JBuilder 3, and on the display detail.*

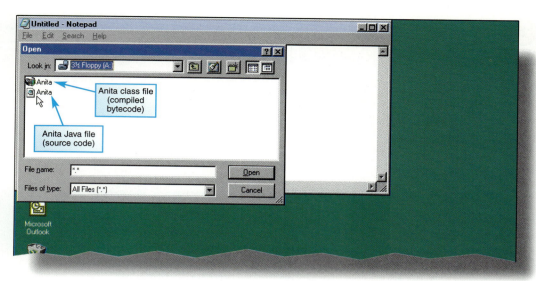

**FIGURE 1-41**

**6** Double-click the source code file, Anita.

*The Open dialog box closes and the Anita file displays in the Notepad workspace (Figure 1-42). The file name displays on the title bar.*

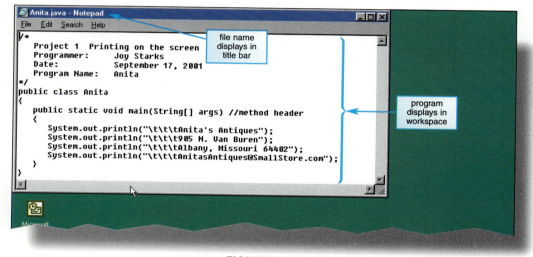

**FIGURE 1-42**

1. Type complete path and name of file in File name box

When using the Open dialog box, if you do not choose All Files (*.*) in the Files of type list, Notepad will display only files with the extension .txt. Because Java programs have the extension .java, Notepad does not display Java source code files automatically.

### Importing Packages

You will make modifications to the source code in order to direct the output to a Web window. The classes and methods needed to create such a window are not immediately available unless you tell the compiler, through the coding, to access the storage location. The JDK includes packages as part of the standard installation, packages that are used when creating an applet. **Packages** are collections of classes, sometimes called libraries, which contain portable Java bytecode files. Because there are hundreds of Java classes, the package is a convenient way to group them and maintain some order among this huge collection.

Some of the more significant packages and their descriptions are listed in Table 1-4. See Appendix A for information on downloading the JDK help files that contain a complete listing of which class resides in which package.

| TABLE 1-4    JDK Provided Packages | |
|---|---|
| **PACKAGE NAME** | **DESCRIPTION** |
| java.applet | classes to facilitate using applets |
| java.awt | Abstract Window Toolkit; classes to facilitate graphics user interfaces |
| java.net | classes used for networking and client/server applications |
| java.io | classes to facilitate input and output |
| java.lang | classes to facilitate data types, threads, strings, and others |
| java.util | classes used for dates, vectors, and others |

The java.lang package is the only package imported automatically without an explicit command; all other packages need an import command. The **import** command is placed at the beginning of java source code, most commonly right after the opening documentation. During compilation, the import command goes to the location where the JDK is stored and loads the appropriate class or classes. You may load all the classes within a package by typing an asterisk (*) or you may load individual classes by using their name.

Follow these steps to edit the Anita program you created earlier in this project and insert two import commands.

 **To Insert the Import Command**

**1** **Make sure the Anita.java file is open in Notepad. Click at the end of line 6. Press the ENTER key.**

*A new line displays in the source code (Figure 1-43).*

```
/*
    Project 1  Printing on the screen
    Programmer:     Joy Starks
    Date:           September 17, 2001
    Program Name:   Anita
*/

public class Anita
{
    public static void main(String[] args) //method header
    {
        System.out.println("\t\t\tAnita's Antiques");
        System.out.println("\t\t\t905 N. Van Buren");
        System.out.println("\t\t\tAlbany, Missouri 64402");
        System.out.println("\t\t\tAnitasAntiques@SmallStore.com");
    }
```

line 6

insertion point displays on new line

**FIGURE 1-43**

**2** **Type** import java.applet.*; **and then press the ENTER key. Type** import java.awt.*; **on the new line.**

The commands to import two packages from the JDK display (Figure 1-44). All the classes will be imported when you include the asterisk.

```
/*
    Project 1  Printing on the screen
    Programmer:    Joy Starks
    Date:          September 17, 2001
    Program Name:  Anita
*/
import java applet.*;
import java.awt.*;
public class Anita
{
    public static void main(String[] args) //method header
    {
        System.out.println("\t\t\tAnita's Antiques");
        System.out.println("\t\t\t905 N. Van Buren");
        System.out.println("\t\t\tAlbany, Missouri 64402");
        System.out.println("\t\t\tAnitasAntiques@SmallStore.com");
```

import statements inserted

**FIGURE 1-44**

Some programmers place the import statements before the block comments instead of after them. Either way is acceptable, just as long as the import statements are placed somewhere before the class header.

As you edit the remainder of the source code in order to adapt this program to run on the Web, you will incorporate methods and classes that Java uses from these two imported packages. Applets inherit certain attributes and manipulating classes from the applet package. The **AWT** or **Abstract Window Toolkit** is a package included with the JDK to provide you with access to color, draw methods, and other GUI facilities commonly used in applets.

## Editing the Applet

Because the purpose of this program now will be to run as an applet on the Web, it is important to change the name of the class. You will change the program name in the documentation, in the class header, and in the file name when you save. Additionally, you will **extend** the class, which means that this new Java class, created specifically as an applet, must be a subclass of the general Applet class supplied with the JDK applet package. The extends command is added to the class header along with the name of the superclass. A superclass is a class that represents a broader, higher category of the subclass object with a common structure and behavior. In this case, Applet is the superclass you will use to create your specific applet subclass for Anita's Antiques.

Perform the following steps to edit an applet.

**To Edit an Applet**

**1** **In the Notepad window, click after the word, Anita, in the documentation line. Without spacing, type Applet as shown in Figure 1-45.**

```
/*
    Project 1  Printing on the screen
    Programmer:     Joy Starks
    Date:           September 17, 2001
    Program Name:   AnitaApplet
*/
import java applet.*;
import java.awt.*;
public class Anita
{
    public static void main(String[] args) //method header
    {
        System.out.println("\t\t\tAnita's Antiques");
        System.out.println("\t\t\t905 N. Van Buren");
        System.out.println("\t\t\tAlbany, Missouri 64402");
        System.out.println("\t\t\tAnitasAntiques@SmallStore.com");
```

edited program name comment

**FIGURE 1-45**

**2** **Click at the end of line 9. Without spacing, type Applet extends Applet to force AnitaApplet to become a subclass of the general Applet.**

*The new method header displays (Figure 1-46).*

line 9

```
/*
    Project 1  Printing on the screen
    Programmer:     Joy Starks
    Date:           September 17, 2001
    Program Name:   AnitaApplet
*/
import java applet.*;
import java.awt.*;
public class AnitaApplet extends Applet
{
    public static void main(String[] args) //method header
    {
        System.out.println("\t\t\tAnita's Antiques");
        System.out.println("\t\t\t905 N. Van Buren");
        System.out.println("\t\t\tAlbany, Missouri 64402");
        System.out.println("\t\t\tAnitasAntiques@SmallStore.com");
```

edited class name and extend command

**FIGURE 1-46**

The relationship of the JDK to its packages, and the packages to their classes, is a perfect example of the superclass, class, and subclass hierarchy. You will learn more about creating subclasses and instances of existing classes in a later project.

## The Paint Method and DrawString Method

The method header of an applet is not usually the main method, as it is in a stand-alone application. Actually, a default method called, **init**, initializes the applet and loads the initial setup of the applet. Because the previous steps extended the Applet class, init and all the applet methods happen automatically. However, in this applet, you will call the **paint** method explicitly in order to graphically draw some text on the applet screen, thereby creating an instance. The paint method takes a graphics argument and returns nothing. It is a common practice to identify the argument as g, although any name may be used.

```
public void paint(Graphics g)
```

Additionally, you will use the drawString method, instead of println. **DrawString**, which is a method of the AWT package, sends a message to a Graphics object. DrawString takes three arguments: a string to display, the horizontal (X) position at which to display the string, and the vertical (Y) coordinate at which to display the string. Notice that you use the variable name from the method header, followed by a dot, followed by the function name. As usual, the arguments are in parentheses. Multiple arguments are **delimited**, or separated, by commas.

```
g.drawString("Anita's Antiques", 15, 20)
```

In the following steps, you will edit the program. Use standard editing techniques to replace and enter the new code, much as you would for a word processing or spreadsheet program (i.e., drag through the text or use the DELETE and BACKSPACE keys). Perform the following steps to complete the applet and save it.

**More About**

**Graphics**

Several demo applets that display graphics and their source code automatically install when you download the JDK. They usually are in a folder, c:\jdk1.2.2\demo. The Sun Microsystems Web site also has free applets that you may download. For more examples of graphics and the source code that created them, visit the Java Programming Web page (www.scsite.com/java/more.htm) and click Graphics Applets.

### To Complete and Save the Applet

**1** Edit the rest of the program as shown in Figure 1-47.

The println methods have been replaced with the drawString method (Figure 1-47). The tab escape characters are replaced by coordinates following the string.

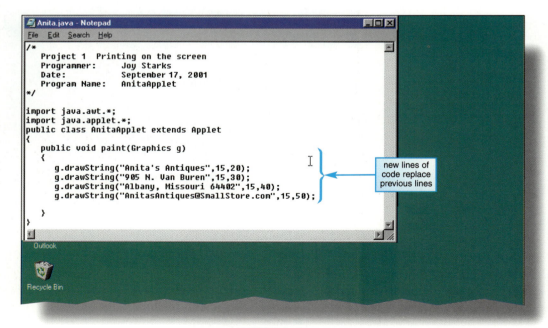

FIGURE 1-47

**2** **Click File on the menu bar and then point to Save As.**

*The File menu displays (Figure 1-48).*

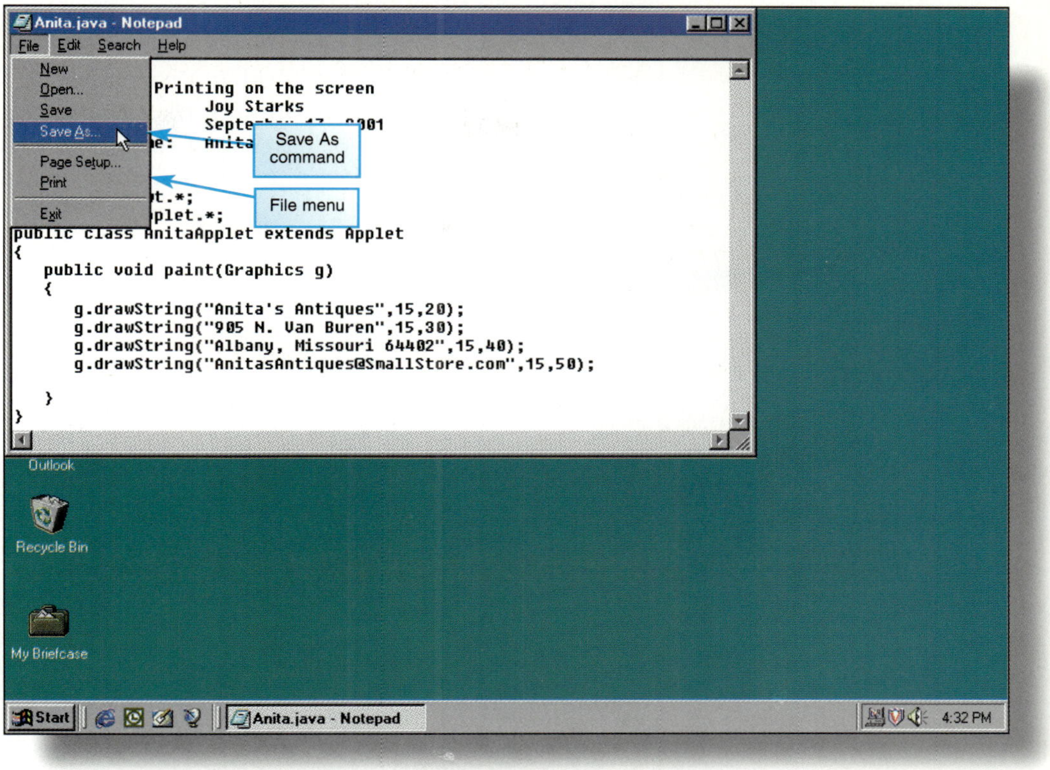

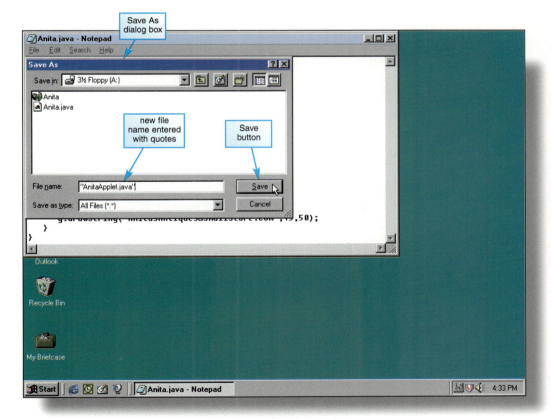

**FIGURE 1-48**

**3** **Click Save As. When the Save As dialog box displays, type** `"AnitaApplet.java"` **in the file name text box. If necessary click 3½ Floppy (A:) in the Save in list. Point to the Save button.**

*The Save As dialog box displays (Figure 1-49).*

**4** **Click the Save button.**

*The applet saves on drive A with the file name AnitaApplet.*

**FIGURE 1-49**

The Graphics argument is an object that models the drawing behavior of a portion of a screen, which means that it will respond to messages from a method requesting that a string be displayed at a particular location. The x-coordinate, as you might expect, is the left position of the string within the window, and the y-coordinate is the bottom or baseline of the string (Figure 1-50). Other methods used with the Graphics object draw shapes, add color, and return font information.

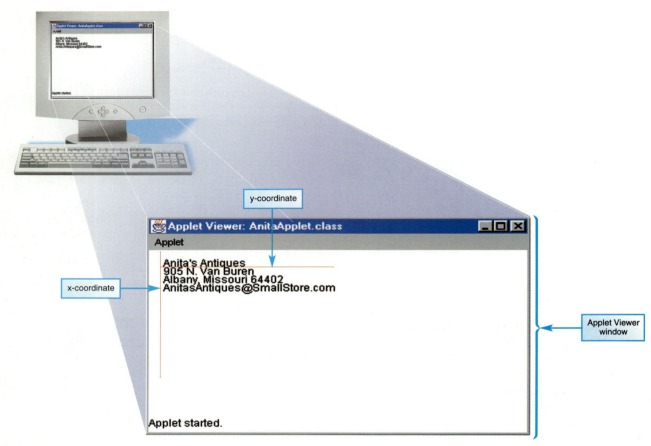

FIGURE 1-50

## Opening the MS-DOS Prompt Window and Compiling the Applet

Perform the following steps to open the MS-DOS Prompt window and compile the applet. For detailed instructions on opening the MS-DOS Prompt window, see pages J 1.9 through J 1.13. For detailed instructions on compiling a program, see pages J 1.20 through J 1.21.

**More About**

### Applet Color

Java's setBackground method allows you to change the background color of an applet window. For instance, the statement setBackground(Color.green); would change the background of the applet window to green.

## TO OPEN THE MS-DOS PROMPT WINDOW AND COMPILE THE APPLET

**1** Click the Start button on the taskbar. Point to Programs. Click MS-DOS Prompt on the Programs submenu.

**2** When the MS-DOS Prompt window opens, if you downloaded Java from the Sun Web site, set the path by typing `path=c:\jdk1.2.2\bin` and then press the ENTER key. If you installed Java from the Inprise CD-ROM, set the path by typing `path=c:\jbuilder3\java\bin` at the command prompt. Press the ENTER key.

**3** Specify drive A by typing `a:` and then press the ENTER key.

**4** Type `javac AnitaApplet.java` and then press the ENTER key.

**5** If an error message displays, correct the error in the Notepad window. Save the AnitaApplet.java file again, and repeat step 4.

*The program compiles.*

Again, possible errors include incorrect location for the Java compiler, typing mistakes, omitting special characters, case-sensitive errors, and file name errors. If you cannot determine your mistake based on what the Java compiler tells you about the error and the information about errors on pages J 1.22 through J 1.23, consult your instructor.

# HTML Host Documents

Because an applet is initiated and executed from within another language or run as a part of a Web page, in order to view the applet in execution, you must create a **host,** or reference program to execute the applet. The applet for this project is called from a Web page. The HTML language is not really a language at all, because it cannot compute. It is a passive tool; in other words, it can present only the information that it carries. It cannot interact with the user to produce new information. That is why a Java applet is ideal for adding interactivity and programming to a Web page. You do not need to know the HTML language in order to program an applet; a few simple HTML commands are all that are necessary to create a host for a Java applet.

## HTML Tags

HTML uses a concept called tags to reference Java applets. A **tag,** or markup, is a code specifying links to other documents, or code specifying how a Web page is to display. A tag has a beginning code word called a **start tag,** which is enclosed in angle brackets < >. The same code must be turned off after it is complete by using a slash before the code word called an **end tag,** again enclosed within angle brackets. The tag at the beginning and end of the source code for a typical Web page is a perfect example. At the beginning, programmers insert a tag such as <HTML>. In order to end the code, programmers would need to insert </HTML>.

```
<HTML>
. . .
</HTML>
```

**More About**

**Tags**

Other attributes that can be set with the applet tag include ALIGN, which sets how the applet is viewed: top, middle, or bottom, and VSPACE and HSPACE, which set the amount of space around the applet.

**More About**

**HTML**

For more information on HTML code, visit the HTML Web page (www.scsite.com/html/more.htm).

In the following series of steps, you will create a simple HTML file to display the AnitaApplet you created earlier.

 **To Create the HTML Host Document**

**1** **With the Notepad window still open, click File on the menu bar and then point to New. Be certain that any currently displayed files have been saved.**

*The New command will clear the workspace (Figure 1-51).*

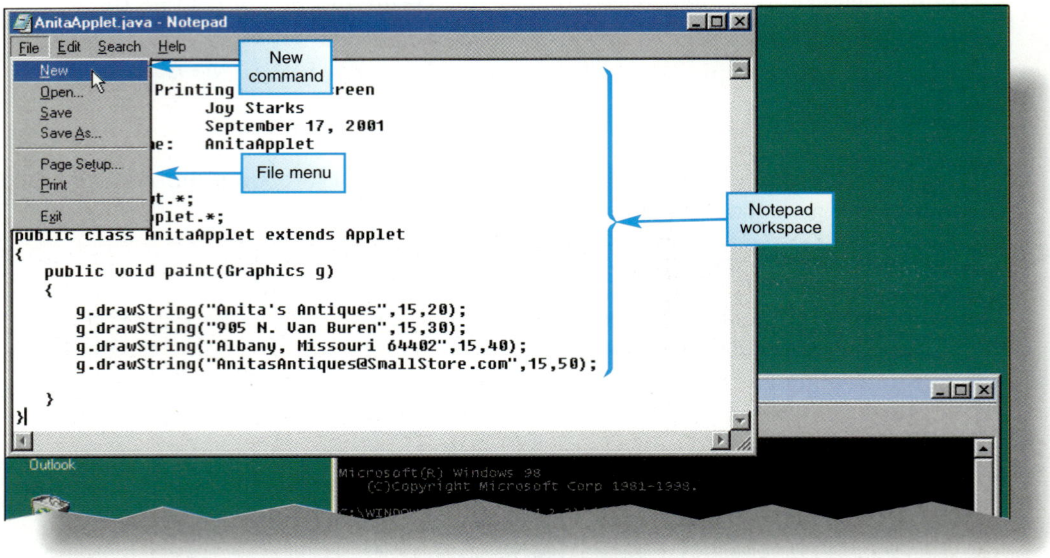

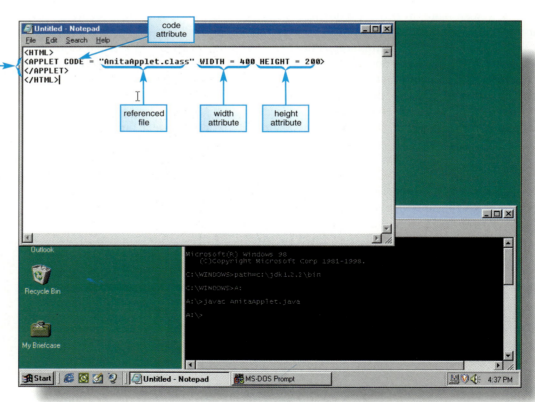

**FIGURE 1-51**

**2** **Click New. In the Notepad workspace, type the code as shown in Figure 1-52.**

*The code attribute specifies the name of the class to be referenced (Figure 1-52). HTML and its tags generally are not case-sensitive. The name of the referenced file, however, must match exactly because it is a Java class.*

**FIGURE 1-52**

**③** **Click File on the menu bar and then click Save As. When the Save As dialog box displays, if necessary, click the Look in box arrow and click 3½ Floppy (A:) in the list. In the File name text box, type "AnitaApplet.html" as the name of the file. Point to the Save button.**

*The file will be saved on drive A with the name AnitaApplet.html (Figure 1-53). The quotation marks must be included to prevent Notepad from saving the file as a simple text file.*

**④** **Click the Save button.**

*The file saves on drive A.*

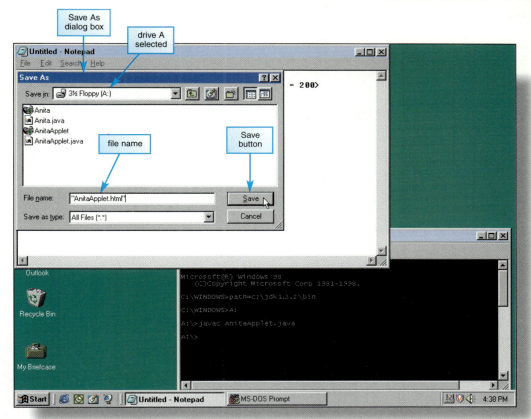

**FIGURE 1-53**

---

The applet tag, nested within the HTML beginning and ending tags, specifies three pieces of information that the Web page will need in order to access the Java applet: the name of the Java bytecode file, the width of the window, and the height of the window in which to run the applet (Figure 1-52).

The width and height attributes in the tag are measured in pixels. A **pixel**, or picture element, is the basic unit of programmable color on a computer display or in a computer image. You can think of it like a dot of light. Dots grouped together form characters and images. The physical size of a pixel depends on how you have set the resolution for your screen. For instance, if your screen resolution is 800 by 600 pixels, a width of 400 pixels means that the applet will display across approximately half the width of your screen.

## Running an Applet Using Applet Viewer

The JDK provides an **appletviewer** command, which is a program to display Web page applets. At the command prompt, you type `appletviewer`, followed by the name of a host document, which is usually an HTML file. Applet Viewer displays each applet referenced by the host document in its own window.

Applet Viewer makes it possible to run a Java applet without using a browser. Applet Viewer ignores any HTML that is not immediately relevant to launching an applet. If the host document does not include a reference to an applet or similar object, Applet Viewer does nothing. If for some reason, you do not want to use Applet Viewer to execute the Java applet, you can display applets using a Web browser by entering the path and name of the host document in the browser's address text box.

**More About**

**The Applet Tag**

If your HTML file does not reference any applets using the OBJECT, EMBED, or APPLET tags, then Applet Viewer does nothing. For more information on the HTML tags that Applet Viewer supports, visit the Java Programming Web page (www.scsite.com/java/more.htm) and click Applet Viewer Tags.

The following step illustrates how to run an applet using Applet Viewer from the command prompt.

## Steps: To Run an Applet Using Applet Viewer

**1** **If the A: prompt is not currently displayed in the MS-DOS window, type** a: **at the command prompt and press the ENTER key. In the MS-DOS Prompt window, type** appletviewer AnitaApplet.html **and then press the ENTER key.**

*The applet displays on the screen (Figure 1-54). The name of the MS-DOS Prompt window changes to APPLET while the program is running.*

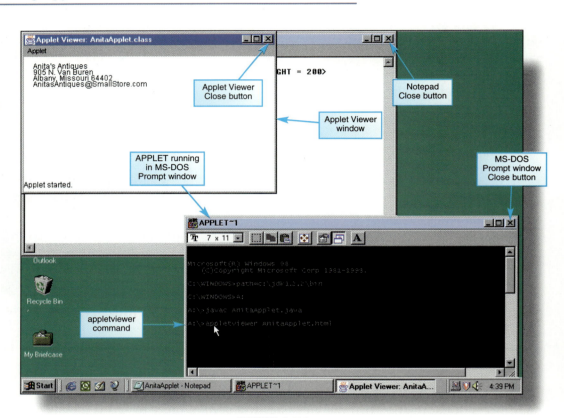

**FIGURE 1-54**

Applet Viewer does not contain any extra features like those in a browser. The advantage of using Applet Viewer is that you do not have to have access to a browser in order to view your applet. It also uses less memory than does a browser.

### Closing the Open Applications

The project now is complete. Perform the following steps to close Applet Viewer, Notepad, and the MS-DOS Prompt windows.

#### TO CLOSE APPLET VIEWER, NOTEPAD, AND THE MS-DOS PROMPT WINDOWS

**1** Click the Close button on the Applet Viewer title bar.

**2** Click the Close button on the Notepad title bar.

**3** Click the Close button on the MS-DOS Prompt title bar.

*The applications close and the Windows desktop displays.*

# Summary

In this project, you learned the basic form of a Java program and an applet. You formatted the desktop to display both the Notepad window, used as an editor for Java source code, and the MS-DOS Prompt window, used to compile and run the Java programs in console, or stand-alone, mode. After inserting proper documentation, you learned the basic syntax of a class and method, along with naming conventions, arguments, and return values. You included sequential commands within the curly braces of the main method. After running and compiling the program, you edited the source code to include commands to create an applet that can run on the Web. Finally, you created a host program to display the applet and run it using Applet Viewer.

# What You Should Know

Having completed this project, you now should be able to perform the following tasks:

▶ Close Applet Viewer, Notepad, and the MS-DOS Prompt Windows *(J 1.42)*

▶ Complete and Save the Applet *(J 1.36)*

▶ Create the HTML Host Document *(J 1.40)*

▶ Edit a Java Program and Save It with the Same File Name *(J 1.25)*

▶ Edit an Applet *(J 1.35)*

▶ Enter and Save Java Source Code *(J 1.17)*

▶ Insert the Import Command *(J 1.33)*

▶ Open and Format the Command Prompt Window *(J 1.9)*

▶ Open the MS-DOS Prompt Window and Compile the Applet *(J 1.39)*

▶ Print the Source Code and Close the Windows *(J 1.28)*

▶ Recompile and Run the Program *(J 1.27)*

▶ Run an Applet Using Applet Viewer *(J 1.42)*

▶ Run the Java Program *(J 1.24)*

▶ Set the Path and Compile the Program *(J 1.20)*

▶ Start Notepad *(J 1.8)*

▶ Start Notepad and Open a Java Source Code File *(J 1.30)*

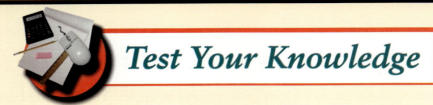

# Test Your Knowledge

## 1 True/False

**Instructions:** Circle **T** if the statement is true or **F** is the statement is false.

T  F  1. Console mode refers to running Java programs from the command prompt.
T  F  2. The Java Virtual Machine does not execute program comments.
T  F  3. Two slashes (//) indicate a line comment.
T  F  4. When a trigger sends a message to an object, an event occurs.
T  F  5. Java code must begin with an access modifier.
T  F  6. Java is not case-sensitive.
T  F  7. The class name should be the same as the file name.
T  F  8. Void means a method has no arguments.
T  F  9. System.out usually is the default display.
T  F  10. Java's println is a method.

## 2 Multiple Choice

**Instructions:** Circle the correct response.

1. IDE stands for _____ .
   a. Integration of Development Engineering
   b. Interactive Diagramming and Environments
   c. Interface Development Environment
   d. Integration of Diagnostic Encapsulation

2. Deciding on an exact sequence of steps to perform is done during the _____ phase of the Program Development Life Cycle.
   a. analysis
   b. design
   c. coding
   d. testing

3. The _____ is a way to interact with the operating system without using any specific application.
   a. command prompt
   b. Notepad
   c. Javac
   d. JBuilder 3

4. A(n) _____ is a piece of data or a data location, which is sent along with a method to help it perform its operation.
   a. identifier
   b. literal
   c. modifier
   d. argument

# *Test Your Knowledge*

5. A(n) _____ is a programming language tool that translates source code into executable code.
   a. interpreter
   b. compiler
   c. IDE
   d. object code generator

6. Which of the following escape codes results in moving the insertion point 8 spaces to the right?
   a. \t
   b. \b
   c. \n
   d. \r

7. A misspelled method most likely would result in a _____ error.
   a. syntax
   b. message
   c. semantic
   d. logic

8. _____ are collections of classes, sometimes called libraries, which contain portable Java bytecode files.
   a. Methods
   b. Classes
   c. Packages
   d. Tables

9. The _____ command is placed at the beginning of java source code to load the appropriate class.
   a. system
   b. println
   c. main
   d. import

10. An extended class created specifically to be used as an applet must be a(n) _____ of the JDK Applet class.
    a. header
    b. superclass
    c. subclass
    d. application

## *Test Your Knowledge*

### 3 Understanding the Desktop

**Instructions:** In Figure 1-55, arrows point to the parts of the two open windows on the desktop. Identify the various parts of those windows in the spaces provided.

**FIGURE 1-55**

# Test Your Knowledge

## 4  Understanding Error Messages

**Instructions:**  Figure 1-56(a) displays a Java program that prints a student's name and address on the screen. Figure 1-56(b) displays the compilation error messages. Rewrite the code to correct the errors.

```
Address.java - Notepad
File  Edit  Search  Help
/*
   Project 1   Printing on the screen
   Programmer:      Joy Starks
   Date:           September 9, 2001
   Program Name:   Address
//

public class Address
{
   public static void main(String[] args)
   {
      System.out.println("\t\t\tJason Frontera")
      System.out.println("\t\t\t1422 Stanley Blvd.");
      System.out.println("\t\t\tAurora, Colorado 80014");
   }
```

**(a) Java Source Code**

```
MS-DOS Prompt
  Tr  7 x 11
A:\>javac Address.java
Address.java:1: Comment not terminated at end of input.
/*
^
Address.java:12: Invalid type expression.
      System.out.println("\t\t\tJason Frontera")
                        ^
Address.java:13: Invalid declaration.
      System.out.println("\t\t\t1422 Stanley Blvd.");
                        ^
Address.java:15: '}' expected.
   }
    ^
4 errors

A:\>
```

**(b) Java Compiler Error Messages**

**FIGURE 1-56**

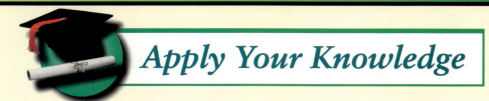

# Apply Your Knowledge

## 1 Writing Java Code from a Flowchart

**Instructions:** Start Notepad. Open the file Apply1.java, from the Student Data Disk (see the inside back cover for instructions on how to obtain a copy of the Data Disk). Using the techniques you learned in the Introduction Project about reading flowcharts and the coding techniques you learned in this project, write the lines of code inside the main method to print the bibliographic entry as described in Figure 1-57.

1. Open the file named Apply1.java on the Data Disk. With the Apply1.java program displayed in the Notepad window, locate the access modifier and class name Apply1. Change the class name to Biblio. Change the name to Biblio in the documentation lines as well.
2. Click inside the main method braces.
3. After studying the flowchart in Figure 1-57, enter the necessary lines of code to produce the output as shown in Figure 1-58.
4. Save the file on your floppy disk with the name "Biblio.java".
5. Open the MS-DOS Prompt window. If you downloaded JDK from the Sun Web site, set the path to the location of your Java bin by typing `path=c:\jdk1.2.2\bin` at the command prompt and press the ENTER key. If you installed the Java compiler from the JBuilder 3 CD-ROM that accompanies this text, type `path=c:\jbuilder3\java\bin` and press the ENTER key.
6. Change to drive A by typing `a:` and then press the ENTER key.
7. Compile your program by typing `javac Biblio.java` at the prompt. If the compilation is successful, proceed to step 8. Otherwise, return to step 3 and correct the errors.
8. Run the program by typing `java Biblio` at the prompt. If the program runs correctly, return to Notepad and print a copy for your instructor. Otherwise, return to step 3 and correct the errors.

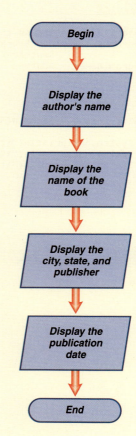

FIGURE 1-57

```
MS-DOS Prompt                                    _ □ ×
Tr  7 x 11 ▼  [:]  ▶■  ■■  ⊞  ☜  ⬚  A

A:\>


Shelly, Gary B., Thomas J. Cashman, and Joy Starks.
        Java Programming: Introductory Concepts and Techniques.
        Cambridge, MA: Course Technology, 2001.



A:\>
```

FIGURE 1-58

# *In the Lab*

## *1* Writing, Compiling, and Running a Java Program

**Problem:** In order to practice writing, compiling, and running Java, you decide to create a Java program that displays your name and address on the screen similar to the display in Figure 1-59.

**FIGURE 1-58**

**Instructions:**

1. To start Notepad, click the Start button. On the Start menu, click Programs and then click Accessories. On the Accessories menu, click Notepad.
2. Type the lines of code below, inserting your name and address in the appropriate places. (Remember: Java is case-sensitive.)
3. Save the program with the filename "Address.java" on your floppy disk.

```
/*
    Project 1, In the Lab 1, Printing my name and address on the screen
    Programmer:    Your Name
    Date:          September 9, 2001
    Program Name: Address
*/
public class Address
{
    public static void main(String[] args)
    {
        System.out.println("\t\t\tYour Name");
        System.out.println("\t\t\tYour Street Address");
        System.out.println("\t\t\tYour City, State, and Zip Code");
    }
}
```

4. To open the MS-DOS Prompt window, click the Start button. On the Start menu, click Programs and then click MS-DOS Prompt. Set your path and specify the floppy disk drive as explained on pages J 1.20 through J 1.21.
5. Compile the program by typing javac Address.java at the command prompt.
6. If necessary, fix any errors in the Notepad window and then save the program again. Once the program compiles correctly, run the program by typing java Address at the command prompt.
7. In the Notepad window, use the Print command on the File menu to print a copy of the coding for your instructor.
8. Close both the Notepad window and the MS-DOS Prompt window using the close button on each title bar.

# In the Lab

## 2 Creating a Display Using Escape Code Sequences

**Problem:** Computer applications typically display a splash screen for users to view while waiting for the entire application to load. The computer science department at Middle Illinois College wants to display a splash screen with the school's initials, MIC, before each application. The display should use the characters themselves to make large versions of the letters M, I, and C (Figure 1-60).

**Instructions:**

1. Start Notepad.
2. Using a block comment beginning with /* type the text from the problem statement above. At the end of the text, type */ to finish the comment.
3. Enter the following code in the Notepad window, using the escape code sequence \t as indicated.
4. Add two or three more lines of code to complete the school's initials.

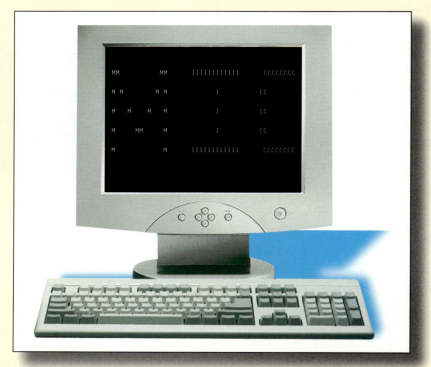

**FIGURE 1-60**

```
public class MIC
{
        public static void main(String[] args)
        {
                System.out.println("\tMM          MM\tIIIIIIIIIIII\t CCCCCCCC");
                System.out.println("\tM M        M M\t     I     \tCC");
                System.out.println("\tM   M    M   M\t     I     \tCC");
                //Add new code here
        }
}
```

5. Save the program with the filename "MIC.java" on your floppy disk.
6. Open the MS-DOS Prompt window. If necessary, set your path. Compile your program by typing javac MIC.java at the command prompt.
7. If there are no compilation errors, execute the program by typing java MIC at the command prompt.
8. In the Notepad window, use the Print command on the File menu to print a copy of the coding for your instructor.
9. Close both the Notepad window and the MS-DOS Prompt window using the close button on each title bar.

# In the Lab

## 3 Creating an Applet with a Background Color

**Problem:** In preparation for creating your own personal Web page, you would like to view some possible background colors that will be easy to read with black text. You decide to write a Java applet that displays black words on a colored background. You will use the setBackground method, which accepts a color argument in applets.

**Instructions:**

1. Start Notepad.
2. Type the following code, inserting your name as the programmer:

```
/*
        Project 1, In the Lab 3, Creating an Applet with a Background Color
        Programmer:    Your Name
        Date:          September 9, 2001
        Program Name: ColorApplet
*/
import java.awt.*;
import java.applet.*;
public class ColorApplet extends Applet
{
    public void paint(Graphics g)
    {
        setBackground(Color.yellow);
        g.drawString("Java is Cool!",15,20);
    }
}
```

3. Save the program with the filename "ColorApplet.java" on your floppy disk.
4. On the Notepad menu bar, click File and then click New. Type the following HTML code.

```
<HTML>
<APPLET CODE = "ColorApplet.class" WIDTH = 400 HEIGHT = 200>
</APPLET>
</HTML>
```

5. Save the HTML program with the filename "ColorApplet.html" on your floppy disk.
6. Open the MS-DOS Prompt window. If necessary, set your path. Compile your program by typing `javac ColorApplet.java` at the command prompt.
7. If there are no compilation errors, execute the applet by typing `appletviewer ColorApplet.html` at the command prompt.
8. Close the applet by clicking the Close button on the Applet Viewer title bar. Open the Java file named "ColorApplet.java" again. Change the word yellow to pink. Recompile and view the applet again. Try various colors.
9. Close Applet Viewer, Notepad, and the MS-DOS Prompt windows by clicking the Close button on each title bar.

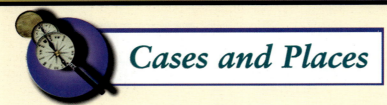

# Cases and Places

The difficulty of these case studies varies:
▶ are the least difficult; ▶▶ are more difficult; and ▶▶▶ are the most difficult.

**1** ▶ Steve's Swimwear plans to move its line of swimwear to the Web next year. In preparation for Steve to begin e-commerce, write a Java program to display the name of the store on the screen. Use appropriate documentation lines. Compile the program and execute it. Once the program executes with no errors, edit the program to include Steve's e-mail address (SwimWithSteve@swimwear.com). Save, compile, and execute the program again. Convert the program to display as an applet. When it is complete, with no compilation errors, write the HTML code to run the applet.

**2** ▶ Using the techniques from In the Lab 2 on page J 1.50, write a Java program to print your school's initials on the screen. Use the escape code characters and spacing to print the letters in the correct locations. Compile and execute your program. Print the source code.

**3** ▶▶ Every applet you write is an instance of the Applet class. Use one of the following help sources to look for topics related to the Applet class: Sun's Java Web site http://java.sun.com/, Java API, Java Reference on the JBuilder 3 Help menu, other IDEs, or a Java reference book. Print out or write down what you found about the hierarchy of the Applet class. Create a hierarchy chart.

**4** ▶▶ The Web contains many sites that boast of free Java applets that you may download. Search for Java applets using a search engine on the Web. When you find a page with some applets, use your browser's View Source command to look at the coding. Within that code, look for tags such as <APPLET CODE = >. Print two examples to submit to your instructor.

**5** ▶▶▶ Companies sometimes use a splash screen on the Web to give the user something to look at while the longer, graphic intensive Web page downloads. Write a splash screen applet that displays the name of your company or school, the address, the Web address, and the toll-free phone number. Position the lines using the g.drawString method with the x and y coordinates. Position the applet window using WIDTH and HEIGHT attributes of the applet tag. Use both Applet Viewer and a browser to look at the splash screen. Compare the two results. Print both the source code for the applet and the HTML file.

**6** ▶▶▶ In preparation for future Java programs, create a Java program named Center that displays a centered, opening screen with information about your program. Include the name of your program, your name, your instructor's name, the date, and any other necessary information. When maximized, the MS-DOS Prompt window displays approximately 25 lines that are 80 characters across. To center vertically, divide the number of lines of text by 25 (dropping any remainder) to determine how many blank lines (\n) to insert before each text line. To center horizontally, count your characters in the line of text, divide that by 2 (dropping any remainder), and then subtract that from 40 to determine how many spaces you should indent from the left margin. Remember that each tab character (\t) moves the text approximately 8 characters to the right. Use the SPACEBAR to insert fewer than 8 spaces. Compile and execute your program. Save your program for future use on a floppy disk.

Java Programming

# Java Programming

# Manipulating Data Using Methods

## OBJECTIVES

You will have mastered the material in this project when you can:

- Enter sample data into a Java program
- Identify primitive data types
- Use proper naming conventions when creating identifiers
- Declare Java variables
- Use operators and parentheses correctly in formulas
- Use variables in output
- Round an answer using the Math.round method
- Find the exponential power of a number using the Math.pow method
- Wrap input streams from a keyboard buffer
- Create Java constructors
- Input data with the readLine method
- Convert strings to numbers using the parse method
- Add interactive components into an applet
- Implement the Java ActionListener
- Execute an interactive applet
- Identify Java source code files and Java class files on a storage device

# A Circus Without Animals

## Cirque du Soleil Stirs the Creative Spirit

A circus without elephants? Without a ringmaster's whistle, top hat, and tails? Yes, when the circus is Cirque du Soleil, a dazzling theatrical experience blending nonstop acrobatics, gymnastics, pantomime, dance, comedy, music, and lighting.

Cirque du Soleil, a French name that translates to Circus of the Sun, has humble beginnings as a festival of street performers in Quebec in 1984. Since that time, more than 23 million people in 120 cities have been mesmerized by a Cirque performance. Four of the shows are based permanently in the United States: *Alegría* in Biloxi, Mississippi; *Mystère* and *O* in Las Vegas; and *La Nouba* at the Walt Disney World Resort near Orlando, Florida. In addition, *Dralion*, *Quidam*, and *Saltimbanco* are traveling throughout North America, Europe, and Asia and are being performed in a giant tent containing an intimate, single ring.

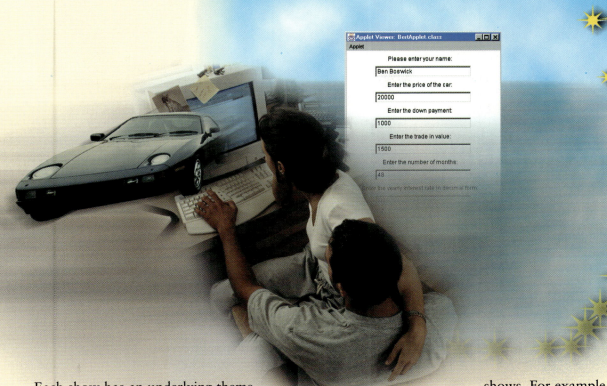

Each show has an underlying theme based on such universal contrasts of reality and fantasy, good and evil, love and loneliness, and childhood and adulthood. Dancers, illusionists, and musicians are among the approximately 75 cast members who interpret these messages accompanied by synthesizers, electric guitars, reed instruments, percussion, and voice. More than 30 percent of the 450 full-time artists currently performing in the shows have an athletic background, particularly in gymnastics.

Each weekend, more than 50,000 people throughout the world witness Cirque's magic. Each day, more than 5,000 visit Cirque's Website, www.cirquedusoleil.com. This creative display of graphics and innovative effects features details of each production, RealVideo of *Mystère*, and virtual reality tours of the International Headquarters in Montreal. Lighting booths, costume shops, training rooms, and the lifts and platforms beneath the stage are displayed.

The Join Cirque section of the Web site describes diverse employment opportunities ranging from accountants to Web architects throughout the world. In addition, the site uses a flexible Java applet, Affiche.class (French for Displays), to show immediate needs for performers in specific

shows. For example, if a dancer is needed for *Mystère*, the Web designers insert the words "DANCER WANTED —- DANCER WANTED —- DANCER WANTED" as the value in the text1 parameter code. When an interested viewer clicks the link below this text, the qualifications for the job and application procedures display.

The site also contains a handy online form to subscribe to the *Dralion* Internet Club, which gives members the opportunity to obtain advance tickets and to view audio and video clips of that show. Also available are a *Dralion* screensaver and wallpapers.

Likewise, you will create a practical Java applet in this project by developing a prototype program for a new car showroom kiosk. A shopper will enter values regarding the car price, loan terms, and down payment, and the program will process this data and then display a monthly payment.

Cirque returns nearly 1 percent of its box-office revenues to assist at-risk youth through the use of circus arts. This international philanthropic activity is an extension of Cirque's quest to awaken dreams and to kindle the imagination. Indeed, Cirque is much more than a circus.

Java Programming

# Manipulating Data Using Methods

**CASE PERSPECTIVE**

Bert's car dealership, Bert's Banner Cars, wants to create an interactive kiosk in the new car show room. The kiosk, with a keyboard and screen, would run a question and answer program for customers to calculate sample monthly payments. Bert is hoping that this kiosk will ease the car buying process for customers.

Once customers have received the appropriate information from a salesperson at the dealership, Bert would like the program at the kiosk to prompt the customers for the price of the new car, their estimated down payment, their trade-in value, the current interest rate, and the number of payments to be made. After the user enters the information, Bert wants to display a message with the customer's projected monthly payment.

You decide to use the Java skills you have acquired to create a prototype program for Bert to consider. With some sample data that Bert provides, you can test your formula and then create an interactive stand-alone program for the kiosk. You also decide to create an applet to run from Bert's Web page.

# Introduction

Manipulating data is integral to creating useful computer programs. Programmers must know how to retrieve and store different kinds of data efficiently. Data may come from a variety of sources, such as users, files, and other programs, as well. It is not unusual to imbed certain kinds of data, such as constant values that will not change, within the computer program and obtain other kinds of data, such as current rates or prices, from external files and users.

Java offers numerous ways to retrieve and manipulate data. Using lines of code that assign values to variables, Java can be used to store data temporarily for processing. Using classes and methods, Java can be used to set fields to specific values and create instances. When users provide data, Java can accept a stream of character input from a keyboard and then, using a method, can read the line and process it.

# Project Two — Bert's Loan Kiosk

**ANALYZING THE PROBLEM** Bert wants a computer program that calculates a monthly payment on a car loan. Input values will include the customer's name, the price of the car, the amount of the down payment, the amount of the trade-in, the interest rate, and the number of payments. Output should include the customer's name and a message with the monthly payment amount (Figure 2-1a). Processing will involve using a standard formula that computes compound interest and then calculates a monthly payment.

The portability of Java across platforms makes it a good programming language to use for this type of application.

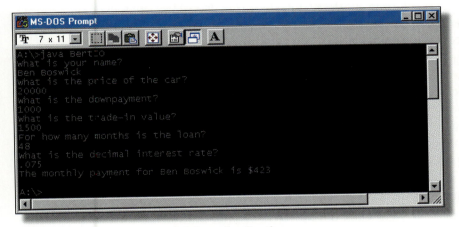

(a) Java Application

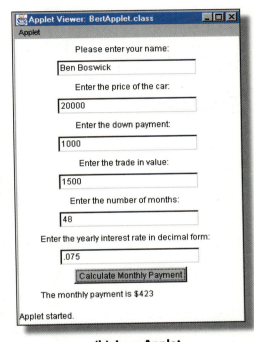

(b) Java Applet

**FIGURE 2-1**

**DESIGNING THE PROGRAM** The structure of the program will be sequential in nature. As you may remember from the Introduction Project, sequential processing means the computer is instructed to perform one action after another without skipping any steps or making any decisions that would affect the flow of the logic.

The program itself will be designed in three stages. The first stage will manipulate sample data that you will store in the code itself. By using sample data in the calculations, you will be able to test the formula and compare the results with known correct values. Second, you will modify the program to accept input from the keyboard. After storing the user's responses, the program will continue executing in a manner similar to the first stage. Finally, you will convert the application to an applet (Figure 2-1b). Each stage of the program should contain appropriate documentation and be saved for future use.

**CODING THE PROGRAM** You will create Java source code using the syntax and commands of the Java programming language. The following pages present a series of step-by-step instructions to write the code for each of the three stages as described in the preceding paragraph.

**TESTING THE PROGRAM** You will test the program by inserting sample data, compiling, and then executing it in console mode.

> **More About**
>
> **Flowcharts**
>
> For more information on flow-charting sequential projects like this one, visit the Java Programming Web Page (www.scsite.com/java/more.htm) and then click Project 2 Flowchart.

**FORMALIZING THE SOLUTION**  You will review the source code, use proper documentation, edit, recompile, and print a copy.

**MAINTAINING THE PROGRAM**  You will modify the program to accept user input and then convert it to an applet.

# Starting a New Java Program

In Project 1, you learned how to set up the desktop, opening both Notepad and the MS-DOS Prompt windows. Complete the following steps to set up the desktop.

## TO SET UP THE DESKTOP

1. Click the Start button on the taskbar, point to Programs on the Start menu, and then point to Accessories on the Programs submenu. Click Notepad on the Accessories submenu.

2. In order to display both the Notepad window and the MS-DOS Prompt window on the desktop, drag the title bar of the Notepad window to the upper-left corner of the desktop. Drag the lower-right corner of the Notepad window so that it covers approximately one-third of the desktop.

3. With the Notepad window still open, click the Start button again. Point to Programs on the Start menu and then click MS-DOS Prompt (Windows 95 or 98) or Command Prompt (Windows NT).

4. If your system displays the MS-DOS Prompt window as a black, full screen, press and hold the ALT key while pressing the TAB key to minimize the window.

5. On the taskbar, right-click the MS-DOS Prompt button and then click Properties on the shortcut menu.

6. When the MS-DOS Prompt Properties dialog box displays, click the Font tab. In the Font size box, scroll, and then click the 7 x 11 or a similar font size.

7. Click the Screen tab. In the Usage area, click the Window option button to select it. In the Window area, make certain that the Display toolbar check box contains a check mark.

8. Click the OK button. If the MS-DOS Prompt window does not display, click the MS-DOS Prompt button so that the window displays. Drag it to the lower-right corner of the screen. If necessary, click in the MS-DOS Prompt window to activate it.

9. If you downloaded Java from the Sun Microsystems Web site, type `path=c:\jdk1.2.2\bin` at the prompt. If you installed the Java compiler from the JBuilder 3 CD-ROM that may accompany this text, type `path=c:\jbuilder3\java\bin` and then press the ENTER key.

10. With a floppy disk inserted in drive A, change to drive A by typing `a:` and then press the ENTER key.

*The desktop displays the Notepad window in the upper-left portion of the screen and the MS-DOS Prompt window in the lower-right portion of the screen (Figure 2-2).*

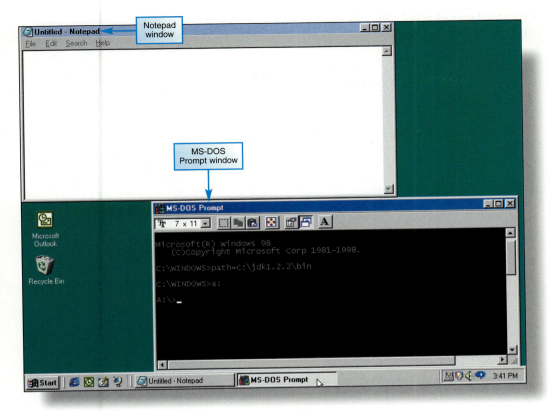

FIGURE 2-2

## Entering Beginning Code

Similar to the program in Project 1, the program in this project for Bert's Banner Cars will include comments, an access modifier with the class name Bert, and a main method. Complete the following steps to enter beginning code.

 **To Enter Beginning Code**

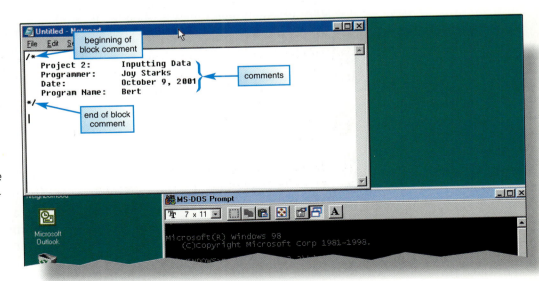

**1** **Click the Notepad window. Type the comments as shown in Figure 2-3, pressing the ENTER key after each line. Insert your own name as the programmer and the current date.**

*The comments display (Figure 2-3). The beginning and ending block symbols delineate the indented comments.*

FIGURE 2-3

**Other Ways**

1. To start Notepad, right-click desktop, click New, click Text Document, double-click New Text Document icon on desktop

2. To open MS-DOS Prompt window, click Start button, click Run, type Command.com press ENTER key

**2** Type `public class Bert` **and then press the ENTER key. Type the opening brace and then press the ENTER key.**

The access modifier and class name display (Figure 2-4). The brace indicates the beginning of the class contents.

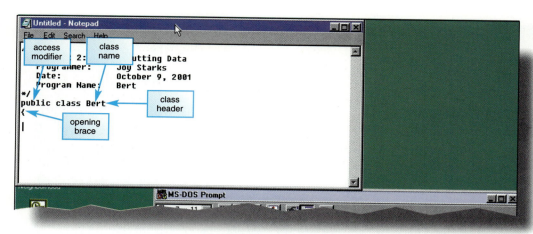

**FIGURE 2-4**

**3** In order to indent the code, press the SPACEBAR **three times. Type** `public static void main(String[] args)` **and then press the ENTER key. Press the SPACEBAR three times, type the opening brace, and then press the ENTER key.**

The main method header that begins most Java programs displays (Figure 2-5).

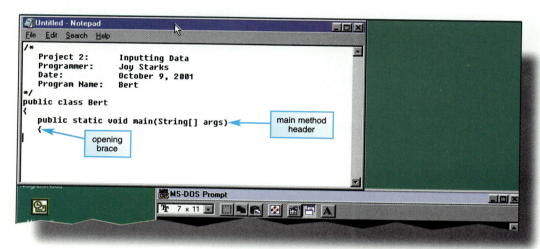

**FIGURE 2-5**

The indentation is not mandatory; Java ignores the space characters. However, it is good programming practice to make the code easy to read by using consistent indentation and to indent all code identically within a given set of braces. Two-space or three-space indentations are used by many programmers. You may use the TAB key to indent, although the TAB key's five space standard may make longer lines wrap around, defeating the goal of easy reading.

# Storing Data

**Data** are small pieces of unprocessed information such as words, texts, or numbers that a computer program uses in order to perform operations and produce output. Data are raw facts used in reasoning or calculations. These data — datum is the singular form of the word — may come from the program itself, from users of the program, or from external files. For a computer program to make use of these pieces of data, they must be stored in the memory of the computer. Each storage location is **allocated**, or set up, before it is used with a declaration statement. The **declaration statement** identifies the type of data to store and assigns a logical name for the storage location.

## Java Data Types

In Java, before you can store a piece of data, the storage location must be declared. **Declaring** means using a descriptive word or abbreviation to identify the type, or data type. A **data type** is a classification of a particular type of information that is a built-in feature of Java. It tells the computer how to interpret and store the data. It is easy for humans to distinguish between different types of data. You usually can tell at a glance whether a number is a percentage, a time, or an amount of money through special symbols, such as % or $, that indicate the data's type. Similarly, a computer uses special internal codes to keep track of the different types of data it processes.

Java is a **strongly typed language**, which means it enforces a set of rules about how you use the objects you create — especially when using data. For instance, you cannot declare a variable location as a single integer in Java and then try to insert a string of characters into that same location. First, there would not be enough room, because each data type has internal sizes associated with it. Second, the Java compiler would be confused and would possibly try to **cast**, or convert, the data from its original form to the declared data type with unpredictable results.

In this project, you will use some of Java's primitive data types. **Primitive data types** are data types that are structured by Java to hold simple kinds of data. Java's primitive data types help programmers by restricting the kind of data allowed in the declared variable location; Java displays an error message during compilation if you try to store some other type of value in that variable. The eight primitive data types are listed in Table 2-1. You will learn about other data types in a future project.

### More About
**Integers**

An integer is a positive or negative whole number. Java provides several types of integers, which are based on the number of bits in the integer's internal representation, such as byte, int, short, and long. You should choose the representation with the narrowest scope for your situation. When an integer literal, or actual value, is used in a Java program, it is considered an int value unless you type an L (designating long) after the value.

| Table 2-1 | Java Primitive Data Types |
|-----------|---------------------------|
| TYPE | DESCRIPTION |
| boolean | stores data in only one of two states, as a logical value of true or false |
| byte | stores whole number values in 8-bit signed locations from −128 to +127 |
| char | stores any one of the 65,436 single characters of the Unicode set, which includes characters and symbols from many languages |
| double | stores numbers with up to 14 or 15 decimal places as double-precision, floating-point values |
| float | stores numbers with up to 6 or 7 decimals as floating-point values |
| int | stores whole number values in 32-bit signed locations from $-2^{31}$ to $+2^{31}-1$ |
| long | stores whole number values in 64-bit signed locations from approximately $-9*10^{18}$ to $+9*10^{18}-1$ |
| short | stores whole number values in 16-bit signed locations from −32,768 to +32,767 |

### More About
**Data Types**

Java's primitive data types are not considered objects. However, each primitive data type has a wrapper class, which encapsulates and helps perform certain data conversions like the parse method. For example, int is a primitive data type, but Integer is a wrapper class.

## Variables and Identifiers

Along with the data type, each storage location is referenced by an identifier. An **identifier** is a word that the programmer chooses to label a storage address in memory. Every time the programmer needs to access that location, he or she uses the identifier name. Internally, storage locations have computer-assigned numeric addresses. Using an identifier is easier than remembering a nondescriptive number.

Identifiers also are used to represent classes, objects, and methods, but when referencing pieces of data, the identifier is naming the location for a variable or constant. A **variable** is a storage location for data that may change during the processing of the computer program. Examples might include calculated amounts, user-entered data, and accumulated totals. A **constant** is a value that does not change during the course of the program, such as a standard rate, a maximum or minimum value, or a constant scientific value such as *pi* or the boiling point of water.

### More About
**Casting**

In general, when a numeric expression contains values or operands of different data types, Java will promote the smaller type to a larger type. This is called implicit casting. An explicit cast is performed when the programmer forces a data type change by including the data type in parentheses before the value.

Identifiers should be meaningful to the purpose of the program. For instance, in a payroll program the name, x, is not as meaningful as the name, grosspay. Even though the programmer chooses the names of the identifiers, Java imposes a few rules to which programmers must adhere.

▶ The first character of an identifier must be a letter. Subsequent characters can be letters or numbers.

▶ Identifiers may not contain special characters such as percent signs or number signs. Identifiers may contain underscores (_) and the dollar sign ($), which are considered letters in Java.

▶ Identifiers may not contain spaces.

▶ Identifiers are case-sensitive.

▶ Identifiers may be spelled using any alphabet of any spoken language.

▶ Reserved words that are part of the Java language may not be used as identifiers (see Appendix B).

It is common practice among Java programmers to begin variable identifiers and object instances with a lowercase letter. Classes usually begin with a capital letter. Constants commonly are named in all uppercase letters. Java is case-sensitive, so you must be careful when typing code. Restrictions such as these may slow down the typing task, but it is easier to locate certain kinds of identifiers if a naming scheme is used.

Table 2-2 lists some legal and illegal examples of Java identifiers.

| Table 2-2 | Examples of Legal and Illegal Java Identifiers | |
|---|---|---|
| **LEGAL** | **ILLEGAL** | **EXPLANATION** |
| firstName first_Name | First Name | Java does not allow spaces; if spacing is desired for legibility, use an underscore (_) between words or capitalize the second word. |
| employee7 | 7employee | Identifiers must begin with a letter. |
| $amount | $amt.cents | The dollar sign ($) is allowed; however, special characters such as the period (.) are not allowed. |
| totalSales | Sales&Tax | Special characters (&) are not allowed. |
| invNo7123 | 7123 | Identifiers may not begin with a number. |
| numberOfPeople | public | The reserved word, public, is not allowed. |

## Declaring Variables

**Declaring a variable** means listing the data type and the identifier before it is used in the program.

```
int grandTotal;
```

This example code tells Java that an integer will be stored, and that you plan to reference it with the word grandTotal as an identifier. Declarations must take place before variables can be used; however, you may combine the declaration of a variable with its first value or assignment. In the following example, the interest rate is declared a float and assigned a value of nine percent in the same line.

```
float interestRate = .09;
```

## Field Declarations

Some Java programmers refer to the declaration of a variable as a field declaration. Field declarations may include an access modifier that determines how the field can be accessed and its scope. For example, private double width; declares that the identifier width will not be available to other classes.

## Reference Variables

Java programmers use the term, reference variable, when the declaration is associated with an object. For instance, if you create an object called, Person, then the declaration would be Person student; which tells Java that student always must refer to a Person data type.

## Declaration Syntax

Every Java statement must end with a semicolon, but you can declare multiple identifiers of the same data type on the same line, as long as they are separated by commas. Identifiers, or variables, must be declared before they can be used, and the names are case-sensitive.

As you declare your variables and add more lines of code, you will benefit by having a bigger window to display more workspace. Perform the following steps to maximize the Notepad window and then code the declaration statements of the program for Bert's Banner Cars.

 **To Maximize the Notepad Window and Declare Variables**

**1** If necessary, click the Notepad window to activate it. Point to the Maximize button on the Notepad title bar.

*The title bar displays buttons to minimize, maximize, and close the window (Figure 2-6).*

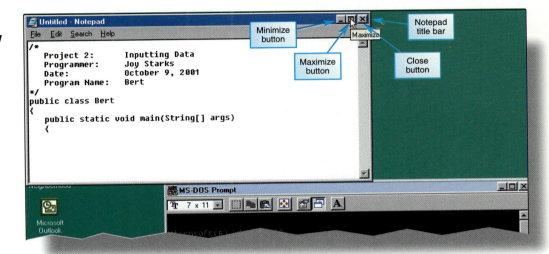

FIGURE 2-6

**2** Click the Maximize button and then click below the lines of code in the Notepad window on line 11.

*The insertion point displays on line 11 (Figure 2-7).*

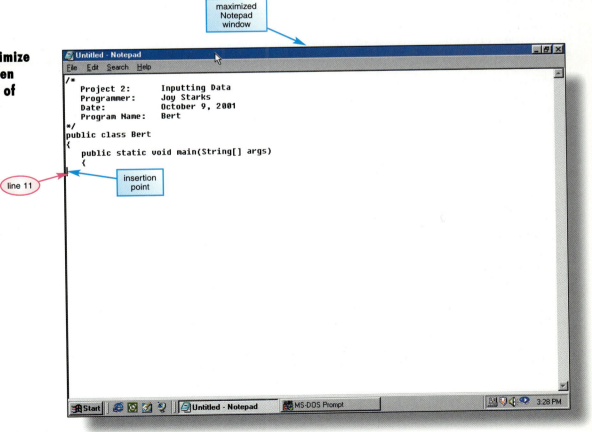

FIGURE 2-7

**3** **Type the declaration section of code as shown in Table 2-3 using proper indentation.**

The declaration for the pieces of data display (Figure 2-8). No assignment of values is made.

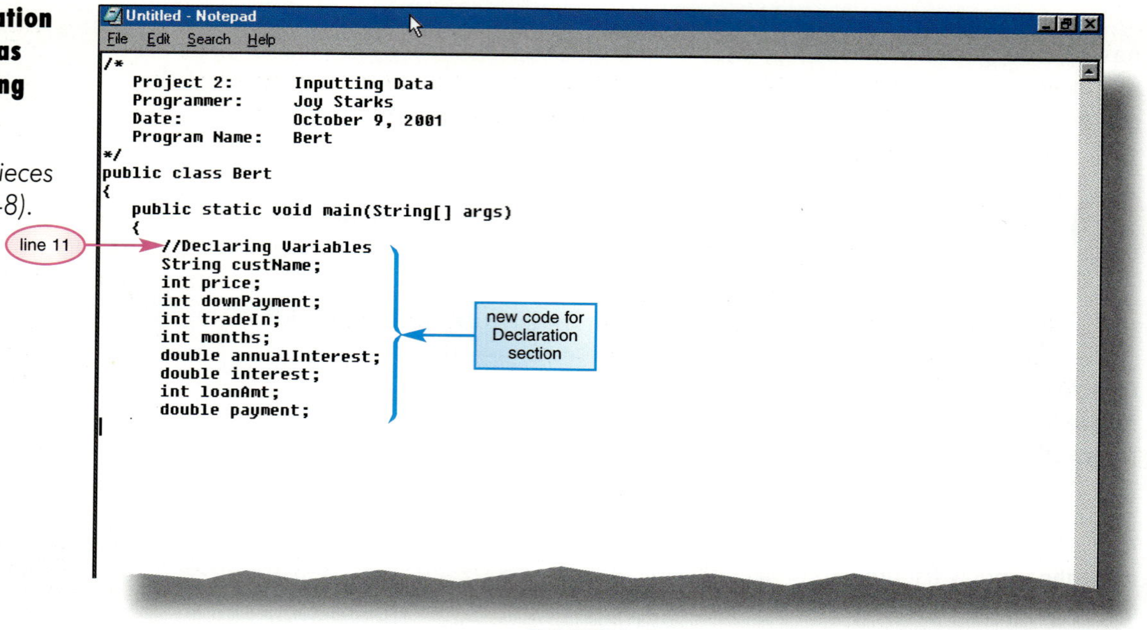

```
/*
   Project 2:      Inputting Data
   Programmer:     Joy Starks
   Date:           October 9, 2001
   Program Name:   Bert
*/
public class Bert
{
   public static void main(String[] args)
   {
      //Declaring Variables
      String custName;
      int price;
      int downPayment;
      int tradeIn;
      int months;
      double annualInterest;
      double interest;
      int loanAmt;
      double payment;
```

line 11

new code for Declaration section

**FIGURE 2-8**

### Table 2-3

| LINE | CODE |
| --- | --- |
| 11 | //Declaring Variables |
| 12 | String custName; |
| 13 | int price; |
| 14 | int downPayment; |
| 15 | int tradeIn; |
| 16 | int months; |
| 17 | double annualInterest; |
| 18 | double interest; |
| 19 | int loanAmt; |
| 20 | double payment; |

If you want to declare variables of different types, you must use a separate statement for each type; however, if you have several variables of the same type, you may list the data type once, and then include each variable on the same line separated by commas.

```
double price, salary;
```

It may be helpful to remember that integers are whole numbers, whereas the double data type represents a double-precision, floating-point value. Table 2-1 on page J 2.9 describes a double as a number that is precise up to 14 decimal places. The word floating comes from scientists who refer to large numbers in scientific notation. For instance, 1,200,000 can be notated as 1.2 times 10 to the power of 6. The decimal point floated six places to the left.

**Precision** refers to the amount of storage allocated to hold the fractional part of a number. The higher that storage amount, the more precise the number.

# Using Sample Data

Programmers use sample data to test their programs. **Sample data**, or test data, are pieces of information used in lieu of the real data in order to see if a program is functioning properly. For instance, if a programmer wants to test a formula to accumulate a total of all purchased items and then calculate sales tax, he or she might create a fictitious list of items to be purchased. The programmer then would use these amounts, instead of a real customer's bill, to practice adding the amounts together and multiplying by a percentage. By inputting sample data into the computer, the programmer manipulates data that would not affect a real customer. Additionally, results from sample data can be checked against the already known correct answers to assure that all formulas and calculations are correct.

## Writing Code with Sample Data

You will use assignment statements to store sample data values in the computer's memory. An **assignment statement** is a line of code beginning with a location, followed by an equal sign (=) and the new value.

```
location = value
```

The value may be a number, a string, a formula, or reference to another piece of data. The location may be a variable identifier or an attribute of an object.

Perform the following step to assign sample data to the program.

**More About**

### The Scope of Sample Data

An identifier's scope is simply that portion of the class where it may be used. Fields or instance variables in Java have class scope that extends throughout the entire body of the class definition in which they are declared. Class scope identifiers will not retain their value in other classes.

 **To Assign Sample Data**

**1** In the Notepad window, position the insertion point below the previous code in the workspace on line 21. Press the ENTER key to insert a blank line and then type the comment and code as displayed in Table 2-4 using proper indentation. After the last line of code is entered, press the ENTER key.

*The comments and assignment statements display (Figure 2-9). A blank line between sections of code makes it easier to read and understand.*

```
🗐 Untitled - Notepad                                          _ 🗗 ✕
File  Edit  Search  Help
/*
    Project 2:        Inputting Data
    Programmer:       Joy Starks
    Date:             October 9, 2001
    Program Name:     Bert
*/
public class Bert
{
    public static void main(String[] args)
    {
        //Declaring Variables
        String custName;
        int price;
        int downPayment;
        int tradeIn;
        int months;
        double annualInterest;
        double interest;
        int loanAmt;
        double payment;

        //Assigning Values
        custName = "Ben Boswick";
        price = 20000;
        downPayment = 1000;
        tradeIn = 1500;
        months = 48;
        annualInterest = .075;
```

line 21

new code for Assignment section

**FIGURE 2-9**

| Table 2-4 | |
|-----------|------|
| LINE | CODE |
| 22 | //Assigning Values |
| 23 | custName = "Ben Boswick"; |
| 24 | price = 20000; |
| 25 | downPayment = 1000; |
| 26 | tradeIn = 1500; |
| 27 | months = 48; |
| 28 | annualInterest = .075; |

Notice that assignment statements are code statements and end with a semicolon in Java. Later, when the program accepts data from a user, these assignment statements with sample data will be removed from the program.

**Operators**

Operators need not be preceded and followed by a space. Java basically ignores any white space between commands. Pressing the SPACEBAR key before and after operators simply makes the formulas easier to read.

# Operators

Performing mathematical operations and using formulas in Java is similar to other programming languages. Values stored in the computer may need to be manipulated arithmetically, such as adding or subtracting values; or they may need to be evaluated logically, such as testing to see if the hours worked are greater than 40. Operator symbols in Java are similar to regular algebraic symbols. In the case of formulas, an assignment statement is used. The formula is placed on the right side of the equal sign and the location to store the result is on the left.

```
int answer = 15 + 5;
```

In this example, the result of 20 is stored in an integer variable named, answer. Alternately if the declaration is coded separately, the two lines of code would display as follows.

```
int answer;
answer = 15 + 5;
```

Both ways of assigning a formula's solution to a variable location are acceptable and produce the same result.

Because Java evaluates the code on the right side of the equal sign before assigning the value to the left side, a special case might arise where a value is manipulated and stored back in the same place. For instance, if you wanted to collect the number of hits on a web page, you might write a line of code to add one more to a storage location every time the page is downloaded from the Web server. The result is an accumulated total or counter.

```
counter = counter + 1;
```

In this example, every time Java executes the line of code, one more will be added to the counter. You will use accumulators and counters in a future project.

## Arithmetic Operators

Arithmetic operators manipulate two or more numeric values. Table 2-5 lists the five arithmetic operators, their descriptions, examples, and example results. You may be familiar with most of the arithmetic operators. The unusual ones, with respect to Java, are integer and modular division. **Integer division** is performed when both the dividend and the divisor are integers. Java forces the result to be an integer because it is a primitive data type. **Modular division** is a way to store any truncated remainder value from integer division. The **modulus operator**, %, is sometimes called the remainder operator. It is entered between two integers and performs modular division. Modular division is common to many programming languages.

**More About**

**The Modulus Operator**

The modulus operator can be used by itself without its corresponding integer division. Read as 10 mod 3, the result is 1. You do not have to know that 10/3 is 3. Many times, you want to know only if a remainder exists; therefore, modulus operations can stand alone.

## Table 2-5 Arithmetic Operators in Java

| OPERATOR | DESCRIPTION | EXAMPLE | RESULT |
|---|---|---|---|
| + | Addition | 20 + 3 | 23 |
| - | Subtraction | 20 – 3 | 17 |
| * | Multiplication | 20 * 3 | 60 |
| / | Division with integers | 20 / 3 | 6 (the remainder is dropped because the operands both are integers) |
| / | Division with floating point numbers | 20.0 / 3.0 | 6.6666667 for float<br>6.666666666666667 for double |
| % | Modular division | 20 % 3 | 2 (only the integer remainder is stored) |

The first four arithmetic operators may manipulate any data type. However, if you divide integer values, the remainder will be dropped. Dividing float or double numbers will yield decimal results. If the operands in a division problem are of different data types, Java **promotes** the integers to floating point values before the expression is evaluated. Modular division can be performed only on integers, because an integer remainder results. You will learn about special operators that involve single value arithmetic in a later project.

## Comparison Operators

Comparison operators involve two values, as do arithmetic operators; however, they compare the numbers. The result evaluates to be either true or false. Programmers use the term **boolean** to store a result that only has two states, such as true or false, yes or no, 1 or 0. As an example, the following statement would declare a boolean variable and store a true value if the variable, hours, is greater than 40.

```
boolean isOvertime = ( hours > 40 );
```

Comparison operations are enclosed in parentheses. The identifiers for boolean variables are recognized more easily if a form of the verb, to be, is used as part of the variable name, as in the example above.

Table 2-6 lists the six comparison operators, their descriptions, a true expression, and a false expression.

**More About**

**Operators**

Java actually has 12 different kinds of operators, including parentheses, incremental, unary, type casts, constructors, relational, equality, and Boolean, as well as the traditional operators.

## Table 2-6 Comparison Operators in Java

| OPERATOR | DESCRIPTION | TRUE EXPRESSION | FALSE EXPRESSION |
|---|---|---|---|
| < | less than | (2 < 9) | (9 < 2) |
| > | greater than | (5 > 1) | (1 > 5) |
| <= | less than or equal to | (3 <= 4) | (5 <= 4) |
| >= | greater than or equal to | (8 >= 6) | (3 >= 7) |
| == | equal to | (9 == 9) | (5 == 9) |
| != | not equal to | (4 != 2) | (2 != 2) |

The first four comparison operators sometimes are referred to as **relational operators** because they compare the relation of two values; the last two commonly are called **equality operators.** The double equal sign (==) is used to differentiate "equal to" from the assignment statement's equal sign used in Java. Spaces are not included between comparison operator double symbols.

## Precedence

With both arithmetic and comparison operators, operations enclosed within parentheses indicate precedence. An operation takes **precedence** if it is performed before another operation. After parentheses, multiplication and division are performed before addition and subtraction, in order from the left to the right. Relational operators take precedence over equality operators. When in doubt about the precedence, use parentheses to force the desired operation to take place first.

## Formulas

A **formula** is a mathematical sentence that contains values — variables, constants, or numbers — and operators. Formulas may appear in assignment statements or as a part of a method, in which case the result becomes an argument or parameter. Three formulas will be used in this program.

▶ Divide the annual percentage rate by 12 for a monthly payment
▶ Calculate a loan amount by subtracting the down payment and trade-in values from the price of the car
▶ Calculate a monthly payment with compound interest

The formula for compound interest contains an exponent. Even though Java has no exponentiation operator, it easily is accomplished by using a prewritten method named, pow, which is from the Math class. The **Math class** is part of the java.lang package. It contains methods for a number of useful functions such as rounding, randomizing, and square roots. In this case, pow is a method for expressing exponentiation. The Math class methods have the following general form:

```
Math.method(arguments)
```

For example, if you want Java to calculate 17 to the power of 9, commonly written as $17^9$, you would enter Math.pow(17,9).

Perform the following steps to enter the formulas.

## More About

### Precedence

Formulas that do not contain parentheses are hard to read. Java will perform multiplication, division, and modulus operations, left to right, before performing addition and subtraction. You later will learn about unary operators, which change that order. Unary operators are performed before all other operations and then they are performed right to left. To avoid confusion, use parentheses.

## More About

### Operator Overloading

Operator symbols are overloaded in Java, which means they can be used for more than one type-dependent operation. For example, the plus sign (+) may be used for addition and string concatenation, and the slash (/) is used for both integer and floating-point division.

**Steps** | **To Enter the Formulas**

**1** In the Notepad window, position the insertion point below the code previously entered. Press the ENTER key to insert a blank line and then press the SPACEBAR to indent as shown in Figure 2-10. Type the comment, //Calculations and then press the ENTER key. Indent again, and then type interest = annualInterest/12; to calculate the interest rate. Press the ENTER key.

The formula to divide the yearly interest rate by 12 displays (Figure 2-10).

```
/*
    Project 2:      Inputting Data
    Programmer:     Joy Starks
    Date:           October 9, 2001
    Program Name:   Bert
*/
public class Bert
{
    public static void main(String[] args)
    {
        //Declaring Variables
        String custName;
        int price;
        int downPayment;
        int tradeIn;
        int months;
        double annualInterest;
        double interest;
        int loanAmt;
        double payment;

        //Assigning Values
        custName = "Ben Boswick";
        price = 20000;
        downPayment = 1000;
        tradeIn = 1500;
        months = 48;
        annualInterest = .075;

        //Calculations
        interest = annualInterest/12;
```

insertion point

formula to calculate monthly interest

**FIGURE 2-10**

**2** On the new line 33, indent and then type loanAmt = price-downPayment-tradeIn; to calculate the loan amount. Press the ENTER key.

The formula to calculate the amount of the loan displays (Figure 2-11).

```
/*
    Project 2:      Inputting Data
    Programmer:     Joy Starks
    Date:           October 9, 2001
    Program Name:   Bert
*/
public class Bert
{
    public static void main(String[] args)
    {
        //Declaring Variables
        String custName;
        int price;
        int downPayment;
        int tradeIn;
        int months;
        double annualInterest;
        double interest;
        int loanAmt;
        double payment;

        //Assigning Values
        custName = "Ben Boswick";
        price = 20000;
        downPayment = 1000;
        tradeIn = 1500;
        months = 48;
        annualInterest = .075;

        //Calculations
        interest = annualInterest/12;
        loanAmt = price-downPayment-tradeIn;
```

line 33

formula to calculate amount of loan

insertion point

**FIGURE 2-11**

**3** **On the new line 34, indent and then type** `payment = loanAmt/((1/interest) -(1/(interest*Math .pow(1+interest, months))));` **to calculate the monthly payment. Press the ENTER key.**

The formula to calculate the monthly payment displays (Figure 2-12). Notice this formula uses variables assigned in the previous formulas, as well as the method, pow. The formula is a standard one used by banks and other industries to compute compound interest.

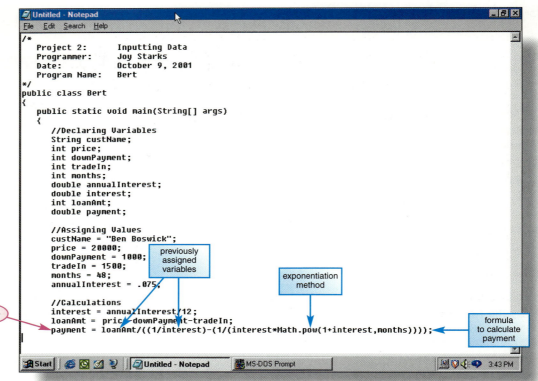

**FIGURE 2-12**

In general, you invoke methods by typing the class name, followed by a period, followed by the method name. Recall that the values inside the parentheses are the arguments — the pieces of information the method needs to perform its task. The Math class is part of the java.lang package, which, as discussed in Project 1, is part of the JDK and needs no previous declaration or import.

Now that you have entered all the formulas, you are ready to code the output to the display.

# Output

After all calculations are performed, the program should display appropriate responses on the screen. Output will include a message with the customer's name and the monthly payment for the car the customer wishes to purchase.

## Using Variables in Output

The System.out.println, used in Project 1, commonly displays a string of characters, but it also can display values from variable locations. Remember that System.out refers to the default output device, usually the monitor. The only way for Java to display the values from variable locations to users is to send them to an output device. An identifier may be used instead of the literal string inside the println argument. In the following example, the value stored in amountBorrowed would display.

```
System.out.println(amountBorrowed);
```

If you want to combine strings of characters and variables on the same line, the code can take one of two forms. First, you can use the method, print, followed by println. The print method does not force a new line after displaying, so that any output following a print method will display on the same line. The following two lines of code display on one line on the screen.

```
System.out.print("The answer is ");
System.out.println(answer);
```

A second way to combine strings and variables on the same line is to use concatenation. Using a plus sign (+), Java allows a **concatenation**, or joining, of these types of data in a single output line of code.

```
System.out.println("The answer is " + answer);
```

In the example, the plus sign (+) concatenates the string with the variable to display both on the same line. Leaving a space after the word, is, keeps the message and the answer from running together in both examples.

## Using Methods in Output

Additionally, programmers may invoke methods in their output. Adding the Math.round method to the above example, would round off any decimal places.

```
System.out.println(Math.round(answer));
```

Math is the name of the class; round is the method; answer is the argument.

Perform the steps on the next page to enter the code to produce output on the screen using variables, concatenation, and a method.

**More About**

**Output**

For more information on outputting to a file for printing on a printer, visit the Java Programming Web Page (www.scsite.com/java/more.htm) and click File Processing.

## Steps To Enter Output Code

**1** **In the Notepad window, position the insertion point below the code previously entered. If necessary, press the ENTER key to begin a new line 36. Indent and then type** `//Output` **as a comment for this section. Press the ENTER key.**

*The insertion point displays on a new line (Figure 2-13).*

Untitled - Notepad
File Edit Search Help
Programmer: Joy Starks
Date: October 9, 2001
Program Name: Bert
*/
public class Bert
{
public static void main(String[] args)
{
//Declaring Variables
String custName;
int price;
int downPayment;
int tradeIn;
int months;
double annualInterest;
double interest;
int loanAmt;
double payment;
//Assigning Values
custName = "Ben Boswick";
price = 20000;
downPayment = 1000;
tradeIn = 1500;
months = 48;
annualInterest = .075;
//Calculations
interest = annualInterest/12;
loanAmt = price-downPayment-tradeIn;
payment = loanAmt/((1/interest)-(1/(interest*Math.pow(1+interest,months))));
//Output
line 36
comment
insertion point
Start
Untitled - Notepad
MS-DOS Prompt
3:48 PM

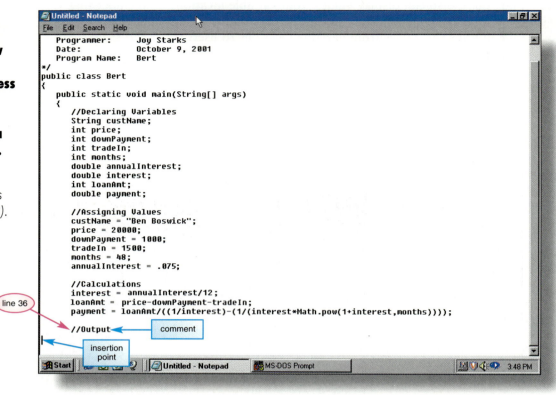

FIGURE 2-13

**2** **Indent and then type** `System.out.print("The monthly payment for " + custName + " is $");` **to enter the code for output on line 37. Press the ENTER key.**

*The output line of code displays (Figure 2-14). The plus signs concatenate strings on either side of the variable. The print method will not create a new line during execution.*

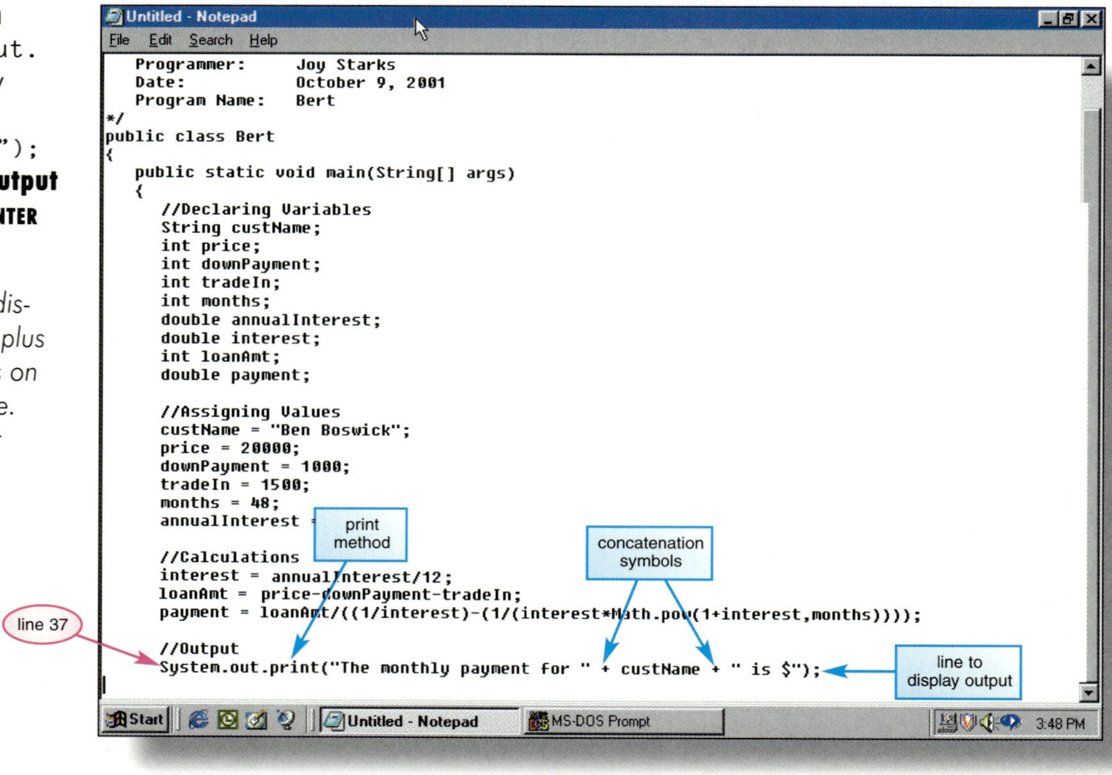

Untitled - Notepad
File Edit Search Help
Programmer: Joy Starks
Date: October 9, 2001
Program Name: Bert
*/
public class Bert
{
public static void main(String[] args)
{
//Declaring Variables
String custName;
int price;
int downPayment;
int tradeIn;
int months;
double annualInterest;
double interest;
int loanAmt;
double payment;
//Assigning Values
custName = "Ben Boswick";
price = 20000;
downPayment = 1000;
tradeIn = 1500;
months = 48;
annualInterest
//Calculations
interest = annualInterest/12;
loanAmt = price-downPayment-tradeIn;
payment = loanAmt/((1/interest)-(1/(interest*Math.pow(1+interest,months))));
//Output
System.out.print("The monthly payment for " + custName + " is $");
print method
concatenation symbols
line 37
line to display output
Start
Untitled - Notepad
MS-DOS Prompt
3:48 PM

FIGURE 2-14

**3** **Indent and then type** System.out. println(Math.round (payment)); **to code the monthly payment output on line 38. Press the ENTER key.**

*The output line displays (Figure 2-15). The rounded monthly payment will display on the same line as the previous data.*

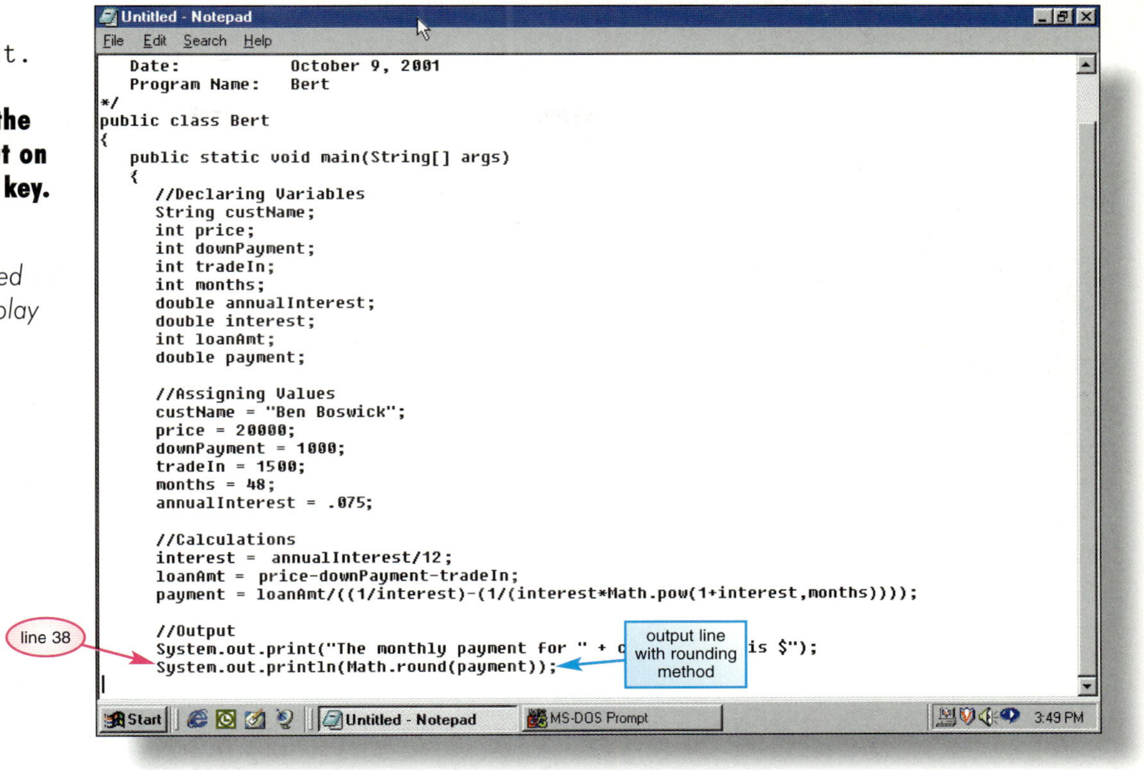

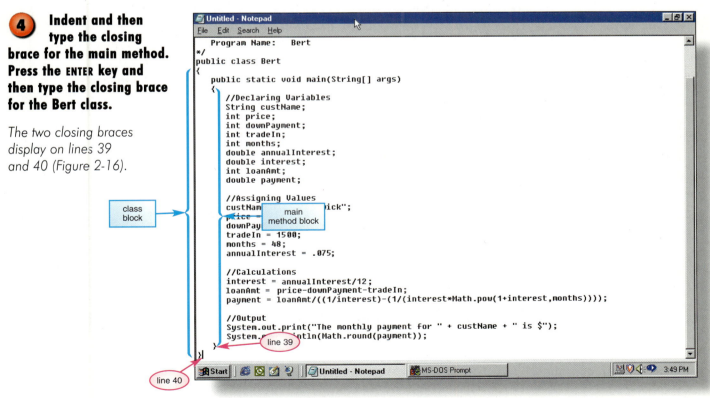

FIGURE 2-15

**4** **Indent and then type the closing brace for the main method. Press the ENTER key and then type the closing brace for the Bert class.**

*The two closing braces display on lines 39 and 40 (Figure 2-16).*

FIGURE 2-16

Your program now is complete. You coded the documentation, the opening class and method headers, the declaration of variables, the assignment of sample data, the calculations, and the output. Figure 2-17 shows a printout of the program code in its entirety. Check for syntax, spelling errors, capitalization, and indentations. When you are confident everything is correct, you are ready to save and compile your program.

```
                                            Bert


/*
    Project 2:       Inputting Data
    Programmer:      Joy Starks
    Date:            October 9, 2001
    Program Name:    Bert
*/
public class Bert
{
    public static void main(String[] args)
    {
        //Declaring Variables
        String custName;
        int price;
        int downPayment;
        int tradeIn;
        int months;
        double annualInterest;
        double interest;
        int loanAmt;
        double payment;

        //Assigning Values
        custName = "Ben Boswick";
        price = 20000;
        downPayment = 1000;
        tradeIn = 1500;
        months = 48;
        annualInterest = .075;

        //Calculations
        interest = annualInterest/12;
        loanAmt = price-downPayment-tradeIn;
        payment = loanAmt/((1/interest)-(1/(interest*Math.pow(1+interest,months))));

        //Output
        System.out.print("The monthly payment for " + custName + " is $");
        System.out.println(Math.round(payment));
    }
}




                                          Page 1
```

**FIGURE 2-17**

# Saving, Compiling, and Executing

You will save the program on a floppy disk, compile the source code with the javac compiler, and then execute the program by running the compiled bytecode.

## Saving the Source Code

To save the source code, you must save the Notepad file with a .java extension. Complete the following steps to save the source code.

### TO SAVE THE SOURCE CODE

**1** With a floppy disk in drive A, click File on Notepad's menu bar, and then click Save As.

**2** When the Save As dialog box displays, type "Bert.java" in the File name text box. You must type the quotation marks around the file name.

**3** If necessary, click the Save in box arrow and then click 3½ Floppy (A:) in the list.

**4** Click the Save button.

*The file is saved on drive A.*

## Compiling the Program

Remember that compiling must be done before executing. The compiler translates the source code into Java bytecode. To compile the program, you must issue the javac command at the command prompt, followed by the name of the file. Complete the following steps to compile the program.

### TO COMPILE THE PROGRAM

**1** If you previously closed the MS-DOS Prompt window, or the MS-DOS Prompt button does not display on your taskbar, re-open it by following steps 3 through 10 on page J 2.6 in this project. Otherwise, click the MS-DOS Prompt button on the taskbar.

**2** In the MS-DOS Prompt window, type `javac Bert.java` at the A: prompt and then press the ENTER key.

*The program compiles. If Java notifies you of compilation errors, fix them in the Notepad window, and then save and compile again.*

## Executing the Program

Now that the program has been compiled into bytecode, you are ready to execute, or run, the program and see the results of your coded calculations. Perform the steps on the next page to execute the program.

**Saving Files**

Notepad's default file type is .txt, which means that Notepad wants to save most of its files as raw text files. Using quotation marks around the complete java file names create an explicit extension. The explicit extension overrides Notepad's default setting to save files as text documents.

**Other Ways**

1. Press ALT+F, press A

## More About

## Repeating Commands

The F3 function key can be used to repeat the most recent command in the MS-DOS Prompt window. For instance, say you compiled and got an error. After you fix the error and save in Notepad, pressing the F3 key will type the compile command again for you.

## TO EXECUTE THE PROGRAM

**1** If necessary, click the MS-DOS Prompt window.

**2** Type java Bert and then press the ENTER key.

*The output displays on the screen (Figure 2-18).*

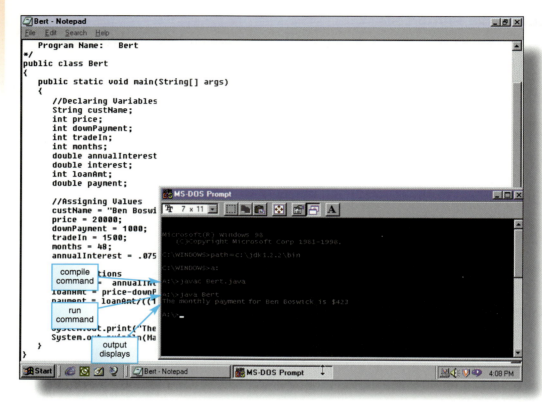

**FIGURE 2-18**

Notice the answer displays on one line. If your screen displays a different monthly payment than what is displayed in Figure 2-18, double check the formulas entered on pages J 2.11 and J 2.12. Fix any errors, save, and recompile. You may want to print a copy of the Bert source code to view as you modify the program for user input instead of sample data. You also may refer back to Figure 2-17 on page J 2.22.

# User Input

Programmers who want to use timely data or data that changes on a regular basis usually do not type the data into their programs. For example, bank transaction data, such as deposits and checks, are recorded electronically. Programmers reference only the external data source in their program. Bank customers, not the programmer, can enter data such as PIN numbers using the ATM machine keyboard. In fact, it is more common to rely on data from external sources than it is to type the data into the program itself. External data allows for flexibility in programming and tailoring of the program to fit the company's or the user's needs.

## Input from the Keyboard

**Interactive** is the term used with programs that allow the user to interact with the program by making choices, entering data, and viewing results. Interactive input and output in Java usually involves a user of the program entering data from a keyboard and viewing results on the screen.

## Streams and Constructors

In Java, data flowing in or out of a program are called a **stream**. The System class, which you used in Project 1, actually has many different streams, which are defined as class variables, including the more popular ones: System.in, System.out, and System.err. Table 2-7 describes these three system classes.

| Table 2-7 | System Classes | | |
|---|---|---|---|
| CLASS | FUNCTION | METHODS USED IN IN CONJUNCTION WITH CLASS | DEFAULT DEVICE |
| System.in | Accepts data from the keyboard buffer wrapped in the InputStreamReader | readLine( ) | keyboard buffer |
| System.out | Sends output to the display or redirects to a designated file | print( ) println( ) flush( ) | monitor |
| System.err | Sends output to the monitor, used for prompts and error messages | print( ) flush( ) | monitor |

Recall that System.out sent a stream to the standard output device, usually the monitor. System.out implemented the method, println, to transfer the stream of characters.

```
System.out.println("Anita's Antiques");
```

The result of System.out.println was a display of the literal string argument on the screen. In the above example, Anita's Antiques would appear on the display. System.in, however, is more complicated. The JDK contains no simple method for input like the println method for output.

System.in actually refers to a buffered input stream. As a user types, the keystrokes are sent to a buffer. A **buffer** is a data area shared by hardware devices or programs, where data are held until they are needed by the processor. Buffering ensures that if a user hits the BACKSPACE key to take out a character, the deleted characters are not sent when the program retrieves characters from the input buffer.

The JDK contains a special reader to read the input buffer called the InputStreamReader. The **InputStreamReader** (**ISR**) is a Java class or object that serves as an intermediary between the input buffer and the Java program. Java programmers use the word, **wrap**, to describe how the ISR envelops the stream from the input buffer. The Java code necessary to reference the buffer is an ISR class method, with System.in as the argument.

```
InputStreamReader(System.in)
```

**More About**

**Buffers**

For more information on computer system buffers, visit the Java Programming Web Page (www.scsite.com/java/more.htm) and click Buffers.

One more step must be completed before you can use the data from the ISR. It must be stored and named in an accessible way as described in the next section.

## Instantiation and Constructors

As you may recall, storage locations must be declared and identified before they can be used. This is true for data from the ISR as well. Because the ISR data are special kinds of data from a buffer, its data type is not a primitive one. Complex data types must be created by the programmer or instantiated from a Java class. **Instantiation** is the process of creating an instance from a previously defined class. In the case of buffers, the previously defined class is called the BufferedReader. **BufferedReader** is a non-primitive class from a package of input and output utilities called java.io, which comes with the JDK.

The code necessary to instantiate is called a constructor, or constructor method. A **constructor** specifies the data type and assigns an identifier just like a declaration statement. The difference is that a constructor uses an assignment statement to declare the variable as an instance. A constructor takes the following form. The equal sign and the word, new, always are included.

```
Class identifier = new Class( );
```

In the case of instantiating for input, the BufferedReader is the class. Most programmers use a variable identifier such as myIn or dataIn to hold their input data. The resulting line of Java code may seem a bit cryptic; however, when broken down into its components, it is easier to understand.

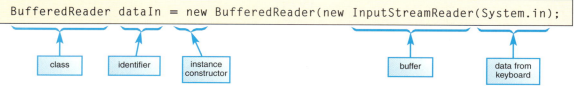

```
BufferedReader dataIn = new BufferedReader(new InputStreamReader(System.in);
```
class    identifier    instance constructor      buffer    data from keyboard

An identifier called dataIn is created from an instance of the BufferedReader class. It will contain the new data from System.in wrapped in the InputStreamReader each time the statement is executed. Figure 2-19 shows the flow of the data stream.

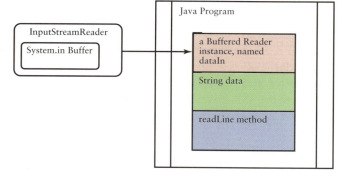

InputStreamReader

System.in Buffer

Java Program

a Buffered Reader instance, named dataIn

String data

readLine method

**FIGURE 2-19**

## Modifying the Bert Program

As you modify this program to accept user input, it is appropriate to give this version of the program a new name, not only to distinguish it from the previous version, but also to better reflect the purpose. You will rename this program BertIO.java. Using a name such as BertIO, instead of BertVersion2, more closely represents the purpose of the program and is easier to remember.

Inserting an import statement before the class header will tell Java to expect references to classes from the java.io package, as it did in Project 1. Additionally, you will enter a constructor, creating a storage allocation for the instance of the buffered stream.

Perform the following steps to edit the code for interactive data input from the user.

### More About

### Class File Names

If you routinely edit, recompile, and execute the same file name, Java allows you to add an optional command to the java statement to re-compile if necessary. By typing java -cs and then the file name, the Java runtime system will recompile if a newer version of bytecode exists.

## To Enter New Code

**1** If necessary, minimize the MS-DOS Prompt window so that the maximized Notepad window displays. Point to the end of the word, Bert, in line 5.

*The mouse pointer displays as an I-beam over previously typed text at the end of the word Bert (Figure 2-20).*

line 5

```
Bert - Notepad
File   Edit   Search   Help
     Program Name:      Bert              mouse
*/                                        pointer
public class Bert
{
     public static void main(String[] args)
     {
          //Declaring Variables
          String custName;
          int price;
          int downPayment;
          int tradeIn;
          int months;
          double annualInterest;
          double interest;
          int loanAmt;
          double payment;

          //Assigning Values
          custName = "Ben Boswick";
          price = 20000;
          downPayment = 1000;
          tradeIn = 1500;
          months = 48;
          annualInterest = .07
```

**FIGURE 2-20**

**2** Click at the end of the word Bert. Without inserting a space, type IO to change the Program Name comment. Point to the end of the block comment.

*The edited comment displays (Figure 2-21).*

```
Bert - Notepad
File   Edit   Search   Help
     Program Name:      BertIO
*/
public class Bert
{
     public static void main(String[] args)
     {                                 comment
          //Declaring Variabl          edited
          String custName;
          int price;
          int downPayment;
          int tradeIn;
          int months;
          double annualInterest;
          double interest;
          int loanAmt;
          double payment;

          //Assigning Values
          custName = "Ben Boswick";
          price = 20000;
          downPayment = 1000;
          tradeIn = 1500;
          months = 48;
          annualInterest = .07
```

mouse pointer

**FIGURE 2-21**

**3** **Click after the block comment. Press the ENTER key twice. Type** `import java.io.*;` **and then press the ENTER key. Point to the end of the word Bert in the class header.**

*The new line of code to import all of the classes in the java.io package displays (Figure 2-22). The semicolon ends the line.*

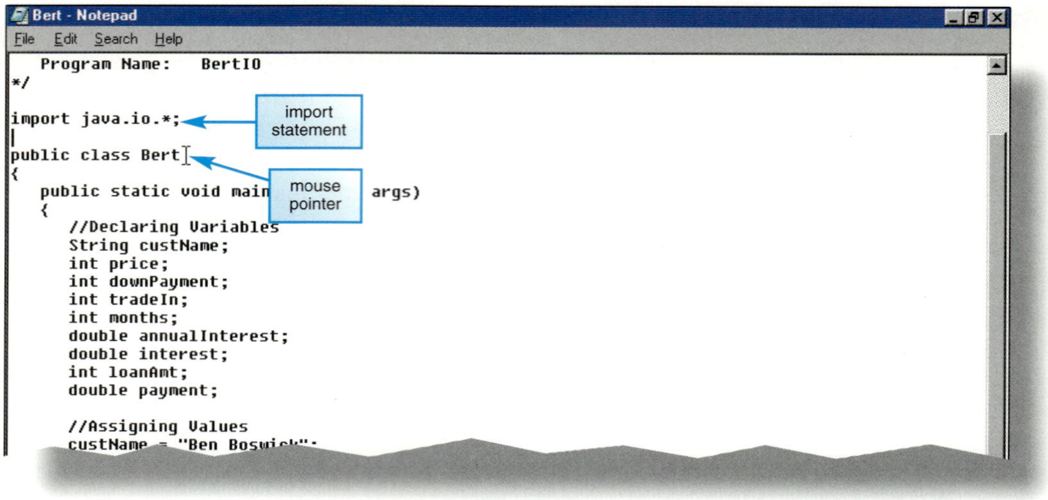

```
    Program Name:   BertIO
*/

import java.io.*;          [import statement]

public class Bert          [mouse pointer]
{
    public static void main(String[] args)
    {
        //Declaring Variables
        String custName;
        int price;
        int downPayment;
        int tradeIn;
        int months;
        double annualInterest;
        double interest;
        int loanAmt;
        double payment;

        //Assigning Values
        custName = "Ben Boswick";
```

**FIGURE 2-22**

**4** **Click after the word, Bert, in the class header. Type** `IO` **to change the class name to BertIO. Point to the opening brace of the main method.**

*The class name now is BertIO (Figure 2-23).*

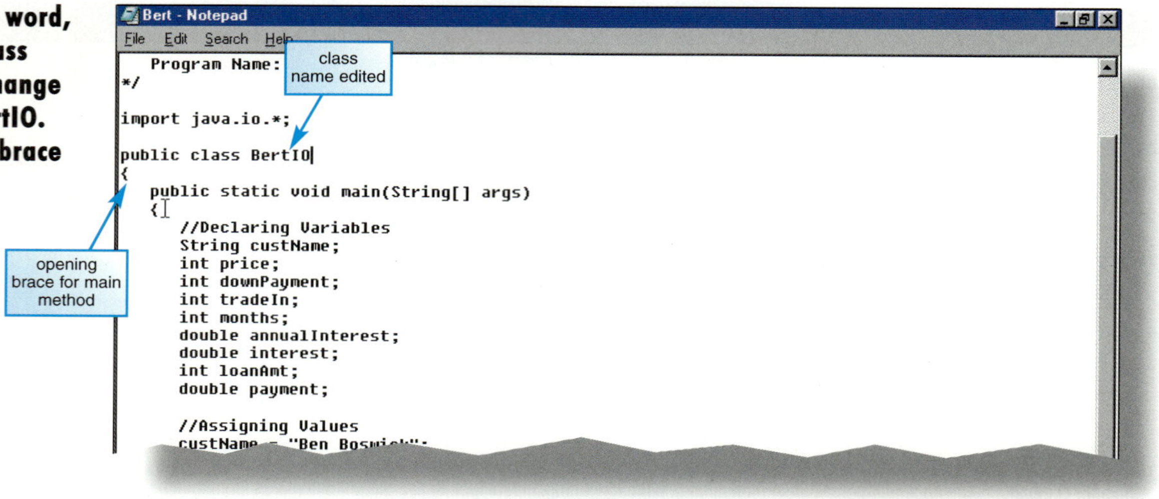

```
    Program Name:      [class name edited]
*/

import java.io.*;

public class BertIO
{
    public static void main(String[] args)
    {                          [opening brace for main method]
        //Declaring Variables
        String custName;
        int price;
        int downPayment;
        int tradeIn;
        int months;
        double annualInterest;
        double interest;
        int loanAmt;
        double payment;

        //Assigning Values
        custName = "Ben Boswick";
```

**FIGURE 2-23**

**5** **Click after the opening brace of the main method. Press the ENTER key.**

*A new line 14 is created (Figure 2-24).*

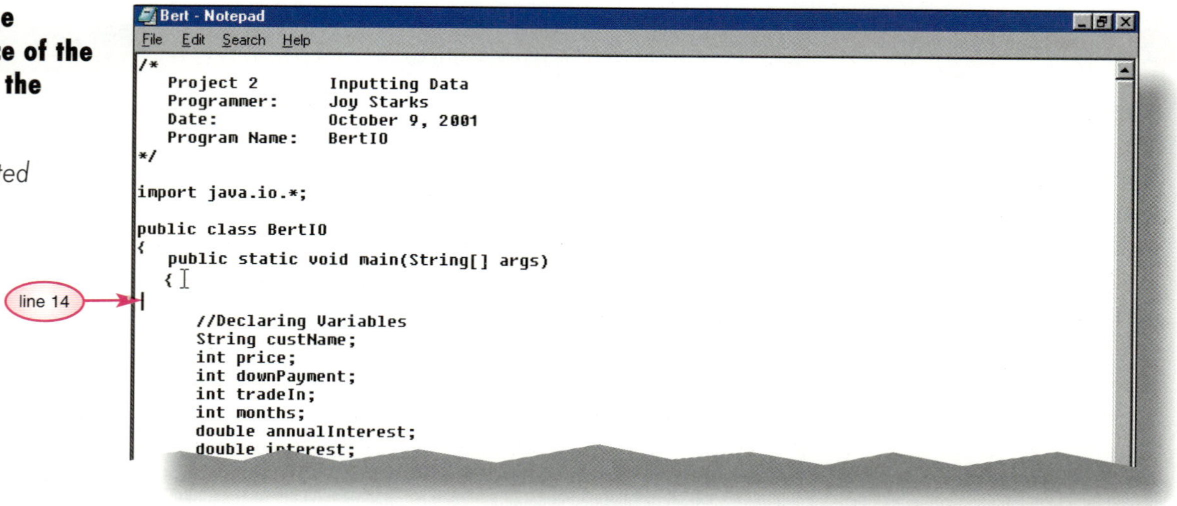

```
/*
    Project 2        Inputting Data
    Programmer:      Joy Starks
    Date:            October 9, 2001
    Program Name:    BertIO
*/

import java.io.*;

public class BertIO
{
    public static void main(String[] args)
    {

[line 14]

        //Declaring Variables
        String custName;
        int price;
        int downPayment;
        int tradeIn;
        int months;
        double annualInterest;
        double interest;
```

**FIGURE 2-24**

**6  Indent and then type**

BufferedReader dataIn = new BufferedReader(new InputStreamReader (System.in)); **to enter the constructor code. Press the ENTER key.**

*The new line of code for the constructor displays (Figure 2-25).*

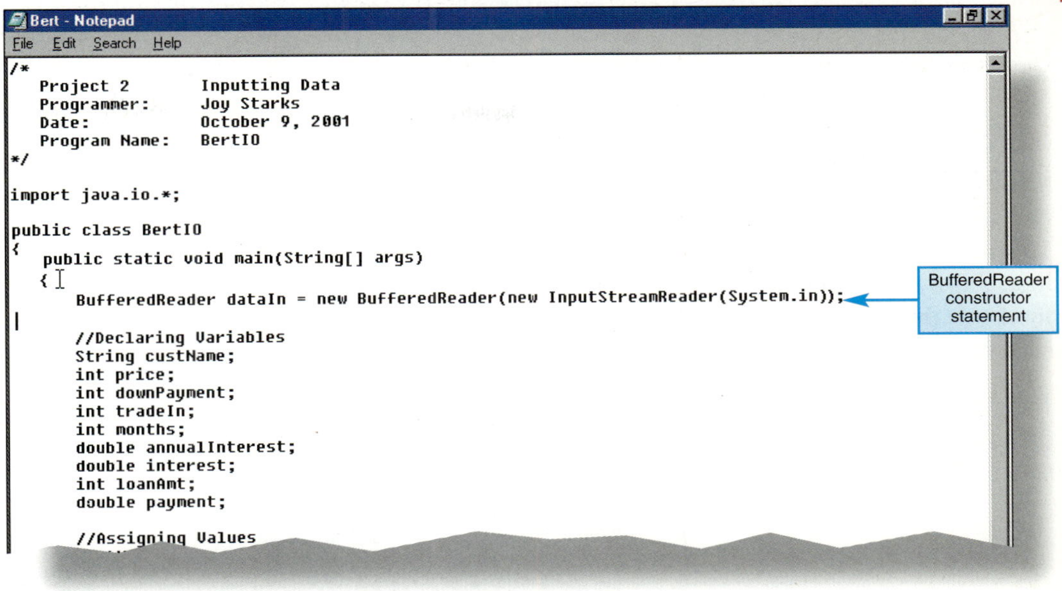

```
/*
    Project 2        Inputting Data
    Programmer:      Joy Starks
    Date:            October 9, 2001
    Program Name:    BertIO
*/

import java.io.*;

public class BertIO
{
    public static void main(String[] args)
    {
        BufferedReader dataIn = new BufferedReader(new InputStreamReader(System.in));

        //Declaring Variables
        String custName;
        int price;
        int downPayment;
        int tradeIn;
        int months;
        double annualInterest;
        double interest;
        int loanAmt;
        double payment;

        //Assigning Values
```

BufferedReader constructor statement

**FIGURE 2-25**

Many users and textbooks create their own classes for input and output to simplify the process of reading from the buffer. However, it is exactly this BufferedReader capability that makes Java easy to adapt to all kinds of input, such as strings, numbers, special characters, and foreign language symbols. It aids in Java's platform independence.

## Data Handling

Users of this program will respond to prompts on the screen in order to enter the data. The sample data will be replaced by prompts that take the form of questions displayed with the System.out.println method. Then, using a method from the BufferedReader class called **readLine**, the data will be moved from the generic dataIn location to a location with an identifier that is more indicative of the data itself. For instance, a customer's name might be moved from dataIn to custName for use later in the program. Like all variables, these identifiers must be declared before being used.

Because the buffer stores input data one character at a time from the keyboard, a piece of data read from the buffer with the method, readLine, is a string of characters, and, therefore, must be declared as such. A string of characters is fine for data such as a person's name, but Java cannot perform mathematical operations on strings. Consequently, the data must be converted from string to numeric data types. Java has a **parse** method that you use to convert input strings to integers or doubles.

When you use the readLine method, you must warn Java that there is a possibility of errors. For instance, a user might not have authority to open a file that Java is trying to read, or the buffer on a particular system might be busy with other input. An easy way to keep the program from aborting prematurely due to these kinds of errors is to add the code: **throws IOException** to the end of the main method header. The program then acknowledges potential failures of this kind and will compile correctly.

Perform the steps on the next page to add exception handling to the main method header, to declare the input variables, and to parse the numbers.

**More** *About*

**Parsing**

Java allows several different parse methods to convert data types, including the wrappers for Long, Short, and Double - all of which convert values. The toString method is available for converting numbers to strings.

**Steps** To Edit Code for Data Handling

**1** **Click at the end of the main method header. Press the SPACEBAR and then type** throws IOException **to finish the line. Point to the end of the Declaring Variables section.**

*The main method now acknowledges possible run-time errors (Figure 2-26).*

```
    Program Name:    BertIO
*/
import java.io.*;

public class BertIO
{
    public static void main(String[] args) throws IOException
    {
        BufferedReader dataIn = new BufferedReader(new InputStreamReader(System.in);

        //Declaring Variables
        String custName;
        int price;
        int downPayment;
        int tradeIn;
        int months;
        double annualInterest;
        double interest;
        int loanAmt;
        double payment;

        //Assigning Values
        custName = "Ben Boswick";
        price = 20000;
        downPayment = 1000;
        tradeIn = 1500;
        months = 48;
        annualInterest = .075;

        //Calculations
        interest = annualInterest/12;
        loanAmt = price-downPayment-tradeIn;
        payment = loanAmt/((1/interest)-(1/(interest*Math.pow(1+interest,months))));
```

throw statement added to main method header

mouse pointer

Bert - Notepad

Start | Bert - Notepad | MS-DOS Prompt | 4:18 PM

**FIGURE 2-26**

**2** **Click after the last variable declaration and then press ENTER. Type the five new string declarations beginning on line 21 using proper indentation. Table 2-8 on page J 2.33 displays the new code.**

*Notice these variables begin with the letters, str, to differentiate them from their integer counterparts (Figure 2-27).*

```
    Program Name:    BertIO
*/
import java.io.*;

public class BertIO
{
    public static void main(String[] args) throws IOException
    {
        BufferedReader dataIn = new BufferedReader(new InputStreamReader(System.in));

        //Declaring Variables
        String custName;
        int price;
        int downPayment;
        int tradeIn;
        int months;
        double annualInterest;
        double interest;
        int loanAmt;
        double payment;
        String strPrice;
        String strDownPayment;
        String strTradeIn;
        String strMonths;
        String strAnnualInterest;

        //Assigning Values
        custName = "Ben Boswick";
        price = 20000;
        downPayment = 1000;
        tradeIn = 1500;
        months = 48;
        annualInterest = .075;
```

line 21

new String declarations

Bert - Notepad

**FIGURE 2-27**

**3** **Drag through the Assigning Values section of the code to select it.**

*The comment line and assignments of sample data are selected (Figure 2-28).*

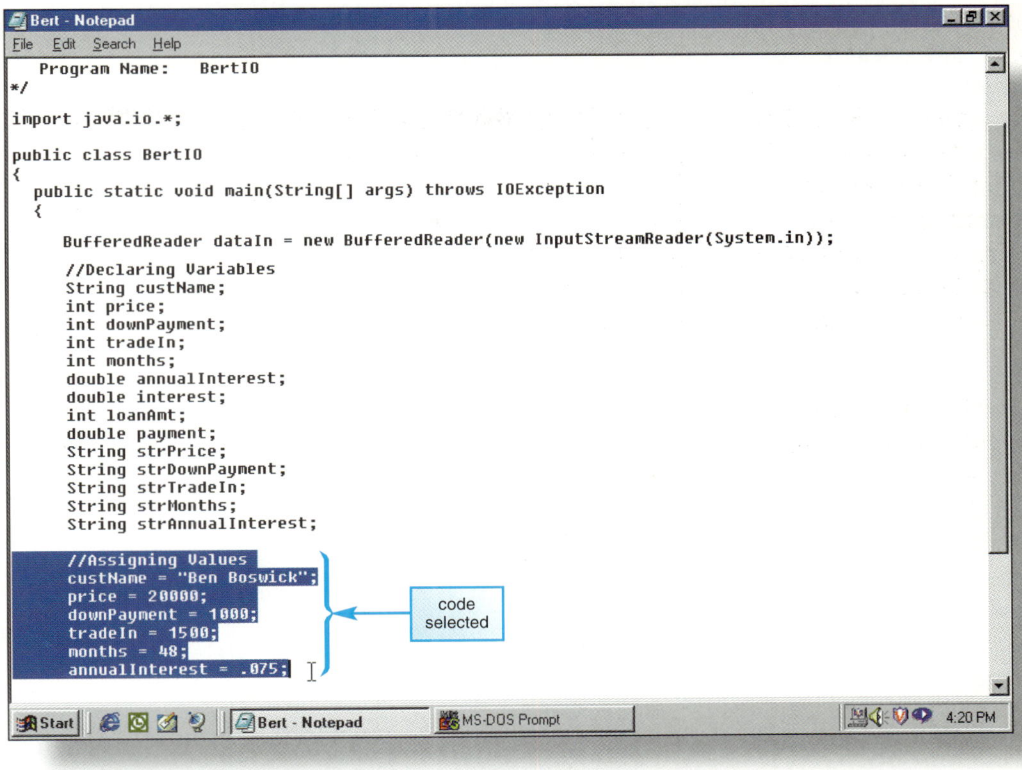

**FIGURE 2-28**

**4** **Right-click the selected area. When the shortcut menu displays, point to Delete.**

*The shortcut menu displays (Figure 2-29).*

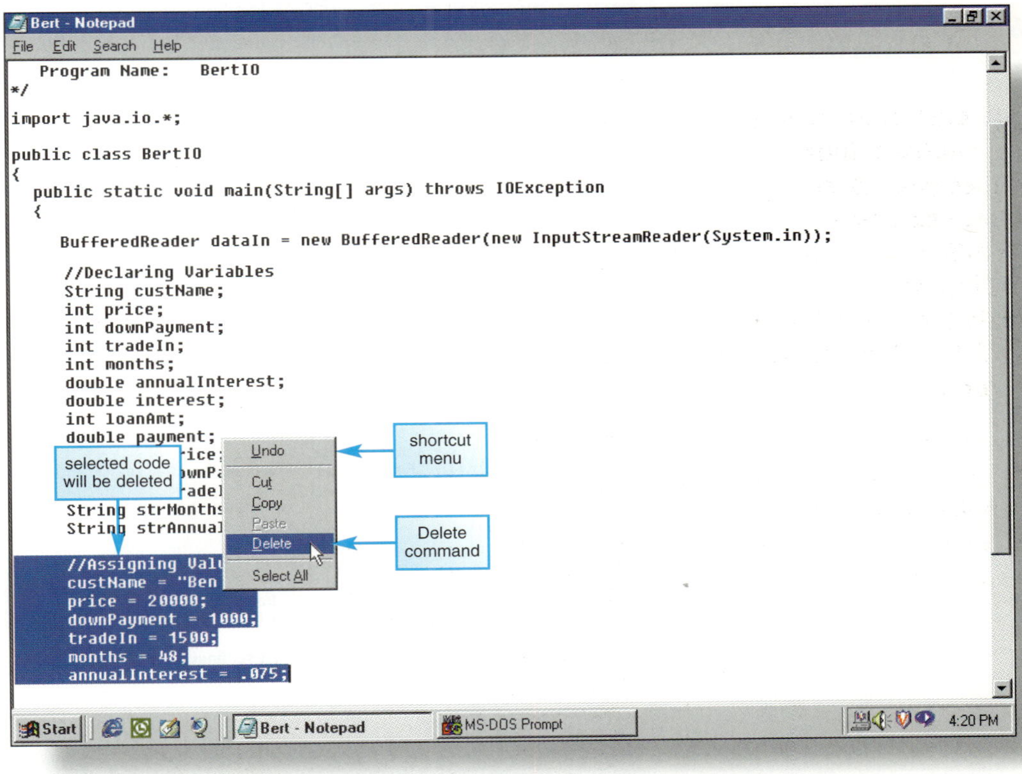

**FIGURE 2-29**

**5** **Click Delete. In the space where the Assigning Values section was, type the Get Input from User section of code beginning on line 27 using proper indentation. Table 2-9 on page J 2.33 displays the new code.**

*The System.out.println method displays the prompt as the argument for each question (Figure 2-30). The assignment statements below each prompt transfer data from the buffer to the appropriate variable location. Indentation and line spacing make the code easy to read.*

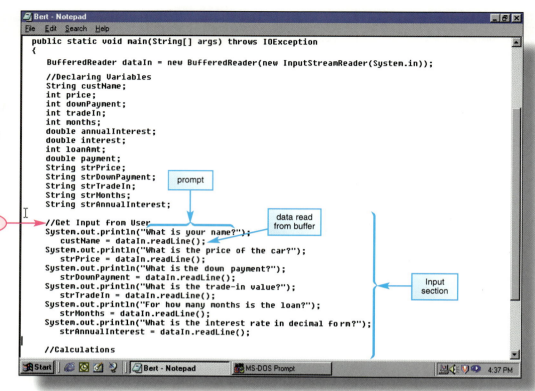

```
public static void main(String[] args) throws IOException
{
    BufferedReader dataIn = new BufferedReader(new InputStreamReader(System.in));

    //Declaring Variables
    String custName;
    int price;
    int downPayment;
    int tradeIn;
    int months;
    double annualInterest;
    double interest;
    int loanAmt;
    double payment;
    String strPrice;
    String strDownPayment;          prompt
    String strTradeIn;
    String strMonths;
    String strAnnualInterest;
                                                      data read
    //Get Input from User                             from buffer
    System.out.println("What is your name?");
        custName = dataIn.readLine();
    System.out.println("What is the price of the car?");
        strPrice = dataIn.readLine();
    System.out.println("What is the down payment?");
        strDownPayment = dataIn.readLine();
    System.out.println("What is the trade-in value?");    Input
        strTradeIn = dataIn.readLine();                   section
    System.out.println("For how many months is the loan?");
        strMonths = dataIn.readLine();
    System.out.println("What is the interest rate in decimal form?");
        strAnnualInterest = dataIn.readLine();

    //Calculations
```

line 27

**FIGURE 2-30**

**6** **Press the ENTER key, then type the Conversions section of code beginning at line 41 using proper indentation. Table 2-10 on page J 2.33 displays the new code.**

*The parse method displays in each assignment statement (Figure 2-31).*

```
    int downPayment;
    int tradeIn;
    int months;
    double annualInterest;
    double interest;
    int loanAmt;
    double payment;
    String strPrice;
    String strDownPayment;
    String strTradeIn;
    String strMonths;
    String strAnnualInterest;

    //Get Input from User
    System.out.println("What is your name?");
        custName = dataIn.readLine();
    System.out.println("What is the price of the car?");
        strPrice = dataIn.readLine();
    System.out.println("What is the down payment?");
        strDownPayment = dataIn.readLine();
    System.out.println("What is the trade-in value?");
        strTradeIn = dataIn.readLine();
    System.out.println("For how many months is the loan?");
        strMonths = dataIn          ();       parse
    System.out.println("         e interest rate in decimal form?");   method
        strAnnualInterest          readLine();

    //Conversions
    price = Integer.parseInt(strPrice);
    downPayment = Integer.parseInt(strDownPayment);
    tradeIn = Integer.parseInt(strTradeIn);             Conversion
    months = Integer.parseInt(strMonths);               section
    annualInterest = Double.parseDouble(strAnnualInterest);

    //Calculations
```

line 41

**FIGURE 2-31**

**Table 2-8**

| LINE | CODE |
|---|---|
| 21 | String strPrice; |
| 22 | String strDownPayment; |
| 23 | String strTradeIn; |
| 24 | String strMonths; |
| 25 | String strAnnualInterest; |

**Table 2-9**

| LINE | CODE |
|---|---|
| 27 | //Get Input from User |
| 28 | System.out.println("What is your name?"); |
| 29 | custName = dataIn.readLine(); |
| 30 | System.out.println("What is the price of the car?"); |
| 31 | strPrice = dataIn.readLine(); |
| 32 | System.out.println("What is the downpayment?"); |
| 33 | strDownPayment = dataIn.readLine(); |
| 34 | System.out.println("What is the trade-in value?"); |
| 35 | strTradeIn = dataIn.readLine(); |
| 36 | System.out.println("For how many months is the loan?"); |
| 37 | strMonths = dataIn.readLine(); |
| 38 | System.out.println("What is the decimal interest rate?"); |
| 39 | strAnnualInterest = dataIn.readLine(); |

**Table 2-10**

| LINE | CODE |
|---|---|
| 41 | //Conversions |
| 42 | price = Integer.parseInt(strPrice); |
| 43 | downPayment = Integer.parseInt(strDownPayment); |
| 44 | tradeIn = Integer.parseInt(strTradeIn); |
| 45 | months = Integer.parseInt(strMonths); |
| 46 | annualInterest = Double.parseDouble(strAnnualInterest); |

The interactive version of the program now is complete. You added the import statement, changed the name of the class, and declared the necessary string variables. You then entered code to prompt the user and to accept a string answer from the buffer. Finally, you included the parse method to convert the strings to numbers in order to use them in later calculations.

Figure 2-32 on the next page shows the printout of the program code in its entirety. Check for syntax, proper spelling, capitalization, and indentations. When you are confident everything is correct, you are ready to save and compile your program.

```
                                    BertIO


        tradeIn = Integer.parseInt(strTradeIn);
        months = Integer.parseInt(strMonths);
        annualInterest = Double.parseDouble(strAnnualInterest);

        //Calculations
        interest = annualInterest/12;
        loanAmt = price-downPayment-tradeIn;
        payment = loanAmt/((1/interest)-(1/(interest*Math.pow(1+interest,months))));

        //Output
        System.out.print("The monthly payment for " + custName + " is $");
        System.out.println(Math.round(payment));
    }
}
```

Page 2

```
                                    BertIO


        /*
            Project 2         Inputting Data
            Programmer:       Joy Starks
            Date:             October 9, 2001
            Program Name:     BertIO
        */

        import java.io.*;

        public class BertIO
        {
            public static void main(String[] args) throws IOException
            {

                BufferedReader dataIn = new BufferedReader(new InputStreamReader(System.in));

                //Declaring Variables
                String custName;
                int price;
                int downPayment;
                int tradeIn;
                int months;
                double annualInterest;
                double interest;
                int loanAmt;
                double payment;
                String strPrice;
                String strDownPayment;
                String strTradeIn;
                String strMonths;
                String strAnnualInterest;

                //Get Input from User
                System.out.println("What is your name?");
                    custName = dataIn.readLine();
                System.out.println("What is the price of the car?");
                    strPrice = dataIn.readLine();
                System.out.println("What is the down payment?");
                    strDownPayment = dataIn.readLine();
                System.out.println("What is the trade-in value?");
                    strTradeIn = dataIn.readLine();
                System.out.println("For how many months is the loan?");
                    strMonths = dataIn.readLine();
                System.out.println("What is the interest rate in decimal form?");
                    strAnnualInterest = dataIn.readLine();

                //Conversions
                price = Integer.parseInt(strPrice);
                downPayment = Integer.parseInt(strDownPayment);
```

Page 1

**FIGURE 2-32**

# Executing an Interactive Program

Java program names must be the same as the class statement at the beginning of the code. Therefore, when you save the program, you must use the Save As command and indicate the new file name. You also will use the new file name when you compile the program.

## Saving and Compiling

You will save this new version of the program that accepts input from the user with the file name BertIO.java. Perform the following steps to save the file on a floppy disk with a new name and then compile it. Perform the following steps to save and compile the source code.

### TO SAVE AND COMPILE THE SOURCE CODE

1. With a floppy disk in drive A, click File on Notepad's menu bar, and then click Save As.
2. When the Save As dialog box displays, type "BertIO.java" in the File name text box.
3. If necessary, click the Save in box arrow and then click 3½ Floppy (A:) in the list.
4. Click the Save button.
5. Click the MS-DOS Prompt button on the taskbar. At the A: prompt, type javac BertIO.java and press the ENTER key to compile the program. If you have errors, correct them in the Notepad window and repeat the steps.

*The command prompt again displays as the file on drive A is compiled successfully.*

Again, if you want to print a copy of your program, the Notepad File menu contains the Print command, which sends a copy of your code to the default printer.

Other Ways

1. To save in Notepad, press ALT+F, press A

## Running the Program

When you run an interactive Java program, the compiled bytecode runs in the MS-DOS Prompt window, pausing every time the readLine method is executed in order for the user to enter the data requested in the prompt. To test the program, programmers typically use the same sample data that they used in creating the original version of the code, this time entering it from a user's perspective as the program runs.

Perform the steps on the next page to run the interactive program, BertIO from the prompt line.

## To Run the Program

**1** **At the A: prompt in the MS-DOS Prompt window, type** java BertIO **and then press the ENTER key.**

*The first prompt displays (Figure 2-33). The MS-DOS Prompt button on the taskbar changes to reflect the running Java program.*

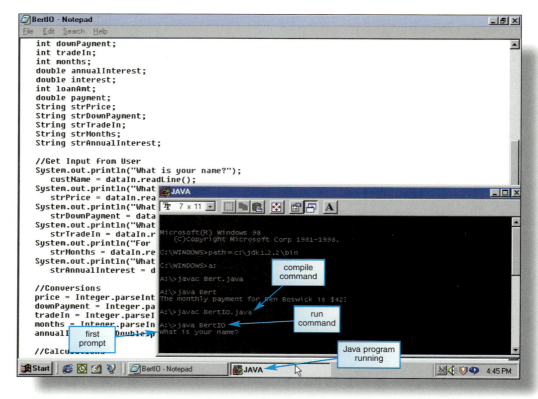

FIGURE 2-33

**2** **Type** Ben Boswick **and then press the ENTER key.**

*The customer name is entered and the next prompt displays (Figure 2-34).*

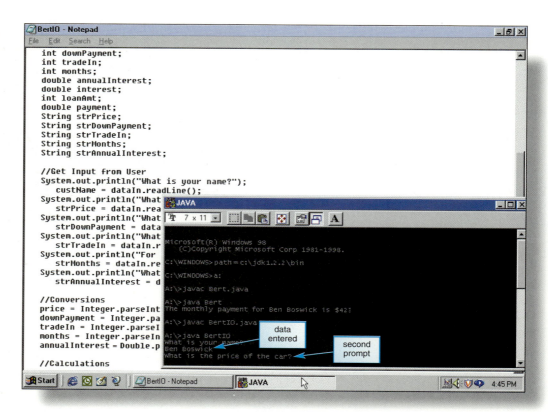

FIGURE 2-34

**3** **Type** 20000 **in response to the prompt for the price of the car. Press the ENTER key.**

*The price is entered and the next prompt displays (Figure 2-35). When entering numbers, do not type a comma.*

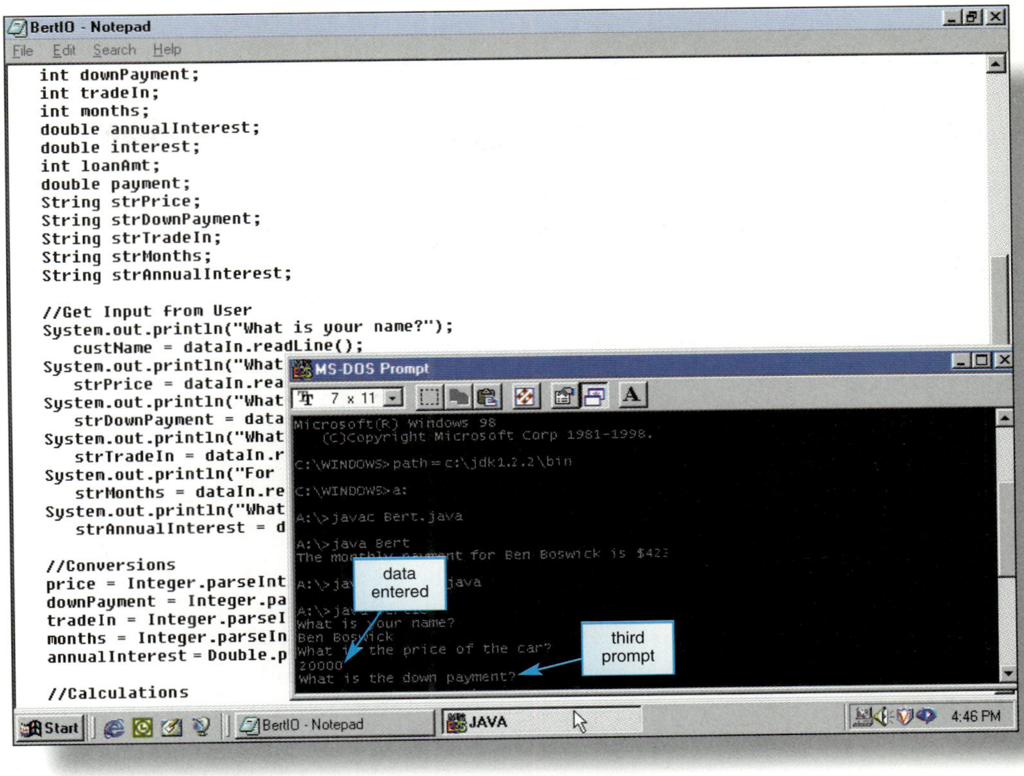

```
int downPayment;
int tradeIn;
int months;
double annualInterest;
double interest;
int loanAmt;
double payment;
String strPrice;
String strDownPayment;
String strTradeIn;
String strMonths;
String strAnnualInterest;

//Get Input from User
System.out.println("What is your name?");
   custName = dataIn.readLine();
System.out.println("What
   strPrice = dataIn.rea
System.out.println("What
   strDownPayment = data
System.out.println("What
   strTradeIn = dataIn.r
System.out.println("For
   strMonths = dataIn.re
System.out.println("What
   strAnnualInterest = d

//Conversions
price = Integer.parseInt
downPayment = Integer.pa
tradeIn = Integer.parseI
months = Integer.parseIn
annualInterest = Double.p

//Calculations
```

MS-DOS Prompt

```
Microsoft(R) Windows 98
  (C)Copyright Microsoft Corp 1981-1998.
C:\WINDOWS>path=c:\jdk1.2.2\bin
C:\WINDOWS>a:
A:\>javac Bert.java
A:\>java Bert
The monthly payment for Ben Boswick is $423
A:\>ja             java
A:\>ja
What is your name?
Ben Boswick
What is the price of the car?
20000
What is the down payment?
```

data entered

third prompt

**FIGURE 2-35**

**4** **At the next four prompts, enter the corresponding sample data of** 1000 **for the down payment,** 1500 **for the trade-in,** 48 **for the number of months, and** .075 **for the interest rate, pressing the ENTER key after each entry.**

*The final answer displays (Figure 2-36).*

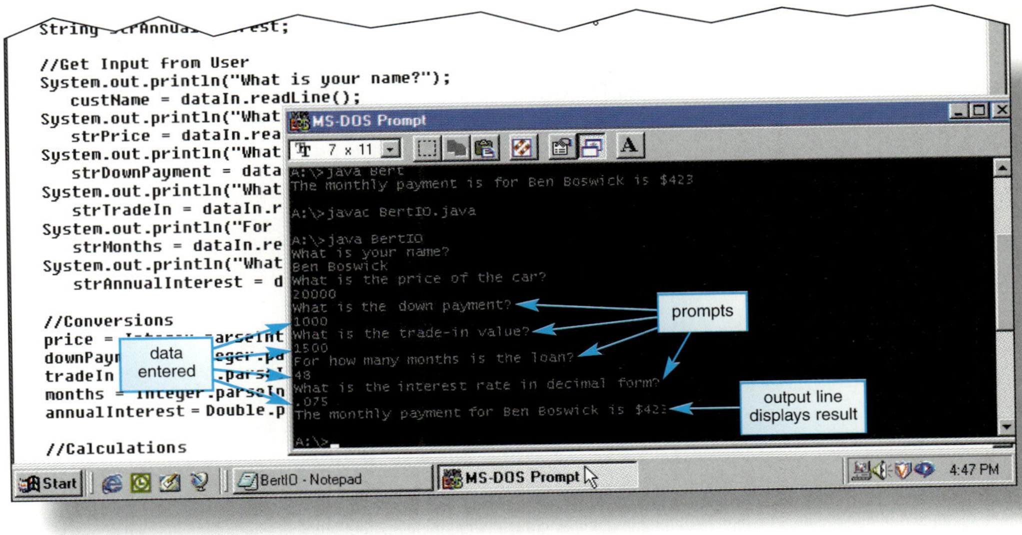

```
String strAnnua      est;

//Get Input from User
System.out.println("What is your name?");
   custName = dataIn.readLine();
System.out.println("What
   strPrice = dataIn.rea
System.out.println("What
   strDownPayment = data
System.out.println("What
   strTradeIn = dataIn.r
System.out.println("For
   strMonths = dataIn.re
System.out.println("What
   strAnnualInterest = d

//Conversions
price =          arseInt
downPayment     eger.pa
tradeIn         .pars
months = Integer.parseIn
annualInterest = Double.p

//Calculations
```

data entered

MS-DOS Prompt

```
A:\>java Bert
The monthly payment is for Ben Boswick is $423
A:\>javac BertIO.java
A:\>java BertIO
What is your name?
Ben Boswick
What is the price of the car?
20000
What is the down payment?
1000
What is the trade-in value?
1500
For how many months is the loan?
48
What is the interest rate in decimal form?
.075
The monthly payment for Ben Boswick is $423
A:\>
```

prompts

output line displays result

**FIGURE 2-36**

Interactive programs allow programmers the flexibility of running the program many times, using various sample data, without having to recompile. Obviously, many things could go wrong when users begin to enter data, such as entering incorrect information or unrealistic data. This project does not attempt to account for all of the possible errors that might occur; however, if the program is run with sensible data and the data are entered correctly, the correct answer will display.

# Moving to the Web

The final version of the program for Bert's Banner Cars is to create an applet. Recall that an applet is a program called from within another environment, usually a Web page. In order to convert the BertIO program from running at the command prompt into a program that will display as part of a Web page, you will need to create three kinds of applet objects. You will use labels, text fields, and buttons in the applet for Bert's Banner Cars.

## Converting the Program to an Applet

In Project 1, you learned that an applet uses Java packages that are different from an application. Instead of the java.io package, an interactive applet must import the JDK-supplied java.awt package as well as the java.applet package. Applets must extend the program's class in the class header, in order to inherit attributes from the applet package.

This applet will be interactive, which requires implementing an interface handler provided with the JDK called **ActionListener**. ActionListener is contained in a special part of the java.awt package used for applet events. ActionListener listens for events such as mouse clicks during execution of the applet.

Perform the following steps to insert import statements into the BertIO program, extend the Applet, implement the ActionListener, and change the applet's name.

### Applets on the Web

On the Web, Java applets can be used for client/server applications, such as graphing and charting stock purchases; for drag-and-drop applications, such as dropping items in a shopping cart; for Internet games; for smooth animation; and for a wide variety of multimedia applications.

 **To Enter Code**

**1** If necessary, minimize the MS-DOS Prompt window so that the maximized Notepad window displays. Point to the scroll box on the vertical scroll bar.

*The Notepad window displays and is maximized (Figure 2-37).*

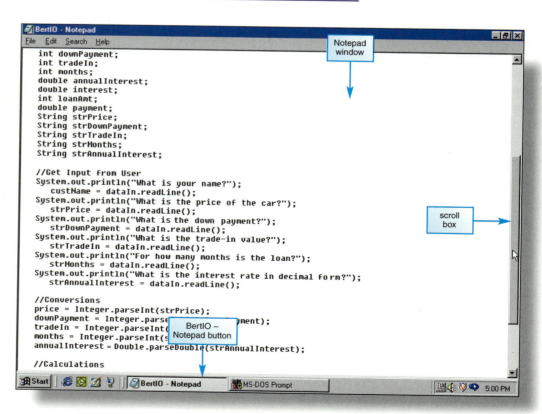

**FIGURE 2-37**

**2** Drag the scroll box to the top of the scroll bar. Drag through the text import java.io.*; to select it.

*The line of code displays selected (Figure 2-38).*

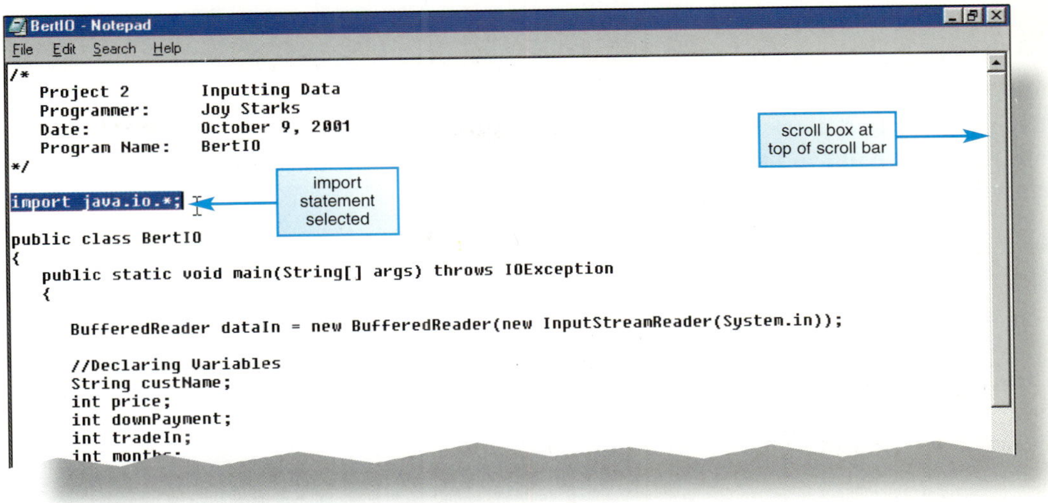

```
/*
    Project 2        Inputting Data
    Programmer:      Joy Starks
    Date:            October 9, 2001
    Program Name:    BertIO
*/

import java.io.*;

public class BertIO
{
    public static void main(String[] args) throws IOException
    {
        BufferedReader dataIn = new BufferedReader(new InputStreamReader(System.in));

        //Declaring Variables
        String custName;
        int price;
        int downPayment;
        int tradeIn;
        int months;
```

scroll box at top of scroll bar

import statement selected

**FIGURE 2-38**

**3** With the text still selected, press the DELETE key and then type the new import statements as shown in Figure 2-39.

*The commands to import the Java packages display (Figure 2-39).*

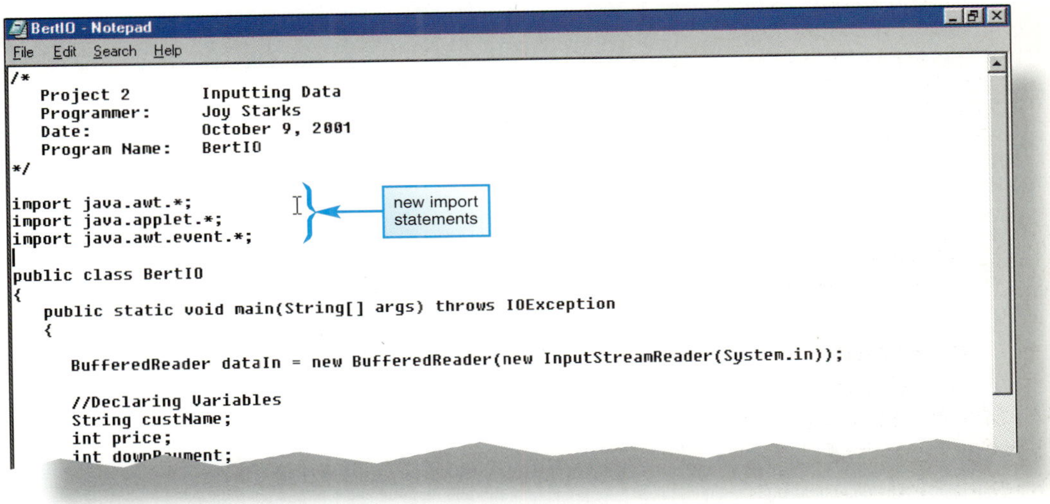

```
/*
    Project 2        Inputting Data
    Programmer:      Joy Starks
    Date:            October 9, 2001
    Program Name:    BertIO
*/

import java.awt.*;
import java.applet.*;
import java.awt.event.*;

public class BertIO
{
    public static void main(String[] args) throws IOException
    {
        BufferedReader dataIn = new BufferedReader(new InputStreamReader(System.in));

        //Declaring Variables
        String custName;
        int price;
        int downPayment;
```

new import statements

**FIGURE 2-39**

**4** Select the text, BertIO, in the block comment.

*The name of the class displays selected (Figure 2-40).*

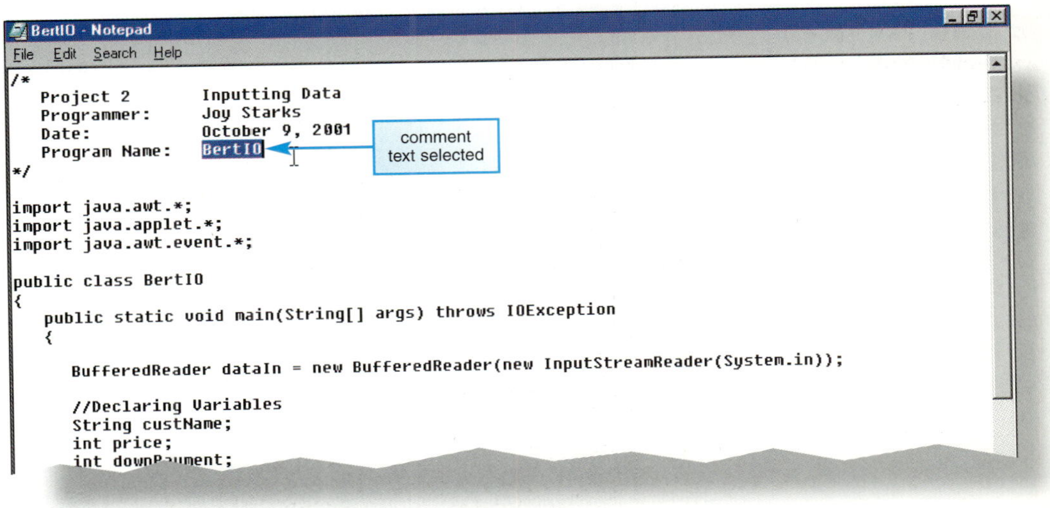

```
/*
    Project 2        Inputting Data
    Programmer:      Joy Starks
    Date:            October 9, 2001
    Program Name:    BertIO
*/

import java.awt.*;
import java.applet.*;
import java.awt.event.*;

public class BertIO
{
    public static void main(String[] args) throws IOException
    {
        BufferedReader dataIn = new BufferedReader(new InputStreamReader(System.in));

        //Declaring Variables
        String custName;
        int price;
        int downPayment;
```

comment text selected

**FIGURE 2-40**

**5** **With the text still selected, press the DELETE key and then type** BertApplet **to replace the existing text. Point to the class header.**

*BertApplet replaces the old class name (Figure 2-41).*

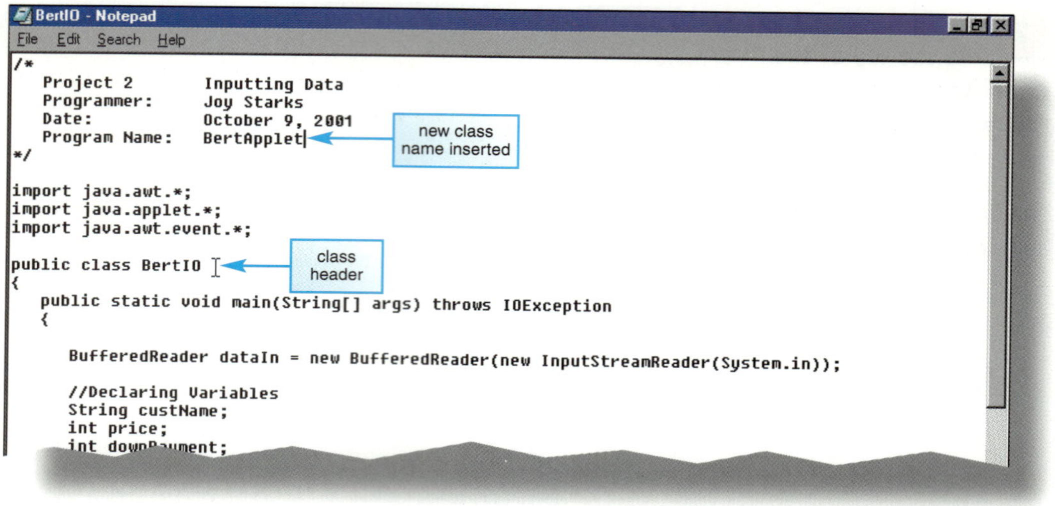

FIGURE 2-41

**6** **Drag through the text, BertIO, in the class header.**

*The class name in the class header displays selected (Figure 2-42).*

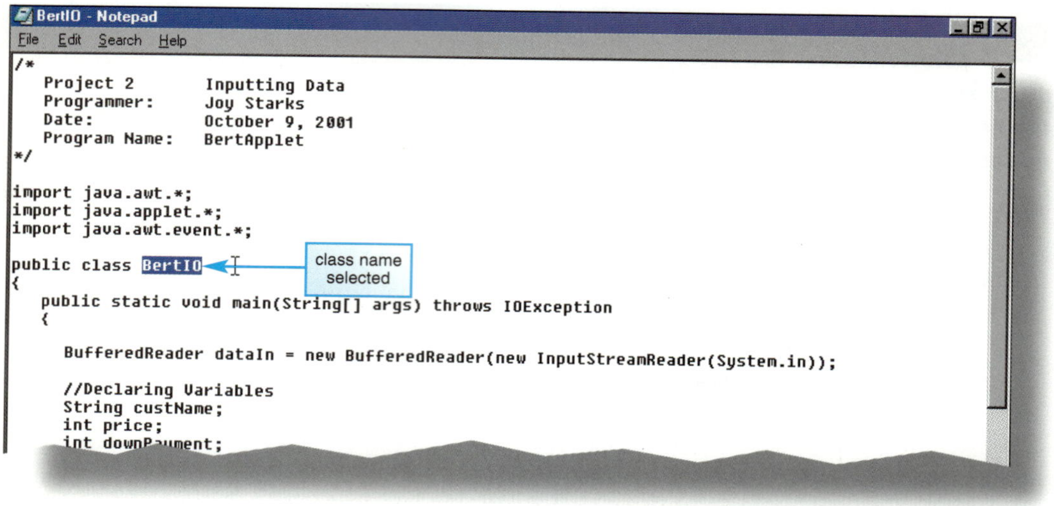

FIGURE 2-42

**7** **With the text still selected, press the DELETE key and then type** BertApplet extends Applet implements ActionListener **in the class header.**

*The class header displays the new class name, extension, and implementation (Figure 2-43).*

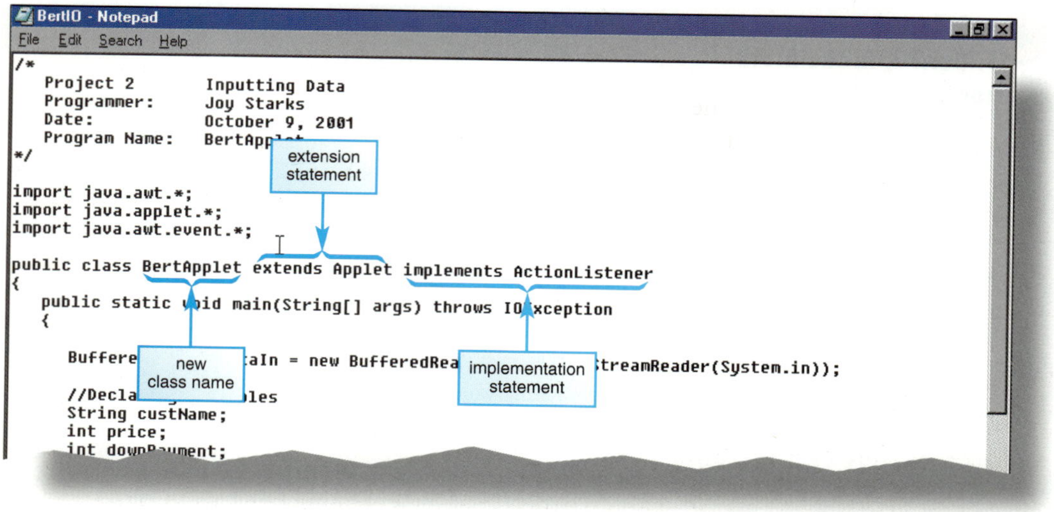

FIGURE 2-43

**Import statements** allow you to refer to a library class by its short name rather than spelling out the entire package and class name each time you want to use it. In the previous step, instead of referring to java.awt.event.ActionListener, the programmer simply uses the name of the event ActionListener in the code. The **asterisk** (*) is a wild card character that matches any public class name in the java.awt.event package.

In general, the purpose of importing classes is to avoid having to write common routines that already exist in Java.

## Label Components

The java.awt package contains components that you can use in applets. A typical component called a **label**, is a class that displays text on the screen. Labels are assigned a string of characters, or a text value, by the programmer. A common usage is to create a constructor that assigns the string of characters to the component.

```
Label identifier = new identifier("message");
```

Recall that a constructor is a special kind of assignment statement that creates an instance of a class. The label instance is constructed during compilation. During execution, the label, displaying its message, is added to the applet window.

## Text Field Components

A second kind of component that holds and displays text is a text field. A **text field** is a class that creates a box in which users enter text. Like the label, it displays inside the applet window. In the constructor, the programmer enters a width argument, which is the number of characters a user may input during execution. The difference between labels and text fields is a conceptual one. Only the programmer manipulates the text of a label, whereas a text field is created by the programmer for manipulation by the user. A common usage is to create a text field component that the user will fill in during execution.

```
TextField identifier = new TextField(width);
```

## Button Components

A third type of component is a button. Most computer users are very familiar with command buttons. When you click a button you expect something to happen. Typically, buttons inherit their characteristics, such as color and shape, from the operating system, but programmers may determine the caption on the button, as well as the actions to be performed when it is clicked. In the constructor, the programmer enters a caption argument, which is the string of characters that displays on the face of the button during execution. The construct, or code, for a button is similar to a label constructor.

```
Button identifier = new Button("caption");
```

## Programming Conventions

Component identifiers must follow the same Java naming rules as variable identifiers, but programmers differ in their specific naming conventions. A **naming convention** is the way you use words, case, prefixes, and underscores to name the identifiers in your program. The main reason for using a consistent set of naming conventions within a given program is to standardize the structure and coding style of an application, so that you and others may read and understand the code. For example, if you consistently use title case — capitalized first letters — for identifiers with more than one word, your program is easier to read and edit.

Some programmers name their applet components with a three-letter prefix similar to the ones used in the Visual Basic programming languages, such as lblTitle or txtName. Others use no component-specific letters, simply calling their components, label, title, or name. Such a convention makes it difficult in longer programs to remember and identify what kind of component is being used. In this text, the naming convention will identify the purpose beginning with a lowercase letter, followed by the component in title case. For example, a label might be named, titleLabel, and a text field, nameField. When naming buttons, the purpose will include a verb whenever possible, or a response caption such as OK. That purpose and/or response will be followed by the word Button. For example, a button might be named, calcButton or okButton. Whatever naming convention you decide to use in your own programs, your goals should be easy reading and consistency.

Recall that when you coded the prompt for the user, followed by the allocation of storage for the answer, you indented the allocation of storage to easily pair the two. You will do the same for the creation of labels and text fields that go together. This kind of indentation rule is part of a programmer's **coding convention**.

Unfortunately, there are no hard and fast rules about coding conventions, but as Java takes a firmer hold in application development, a system of standardized indentations and spacings will follow.

Perform the following steps to create label, text field, and button components in the applet.

## To Create Applet Components

**1** **Select the text from the main method header through the Get Input from User section.**

*The text is selected (Figure 2-44).*

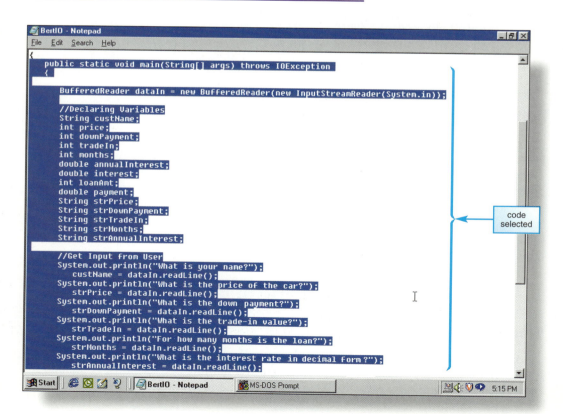

**FIGURE 2-44**

**2** **Right-click the selected area and point to Delete on the shortcut menu.**

*The shortcut menu displays (Figure 2-45).*

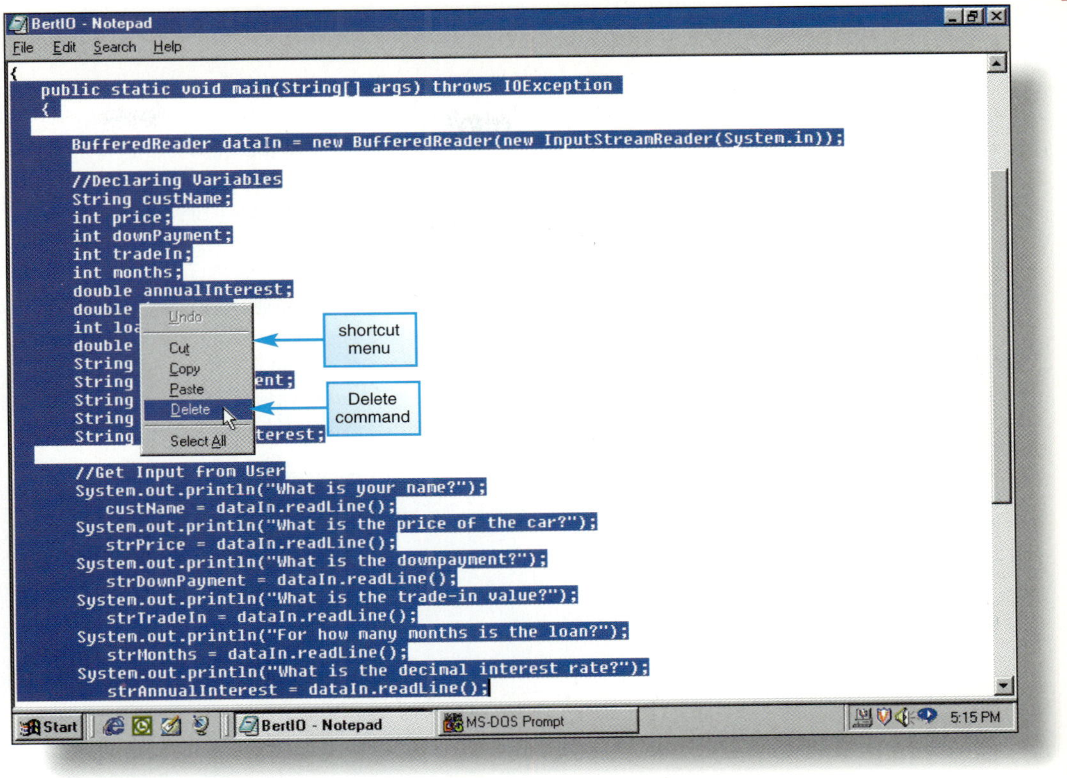

**FIGURE 2-45**

**3** **Click Delete and then type the lines to display the labels, text boxes, and button as shown in Table 2-11 on the next page. Use proper indentation.**

*The constructor lines display (Figure 2-46).*

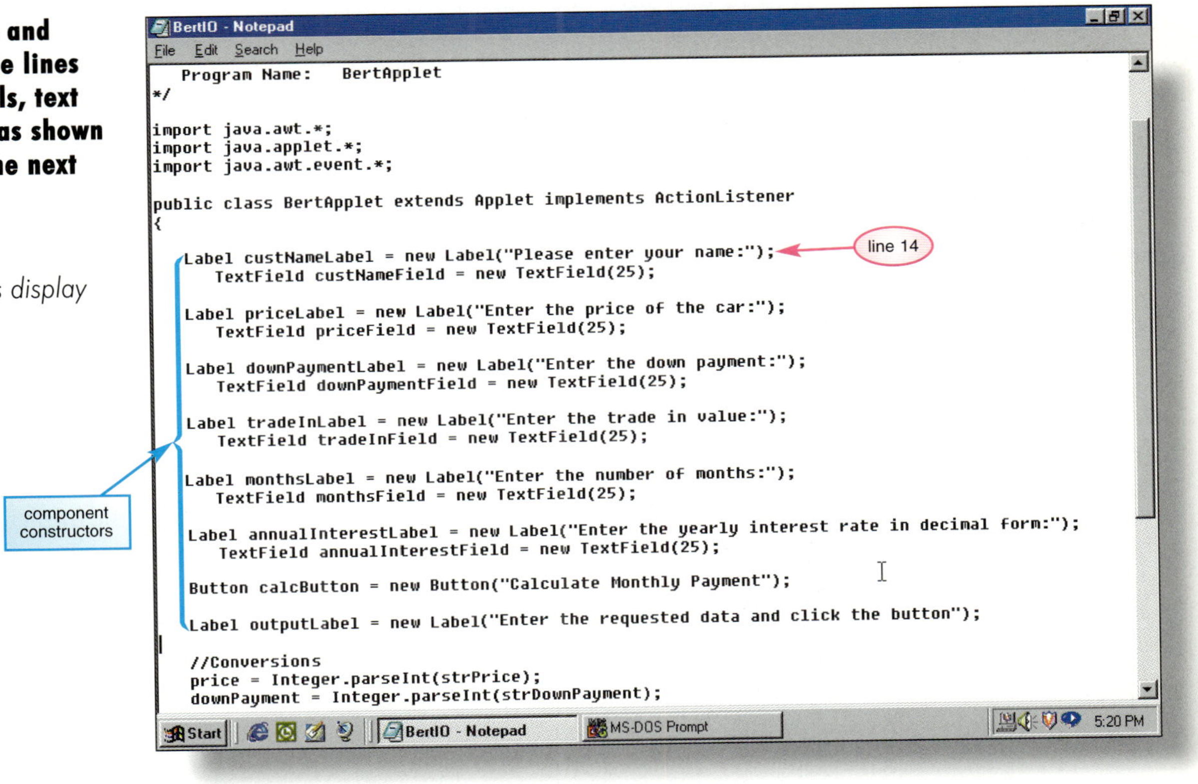

**FIGURE 2-46**

**Table 2-11**

| LINE | CODE |
|------|------|
| 14 | Label custNameLabel = new Label("Please enter your name:"); |
| 15 | TextField custNameField = new TextField(25); |
| 16 | |
| 17 | Label priceLabel = new Label("Enter the price of the car:"); |
| 18 | TextField priceField = new TextField(25); |
| 19 | |
| 20 | Label downPaymentLabel = new Label("Enter the down payment:"); |
| 21 | TextField downPaymentField = new TextField(25); |
| 22 | |
| 23 | Label tradeInLabel = new Label("Enter the trade in value:"); |
| 24 | TextField tradeInField = new TextField(25); |
| 25 | |
| 26 | Label monthsLabel = new Label("Enter the number of months:"); |
| 27 | TextField monthsField = new TextField(25); |
| 28 | |
| 29 | Label annualInterestLabel = new Label("Enter the yearly interest rate in decimal form:"); |
| 30 | TextField annualInterestField = new TextField(25); |
| 31 | |
| 32 | Button calcButton = new Button("Calculate Monthly Payment"); |
| 33 | |
| 34 | Label outputLabel = new Label("Enter the requested data and click the button"); |

## More About

### Applets

Applets do not include a main method because they do not start themselves. An applet is added to an already running program: the browser. The browser has predefined means for getting each applet to do what it wants. It does this by calling methods that it knows the applet may have, such as init, paint, or start.

You may save this program now by following the steps on page 2.23 or wait until you have finished entering the code and then save it.

Component objects have become more stable over time. With the advent of graphical user interfaces (GUI) in the 1980s, users have certain expectations of text boxes, and expect buttons to be "clickable." Java takes advantages of those expectations and provides the pre-built classes for typical GUI components. Programmers have these kinds of tools at their fingertips, with many ways to manipulate them.

### The Init Method

The constructors for labels, text fields, and buttons are merely storage locations until the applet actually is displayed on the screen. Recall that in Project 1, you used the paint method to draw a string of text in the applet window. The init method is another applet method that is initialized when the applet actually begins to display on the screen or in the browser. The container method, add, is used to add the previously declared objects to the applet. A **container method** is a special method to manipulate a component that resides inside a larger structure such as a window, frame, or panel.

Perform the following steps to code the init method, which adds the components to the applet container.

**Table 2-12**

| LINE | CODE |
|------|------|
| 37 | { |
| 38 | add(custNameLabel); |
| 39 | add(custNameField); |
| 40 | add(priceLabel); |
| 41 | add(priceField); |
| 42 | add(downPaymentLabel); |
| 43 | add(downPaymentField); |
| 44 | add(tradeInLabel); |
| 45 | add(tradeInField); |
| 46 | add(monthsLabel); |
| 47 | add(monthsField); |
| 48 | add(annualInterestLabel); |
| 49 | add(annualInterestField); |
| 50 | add(calcButton); |
| 51 | add(outputLabel); |

**Steps** **To Code the Init Method**

**1** **In the Notepad window, position the insertion point below the last label constructor. Press the ENTER key to insert a blank line. Indent three spaces and then type** `public voic init()` **to code the init method header. Press the ENTER key again.**

*The init header displays (Figure 2-47).*

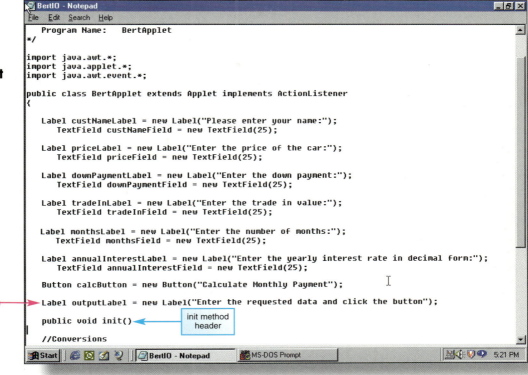

```
    Program Name:    BertApplet
*/

import java.awt.*;
import java.applet.*;
import java.awt.event.*;

public class BertApplet extends Applet implements ActionListener
{

    Label custNameLabel = new Label("Please enter your name:");
       TextField custNameField = new TextField(25);

    Label priceLabel = new Label("Enter the price of the car:");
       TextField priceField = new TextField(25);

    Label downPaymentLabel = new Label("Enter the down payment:");
       TextField downPaymentField = new TextField(25);

    Label tradeInLabel = new Label("Enter the trade in value:");
       TextField tradeInField = new TextField(25);

    Label monthsLabel = new Label("Enter the number of months:");
       TextField monthsField = new TextField(25);

    Label annualInterestLabel = new Label("Enter the yearly interest rate in decimal form:");
       TextField annualInterestField = new TextField(25);

    Button calcButton = new Button("Calculate Monthly Payment");

    Label outputLabel = new Label("Enter the requested data and click the button");

    public void init()

    //Conversions
```

line 34 → init method header

**FIGURE 2-47**

**2** **Type the rest of the init method as shown in Table 2-12 using proper indentation. After the last line of code is entered, press the ENTER key.**

*The code to add the labels, fields, and button displays (Figure 2-48).*

```
    Label downPaymentLabel = new Label("Enter the down payment:");
       TextField downPaymentField = new TextField(25);

    Label tradeInLabel = new Label("Enter the trade in value:");
       TextField tradeInField = new TextField(25);

    Label monthsLabel = new Label("Enter the number of months:");
       TextField monthsField = new TextField(25);

    Label annualInterestLabel = new Label("Enter the yearly interest rate in decimal form:");
       TextField annualInterestField = new TextField(25);

    Button calcButton = new Button("Calculate Monthly Payment");

    Label outputLabel = new Label("Enter the requested data and click the button");

    public void init()
    {
        add(custNameLabel);
        add(custNameField);
        add(priceLabel);
        add(priceField);
        add(downPaymentLabel);
        add(downPaymentField);
        add(tradeInLabel);
        add(tradeInField);
        add(annualInterestLabel);
        add(annualInterestField);
        add(monthsLabel);
        add(monthsField);
        add(calcButton);
        add(outputLabel);
```

line 37 → add methods inserted

**FIGURE 2-48**

Notice that the code to construct the labels, fields, and button comes before the init method. This will speed processing during execution as the init method will already have the compiled data to add to the applet on the screen.

The final set of code will create the event behind the calculate button.

### The ActionListener

Recall that the ActionListener, implemented at the beginning of the program, is a part of the java.awt.event package. The ActionListener detects keystrokes and mouse clicks. The programmer decides which component is going to be the external trigger for the user. The programmer then uses a method called addActionListener to make the component active.

```
calcButton.addActionListener(this);
```

In this example, the calcButton will be the hot component. The addActionListener method only needs one argument to perform its method. Recall that an argument is the information a function, procedure, or method needs in order to do its job. In the applet program, you will use a reserved word, this, as an argument. (See Appendix B for a complete list of reserved words in Java.) The reserved word, this, refers back to the container. In other words, you are asking the ActionListener to add an active button to this applet.

Although the reasons to use a keyword that refers back to the object itself are rather confusing, you can think of it as the ActionListener making the applet listen for the click, and the keyword, this, identifying the "clickable" component.

Once a click is received, a Java applet must perform a task; in this case, it must calculate the monthly payment just as it did in the previous two versions of the program. The **ActionPerformed** method is executed when the click occurs. Text field data items, entered by the user, are retrieved and converted to numbers. The formulas are calculated and the answer is sent back to the applet. The **getText** and **setText** methods are part of the java.awt package. Anytime you use a text box in Java, you can use these methods to easily transfer data back and forth from the applet user to the program, just as you did with the ISR when the program was a stand-alone application.

Finally, the ActionPerformed method (Table 2-13) will hold the code to perform the calculations.

**More About**

**The Java AWT Package**

See Appendix A for information on browsing the Java SDK documentation. Sun Microsystems provides a complete listing of the methods and classes for each of the packages.

**Table 2-13**

| LINE | CODE |
|------|------|
| 55 | `public void actionPerformed(ActionEvent e)` |
| 56 | `{` |
| 57 | `    //Converting input to values` |
| 58 | `    int price = Integer.parseInt(priceField.getText());` |
| 59 | `    int downPayment = Integer.parseInt(downPaymentField.getText());` |
| 60 | `    int tradeIn = Integer.parseInt(tradeInField.getText());` |
| 61 | `    double annualInterest = Double.parseDouble(annualInterestField.getText());` |
| 62 | `    int months = Integer.parseInt(monthsField.getText());` |
| 63 | |
| 64 | `    //Variables used in formulas and output` |
| 65 | `    double interest;` |
| 66 | `    int loanAmt;` |
| 67 | `    double payment;` |
| 68 | |
| 69 | `    //Calculation` |
| 70 | `    interest = annualInterest/12;` |
| 71 | `    loanAmt = price-downPayment-tradeIn;` |
| 72 | `    payment = loanAmt/((1/interest)-(1/(interest*Math.pow(1+interest,months))));` |
| 73 | |
| 74 | `    //Output` |
| 75 | `    outputLabel.setText("The monthly payment is $" + Math.round(payment));` |
| 76 | `    }` |
| 77 | `}` |

Perform the following steps to enter the code for the ActionListener and the ActionPerformed method.

 **Steps** **To Code the ActionListener**

**1** **In the Notepad window, position the insertion point directly below the last add command. Indent as shown in Figure 2-49, type** calcButton. addActionListener (this); **and then press the ENTER key. Indent three spaces and then type a closing brace to complete the init method.**

*The last line of the init method calls the ActionListener (Figure 2-49).*

```
Label tradeInLabel = new Label("Enter the trade In ...de:");
    TextField tradeInField = new TextField(25);

Label monthsLabel = new Label("Enter the number of months:");
    TextField monthsField = new TextField(25);

Label annualInterestLabel = new Label("Enter the yearly interest rate in decimal form:");
    TextField annualInterestField = new TextField(25);

Button calcButton = new Button("Calculate Monthly Payment");

Label outputLabel = new Label("Enter the requested data and click the button");

public void init()
{
    add(custNameLabel);
    add(custNameField);
    add(priceLabel);
    add(priceField);
    add(downPaymentLabel);
    add(downPaymentField);
    add(tradeInLabel);
    add(tradeInField);
    add(annualInterestLabel);
    add(annualInterestField);
    add(monthsLabel);
    add(monthsField);
    add(calcButton);
    add(outputLabel);
    calcButton.addActionListener(this);
}
```
*closing brace*
*addActionListener method inserted*
*line 53*

🏁Start | 🌐🟦🟩🖊🦅 | 📄BertIO - Notepad | 📺MS-DOS Prompt | 🔊🔆🔴 5:22 PM

**FIGURE 2-49**

**2** **Press the ENTER key twice. Enter the actionPerformed event as shown in Table 2-13 using proper indentation.**

*The new actionPerformed method with an ActionEvent e argument displays (Figure 2-50). Braces close both the event and the applet class.*

**BertIO - Notepad**
File  Edit  Search  Help
```
    add(tradeInLabel);
    add(tradeInField);
    add(monthsLabel);
    add(monthsField);
    add(annualInterestLabel);
    add(annualInterestField);
    add(calcButton);
    add(outputLabel);
    calcButton.addActionListener(this);
}

public void actionPerformed(ActionEvent e)
{
    //Converting input to values
    int price = Integer.parseInt(priceField.getText());
    int downPayment = Integer.parseInt(downPaymentField.getText());
    int tradeIn = Integer.parseInt(tradeInField.getText());
    double annualInterest = Double.parseDouble(annualInterestField.getText());
    int months = Integer.parseInt(monthsField.getText());

    //Variables used in formulas and output
    double interest;
    int loanAmt;
    double payment;

    //Calculations
    interest = annualInterest/12;
    loanAmt = price-downPayment-tradeIn;
         = loanAmt/((1/interest)-(1/(interest*Math.pow(1+interest,months))));

    outp            "The monthly payment is $" + Math.round(payment)); ;
    }
}
```
*ActionEvent argument*
*line 55*
*new code*
*closing brace for entire class*
*closing brace for actionPerformed method*

**FIGURE 2-50**

🏁Start | 🌐🟦🟩🖊🦅 | 📄BertIO - Notepad | 📺MS-DOS Prompt | 🔆🔊🔴 5:22 PM

**3** Drag through the remaining code left from the BertIO version of the program.

*The code displays selected (Figure 2-51).*

**4** Right-click the selected text and then click Delete on the shortcut menu.

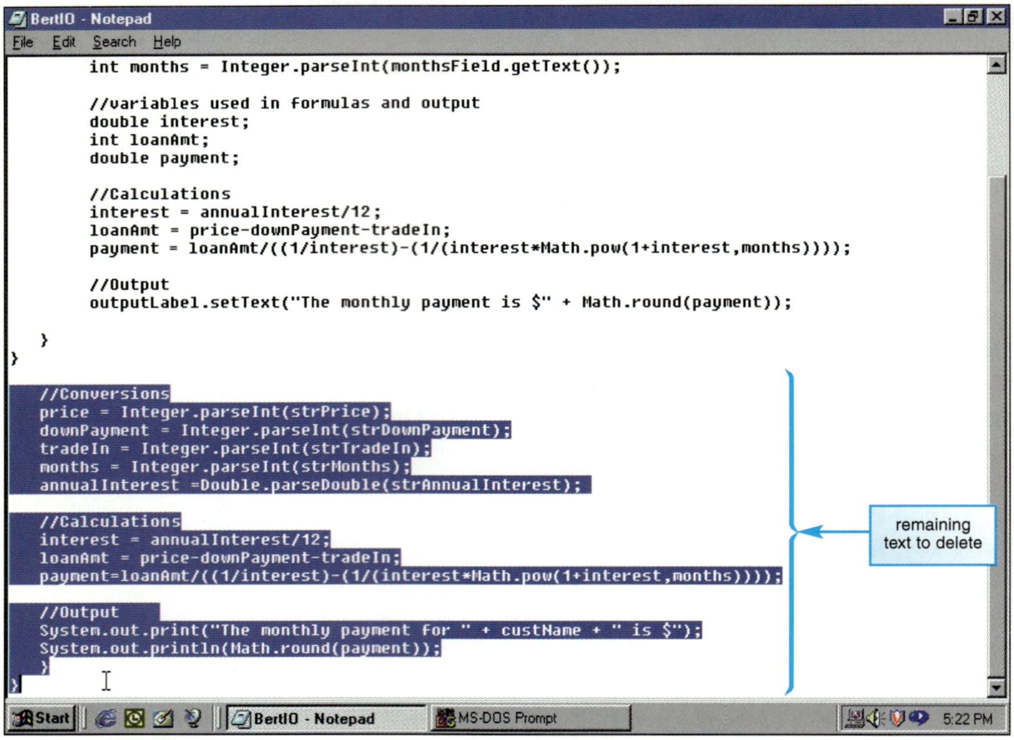

```
                    int months = Integer.parseInt(monthsField.getText());

                    //variables used in formulas and output
                    double interest;
                    int loanAmt;
                    double payment;

                    //Calculations
                    interest = annualInterest/12;
                    loanAmt = price-downPayment-tradeIn;
                    payment = loanAmt/((1/interest)-(1/(interest*Math.pow(1+interest,months))));

                    //Output
                    outputLabel.setText("The monthly payment is $" + Math.round(payment));

            }
    }

        //Conversions
        price = Integer.parseInt(strPrice);
        downPayment = Integer.parseInt(strDownPayment);
        tradeIn = Integer.parseInt(strTradeIn);
        months = Integer.parseInt(strMonths);
        annualInterest =Double.parseDouble(strAnnualInterest);

        //Calculations
        interest = annualInterest/12;
        loanAmt = price-downPayment-tradeIn;
        payment=loanAmt/((1/interest)-(1/(interest*Math.pow(1+interest,months))));

        //Output
        System.out.print("The monthly payment for " + custName + " is $");
        System.out.println(Math.round(payment));
    }
```

remaining text to delete

**FIGURE 2-51**

The applet version of the program now is complete. You added the import statements, changed the name of the class, and constructed the applet components. You then entered code for the init() method. Finally, you included the actionPerformed event to convert the text to numbers, to calculate, and to display the answer.

Figure 2-52 shows the applet code in its entirety. Check your own code for syntax, proper spelling, capitalization, and indentations. When you are confident everything is correct, you are ready to save and compile your program.

```
                              BertApplet


        add(calcButton);
        add(outputLabel);
        calcButton.addActionListener(this);
    }

    public void actionPerformed(ActionEvent e)
    {
        //Converting input to values
        int price = Integer.parseInt(priceField.getText());
        int downPayment = Integer.parseInt(downPaymentField.getText());
        int tradeIn = Integer.parseInt(tradeInField.getText());
        double annualInterest = Double.parseDouble(annualInterestField.getText());
        int months = Integer.parseInt(monthsField.getText());

        //Variables used in formulas and output
        double interest;
        int loanAmt;
        double payment;

        //Calculations
        interest = annualInterest/12;
        loanAmt = price-downPayment-tradeIn;
        payment = loanAmt/((1/interest)-(1/(interest*Math.pow(1+interest,months))));

        //Output
        outputLabel.setText("The monthly payment is $" + Math.round (payment));

    }
}




                               Page 2
```

## Wordwrap in Notepad

As your Java programs get more complicated, the statements may wrap to the next line, making them more difficult to read. Consider printing your programs in Landscape orientation. The larger page width increases the number of characters per line. On Notepad's File menu, click Page Setup and then click the Landscape option button.

```
                              BertApplet


    /*
        Project 2        Inputting Data
        Programmer:      Joy Starks
        Date:            October 9, 2001
        Program Name:    BertApplet
    */

    import java.awt.*;
    import java.applet.*;
    import java.awt.event.*;

    public class BertApplet extends Applet implements ActionListener

    {
        Label custNameLabel = new Label("Please enter your name:");
            TextField custNameField = new TextField(25);

        Label priceLabel = new Label("Enter the price of the car:");
            TextField priceField = new TextField(25);

        Label downPaymentLabel = new Label("Enter the down payment:");
            TextField downPaymentField = new TextField(25);

        Label tradeInLabel = new Label("Enter the trade in value:");
            TextField tradeInField = new TextField(25);

        Label monthsLabel = new Label("Enter the number of months:");
            TextField monthsField = new TextField(25);

        Label annualInterestLabel = new Label("Enter the yearly interest
    rate in decimal form:");
            TextField annualInterestField = new TextField(25);

        Button calcButton = new Button("Calculate Monthly Payment");

        Label outputLabel = new Label("Enter the requested data and click
    the button");

        public void init()
        {
            add(custNameLabel);
            add(custNameField);
            add(priceLabel);
            add(priceField);
            add(downPaymentLabel);
            add(downPaymentField);
            add(tradeInLabel);
            add(tradeInField);
            add(monthsLabel);
            add(monthsField);
            add(annualInterestLabel);
            add(annualInterestField);


                               Page 1
```

**FIGURE 2-52**

## Saving And Compiling

Perform the following steps to save and compile the applet.

### TO SAVE AND COMPILE THE APPLET

**1** Click the Notepad window.

**2** With a floppy disk in drive A, click File on the menu bar and then click Save As.

**3** When the Save As dialog box displays, type "BertApplet.java" in the File name text box. You must type the quotation marks around the file name.

**4** Click the Save in box arrow and then click 3½ Floppy (A:) in the list.

**5** Click the Save button.

**6** If the MS-DOS Prompt window is not on your desktop, open it, set your path, and change to drive A. Otherwise, click the MS-DOS Prompt button on the taskbar.

**7** At the A: prompt in the MS-DOS Prompt window, type javac BertApplet.java and then press the ENTER key.

**8** If you have errors, fix them in the Notepad window. Save the BertApplet.java file again, and repeat step 7.

*The program compiles.*

<aside>
### More About

### Editing in the MS-DOS Prompt Window

If you type doskey at the command prompt and then press the ENTER key, the operating system remembers your typed commands. You can add this command to your autoexec.bat file or type it each time you open a MS-DOS Prompt session. You then can use the arrow keys to display previously typed commands, which saves you time and eliminates the tedium of typing the commands again. The F3 key displays only the most recent command, whereas using doskey and the arrow keys keeps a record of all your previous command entries.
</aside>

# The HTML Host Document and Interactive Applets

You may remember that, in order to execute an applet in a browser or with Applet Viewer, you need a host document. This short, HTML file tells the browser, through the use of tags, the name of the applet and the size of the window. HTML hosts may contain other tags as well.

## Creating the Host Document

You will use the <HTML> tag and the <APPLET> tag in the host document. Perform the following steps to create the HTML host document using Notepad.

### TO CREATE THE HTML HOST DOCUMENT

**1** If necessary, start Notepad. Be certain that you have saved any files that may display.

**2** Click File on the menu bar and then click New.

**3** In the Notepad workspace, type the code as shown in Figure 2-53.

**4** Click File on the menu bar and then click Save As. When the Save As dialog box displays, if necessary, click the Look in box arrow and click 3½ Floppy (A:) in the list. In the File name text box, type "BertApplet.html" as the name of the file.

**5** Click the Save button.

*The file saves on the floppy disk.*

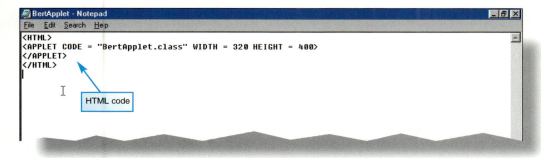

```
BertApplet - Notepad
File   Edit   Search   Help
<HTML>
<APPLET CODE = "BertApplet.class" WIDTH = 320 HEIGHT = 400>
</APPLET>
</HTML>
```

HTML code

**FIGURE 2-53**

The applet tag nested within the HTML beginning and ending tags specifies three pieces of information that the Web page will need in order to access the Java applet: the name of the Java bytecode file, the width of the window, and the height of the window in which to run the applet.

## Running an Interactive Applet Using Applet Viewer

Using the JDK Applet Viewer makes it possible to run a Java applet without using a Web browser. However, whether you use Applet Viewer or a browser, you can interact with the applet when prompted by entering data into text boxes and clicking buttons.

The following steps illustrate how to run an interactive applet using Applet Viewer from the command prompt.

**Steps** **To Run an Interactive Applet Using Applet Viewer**

**1** **Click the MS-DOS Prompt button on** the taskbar. Type `appletviewer BertApplet.html` **and then press the ENTER key.**

*The applet displays on the screen (Figure 2-54).*

Applet Viewer window

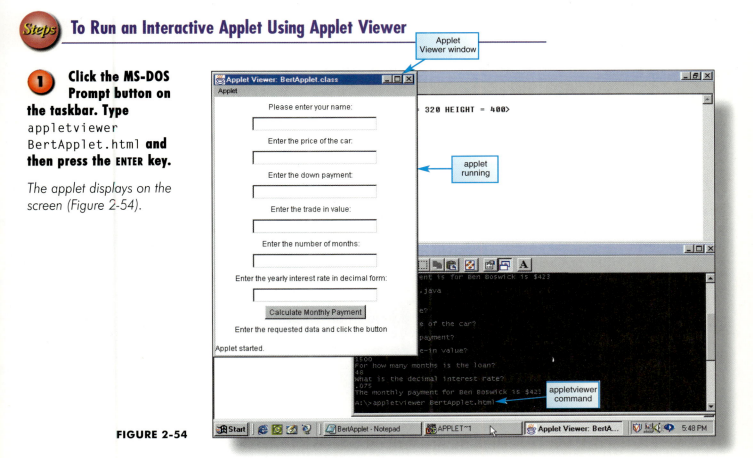

**FIGURE 2-54**

**2** Click the first text box. Enter the sample information as shown in Figure 2-55. You may use the TAB key to move from field to field, or you may use your mouse to click inside each text box. When you are finished, point to the Calculate Monthly Payment button.

*Each text box displays the sample data (Figure 2-55).*

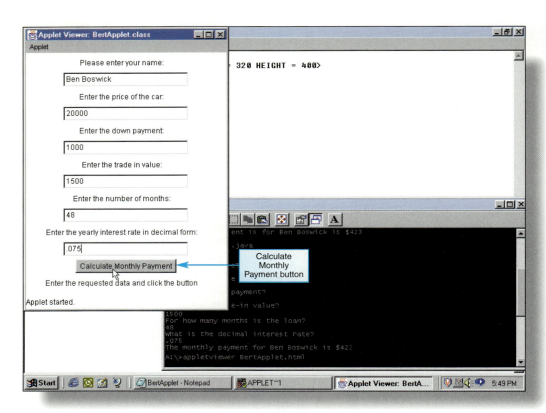

**FIGURE 2-55**

**3** Click the Calculate Monthly Payment button. Point to Applet Viewer's Close button.

*The monthly payment for the sample data displays (Figure 2-56).*

**4** Click the Close button. Click the Close buttons on the Notepad and the MS-DOS Prompt windows.

*Applet Viewer, Notepad, and the MS-DOS window close and the Windows desktop displays.*

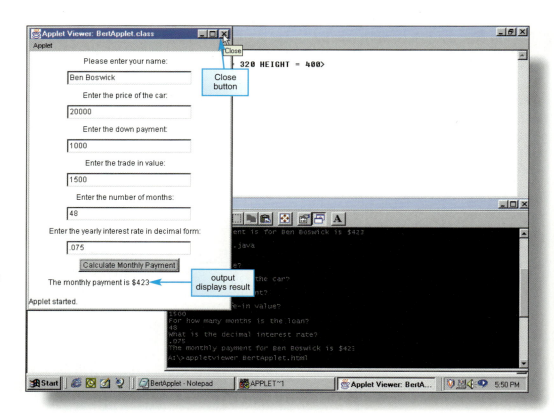

**FIGURE 2-56**

Each time you execute the applet with Applet Viewer, you can enter different data. In a later project, you will learn how to write a clear event that will clear the sample data for the next person, without having to close and execute the program again.

# File Management

Performing the steps to code, save, compile, modify, and so on, creates several files on your storage device. File naming conventions and the operating system's capability of displaying icons associated with different file types can help you keep everything in logical order. In this project, you created a java file, which when compiled, created a class file on your floppy disk. You also modified that file twice, saving and compiling it both times. You created a HTML host file on your floppy disk, as well, for a total of seven files. Figure 2-57 displays a list of files on a floppy disk. Your icons may appear differently, based on your installation of the JDK and your default browser.

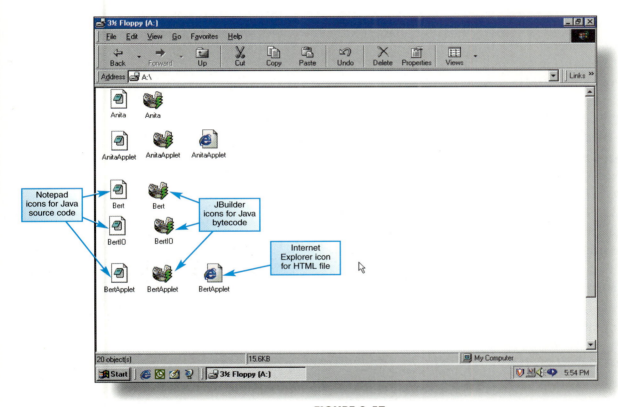

**FIGURE 2-57**

# Project Summary

In this project, you learned how to write assignment statements in Java to store sample data with proper identifiers. You learned how to code formulas with mathematical operators. Two methods from the Math class, round and pow, were used to calculate a monthly payment. Output included variables, calculated amounts, and string data. You then modified the program to accept data from a user. The stand-alone version of the application read data from a buffer wrapped by the InputStreamReader (ISR). The readLine method made the program pause and wait for user input. You converted the application to an interactive applet. Using constructors for each of the components, you added labels, text fields, and a button. With the init method, you added the components to the applet. Finally, running the HTML host produced an applet that allowed user input and calculated when a button was clicked.

# What You Should Know

Having completed this project, you should be able to perform the following tasks:

▶ Assign Sample Data *(J 2.13)*
▶ Code the ActionListener *(J 2.47)*
▶ Code the Init Method *(J 2.45)*
▶ Compile the Program *(J 2.23)*
▶ Create Applet Components *(J 2.42)*
▶ Create the HTML Host Document *(J 2.50)*
▶ Edit Code for Data Handling *(J 2.30)*
▶ Enter Beginning Code *(J 2.7)*
▶ Enter Code *(J 2.38)*
▶ Enter New Code *(J 2.27)*
▶ Enter Output Code *(J 2.20)*
▶ Enter the Formulas *(J 2.17)*
▶ Execute the Program *(J 2.24)*
▶ Maximize the Notepad Window and Declare Variables *(J 2.11)*
▶ Run an Interactive Applet Using Applet Viewer *(J 2.51)*
▶ Run the Program *(J 2.36)*
▶ Save and Compile the Applet *(J 2.50)*
▶ Save and Compile the Source Code *(J 2.35)*
▶ Save the Source Code *(J 2.23)*
▶ Set Up the Desktop *(J 2.6)*

# *Test Your Knowledge*

## 1 True/False

**Instructions:** Circle **T** if the statement is true or **F** is the statement is false.

T  F    1. The Java programming language is considered a strongly typed language.
T  F    2. Java's use of primitive data types means Java is a primitive language.
T  F    3. Math.pow is an operator to perform exponentiation.
T  F    4. Declaring a variable involves listing the data type and the identifier.
T  F    5. The following statement evaluates to true in Java: (7 == 7).
T  F    6. Programmers use the term boolean to refer to a result that has only one state.
T  F    7. Java's add method adds two numbers together.
T  F    8. A buffer is a data area shared by hardware devices or programs, where data are held until they are needed.
T  F    9. The parse method can convert integers to strings.
T  F   10. Modular division truncates any remainder.

## 2 Multiple Choice

**Instructions:** Circle the correct response.

1. In Java, the process of joining two strings with a plus sign is called _____ .
   a. combination
   b. concatenation
   c. encapsulation
   d. compilation
2. Data flowing in or out of a program in Java are called _____ data.
   a. streaming
   b. sinuous
   c. buffering
   d. constructing
3. ISR stands for _____ .
   a. Internal Synchronous Reset
   b. Input Standard Return
   c. Intermediary System Reader
   d. Input Stream Reader
4. _____ is the process of creating an instance of an object with a constructor.
   a. Instantiation
   b. Buffering
   c. Wrapping
   d. Streaming

*(continued)*

# Test Your Knowledge

**Multiple Choice** (continued)

5. If Java tries to open a non-existent file, _____ .
   a. the program needs to acknowledge the potential failure ahead of time
   b. the program throws an exception
   c. the program could abort prematurely
   d. all of the above

6. _____ listens for events in an applet.
   a. A component object
   b. The compiler
   c. ActionListener
   d. The Init method

7. All of the following are applet component objects *except* _____ .
   a. labels
   b. mice
   c. text fields
   d. buttons

8. ActionPerformed is an example of a(n) _____ .
   a. class
   b. instance
   c. object
   d. event

9. The main reason for using a consistent set of _____ is to standardize the structure and coding style of an application, so that you and others easily may read and understand the code.
   a. naming conventions
   b. instantiations
   c. methods
   d. programming applications

10. When evaluating the expression  4 + 8 / 2 * 3 − 2, which of the following is the correct answer?
    a. 16
    b. 22
    c. 6
    d. 14

# Test Your Knowledge

## 3 Understanding the Code

**Instructions:** In Figure 2-58, arrows point to sections of Java code. Identify the code in the spaces provided using the appropriate word(s) from the following list.

| | | | |
|---|---|---|---|
| comment | constructor | calculation | concatenation |
| declaration section | conversion | input from buffer | output section |
| | class name | package name | |

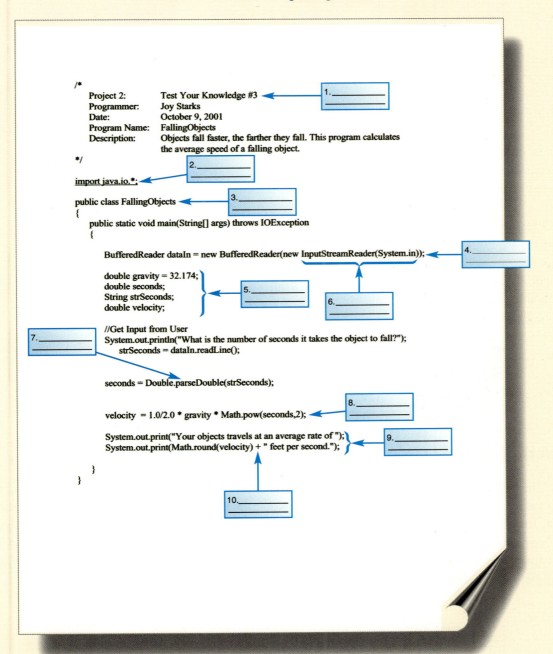

```
/*
    Project 2:       Test Your Knowledge #3          1._____
    Programmer:      Joy Starks
    Date:            October 9, 2001
    Program Name:    FallingObjects
    Description:     Objects fall faster, the farther they fall. This program calculates
                     the average speed of a falling object.
*/
                                          2._____
import java.io.*;

public class FallingObjects            3._____
{
    public static void main(String[] args) throws IOException
    {
        BufferedReader dataIn = new BufferedReader(new InputStreamReader(System.in));   4._____

        double gravity = 32.174;
        double seconds;                5._____
        String strSeconds;                        6._____
        double velocity;

        //Get Input from User
7._____  System.out.println("What is the number of seconds it takes the object to fall?");
            strSeconds = dataIn.readLine();


        seconds = Double.parseDouble(strSeconds);

                                                  8._____
        velocity = 1.0/2.0 * gravity * Math.pow(seconds,2);

        System.out.print("Your objects travels at an average rate of ");   9._____
        System.out.print(Math.round(velocity) + " feet per second.");

    }
}
                          10._____
```

**FIGURE 2-58**

## Test Your Knowledge

### 4 Identifying Applet Components

**Instructions:** Figure 2-59 displays a Java applet. Identify the various parts of the applet in the spaces provided.

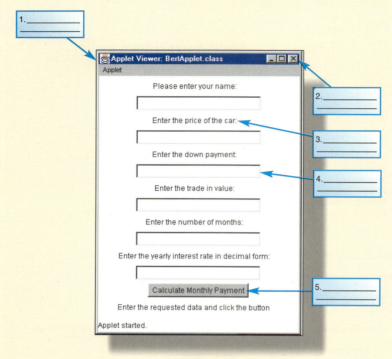

**FIGURE 2-59**

## Apply Your Knowledge

### 1 Converting from Sample Data to User Input

**Instructions:** In order to start Notepad, click the Start button on the taskbar. Point to Programs and then point to Accessories on the Programs submenu. Click Notepad on the Accessories submenu. Open the file Apply2.java, from the Data Disk (see inside back cover for instructions on how to obtain a copy of the Data Disk). The program converts any number of coins into dollars and cents. Change the lines of code that assign sample data into lines of code that prompt the user and store the answers. The resulting prompts display with the calculated answer as shown in Figure 2-60.

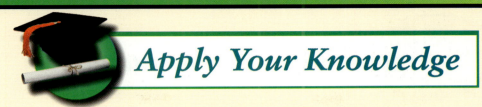

*Apply Your Knowledge*

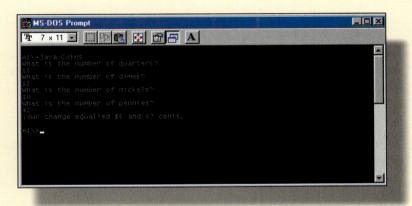

**FIGURE 2-60**

1. With the Apply2.java program displayed in the Notepad window, substitute your name and date in the block comment at the beginning.
2. In the class header, select the class name, Apply2. Type `Coins` as the new class name. Edit the name of the class in the documentation lines as well.
3. Save the file on your floppy disk with the name "Coins.java" as the file name.
4. Add four additional variable declarations for string inputs by typing:

```
String strQuarters;
String strDimes;
String strNickels;
String strPennies;
```

5. Delete the Assigning Values section of code. Replace it with the following:

```
System.out.println("What is the number of quarters?");
        strQuarters = dataIn.readLine();
System.out.println("What is the number of dimes?");
        strDimes = dataIn.readLine();
System.out.println("What is the number of nickels?");
        strNickels = dataIn.readLine();
System.out.println("What is the number of pennies?");
        strPennies = dataIn.readLine();
```

6. Delete the Calculations section of code. Replace the statements that multiply the number of coins by their face value, to lines of code that parse the values the user inputs by typing the following:

```
quarters = Integer.parseInt(strQuarters) * 25;
dimes = Integer.parseInt(strDimes) * 10;
nickels = Integer.parseInt(strNickels) * 5;
pennies = Integer.parseInt(strPennies) * 1;
```

*(continued)*

# Apply Your Knowledge

**Converting from Sample Data to User Input** *(continued)*

7. Save the file again by clicking the Save command on the Notepad File menu.
8. Open the MS-DOS Prompt window. If you downloaded JDK from the Sun Web site, set the path to the location of your Java bin by typing `path=c:\jdk1.2.2\bin` at the command prompt and press the ENTER key. If you installed the Java compiler from the JBuilder3 CD-ROM that accompanies this text, type `path=c:\jbuilder3\java\bin` and press the ENTER key.
9. Change to your floppy disk drive by typing `a:` and then press the ENTER key.
10. Compile your program by typing `javac Coins.java` at the prompt. If the compilation is successful, proceed to step 11. Otherwise, correct the errors and return to step 7.
11. Run the program by typing `java Coins` at the prompt. Remember that Java is case-sensitive and that the name of the file must match the class name exactly. If the program runs correctly, return to Notepad and print a copy for your instructor. Otherwise, return to step 7 and correct the errors.

# In the Lab

## 1 Income to Debt Ratio Calculator

**Problem:**   Many financial institutions make decisions about extending credit and financing majors purchases based on a customer's income to debt ratio. This ratio is the percentage of a customer's income that is spent paying off other debts such as mortgages, automobile loans, credit cards, etc. Typically, all debts are added together and then that total is divided by the monthly income. Customers with a lower income to debt ratio are more likely to qualify for a loan.

As an intern at the Employee's Credit Union, you have been asked to create an interactive income to debt ratio calculation program that can run as a stand-alone application. Figure 2-61 displays the results from executing the program.

```
MS-DOS Prompt
A:\>javac DebtRatio.java

A:\>java DebtRatio
What is your monthly income?
1600
What is the amount of your mortage or rent?
Enter zero if you do not have a mortage or pay rent.
500
What is the amount of your auto loan?
Enter zero if you do not have an auto loan.
332
What is the total amount of your other debts.
Enter zero if you have no other debt.
0
Your income to debt ratio is 0.52
A:\>
```

**FIGURE 2-61**

# In the Lab

**Instructions:** Perform the following tasks.

1. To start Notepad, click the Start button. On the Start menu, point to Programs and then point to Accessories. On the Accessories submenu, click Notepad.
2. Begin your code by typing a block comment with the Lab Assignment number, your name, the current date, and the program name, DebtRatio.java.
3. Type the following lines that import the java.io package and begin blocks for the class header and main method header:

```
import java.io;
public class DebtRatio
{
    public static void main(String[] args) throws IOException
    {
```

4. Type the constructor for the buffered input:

```
BufferedReader dataIn = new BufferedReader(new InputStreamReader(System.in));
```

5. Declare the following variables to be Strings: strMonthlyIncome, strMortgage, strAutoLoan, and strOtherDebt.
6. Declare the following variables to be doubles: monthlyIncome, mortgage, autoLoan, otherDebt, and ratio.
7. Create an input section beginning with an appropriate line comment. Type the System.out.println methods to display the prompts as shown in Figure 2-61. In order to accept user input, type an indented readLine method for each string variable. The first two lines are as follows. Type them and the remaining prompts and readLine methods.

```
System.out.println("What is your monthly income?");
        strMonthlyIncome = dataIn.readLine();
```

8. Create a conversion section, beginning with an appropriate line comment, to parse each of the inputted values. For example, for the first input value, the code would be:

```
monthlyIncome = Double.parseDouble(strMonthlyIncome);
```

9. Create a calculation section, beginning with an appropriate line comment, to calculate the income to debt ratio by typing:

```
ratio = (mortgage + autoLoan + otherDebt) / monthlyIncome;
```

*(continued)*

# In the Lab

**Income to Debt Ratio Calculator** *(continued)*

10. Create an output section, beginning with an appropriate line comment. Enter the code to display the answer by typing:

```
System.out.print("Your income to debt ratio is " + ratio);
```

11. Close both the main and class methods with closing braces.
12. Save the program with the file name "DebtRatio.java" on your floppy disk.
13. Open the MS-DOS Prompt window and set the path.
14. Compile your program by typing `javac DebtRatio.java` at the command prompt. Remember that Java is case-sensitive with respect to the name of the file.
15. If there are no compilation errors, execute the program by typing `java DebtRatio` at the command prompt. Enter the sample data from Figure 2-61 on the previous page. Run the program again with your own personal data.
16. In the Notepad window, use the Print command on the File menu to print a copy of the coding for your instructor.
17. Close Notepad and the MS-DOS Prompt windows by clicking the Close button on each title bar.

## 2 Interactive IO with Java

**Problem:** You would like a program to help you balance your checkbook. You decide to write a stand-alone Java application that accepts the beginning balance, the total of the checks you wrote, the total of your deposits, and the fees charged by the bank as inputs, and then display what the ending balance should be. Figure 2-62 displays the results from executing the application.

**FIGURE 2-62**

**Instructions:**

1. Open the Notepad window.
2. Begin your code by typing a block comment with the Lab Assignment number, your name, the current date, and the program name, Balance.java.
3. Type the import statement, class header, and main method header and their opening braces. Remember to use the phrase, throws IOException, as you will be using interactive statements.
4. Type a constructor for the Buffered Reader as described in this project on pages J 2.26 through J 2.29.

# In the Lab

5. Declare both string and float variables for beginning balance, total deposits, total checks, and total fees. Declare a float variable for ending balance.
6. Using System.out.println methods, enter lines of code to prompt the user for each of the input variables as shown in Figure 2-62. Include a readLine method to accept each input and assign it to its corresponding declared string variable.
7. Enter code to convert each input variable to doubles or floats. For example, for the first input value, the code would be:

```
begBalance = Float.parseFloat(strBegBalance);
```

8. Write a formula that takes the beginning balance plus the total deposits, minus the checks and fees, and assigns the value to the ending balance.
9. Write an output section that displays an appropriate message and the ending balance on the screen.
10. Label each section with an appropriate line comment.
11. Save the program with the filename "Balance.java" on your floppy disk.
12. Open an MS-DOS Prompt window and set the path.
13. Compile your program by typing javac Balance.java at the command prompt. Remember that Java is case-sensitive with respect to the name of the file.
14. If there are no compilation errors, execute the program by typing java Balance at the command prompt. Enter the sample data from Figure 2-62. Run the program again with your own personal data.
15. In the Notepad window, use the Print command on the File menu to print a copy of the code for your instructor.
16. Close both the Notepad window and the MS-DOS Prompt windows by clicking the Close button on each title bar.

## 3 Creating an Applet

**Problem:** As webmaster for a chain of appliance stores, you have been asked to create an applet that will display as part of the store's e-commerce site. The applet will calculate the annual cost of running an appliance. Using text boxes, the applet will ask the user for the cost per kilowatt-hour in cents, and the number of kilowatt-hours the appliance uses in a year. Figure 2-63 displays the results from executing the applet.

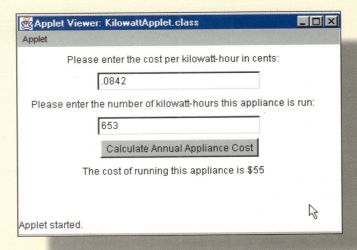

**FIGURE 2-63**

*(continued)*

# In the Lab

**Instructions:**

1. Open the Notepad window, and begin your code by typing a block comment with the Lab Assignment number, your name, the current date, and the program name, KilowattApplet.java.

2. Type lines of code to import the following packages:

```
import java.awt.*;
import java.applet.*;
import java.awt.event.*;
```

3. Type the following class header and opening brace:

```
public class KilowattApplet extends Applet implements ActionListener
{
```

4. Type the following Label constructor and a TextField constructor where costKwhr is the cost per kilowatt-hour:

```
Label costKwhrLabel = new Label("Please enter the cost per kilowatt-hour in cents:");
TextField costKwhrField = new TextField(25);
```

5. Type a similar Label and TextField constructor for the number of kilowatt-hours the appliance uses in a year.

6. Construct a button for the user to click by typing:

```
Button calcButton = new Button("Calculate Annual Appliance Cost");
```

7. Type a Label constructor to display the average.

8. Create an init method to add all of the above controls to the applet interface. The first few lines are as follows:

```
public void init()
{
    add(costKwhrLabel);
    add(costKwhrField);
```

9. Type the following command to add the ActionListener to the calcButton and close the init method with a brace:

```
    calcButton.addActionListener(this);
}
```

# In the Lab

10. Create an actionPerformed event to convert the input and perform the calculations. The event header and first conversion are done for you. Enter the following lines and a line to accept the kilowatt-hours that the appliance uses in a year.

```
public void actionPerformed(ActionEvent e)
{
   //Converting input to values
   double costKwhr = Double.parseDouble(costKwhrField.getText());
```

11. Type a similar line to convert the annual kilowatt-hours.
12. Declare a float variable to hold the average, by typing the following:

```
//Variables used in formulas and output
double average;
```

13. Write a line of code to perform the calculation, which multiplies the cents by the kilowatt-hours in a year, and assigns it to the variable, average.
14. Round off the displayed result using the Math.round method and assign it to the output Label.
15. Close the init block with a closing brace and then close the applet with a closing brace.
16. Save the program with the file name "KilowattApplet.java" on your floppy disk.
17. Open the MS-DOS Prompt window. Set the path, if necessary. Compile the program by typing javac KilowattApplet.java at the command prompt. If there are compilation errors, fix them and recompile.
18. Print a copy of the coding for your instructor.
19. In the Notepad window, click New on the File menu and type the following code for the HTML file:

```
<HTML>
<APPLET CODE = "KilowattApplet.class" WIDTH = 400 HEIGHT = 200>
</APPLET>
</HTML>
```

20. Save the HTML code with the file name "KilowattApplet.html" on your floppy disk.
21. Execute the program from the MS-DOS Prompt window by typing appletviewer KilowattApplet.html at the command prompt. Enter the sample data from Figure 2-63 on page J 2.63. Run the program again with your own personal data.
22. Close both the Notepad window and the MS-DOS Prompt window by clicking the Close button on each title bar.

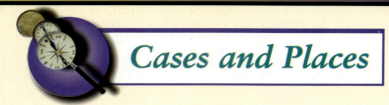

# Cases and Places

The difficulty of these case studies varies:
▶ are the least difficult; ▶▶ are more difficult; and ▶▶▶ are the most difficult.

**1** ▶ Bill's Burgers would like an applet that calculates the sales tax for their front counter help. The applet should let the worker enter the total amount of the customer's order and then calculate a 7 percent sales tax. When the worker clicks a calculate button, the applet should display the amount of the customer's order, the tax, and the total of the customer's order and tax added together.

**2** ▶ Ohm's Law relates the resistance of an electrical device, such as a portable heater, to the electric current flowing through the device and the voltage applied to it. The law is: I = V/R. V is the voltage, measured in volts. R is the resistance, measured in ohms. The answer, I, is the electrical current, measured in amps. Write an applet with two label prompts and text fields. One label will ask the user to input the voltage; the other label will ask the user to input the resistance of a device. The applet then will display the current. Remember that because V and R will be entered as integers; your ActionListener event will have to parse the numbers into double values in order to perform the division.

**3** ▶▶ Your younger brother is studying beginning geometry. He has to calculate the area of several different circles and would like to automate the process. Write a stand-alone application for him that calculates the area of a circle from the radius. The radius will be an integer read in from the keyboard. Create a method that will accept the integer and perform the calculation using the formula $pi\ r^2$; that is, the value of *pi* times the radius, squared. Use the PI method from the Math class for the value of *pi*.

**4** ▶▶ Write a program that will display the number of dollars and cents based on user numeric input. For instance, if the user inputs 543, the program will print out 5 dollars and 43 cents. For this program you will use integer arithmetic and will need to avoid floating point arithmetic. Review the integer remainder modular operator % discussed in the project.

**5** ▶▶▶ Because you are an outstanding student, a local civic organization has awarded you a generous sum of money to pursue your education in England. You also plan to do some sightseeing while you are in Europe. The award money is in U.S. dollars and you want to know how that will convert to British pounds, French francs, Italian lire, German Deutsche marks, and Spanish pesetas. Use the concepts and techniques presented in this project to create an application that will accept the U.S. dollar amount, convert the U.S. dollar amount, and display the English, French, Italian, German and Spanish equivalents. Use the Web, a newspaper, or a local financial institution to obtain the conversion rates.

**6** ▶▶▶ Use the Sun Microsystems Java documentation Web site at http://java.sun.com/docs/searchabledocs.html to find documentation on Java packages. In particular, search the site for methods in the Math class. Make a list of 10 methods and describe their arguments and what they return.

Java Programming

P R O J E C T

# Decision, Repetition, and Components in Java

O B J E C T I V E S

You will have mastered the material in this project when you can:

- Design a program using components
- Test each component individually
- Differentiate between compile-time and run-time errors
- Define an exception
- Code a try and catch construct
- Use the throw statement to construct an exception
- Write a decision structure using the if statement
- Describe the use of AND, OR, and NOT
- Decide when to check data for reasonableness
- Create a user-defined method
- Send arguments and receive return values from a method
- Write a switch structure to test for multiple values in data
- Code a repetition structure using the while statement
- Describe the java.awt, java.applet, and java.awt.event packages
- Add a component with addItemListener in an applet
- Construct a check box group
- Differentiate between applications of a check box and a check box group
- Code an itemStateChanged event

# A Virtual Green Thumb

## Find Your Roots With Garden.com

**W**hether your rhododendrons are the envy of your neighborhood or your crabgrass is making you cranky, you can get back to your roots by digging in the virtual garden at Garden.com. This all-encompassing Web site runs the gamut from an online garden doctor with 24/7 office hours to a chat room filled with green thumb aficionados.

Plan to share the soil with many other nature-loving surfers. Gardening is the foremost recreational pastime for adults, says the Lawn and Garden Marketing and Distribution Association. Sixty-seven million Americans in two-thirds of American households call themselves gardeners, according to the National Gardening Association. They spend, on average, 10 hours per week planting, watering, fertilizing, and pulling weeds.

Garden.com offers more than 20,000 plants and products, Garden Escape Magazine, and weekend project plans. The Plant Finder feature selects plants based on user-specified conditions, such as sun exposure, soil pH and composition, moisture, color and foliage colors, and degree of

maintenance. Another useful feature is the LandscapePlanner, a Java applet stored on the Garden.com server that lets users design their dream gardens. Gardeners begin either by creating their own custom palette from scratch or by choosing a professionally created template, such as a butterfly garden. The custom palette users start their plans by specifying the garden's dimensions on the design canvas, which has gridlines representing a one-foot scale. They then add plants and other accessories, such as furniture, statues, and arbors, by selecting the objects and dragging them to the desired locations on the grid.

The professional templates include a verbal description of the selected plants and the recommended soil and climate conditions, a photo or drawing showing how the finished garden might look at maturity, and links to relevant magazine articles providing additional insight. For example, the butterfly garden template has links to stories on monarch butterflies and on caterpillar cuisine.

Virtual gardeners then can view a list of the plants contained on their templates and make substitutions, additions, and deletions. Once they have finalized their plans, they add the plants to their virtual Wheelbarrow, which is Garden.com's version of a shopping cart. When ready to place an order, they view the Wheelbarrow, enter their name and mailing address, select the form of payment and choose the delivery method. Growers across the country then ship the plants directly to the user in as few as three days.

Placing an online order also is a factor of the Java applet you will create in the project for Candle Line, which sells designer candles and gifts. Your Java modules will accept customer input, test these values, and then calculate shipping charges. Based on the delivery times ranging from 1 to 7 days, you will use decision steps to compute the correct shipping fee and add it to a customer's order.

A delivery from Garden.com can make virtual gardeners' lives blossom as they really dig the results!

Java Programming

# Decision, Repetition, and Components in Java

Java Programming

## CASE PERSPECTIVE

CandleLine.com sells designer candles and personal gifts, catering to customers who want to send gifts for special occasions. CandleLine's e-commerce site is an interactive Web page. As customers choose the candles and gifts they wish to purchase, the items are added to an electronic shopping cart. Approximately 300 people per day are accessing CandleLine's Web site, but many have complained that the shipping charges are a hidden cost. In order to improve customer relations, the company would like to give its customers a choice in shipping methods and a way to calculate their shipping costs before finalizing their order.

You have been asked to create a sample Java program that calculates the shipping cost for customer purchases. Eventually the program will read the total price of purchases as data from the Web page, but for now you will enter the total price as an input value and then have the program calculate shipping charges.

After finalizing the solution, CandleLine wants you to convert the application to an applet that the webmaster eventually can link with the customer shopping cart, implemented from the Web page.

# Introduction

The previous Java programming examples in this book have executed sequentially, from top to bottom without skipping any code or branching to another class, and without making any decisions. Realistically, programs need to interpret data and assess user input, which usually affects the direction the program should take. As discussed in the Introduction Project, a control structure is a standard progression of logical steps to control the sequence of statement execution. The logic controls the order in which the program instructions are executed.

A **sequence** of steps is performed one after another, whereas a **decision**, such as whether or not a user has entered data, is based on a condition. The evaluated condition causes the computer to execute one set of coding instructions as opposed to another. Multiple choices, sometimes presented in the form of menus, assist users in making correct decisions — decisions that then determine the coding path the program will take. Many times, programs must repeat a set of instructions for multiple instances of data or multiple users. A **loop** repeats a section of code while a condition is true or until a condition is met. The **case structure** executes one of several statement blocks depending on the value of an expression. In Java, programmers typically use the case structure when a menu is the best choice for user input.

In Project 2, you learned how to accept user input from the keyboard and manipulate it using Java's arithmetic operators and methods from the Math class. The program worked only if the user entered the data in an acceptable format. No validation of the data occurred. The data was not tested for reasonableness, data type errors, validity within a range, or for consistency errors. An important use of decision structures, in well-written programs, is to verify the correctness of the input data before using it in processing. Programs that terminate abruptly because of invalid input are poorly designed and extremely annoying to users. Allowing the user to try again to enter correct data involves transferring execution back to the beginning of that processing section. Therefore, programmers use a loop to repeat a section of code until valid, correct data has been entered. Java provides data validation techniques using both traditional and object-oriented design and control structures.

Breaking these tasks into small sections of code that can be reused for each data entry is known as **modularization.** In traditional languages, dividing a large problem into simpler sections, called **modules,** makes a program easier to understand and maintain. Most object-oriented languages like Java use the term **component,** which commonly means any of the object-oriented structures such as objects, classes, methods, and events. Eliminating duplicate code, improving understandability, and facilitating reusability are all reasons to write Java code using components.

# **P**roject Three — CandleLine Shipping Charges

**ANALYZING THE PROBLEM**  A computer program is required that will accept the cost of a customer order; then, based on a shipping menu choice, the program will calculate a total charge. The values entered by the user must be valid numbers. Customers may choose the shipping options of priority, express, and standard delivery. Priority shipping is $14.95. Express delivery is $11.95. If the value of the order is more than $75.00, then standard shipping is free; otherwise, it is $5.95. Output will include the value of the order, the shipping charge, and the total of the two charges. Figure 3-1(a) displays the program as an application with sample user input. Figure 3-1(b) displays the program as an applet.

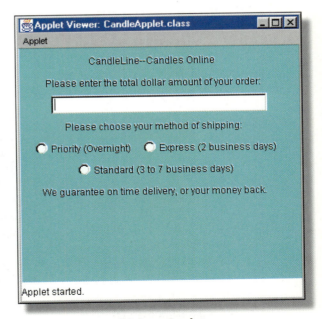

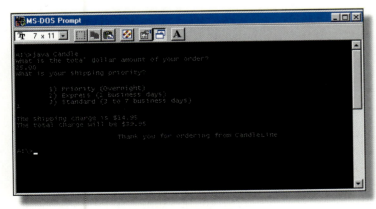

(a) Java Application

(b) Java Applet

**FIGURE 3-1**

**DESIGNING THE PROGRAM**   Because this program will make decisions based on user input, appropriate prompts and messages need to be coded. The program should accept and test a numeric value from the user, display a menu and test for a valid choice, and then calculate and display results. Toward this end, the program will be designed in stages. Programmers commonly create a small portion of code and then thoroughly test it before moving on to the next section. The object-oriented nature of Java lends itself to this kind of design by component, creating reusable portions of code and breaking the programming task down into simpler, more manageable steps. Because this program involves making decisions based on user input, each decision can be designed and tested individually as it is added to the program.

Figure 3-2(a) through Figure 3-2(c) display a flowchart of the logic to input, store, and test the data. Notice that Figure 3-2(a) uses the predefined process symbols to reference Figures 3-2(b) and 3-2(c).

**CODING THE PROGRAM**   You will create Java source code using the syntax and commands of the Java programming language. After creating a Java method to modularize the task of obtaining a shipping cost, you will use Java's ability to catch data type errors as they occur and create a module to display an appropriate error message. Entering a case structure will allow the use of a menu to direct user input. This project presents a series of step-by-step instructions to write the code, explaining its parts.

**TESTING THE PROGRAM**   In this project, you will test the code in each component as you write it. You will compile and run the program at various stages with and without data. Evaluation of the program will take place by deliberately entering incorrect data to test for error checking. Finally, you will test the applet version of the program using Applet Viewer.

**FORMALIZING THE SOLUTION**   You will review the source code, use proper documentation, edit, recompile, and execute the application.

**MAINTAINING THE PROGRAM**   You will modify the program to run as an applet creating options for the three different shipping methods. The applet will calculate in a similar manner to the application.

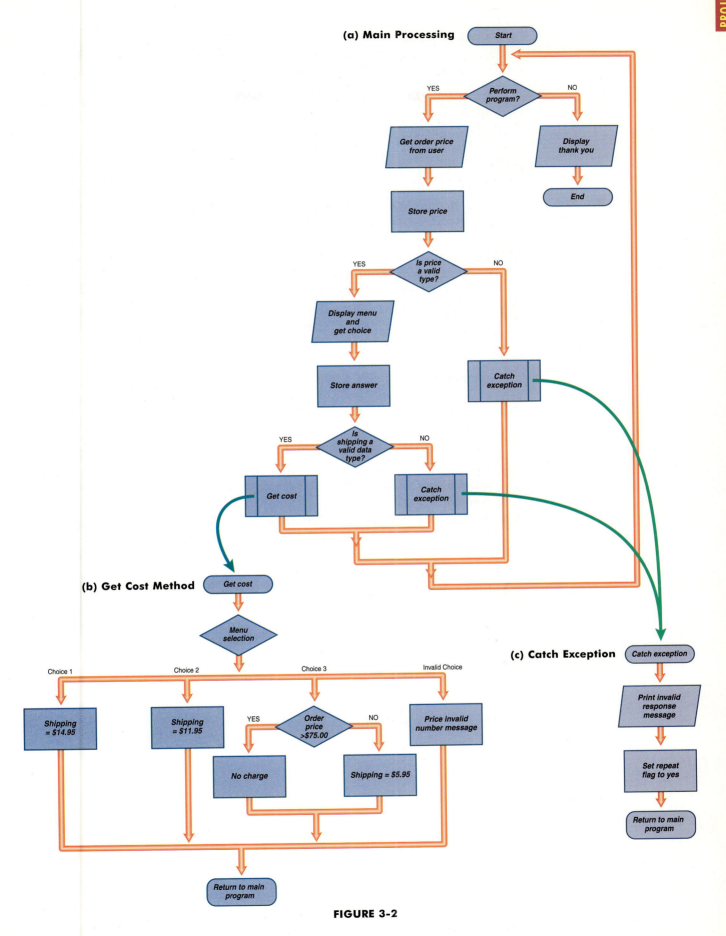

**FIGURE 3-2**

# Starting a New Java Program

Before starting a new Java program, you should set up the Windows desktop by starting Notepad and opening the MS-DOS Prompt window. Perform the following steps to set up the Windows desktop.

### TO SET UP THE DESKTOP

**1** Click the Start button on the taskbar, point to Programs on the Start menu, and then point to Accessories on the Programs submenu. Click Notepad on the Accessories submenu.

**2** In order to display both the Notepad window and the MS-DOS Prompt window on the desktop, drag the title bar of the Notepad window to the upper-left corner of the desktop. Drag the lower-right corner of the Notepad window so that it covers approximately one-third of the desktop.

**3** With the Notepad window still open, click the Start button again. Point to Programs on the Start menu and then click MS-DOS Prompt (Windows 95 or 98) or Command Prompt (Windows NT).

**4** If your system displays the MS-DOS Prompt window as a black, full screen, press and hold the ALT key while pressing the TAB key to minimize the window.

**5** On the taskbar, right-click the MS-DOS Prompt button and then click Properties on the shortcut menu.

**6** When the MS-DOS Prompt Properties dialog box displays, click the Font tab. In the Font size box, scroll to and then click the 7 x 11 or a similar font size.

**7** Click the Screen tab. In the Usage area, click the Window option button to select it. In the Window area, make certain that the Display toolbar check box contains a check mark.

**8** Click the OK button. If the MS-DOS Prompt window does not display, click the MS-DOS Prompt button so that the window displays. Drag it to the lower-right corner of the screen. If necessary, click in the MS-DOS Prompt window to activate it.

**9** If you downloaded Java from the Sun Microsystems Web site, type `path=c:\jdk1.2.2\bin` at the prompt. If you installed the Java compiler from the JBuilder 3 CD-ROM that may accompany this text, type `path=c:\jbuilder3\java\bin` and then press the ENTER key.

**10** With a floppy disk inserted in drive A, change to drive A by typing `a:` and then press the ENTER key.

The desktop displays the Notepad window in the upper-left portion of the screen and the MS-DOS Prompt window in the lower-right portion of the screen (Figure 3-3).

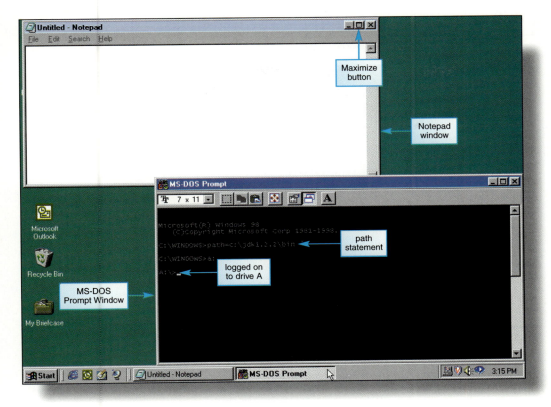

**FIGURE 3-3**

# User Input

Several beginning statements and commands are common to all programs that require user input. These include import statements, comments, the class header, and the method header. Recall from Project 2 that programs requiring user input must import the java.io package. Normally, you should import the entire package by using the wildcard (*) if you plan to use more than one or two classes from that package. General comments and import statements usually precede the class header. In Project 2 you also learned that if there is a possibility that data might be entered incorrectly, you should warn the Java compiler by adding the statement, throws IOException, to the main method header. This statement acknowledges potential failures and allows the program to compile correctly.

## Beginning Code

In the following steps you will create an application for the CandleLine company to calculate shipping charges. You will enter general comments about the program, import the java.io package, create the class named Candle, and enter the main method header. Even though this program has no code inside the braces, Java will compile and execute the program successfully. Programs designed as a kind of template in order to enter code at a later time are called **stubs**.

**Other Ways**

1. To start Notepad, right-click desktop, click New, click Text Document, double-click New Text Document icon on desktop
2. To open MS-DOS Prompt window, click Start button, click Run, type command.com, press ENTER key

**More About**

**The Notepad Window**

Although Notepad is standard on many computer systems, you can use any text-editing program to type your Java source code. As long as the program can save your code as a text file, it will work. Keeping both the Notepad window and the MS-DOS Prompt window open facilitates running and checking the program. You may maximize Notepad to edit longer programs.

## Steps To Enter the Beginning Code

**1** **Maximize the Notepad window by clicking the Maximize button on its title bar. Enter the block comment as shown in Figure 3-4, replacing the programmer name and date shown with your name and the current date.**

*The block comment for the program displays (Figure 3-4).*

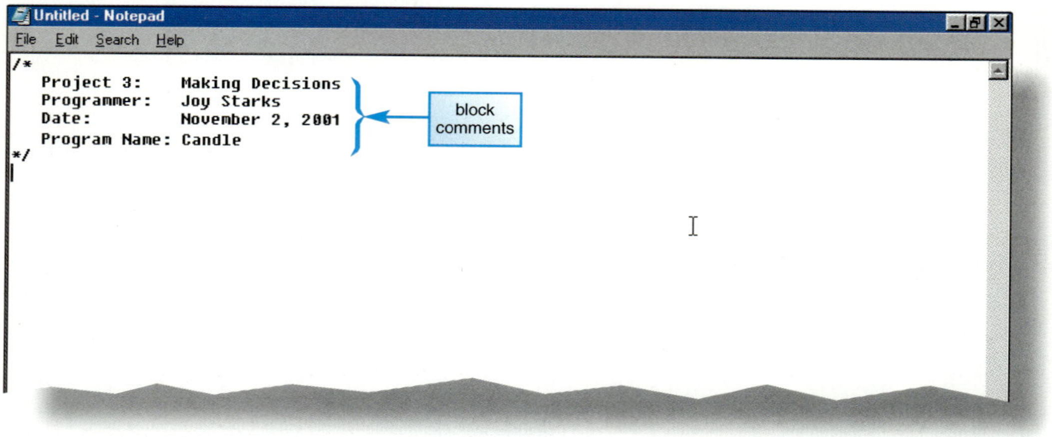
Untitled - Notepad
File Edit Search Help
/*
Project 3: Making Decisions
Programmer: Joy Starks
Date: November 2, 2001
Program Name: Candle
*/
block comments

FIGURE 3-4

**2** **Enter the import statement as shown in Figure 3-5.**

*The java.io package will be imported to handle input and output methods (Figure 3-5).*

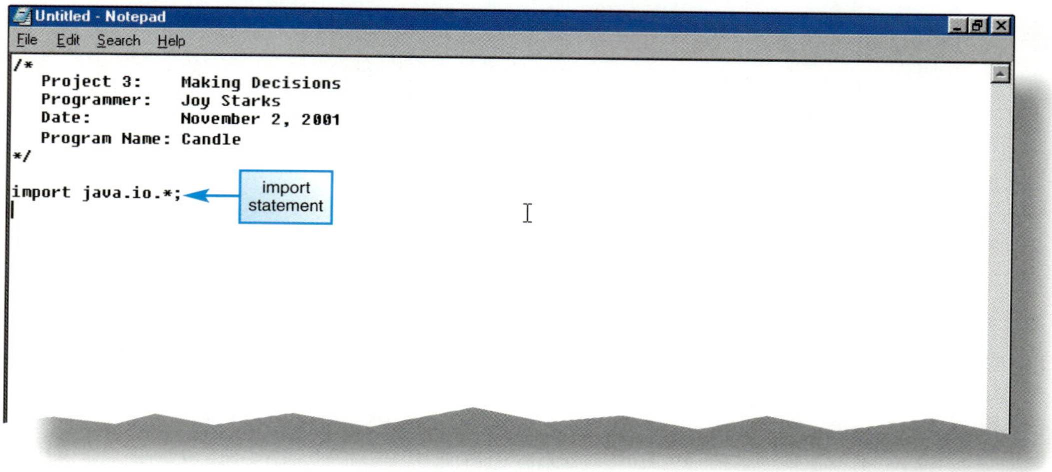
Untitled - Notepad
File Edit Search Help
/*
Project 3: Making Decisions
Programmer: Joy Starks
Date: November 2, 2001
Program Name: Candle
*/
import java.io.*;
import statement

FIGURE 3-5

**3** **Create the program stub by entering the class header and main method headers along with their opening and closing braces, as shown in Figure 3-6. Use proper indentation.**

*The name of the class will be Candle (Figure 3-6). The main method warns the compiler of a possible IOException.*

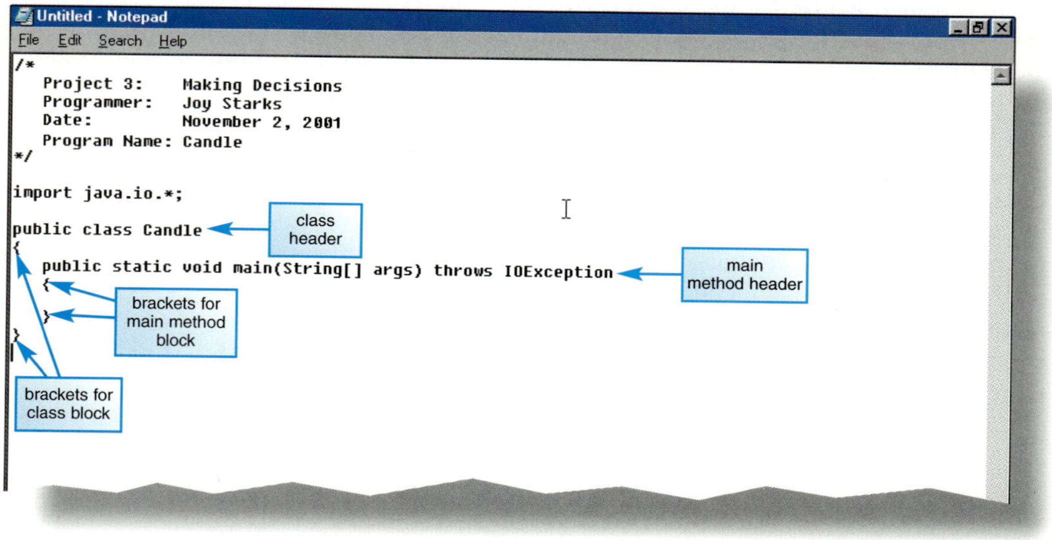
Untitled - Notepad
File Edit Search Help
/*
Project 3: Making Decisions
Programmer: Joy Starks
Date: November 2, 2001
Program Name: Candle
*/
import java.io.*;
public class Candle
{
public static void main(String[] args) throws IOException
{
}
}
class header
main method header
brackets for main method block
brackets for class block

FIGURE 3-6

Remember that the name of the class must match exactly the name of the Java source code file that you save. You will save the source code with the name "Candle.java" on a floppy disk in the next series of steps.

# Component Modularity

The object-oriented nature of Java lends itself to component modularity. **Modularity** means breaking a large program's source code down into smaller sections. Java source code needs only one public class header and one main method in order to compile. After that, it does not matter how many sections of code or components you add. **Components** might include classes, methods, blocks of code, or even calls to classes that are external of the program.

Designing component modularity from the beginning creates reusable portions of code, and breaks the programming task down into simpler, more manageable steps. Because this program involves making decisions based on user input, each decision can be designed and tested individually as it is added to the program, catching errors along the way.

## Saving, Compiling, and Executing the Program Stub

Perform the following steps to save, compile, and execute the program stub.

### TO SAVE, COMPILE, AND EXECUTE THE SOURCE CODE

**1** With a floppy disk in drive A, click File on the Notepad menu bar, and then click Save As.

**2** When the Save As dialog box displays, type "Candle.java" in the File name text box. You must type the quotation marks around the file name.

**3** Click the Save in box arrow and then click 3½ Floppy (A:) in the list.

**4** Click the Save button.

**5** Click the MS-DOS Prompt button on the taskbar. If necessary, enter the path statement and log onto drive A. Type javac Candle.java and then press the ENTER key to compile the program.

**6** If your program contains errors, fix them in the Notepad window and then recompile the program in the MS-DOS Prompt window.

**7** When your program compiles successfully, execute it by typing java Candle at the command prompt and then press the ENTER key.

*The program compiles but produces no visible output (Figure 3-7 on the next page). The program stub has no active statements or commands.*

**More About**

### Run Errors

If you receive this error, "Exception in thread "main" java.lang.NoClassDefFound Error:" it means Java cannot find your compiled bytecode file. One of the places in which Java tries to find your bytecode file is your current directory. If you do not store your files on drive A, you should change your current directory to that folder. Alternately, you permanently can change the classpath. For more information on changing the classpath, visit the Java Programming Web page (www.scsite.com/java/more.htm) and click Classpath Statements.

**More About**

### Compile Errors

If you receive an error when you try to compile, such as "Bad command or file name" (Windows 9X or 2000) or "The name specified is not recognized as an internal or external command, operable program or batch file" (Windows NT), the operating system cannot find the Java compiler, javac. You may have forgotten to set the path or your path could be incorrect. If you do not know where your system installation of JDK is located, click the Start button, click Find, click Files or Folders, and then type javac.exe in the Named text box.

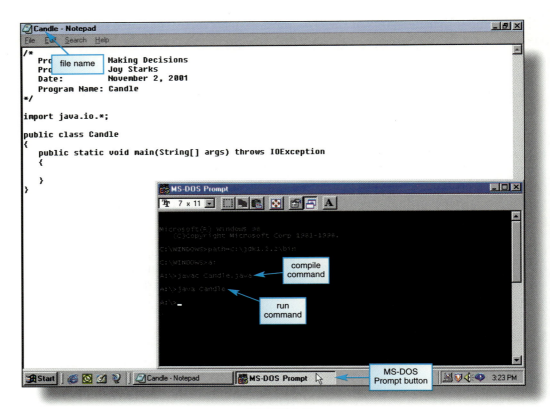

**FIGURE 3-7**

# Exception Handling

Checking for an IOException during compilation is only the first step in handling potential errors. An IOException is an example of a **compile-time** exception — an event that occurs when you try to compile a program. An **exception** is a Java event that generates a new, logical object resulting from an unusual or erroneous situation. The **object** exception contains information about the exception, such as its location and type. **Run-time** exceptions and errors happen when the program is running and Java encounters a problem. When an exception occurs, the JVM run-time environment **throws** the object exception to the processor who looks for a **handler**, or a way to handle the problem. And, unless the programmer codes a way to **catch** the exception, the program will terminate prematurely and display an exception error message. For example, if Java expects an integer input, and the user types a decimal point, a number format exception displays and the program terminates. A **number format exception** indicates an operation was attempted using a number in an illegal format. The number format exception is only one of more than 100 different kinds of exceptions that Java throws. Appendix D lists some sample input and output exceptions.

Java also can throw an **error**, such as an out of memory error, which is a more serious problem representing an unrecoverable situation. Errors sometimes are called **unchecked exceptions** because programmers should not attempt to fix these kinds of system problems.

**Exception handling** is the general concept of planning for possible exceptions from the beginning by directing the program to deal with them gracefully, without aborting prematurely. Java provides several ways — both object-oriented and traditional — to write code that checks for exceptions.

## Try and Catch

One object-oriented way to handle user input errors is to include the lines of code that might cause exceptions inside a **try and catch construct**. The **try statement** identifies a block of statements that potentially may throw an exception. If an exception occurs, the try block transfers execution to a handler. Table 3-1 shows the general form of the **try block**.

| Table 3-1 | The try Block |
|---|---|
| **General form:** | ```
try
{
    . . . lines of code that might generate an exception;
    . . .throw new exception;
}
``` |
| **Comment:** | **Try** and **throw new** are reserved words. All statements within the try block braces are monitored for exceptions. Programmers may **explicitly**, or intentionally, cause an exception by typing the words, throw new, followed by the name of a standard Java exception object. A try block must be followed by a catch block. |
| **Examples:** | ```
try
{
    answer = 23 / 0; //Java throws exception automatically
    throw new DivideByZeroException(); //programmer explicitly throws exception
}
``` |

The try block notifies the JVM that you plan to deal with exceptions rather than just allowing them to happen. Any exception occurring as a result of code within the try block will not terminate the program.

The try block must be followed by a **catch block.** This is the destination of the thrown exception; in other words, execution will be transferred to the catch block when an exception occurs. The **catch statement** consists of the keyword catch, followed by a parameter declaration that identifies the type of exception being caught and an identifier name. The identifier name holds a Java-assigned error value that can access more information about the error through the use of messages. Inside the catch block, programmers include statements to either describe the error to the user or fix the error through programming. Table 3-2 shows the general form of the catch block.

| Table 3-2 | The catch Block |
|---|---|
| **General form:** | ```
catch (exception identifier)
{
    . . . lines of code that handle the exception;
}
``` |
| **Comment:** | **Catch** is a reserved word. **Exception** is the name of a standard Java exception. **Identifier** is a variable name to hold a Java-assigned error value. Catch blocks optionally may be followed by a finally block to continue more processing. |
| **Examples:** | ```
catch(ArithmeticException errNum)
{
    System.out.println("An arithmetic error has occurred. " +
    errNum.getMessage());// message prints with Java-generated data
}
``` |

For example, if a user error causes a program to try to divide by zero, the program normally would abort with the following error message.

```
Exception in thread "main" java.lang.ArithmeticException: / by zero
```

However, if the code is put in a try block and the same error occurs, execution is thrown to the catch block. The programmer then can display a more descriptive message to the user, and perhaps let the user re-enter the information.

Java may generate the exception, as in the division by zero example above, or you may use the keywords, **throw new**, to explicitly or intentionally throw the exception yourself. For instance, Java would throw an ArithmeticException if you tried to calculate an average with no numbers. You might decide to throw the exception if the value were zero, as well. A decision structure could test for the zero value with a resulting throw to the same exception.

```
throw new ArithmeticException();
```

Alternately, you might want to create a new exception type. For example, when a user enters the wrong password you might enter the following line of code.

```
throw new WrongPasswordException();
```

The program then would call the class, WrongPasswordException. That new class must be defined by the programmer and be accessible to the class that contains the throw statement.

The throw statement causes execution to be transferred to the catch block. That way, control passes to the same error handling routine whether the exception is caught by the JVM, as in a data type error, or caught by a programmer testing for an invalid or unreasonable number.

As with the traditional control structures, the try and catch, object-oriented structure can be nested within any other structure. In addition, you can have more than one catch block in the same program or even within the same method, if you are trying to throw multiple exceptions. The try and catch blocks may be followed by an optional block, named with the reserved word, **finally**, which is placed after the catch block. The finally block can be used to perform an end of processing routine associated with the try and catch.

Table 3-3 displays the variable declaration and the try block for the Candle application. Table 3-4 displays the catch block. The catch block will execute only if a number format exception occurs when the program tries to parse the user input (lines 26 and 34).

## Checked and Unchecked Exceptions

Java considers as unchecked some unusual exceptions from the RunTimeException subclass. In other words, exceptions listed in that subclass do not have to be caught within your program because they happen so rarely. A checked exception either must be caught within the method in which it is thrown, or the method must declare that it throws the exception in its header. For more information about the RunTimeException subclass, see the Java Documentation as described in Appendix A.

## Handling Multiple Exceptions

If you anticipate more than one type of exception being thrown in the try block, you can create multiple catch blocks that each catch a different kind of error. For example, if users put in data that does not match your data type declaration it might generate a NumberFormatException. If the user enters zero, even though it is a valid number, Java would generate an ArithmeticException if you try to divide by it. The type of exception is listed in parentheses after the word, catch, in each catch block.

**Table 3-3**

| LINE | CODE |
|------|------|
| 14 | //Declaring Variables |
| 15 | BufferedReader dataIn = new BufferedReader(new InputStreamReader(System.in)); |
| 16 | String strPrice; |
| 17 | String strDays; |
| 18 | double price |
| 19 | int days; |
| 20 | |
| 21 | try |
| 22 | { |
| 23 | //Get input from user |
| 24 | System.out.println("What is the total dollar amount of your order?"); |
| 25 | strPrice = dataIn.readLine(); |
| 26 | price = Double.parseDouble(strPrice); |
| 27 | |
| 28 | System.out.println("What is your shipping priority?"); |
| 29 | System.out.println(); |
| 30 | System.out.println("\t1) Priority (Overnight)"); |
| 31 | System.out.println("\t2) Express (2 business days)"); |
| 32 | System.out.println("\t3) Standard (3 to 7 business days)"); |
| 33 | strDays = dataIn.readLine(); |
| 34 | days = Integer.parseInt(strDays); |
| 35 | } |
| 36 | |

**Table 3-4**

| LINE | CODE |
|------|------|
| 37 | catch (NumberFormatException e) |
| 38 | { |
| 39 | System.out.println("\tYour response was not a valid number."); |
| 40 | System.out.println("\tPlease reenter your order using a numeric value."); |
| 41 | System.out.println(); |
| 42 | } |

In the following steps, you will enter the try and catch blocks. In the try block, you will instantiate the constructor method named BufferedReader (line 15) for the input stream from the keyboard buffer, just as you did in Project 2. You then will declare the variables for data input (lines 16 through 19). Finally, you will code lines to print prompts on the screen and accept user input (lines 24 through 34). In the catch block, you will display an appropriate message to the user if a number format exception occurs (lines 39 and 40). After all code has been entered, you will save the program. Perform the following steps to enter the try and catch blocks and then save the program.

## Steps To Enter the try and catch Blocks

**1 Click the Notepad window between the two braces of the main block on line 14.**

*The insertion point displays on the blank line (Figure 3-8).*

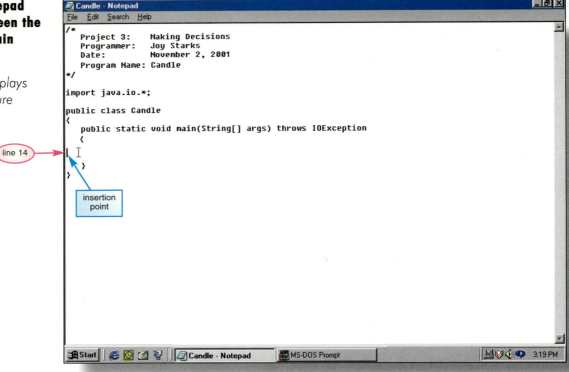

Candle - Notepad
File Edit Search Help
/*
Project 3: Making Decisions
Programmer: Joy Starks
Date: November 2, 2001
Program Name: Candle
*/
import java.io.*;
public class Candle
{
public static void main(String[] args) throws IOException
{
}
}
line 14
insertion point
Start
Candle - Notepad
MS-DOS Prompt
3:19 PM

**FIGURE 3-8**

**2 Using proper indentation, enter the code for the declaration section and the try block as shown in Table 3-3 on the previous page.**

*After the variable declarations, the try block contains the user interface statements for this program (Figure 3-9). As you type, the workspace will scroll.*

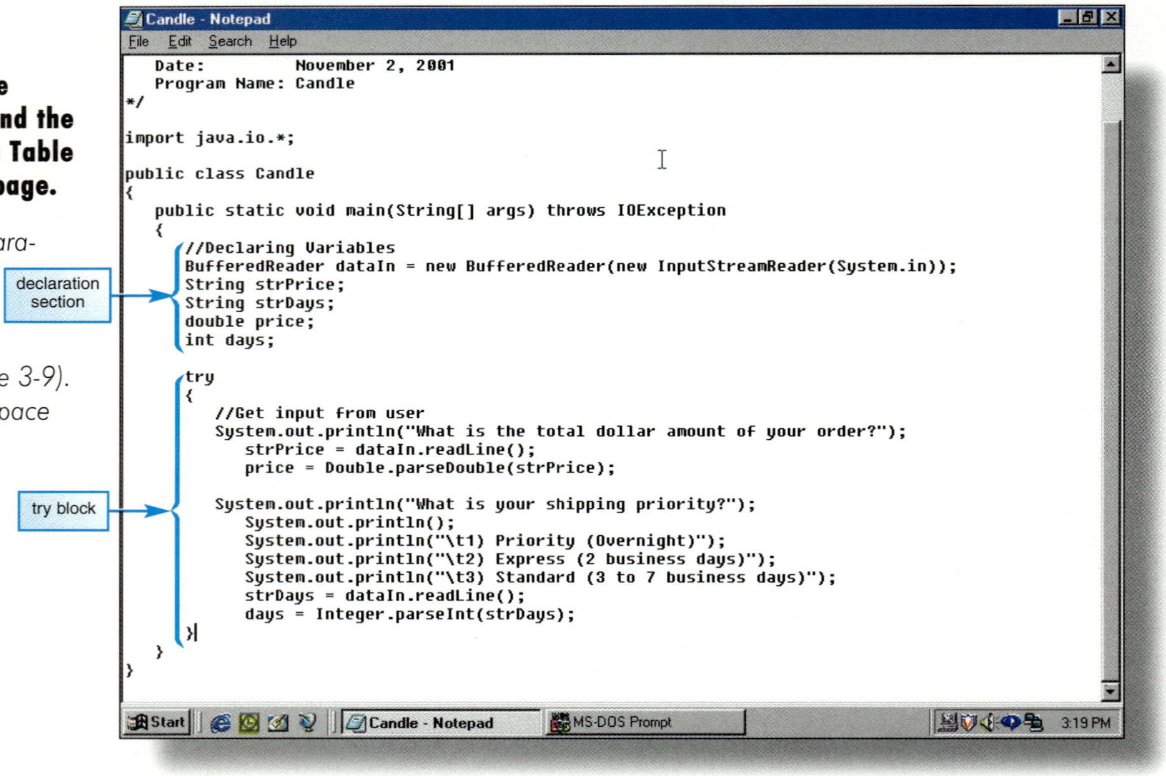

Candle - Notepad
File Edit Search Help
Date: November 2, 2001
Program Name: Candle
*/
import java.io.*;
public class Candle
{
public static void main(String[] args) throws IOException
{
//Declaring Variables
BufferedReader dataIn = new BufferedReader(new InputStreamReader(System.in));
String strPrice;
String strDays;
double price;
int days;
try
{
//Get input from user
System.out.println("What is the total dollar amount of your order?");
strPrice = dataIn.readLine();
price = Double.parseDouble(strPrice);
System.out.println("What is your shipping priority?");
System.out.println();
System.out.println("\t1) Priority (Overnight)");
System.out.println("\t2) Express (2 business days)");
System.out.println("\t3) Standard (3 to 7 business days)");
strDays = dataIn.readLine();
days = Integer.parseInt(strDays);
}
}
}
declaration section
try block
Start
Candle - Notepad
MS-DOS Prompt
3:19 PM

**FIGURE 3-9**

**3** **Press the ENTER key. Using proper indentation, enter the code for the catch block as shown in Table 3-4 on page J 3.15.**

*When an exception occurs, the println methods will print a user-friendly message (Figure 3-10).*

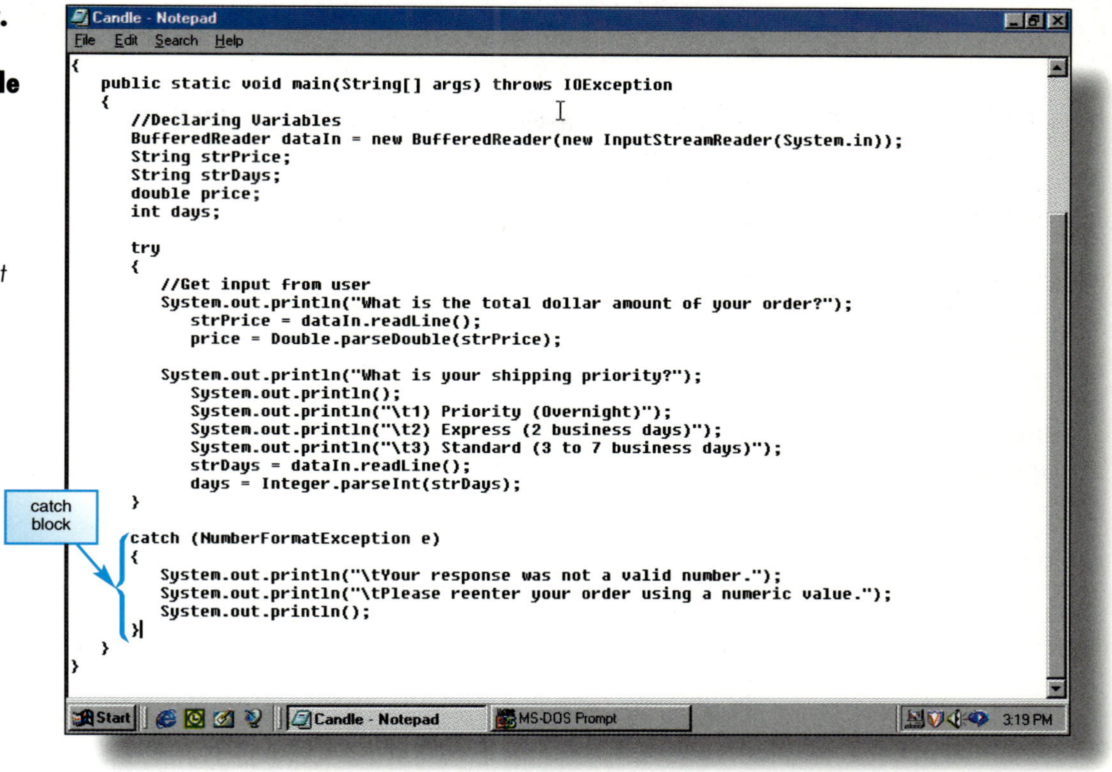

```
{
    public static void main(String[] args) throws IOException
    {
        //Declaring Variables
        BufferedReader dataIn = new BufferedReader(new InputStreamReader(System.in));
        String strPrice;
        String strDays;
        double price;
        int days;

        try
        {
            //Get input from user
            System.out.println("What is the total dollar amount of your order?");
                strPrice = dataIn.readLine();
                price = Double.parseDouble(strPrice);

            System.out.println("What is your shipping priority?");
                System.out.println();
                System.out.println("\t1) Priority (Overnight)");
                System.out.println("\t2) Express (2 business days)");
                System.out.println("\t3) Standard (3 to 7 business days)");
                strDays = dataIn.readLine();
                days = Integer.parseInt(strDays);
        }

        catch (NumberFormatException e)
        {
            System.out.println("\tYour response was not a valid number.");
            System.out.println("\tPlease reenter your order using a numeric value.");
            System.out.println();
        }
    }
}
```

catch block

**FIGURE 3-10**

**4** **Click File on the Notepad menu bar and then point to Save.**

*The File menu displays (Figure 3-11). Because this program has been saved previously with the name Candle, clicking the Save command will save it with the same name, in the same location.*

```
New
Open...
Save
Save As...

Page Setup...
Print

Exit
```

File menu

Save command

```
ic vo       ing[] args) throws IOException

ing v
Reader         new BufferedReader(new InputStreamReader(System.in));
trPric
trDays;
rice;
;

        try
        {
            //Get input from user
            System.out.println("What is the total dollar amount of your order?");          line 24
                strPrice = dataIn.readLine();
                price = Double.parseDouble(strPrice);          line 26

            System.out.println("What is your shipping priority?");
                System.out.println();
                System.out.println("\t1) Priority (Overnight)");          line 30
                System.out.println("\t2) Express (2 business days)");
                System.out.println("\t3) Standard (3 to 7 business days)");
                strDays = dataIn.readLine();
                days = Integer.parseInt(strDays);
        }

        catch (NumberFormatException e)
        {
            System.out.println("\tYour response was not a valid number.");
            System.out.println("\tPlease reenter your order using a numeric value.");
            System.out.println();
        }
    }
}
```

**5** **Click Save.**

*The program is saved on drive A with the same file name.*

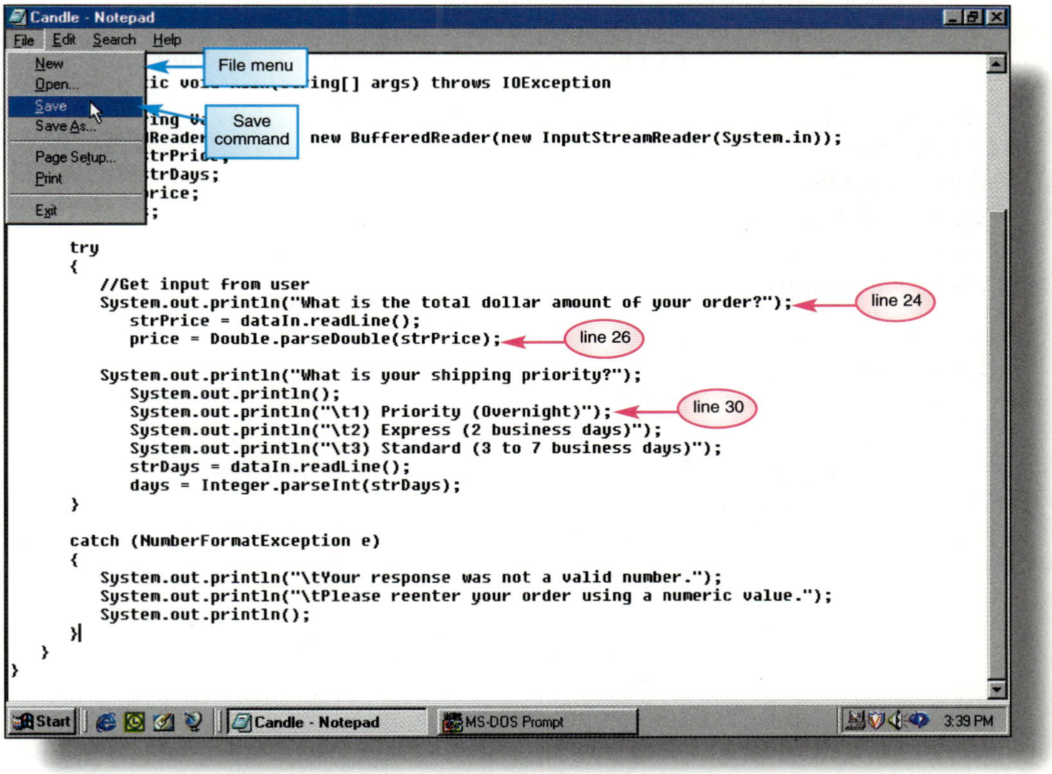

**FIGURE 3-11**

When the program is complete and ready for execution, the first prompt will instruct the user to enter a dollar amount (line 24 in Figure 3-11 on the previous page). Recall that data from the keyboard is sent as a stream of characters to the buffer and then directed to the processor with the readLine method. The string data then is parsed, or converted (line 26). Values with anticipated decimals, such as the price and shipping charge will be converted to doubles.

Lines 30 through 32 will display a small menu, which during execution will accept a numeric value. Because the choices all are whole numbers, the value will be converted to an integer. In an attempt to help the user to enter correct values, the user-friendly menu lists valid choices with explanations. Notice that the menu choices will display indented, for easier reading, due to the \t tab escape character.

In this example, when an exception occurs, a message will display on the screen and the program will terminate. Later in this project, you write code to further test user input and re-direct execution allowing the user to try again.

# Testing Partial Programs

Testing partial programs before moving on to the next section is quite common. You can check for compilation errors with fewer lines of codes, see the results of just one condition or one set of inputs, or debug or look for exceptions within a narrower framework. When testing the running program, you can enter incorrect data to force specific types of exceptions without needing to account for a wide range of errors resulting from combinations of user mistakes.

## Testing for Exceptions

Perform the following steps to compile and then execute the program. During execution, you will enter valid and invalid numbers to test for number format exceptions.

### Steps: To Test the Program for Exceptions

**1** **Click the MS-DOS Prompt button on the taskbar. Type** javac Candle.java **at the command prompt and then press the ENTER key. If there are errors, fix them in the Notepad window and then recompile the program.**

*The command prompt displays after a successful compilation (Figure 3-12).*

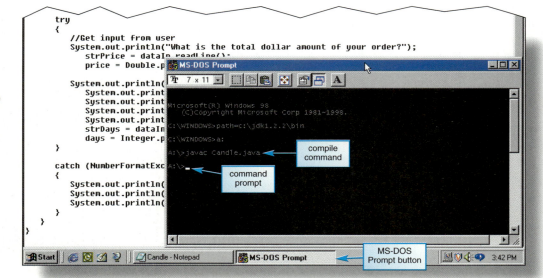

**FIGURE 3-12**

**2** **Type** `java Candle` **and then press the** **ENTER** **key to run the program.**

The program begins to execute and stops, awaiting user input, after displaying the first prompt (Figure 3-13).

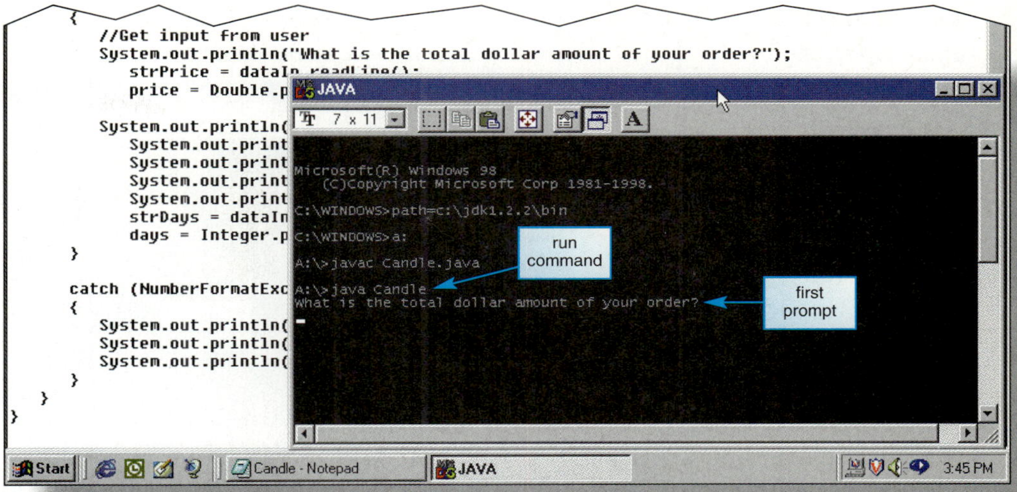

```
        {
        //Get input from user
        System.out.println("What is the total dollar amount of your order?");
            strPrice = dataIn.readline();
            price = Double.p

        System.out.println(
            System.out.print
            System.out.print
            System.out.print
            System.out.print
            strDays = dataIn
            days = Integer.p
        }

        catch (NumberFormatExc
        {
            System.out.println(
            System.out.println(
            System.out.println(
        }
    }
}
```

```
JAVA
Microsoft(R) Windows 98
   (C)Copyright Microsoft Corp 1981-1998.
C:\WINDOWS>path=c:\jdk1.2.2\bin
C:\WINDOWS>a:
A:\>javac Candle.java         run
                              command
A:\>java Candle
What is the total dollar amount of your order?     first
                                                   prompt
```

Start | Candle - Notepad | JAVA | 3:45 PM

**FIGURE 3-13**

**3** **Type** `43` **as the order amount and then press the ENTER key.**

The program accepts the valid number, 43, and displays the next prompt (Figure 3-14).

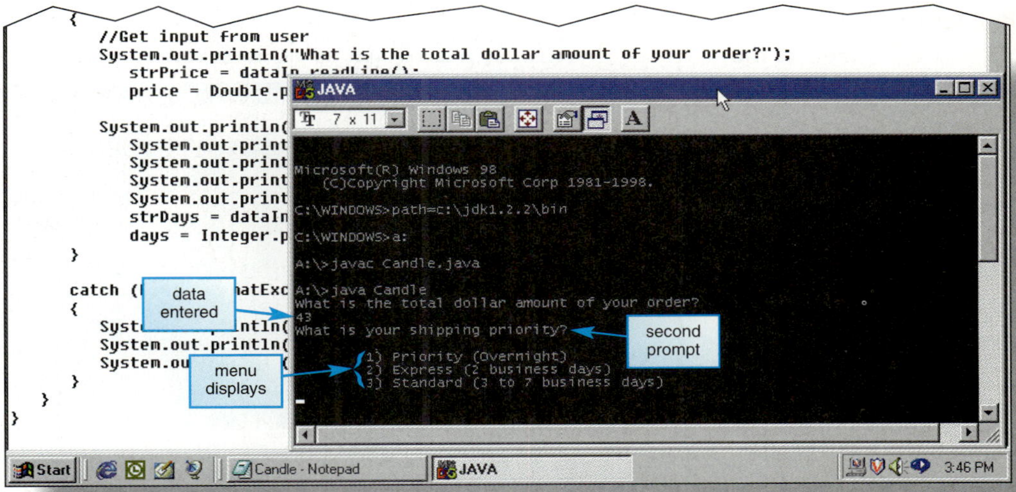

```
        {
        //Get input from user
        System.out.println("What is the total dollar amount of your order?");
            strPrice = dataIn readline();
            price = Double.p

        System.out.println(
            System.out.print
            System.out.print
            System.out.print
            System.out.print
            strDays = dataIn
            days = Integer.p
        }

        catch (          atExc
        {                         data
            Syst             ntln(  entered
            System.out.println(
            System.ou           (
        }                   menu
    }                       displays
}
```

```
JAVA
Microsoft(R) Windows 98
   (C)Copyright Microsoft Corp 1981-1998.
C:\WINDOWS>path=c:\jdk1.2.2\bin
C:\WINDOWS>a:
A:\>javac Candle.java
A:\>java Candle
What is the total dollar amount of your order?
43
What is your shipping priority?     second
                                    prompt
        1) Priority (Overnight)
        2) Express (2 business days)
        3) Standard (3 to 7 business days)
```

Start | Candle - Notepad | JAVA | 3:46 PM

**FIGURE 3-14**

**4** **In response to the menu prompt, type** `1` **to choose Priority (Overnight) delivery. Press the ENTER key.**

The program accepts the valid number, 1, and then finishes (Figure 3-15). The command prompt again displays.

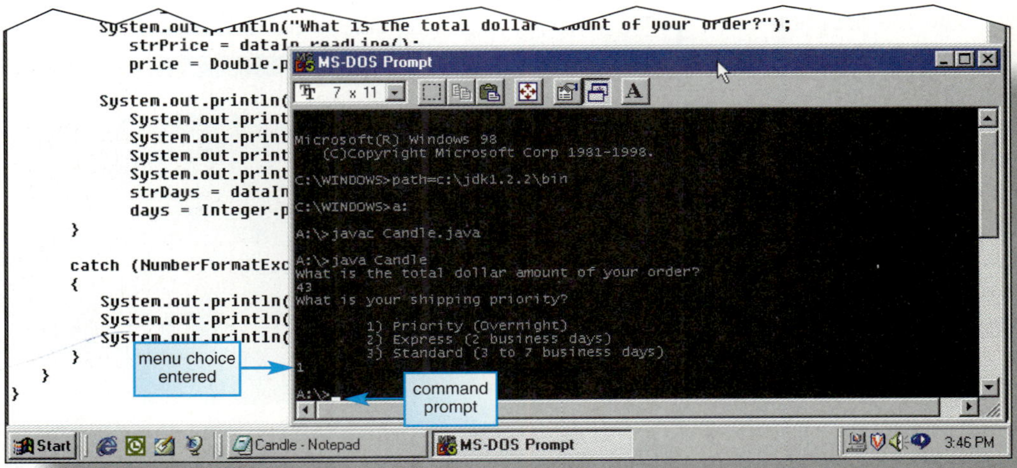

```
        System.out.println("What is the total dollar amount of your order?");
            strPrice = dataIn readline();
            price = Double.p

        System.out.println(
            System.out.print
            System.out.print
            System.out.print
            System.out.print
            strDays = dataIn
            days = Integer.p
        }

        catch (NumberFormatExc
        {
            System.out.println(
            System.out.println(
            System.out.println(
        }               menu choice
    }                   entered
}
```

```
MS-DOS Prompt
Microsoft(R) Windows 98
   (C)Copyright Microsoft Corp 1981-1998.
C:\WINDOWS>path=c:\jdk1.2.2\bin
C:\WINDOWS>a:
A:\>javac Candle.java
A:\>java Candle
What is the total dollar amount of your order?
43
What is your shipping priority?

        1) Priority (Overnight)
        2) Express (2 business days)
        3) Standard (3 to 7 business days)
1
A:\>                command
                    prompt
```

Start | Candle - Notepad | MS-DOS Prompt | 3:46 PM

**FIGURE 3-15**

**5** Run the program again by typing `java Candle` at the command prompt, and then press the ENTER key.

The prompt for the dollar amount of the order again displays (Figure 3-16).

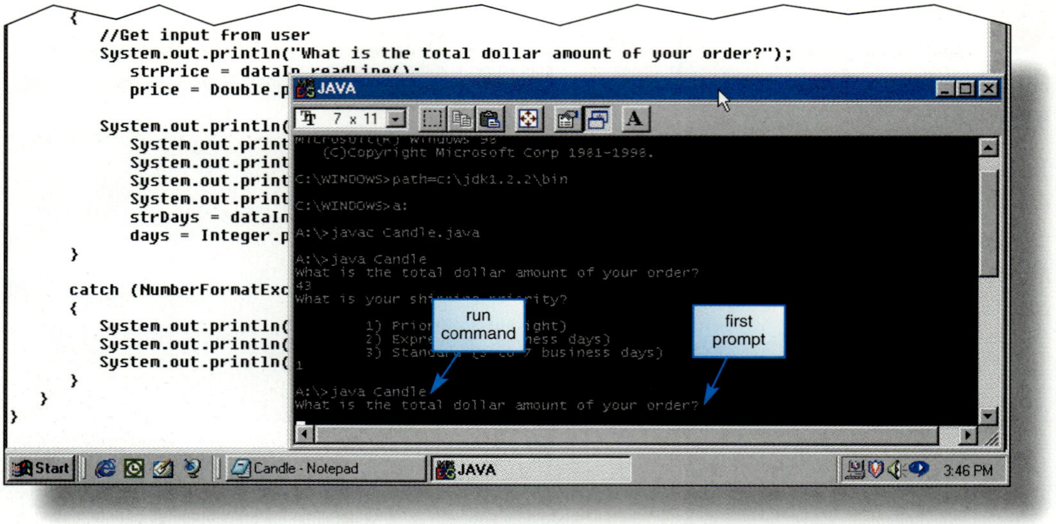

FIGURE 3-16

**6** Type the words, `forty-three` at the prompt and then press the ENTER key.

Java redirects execution to the catch block and displays the error message (Figure 3-17). The words, forty-three, could not be converted to the double data type. The program terminates.

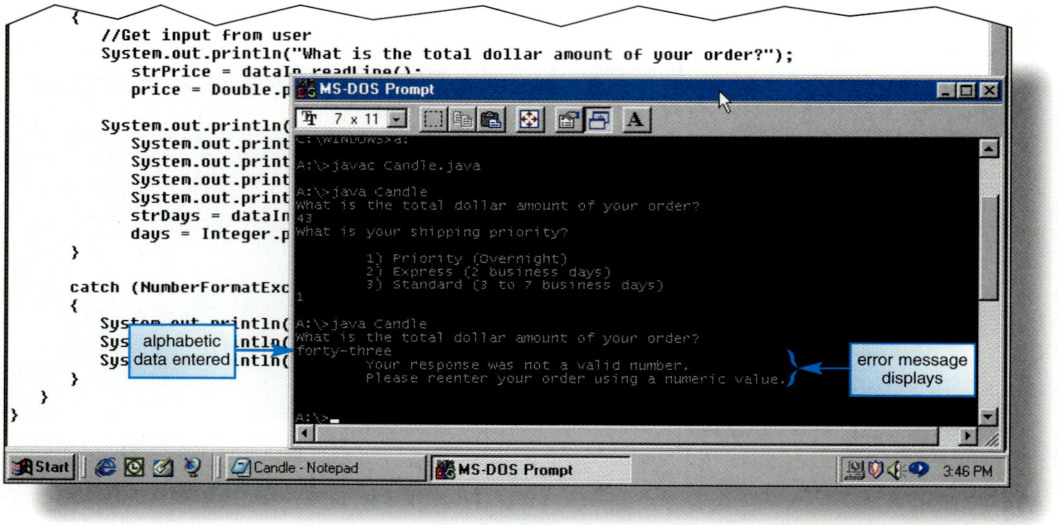

FIGURE 3-17

**7** Run the program again by typing `java Candle` at the command prompt, and then press the ENTER key. When the dollar amount prompt displays, type `59.99` to test a number with decimal points, and then press the ENTER key.

The program accepts the decimal number because the input was converted to a double data type (Figure 3-18). The shipping menu displays.

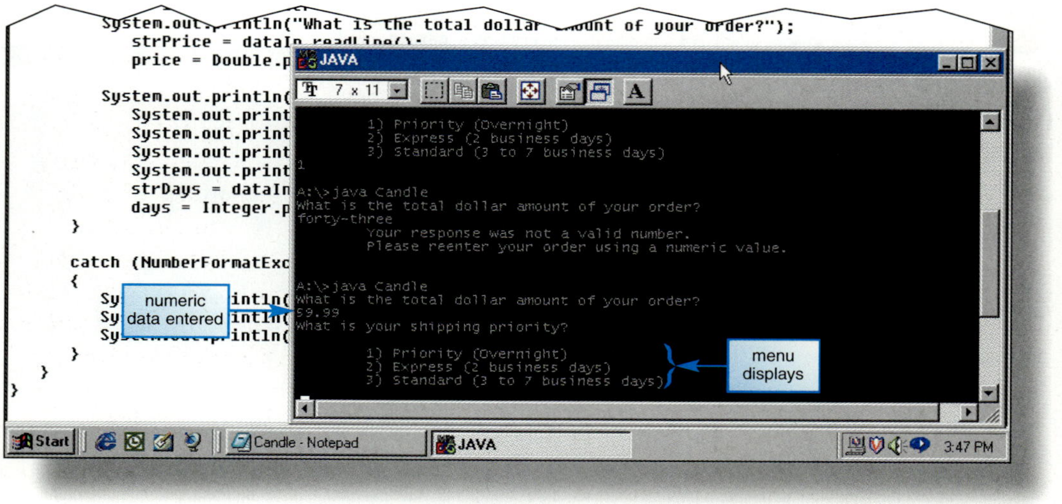

FIGURE 3-18

**8** Type `2.7` in response to the shipping menu prompt and then press the ENTER key.

*Java again redirects execution to the catch block and displays the error message because the input for shipping accepts only an integer (Figure 3-19). The program terminates.*

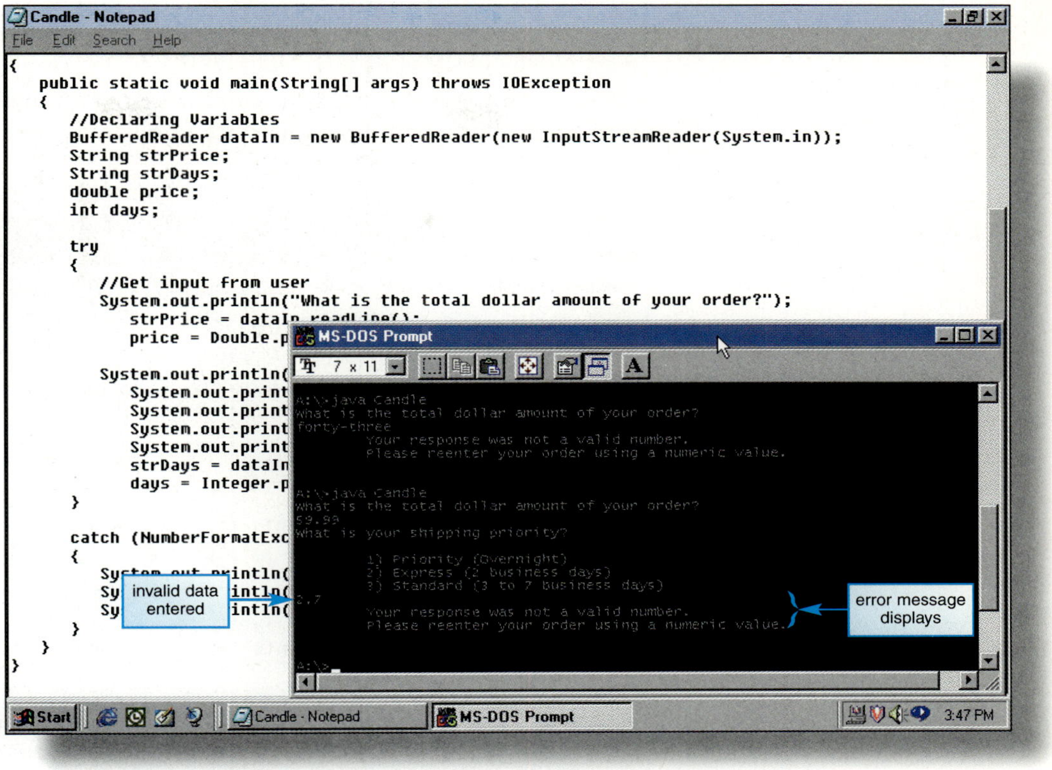

**FIGURE 3-19**

When execution transfers to the catch block, the program performs a validity check. A **validity** check looks for valid data such as correct data types. The exceptions for which you tested in the previous series of steps were both caused by entering values that did not match the type of data the program expects. You did not write the code to test for the condition yourself; you merely caught the JVM interpreter's throw of the number format exception. In the next series of steps, you will write Java statements to test for different kinds of errors.

# The If Decision Structure

Merely because a user has input data that causes no exceptions in Java, it does not mean that it is acceptable data for the program's logic. Java, like other programming languages, has commands that allow the programmer to test or make decisions about data. The decision control structure, also known as the If...Then...Else structure, is used for testing a condition that executes one of two different sets of code. If the condition is true, one set of code is executed; if it is false, then another set of code is executed. These two paths do not have to match in the number of lines of code; for example, the false condition may result in no action being performed, while the true condition might have many lines of code that execute. The only restriction is that the two paths must come back together after the decision structure, in order to continue processing.

The **if** statement in Java can take one of three forms (Table 3-5 on the next page). The first form tests a condition and performs a single action. For example, in a payroll application, if a value named hours equals 40, you might wish to print a message indicating no overtime.

```
if (hours == 40) System.out.println("No overtime is paid");
```

The if statement is followed by a condition in parentheses, which is followed by the resulting code statement. **Conditions** are boolean expressions that evaluate to true or false.

| Table 3-5 The if Construct | |
|---|---|
| **General forms:** | `if (condition) resulting statement;` |
| | `if (condition)`<br>`{`<br>`...statements to execute when true`<br>`}` |
| | `if (condition)`<br>`{`<br>`...statements to execute when true`<br>`}`<br>`else`<br>`{`<br>`...statements to execute when false`<br>`}` |
| **Comment:** | The words, **if** and **else**, are reserved words. The **condition** must evaluate to a boolean expression. If the condition is true, the statements following the if execute; otherwise, the statements following the word else are executed. Either way execution passes out of the construct to the next line of code following the block. |
| **Examples:** | `if (answer == correct)`<br>`{`<br>`    System.out.println("You got it right!");`<br>`    numCorrect = numCorrect + 1;`<br>`}`<br>`else`<br>`{`<br>`    System.out.println("You did not answer it correctly");`<br>`    System.out.println("The correct answer was " + correct);`<br>`    numWrong = numWrong + 1;`<br>`}` |

The second form of the if construct (Table 3-5) allows for multiple statements to execute based on a condition. The resulting statements are enclosed in block braces. For example, if the hours are less than 40 you might want to calculate the grossPay on a rate times hours basis and then display the result.

```
if (hours < 40)
    {
    grossPay = rate * hours;
    System.out.println("The gross pay is "+ grossPay);
    }
```

However, when there are actions to perform when the condition is true, and other actions to perform when the condition is false, you must include the else statement as shown in the third form of the if construct (Table 3-5). As with the if statement, the else statement may be followed by one statement or multiple statements enclosed in braces. The keywords, if and else, are entered in lowercase. Statements within the blocks commonly are indented for easy reading. For example, if the hours are greater than 40, you might want to call an overtime method; otherwise, you might calculate the grossPay as before. Either way the structure comes back together to perform the next sequential step that displays the grossPay.

```
if (hours > 40)
   {
      grossPay = getOvertime(hours);
   }
else
   {
      grossPay = rate * hours;
   }
System.out.println("The gross pay is "+ grossPay);
```

In Project 2, you learned that different types of comparative operators are used in conditions. Comparative operators commonly are broken into three categories: equality, relational, and logical. All three are used to evaluate the relationship between two expressions or values. The values may be variables, constants, numbers, strings, or the result of a function or method.

Table 3-6 displays the equality, relational, and logical operators in Java.

**More About**

**Spacing in Java Syntax**

The Java programming language, like C and C++, is considered a freeform language, which means there are no special rules for positioning white spaces such as blanks, tabs, and new lines. The only limitation is that white space cannot be placed between the two characters of an operator, such as == or ++.

| Table 3-6 | Operator Results in Decision Structures | | | |
|-----------|------------------------------------------|---------|--------|------|
| OPERATOR | MEANING | EXAMPLE | RESULT | TYPE |
| == | equal to | 2 == 2 | true | equality |
| | | 1 == 6 | false | |
| != | not equal to | 7 != 4 | true | equality |
| | | 4 != 4 | false | |
| < | less than | 3 < 5 | true | relational |
| | | 5 < 3 | false | |
| <= | less than or equal to | 4 <= 6 | true | relational |
| | | 7 <= 6 | false | |
| > | greater than | 9 > 7 | true | relational |
| | | 7 > 9 | false | |
| >= | greater than or equal to | 8 >= 8 | true | relational |
| | | 8 >= 10 | false | |
| && | logical AND (both conditions must be true) | (7 > 3) && (0 < 1) | true | logical |
| | | (7 > 3) && (1 < 0) | false | |
| \|\| | logical OR (one of the conditions must be true) | (7 > 3) \|\| (1 < 0) | true | logical |
| | | (3 > 7) \|\| (1 < 0) | false | |
| ! | logical NOT (condition must evaluate to false in order to make the condition true) | ! (5 == 4) | true | logical |
| | | ! (a == a) | false | |

## Reasonableness Check with the if Statement

Input from the user may be checked for **reasonableness**. Any positive number might be a reasonable answer for the dollar amount, as you do not know how many items a customer may have purchased. Negative amounts and the number zero, however, would not be reasonable. If users input a negative number or zero, a message should display notifying them of their error. Because you have already coded a catch block for errors, you may create your own number format exception when the user inputs an unreasonable number. The throw statement, followed by the constructor keyword new, transfers execution to the catch block. Using the catch block for this exception, as well as for the previous exception, is an example of how Java promotes reusable objects.

Perform the following steps to enter code that performs a reasonableness check on the total dollar amount entered by the customer. After saving the program, you will run it and test a value of zero.

### To Code and Test the if Statement

**1** If necessary, click the Notepad window to activate it. Click on line 27 between the two sections requesting user input.

*The insertion point displays between the two sections that prompt the user for input (Figure 3-20).* line 27

```java
Candle - Notepad
File  Edit  Search  Help
public static void main(String[] args) throws IOException
{
    //Declaring Variables
    BufferedReader dataIn = new BufferedReader(new InputStreamReader(System.in));
    String strPrice;
    String strDays;
    double price;
    int days;

    try
    {
        //Get input from user
        System.out.println("What is the total dollar amount of your order?");
            strPrice = dataIn.readLine();
            price = Double.parseDouble(strPrice);

        System.out.println("What is your shipping priority?");
            System.out.println();
            System.out.println("\t1) Priority (Overnight)");
            System.out.println("\t2) Express (2 business days)");
            System.out.println("\t3) Standard (3 to 7 business days)");
            strDays = dataIn.readLine();
            days = Integer.parseInt(strDays);
    }

    catch (NumberFormatException e)
    {
        System.out.println("\tYour response was not a valid number.");
        System.out.println("\tPlease reenter your order using a numeric value.");
        System.out.println();
    }
}
}
```

Start    notepad button    Candle - Notepad    MS-DOS Prompt    3:47 PM

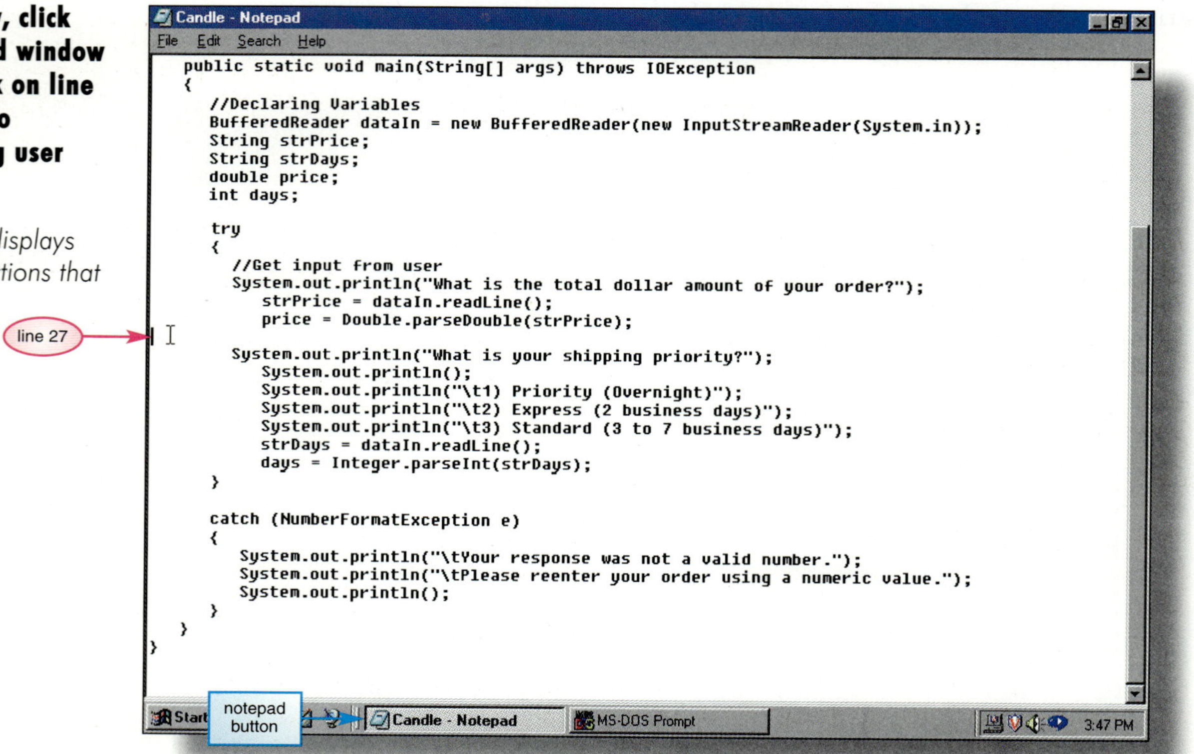

**FIGURE 3-20**

**2** Press the ENTER key to create a blank line. Indent and type the if statement and its block as shown in Figure 3-21. Press the ENTER key again to insert another blank line after the closing brace.

*The if statement, braces, and two statements display (Figure 3-21).*

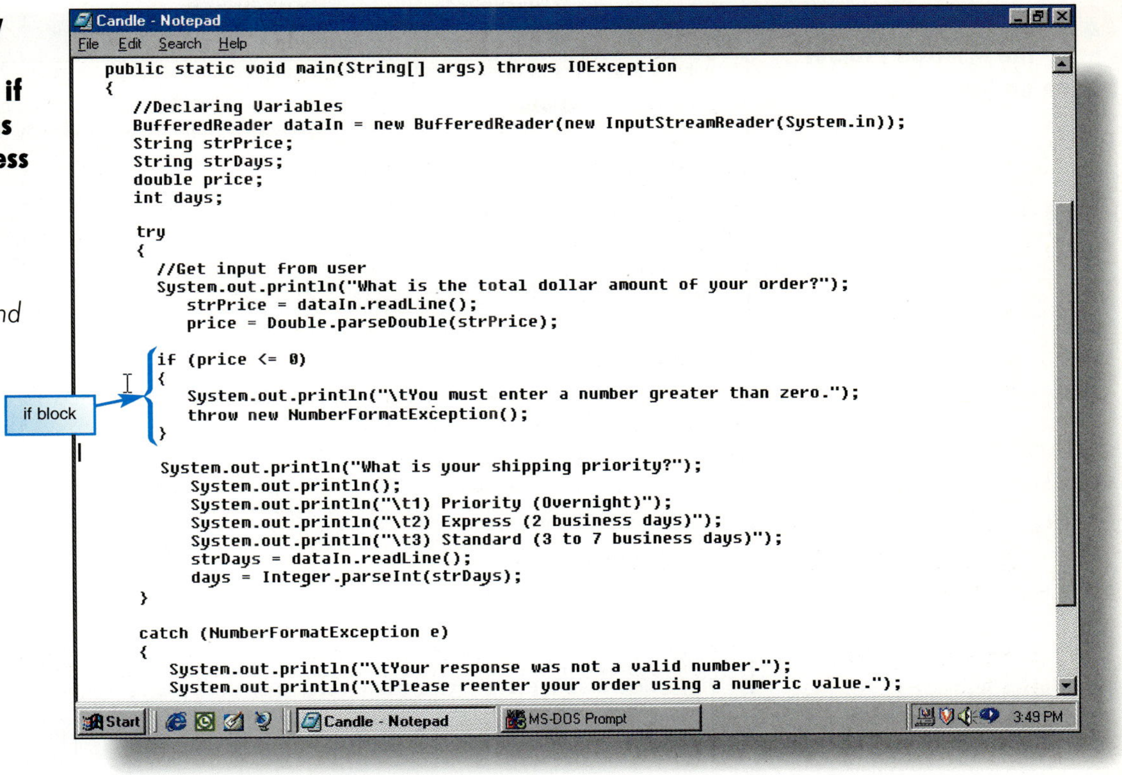

```
Candle - Notepad
File  Edit  Search  Help

public static void main(String[] args) throws IOException
{
    //Declaring Variables
    BufferedReader dataIn = new BufferedReader(new InputStreamReader(System.in));
    String strPrice;
    String strDays;
    double price;
    int days;

    try
    {
        //Get input from user
        System.out.println("What is the total dollar amount of your order?");
        strPrice = dataIn.readLine();
        price = Double.parseDouble(strPrice);

        if (price <= 0)
        {
            System.out.println("\tYou must enter a number greater than zero.");
            throw new NumberFormatException();
        }

        System.out.println("What is your shipping priority?");
        System.out.println();
        System.out.println("\t1) Priority (Overnight)");
        System.out.println("\t2) Express (2 business days)");
        System.out.println("\t3) Standard (3 to 7 business days)");
        strDays = dataIn.readLine();
        days = Integer.parseInt(strDays);
    }

    catch (NumberFormatException e)
    {
        System.out.println("\tYour response was not a valid number.");
        System.out.println("\tPlease reenter your order using a numeric value.");
```

if block

Start | Candle - Notepad | MS-DOS Prompt | 3:49 PM

**FIGURE 3-21**

**3** With your floppy disk in drive A, click File on the menu bar and then point to Save.

*The File menu displays (Figure 3-22). The program will save again in the same location, with the same file name.*

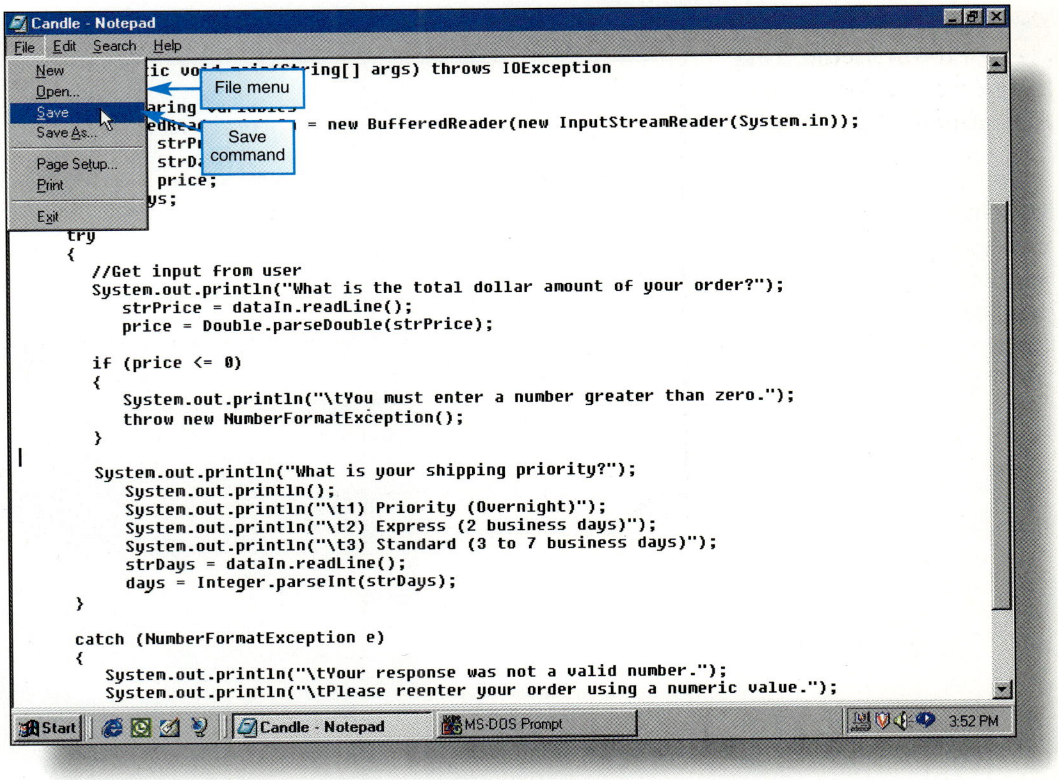

```
Candle - Notepad
File  Edit  Search  Help
New
Open...                    File menu
Save
Save As...                         = new BufferedReader(new InputStreamReader(System.in));
                           Save
Page Setup...              command
Print
Exit

    try
    {
        //Get input from user
        System.out.println("What is the total dollar amount of your order?");
        strPrice = dataIn.readLine();
        price = Double.parseDouble(strPrice);

        if (price <= 0)
        {
            System.out.println("\tYou must enter a number greater than zero.");
            throw new NumberFormatException();
        }

        System.out.println("What is your shipping priority?");
        System.out.println();
        System.out.println("\t1) Priority (Overnight)");
        System.out.println("\t2) Express (2 business days)");
        System.out.println("\t3) Standard (3 to 7 business days)");
        strDays = dataIn.readLine();
        days = Integer.parseInt(strDays);
    }

    catch (NumberFormatException e)
    {
        System.out.println("\tYour response was not a valid number.");
        System.out.println("\tPlease reenter your order using a numeric value.");
```

Start | Candle - Notepad | MS-DOS Prompt | 3:52 PM

**FIGURE 3-22**

**4** Click Save. Point to the MS-DOS Prompt button on the taskbar.

*The Candle.java file is saved on the floppy disk in drive A (Figure 3-23).*

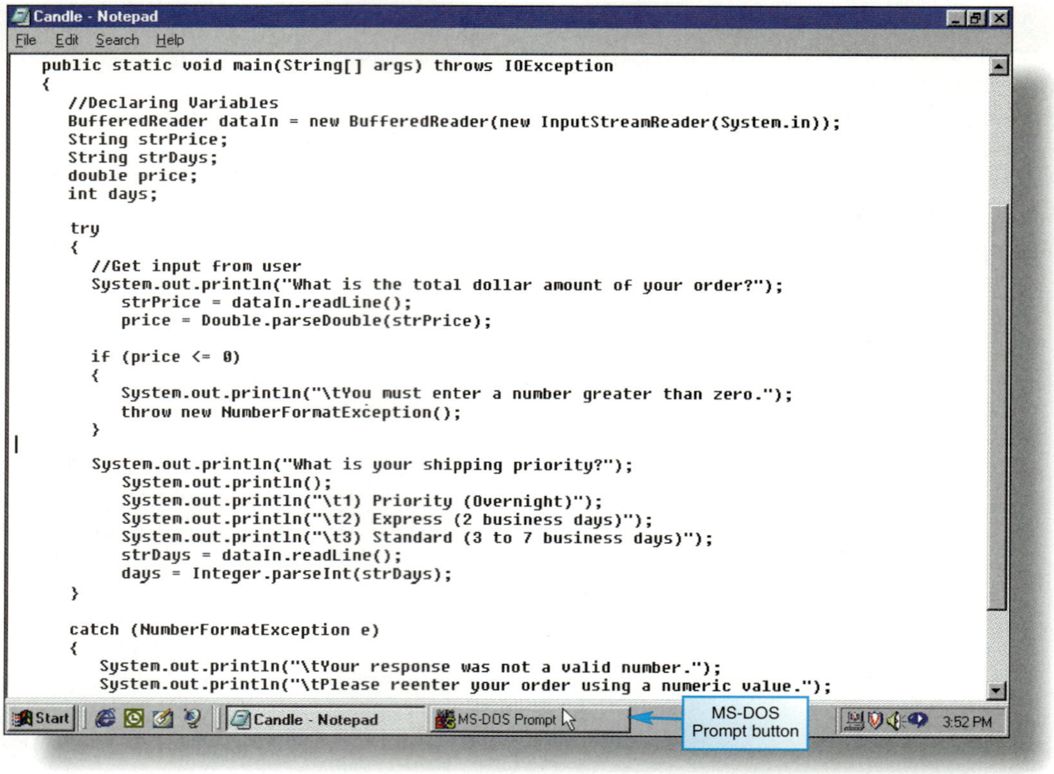

```
Candle - Notepad
File  Edit  Search  Help
    public static void main(String[] args) throws IOException
    {
        //Declaring Variables
        BufferedReader dataIn = new BufferedReader(new InputStreamReader(System.in));
        String strPrice;
        String strDays;
        double price;
        int days;

        try
        {
            //Get input from user
            System.out.println("What is the total dollar amount of your order?");
            strPrice = dataIn.readLine();
            price = Double.parseDouble(strPrice);

            if (price <= 0)
            {
                System.out.println("\tYou must enter a number greater than zero.");
                throw new NumberFormatException();
            }

            System.out.println("What is your shipping priority?");
            System.out.println();
            System.out.println("\t1) Priority (Overnight)");
            System.out.println("\t2) Express (2 business days)");
            System.out.println("\t3) Standard (3 to 7 business days)");
            strDays = dataIn.readLine();
            days = Integer.parseInt(strDays);
        }

        catch (NumberFormatException e)
        {
            System.out.println("\tYour response was not a valid number.");
            System.out.println("\tPlease reenter your order using a numeric value.");
```

MS-DOS Prompt button

**FIGURE 3-23**

**5** Click the MS-DOS Prompt button. Type `javac Candle.java` and then press the ENTER key.

*The program compiles and the command prompt again displays (Figure 3-24). If you have errors, fix them in the Notepad window, save the file, and then recompile.*

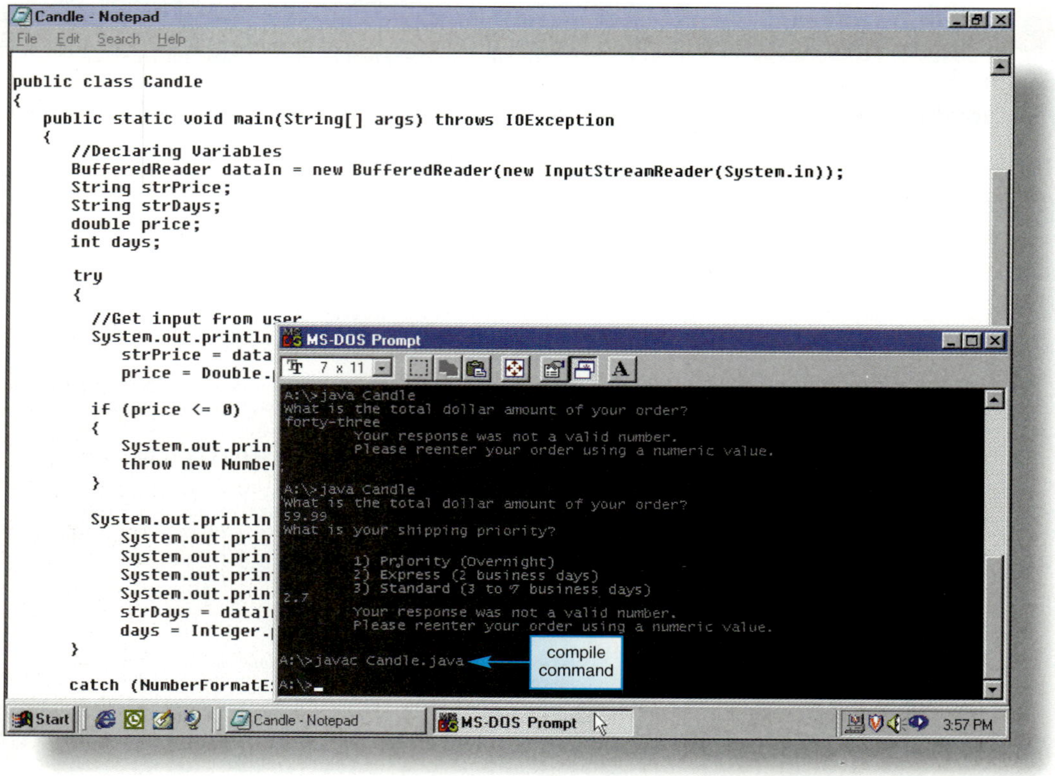

```
Candle - Notepad
File  Edit  Search  Help
public class Candle
{
    public static void main(String[] args) throws IOException
    {
        //Declaring Variables
        BufferedReader dataIn = new BufferedReader(new InputStreamReader(System.in));
        String strPrice;
        String strDays;
        double price;
        int days;

        try
        {
            //Get input from user
            System.out.println
                strPrice = data
                price = Double.

            if (price <= 0)
            {
                System.out.print
                throw new Numbe
            }

            System.out.println
                System.out.prin
                System.out.prin
                System.out.prin
                System.out.prin
                strDays = dataI
                days = Integer.
        }

        catch (NumberFormatE
```

```
MS-DOS Prompt
A:\>java Candle
What is the total dollar amount of your order?
forty-three
        Your response was not a valid number.
        Please reenter your order using a numeric value.

A:\>java Candle
What is the total dollar amount of your order?
59.99
What is your shipping priority?

        1) Priority (Overnight)
        2) Express (2 business days)
        3) Standard (3 to 7 business days)
2.7
        Your response was not a valid number.
        Please reenter your order using a numeric value.

A:\>javac Candle.java
A:\>_
```

compile command

**FIGURE 3-24**

**6** **To test the program, type** `java Candle` **at the command prompt and then press the ENTER key.**

*The program begins to execute and the first prompt displays (Figure 3-25).*

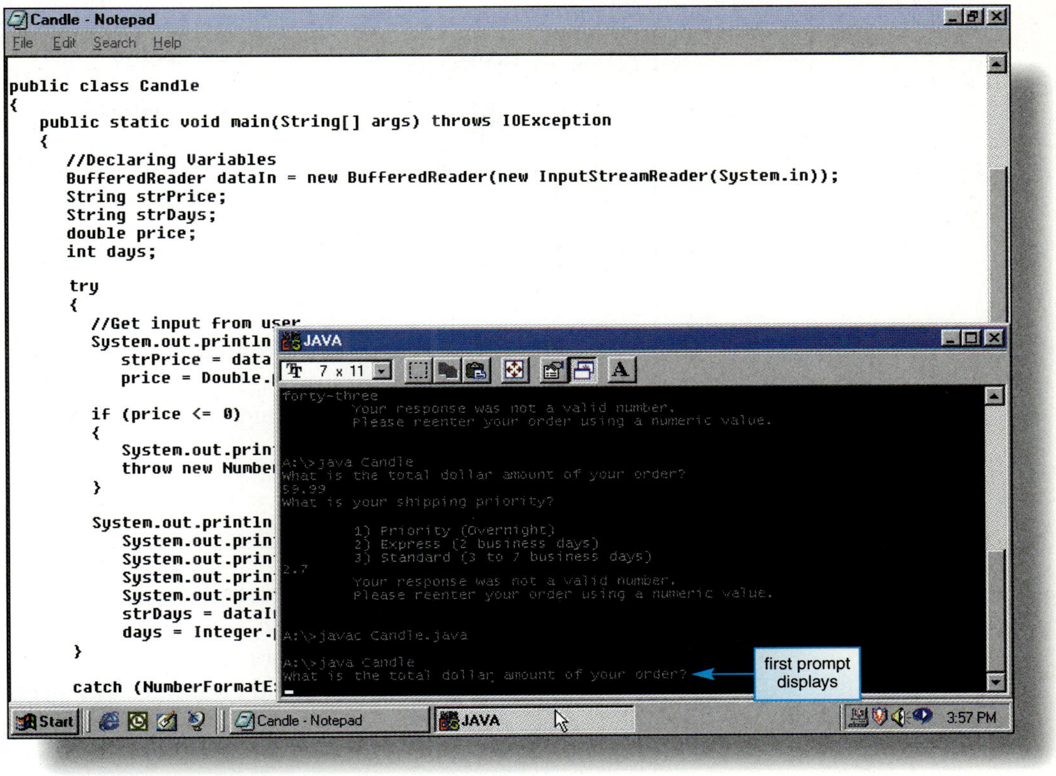

FIGURE 3-25

**7** **Type** `0` **and then press the ENTER key.**

*The program displays the error message (Figure 3-26).*

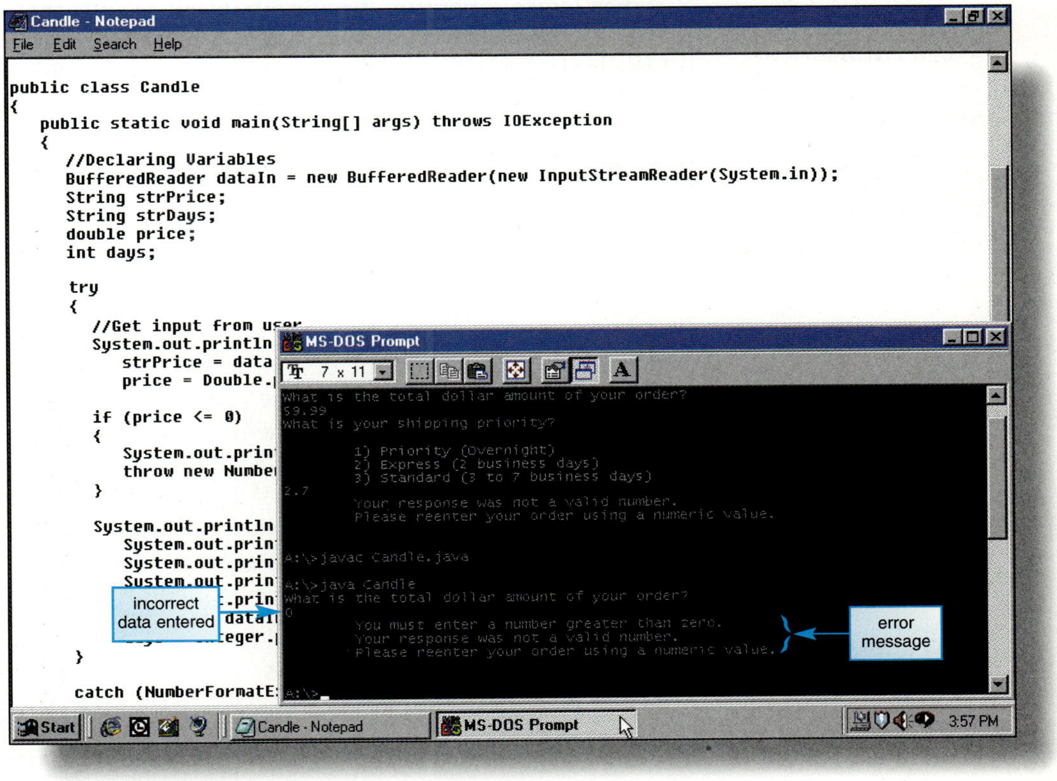

FIGURE 3-26

The previous steps included code that tested for only one condition at a time. While this is common, decision structures may check for more than one possible condition. The logical **AND**, with its operator, &&, typically would be used for situations where you might want to test more than one piece of data at the same time. For example, a program that checks for adult males to register for the selective service might compare the gender with a code for male, and the age with a numeric value. In this case, each condition is enclosed in its own set of parentheses.

```
if ((gender == "male") && (age >= 18))
```

The logical **OR**, with its operator, | |, typically would be used for testing the same piece of data in two different ways. For example, a program that tests an age for possible child or senior discount might compare the age against two different numeric values.

```
if ((age<18) | | (age > 65))
```

The logical **NOT**, with its operator, !, typically would be used for testing a boolean piece of data. For example, a programmer might assign a boolean true value to a variable named, done, in response to a user's input to quit the program. If done were not set, then processing would continue. The decision statement might display as follows.

```
if (!done)
```

The logical operators produce boolean results; that is, they evaluate to true or false. The values or operands used also must be boolean. An important characteristic of the logical AND and OR is that if the left operand is sufficient to decide the condition, the right side never is evaluated. For example if the left side of the AND operator, &&, evaluates to false, the condition automatically is false and the right side need not be evaluated. The left operand was sufficient to decide the condition.

# Creating Methods

Breaking a large program's source code down into smaller sections applies to both the creation process and the design. So far, you have created the program by adding small pieces of code and testing the program after each new addition. Now you will write code to test user input for the menu selection. Java's NumberFormatException checked for an integer, which was a validity check. Checking to see if the menu choice is 1, 2, or 3 is an example of a **range check**. Instead of writing the code in the main method block, you will transfer execution to an external routine in an effort to keep portions of code in their own separate and reusable components. Java calls these external routines programmer-defined or user-defined methods.

## Coding User-Defined Methods

A **method** is the code used to perform an operation or service. In this case, the method will be a service that tests for a correct menu response of 1, 2, or 3, and calculates a shipping cost. In the same manner as Java-defined methods, any method you create must follow certain syntax rules. Creating a method is a two-part process. You must write a call statement and write the code for the method itself.

When you reach the place in the program where the method is to perform its service, you must **call** it. The call is a line of code stating the name of the method along with any data the method needs to do its job enclosed in parentheses. The pieces of data, if any, are called **arguments**, or parameters. If you have no arguments, you still must include the parentheses with nothing inside. The call may be part of another method or statement as in the following example.

```
System.out.println(calculateAverage(payment));
```

The name of the method is calculateAverage. The argument in this example is payment.

Many of the methods you create calculate or assign a value. If you plan to use that value later in the program, you must assign it an identifier name. The following assignment statement, inserted in the main method, calls the user-defined method, getCost.

```
shipping = getCost(price, days);
```

The name of the method is getCost. Price and days are arguments. The answer is returned to a variable named, shipping. Shipping, price, and days must be declared before the call.

When a call statement is encountered, the Java compiler looks for a matching method, either from an imported package, embedded in the application, or from an external class. Table 3-7 displays a stub for the method. In this project, the method will be coded directly below the main method. The method must contain a header (line 56) and a block (lines 57 through 61).

The method header in line 56 contains an access modifier and a method modifier. You may remember that an access modifier specifies the circumstances in which the class can be accessed. The access modifier, public, indicates that the method can be accessed by all objects and can be extended, or used, as a basis for another class. A method modifier, such as static, enables you to set properties for the method, such as where it will be visible and how subclasses of the current class will interact with the method.

| Table 3-7 | |
|---|---|
| LINE | CODE |
| 56 | public static double getCost(double price, int days) |
| 57 | { |
| 58 | double shipping=0; |
| 59 | |
| 60 | return shipping; |
| 61 | } |

If a method returns a value, the data type of the return value comes next. In this case, the method returns a double value. That value must be declared in the body of the method.

You then type the name of the method itself, getCost. The method accepts two values from the code statement that calls it, in this case, the values, price and days, in parentheses. Notice that those two values are included with their data types; this serves as their declaration. They need not be named the same as in the call statement.

The getCost method will execute the code inside its block using the declared values. It will send back the shipping charge to the main method that called it. Because it returns a value, the last line inside the block (line 60) must be is a return statement. The **return** statement indicates to the JVM that the method is finished and that execution may return to the main method. When a method is complete, execution always passes back to the next sequential line that follows the call.

Perform the following steps to declare the shipping variable, insert the code to call the getCost method, and then code a stub for the getCost method itself.

## To Enter Code for the getCost Method

**1** **Click in the Notepad window to activate it. Click on line 21 to the right of the variable declaration for days.**

*The insertion point displays (Figure 3-27).*

```
Candle - Notepad                                               _ 8 X
File  Edit  Search  Help

public class Candle
{
  public static void main(String[] args) throws IOException
  {
    //Declaring Variables
    BufferedReader dataIn = new BufferedReader(new InputStreamReader(System.in));
    String strPrice;
    String strDays;
    double price;
    int days;|           I

    try
    {
      //              from user
      S       println("What is the total dollar amount of your order?");
         = dataIn.readLine();
        price = Double.parseDouble(strPrice);

      if (price <= 0)
      {
        System.out.println("\tYou must enter a number greater than zero.");
        throw new NumberFormatException();
      }

        System.out.println("What is your shipping priority?");
          System.out.println();
          System.out.println("\t1) Priority (Overnight)");
          System.out.println("\t2) Express (2 business days)");
          System.out.println("\t3) Standard (3 to 7 business days)");
          strDays = dataIn.readLine();
          days = Integer.parseInt(strDays);
    }

    catch (NumberFormatException e)

Start    Candle - Notepad    MS-DOS Prompt              3:57 PM
```

*line 21*

*insertion point*

*Notepad button*

**FIGURE 3-27**

**2** **Press the ENTER key. Indent and then type** `double shipping;` **to declare the new variable. Point to the end of the line 41, which parses strDays into days.**

*The variable shipping is declared to be a double data type (Figure 3-28).*

```
Candle - Notepad                                               _ 8 X
File  Edit  Search  Help

public class Candle
{
  public static void main(String[] args) throws IOException
  {
    //Declaring Variables
    BufferedReader dataIn = new BufferedReader(new InputStreamReader(System.in));
    String strPrice;
    String strDays;
    double price;
    int days;
    double shipping;|

    try
    {
      //G          from user
      Sys       println("What is the total dollar amount of your order?");
      s          dataIn.readLine();
        price = Double.parseDouble(strPrice);

      if (price <= 0)
      {
        System.out.println("\tYou must enter a number greater than zero.");
        throw new NumberFormatException();
      }

        System.out.println("What is your shipping priority?");
          System.out.println();
          System.out.println("\t1) Priority (Overnight)");
          System.out.println("\t2) Express (2 business days)");
          System.out.println("\t3) Standard (3 to 7 business days)");
          strDays = dataIn.readLine();
          days = Integer.parseInt(strDays);I

Start    Candle - Notepad    MS-DOS Prompt              3:57 PM
```

*variable declared*

*parse statement*

*line 41*

**FIGURE 3-28**

**3** **Click at the end of the line 41. Press the ENTER key twice and indent. Type** //Call method to get a valid shipping charge **and then press the ENTER key.**

*The comment displays (Figure 3-29).*

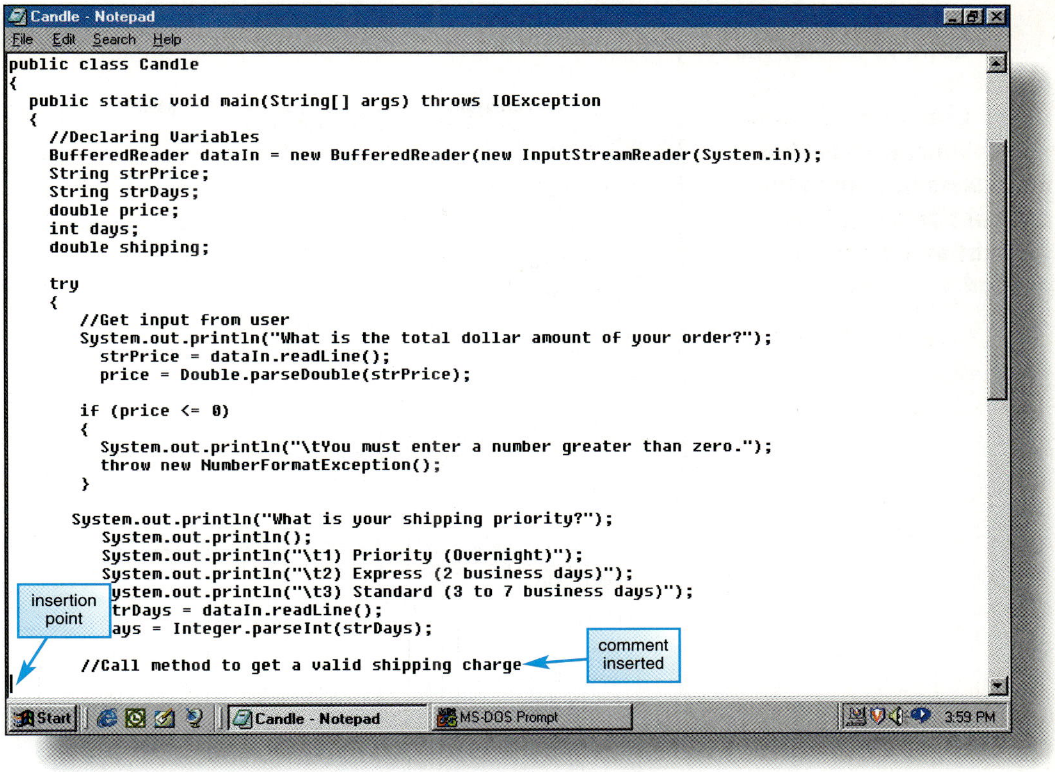

```
Candle - Notepad
File  Edit  Search  Help
public class Candle
{
  public static void main(String[] args) throws IOException
  {
    //Declaring Variables
    BufferedReader dataIn = new BufferedReader(new InputStreamReader(System.in));
    String strPrice;
    String strDays;
    double price;
    int days;
    double shipping;

    try
    {
      //Get input from user
      System.out.println("What is the total dollar amount of your order?");
        strPrice = dataIn.readLine();
        price = Double.parseDouble(strPrice);

      if (price <= 0)
      {
        System.out.println("\tYou must enter a number greater than zero.");
        throw new NumberFormatException();
      }

      System.out.println("What is your shipping priority?");
        System.out.println();
        System.out.println("\t1) Priority (Overnight)");
        System.out.println("\t2) Express (2 business days)");
        System.out.println("\t3) Standard (3 to 7 business days)");
        strDays = dataIn.readLine();
        days = Integer.parseInt(strDays);

      //Call method to get a valid shipping charge
```

insertion point

comment inserted

Start | Candle - Notepad | MS-DOS Prompt | 3:59 PM

**FIGURE 3-29**

**4** **Indent and then type** shipping = getCost(price, days); **to enter the code to call the method. Press the ENTER key twice. Point to the scroll box on the vertical scroll bar.**

*The code to call the method displays (Figure 3-30). This call will send two values, price and days, to the method and return the value, shipping.*

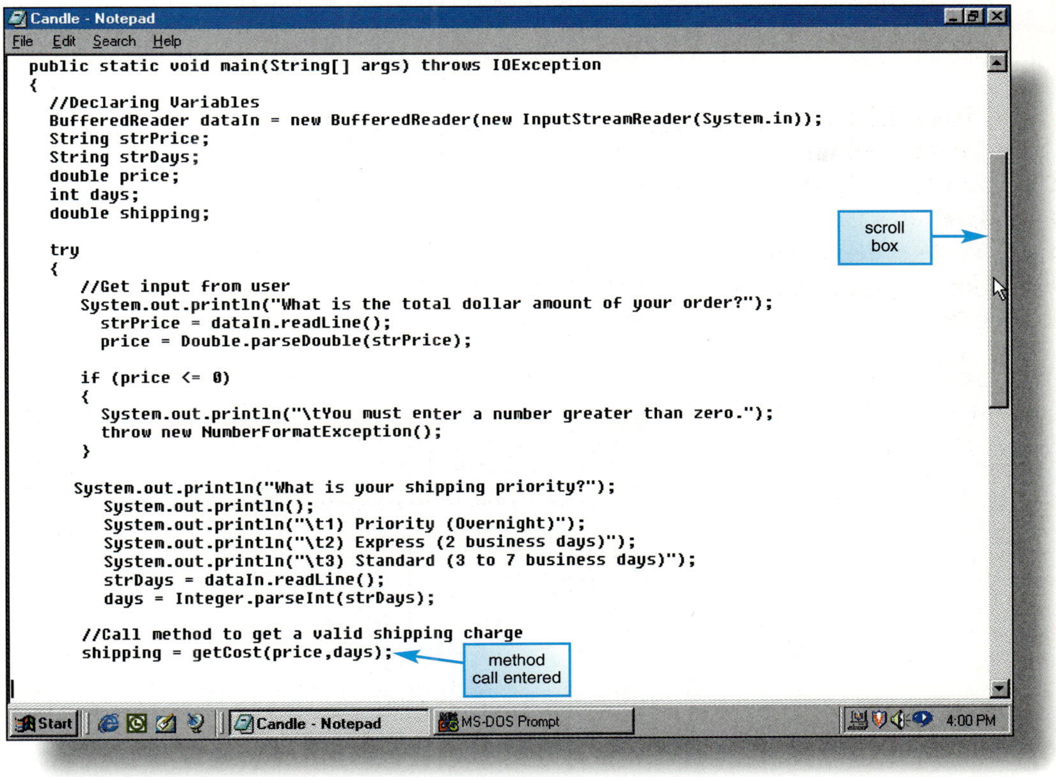

```
Candle - Notepad
File  Edit  Search  Help
  public static void main(String[] args) throws IOException
  {
    //Declaring Variables
    BufferedReader dataIn = new BufferedReader(new InputStreamReader(System.in));
    String strPrice;
    String strDays;
    double price;
    int days;
    double shipping;

    try
    {
      //Get input from user
      System.out.println("What is the total dollar amount of your order?");
        strPrice = dataIn.readLine();
        price = Double.parseDouble(strPrice);

      if (price <= 0)
      {
        System.out.println("\tYou must enter a number greater than zero.");
        throw new NumberFormatException();
      }

      System.out.println("What is your shipping priority?");
        System.out.println();
        System.out.println("\t1) Priority (Overnight)");
        System.out.println("\t2) Express (2 business days)");
        System.out.println("\t3) Standard (3 to 7 business days)");
        strDays = dataIn.readLine();
        days = Integer.parseInt(strDays);

      //Call method to get a valid shipping charge
      shipping = getCost(price,days);
```

scroll box

method call entered

Start | Candle - Notepad | MS-DOS Prompt | 4:00 PM

**FIGURE 3-30**

**5** Drag the scroll box down to display the rest of the program. Click at the end of line 53 after the closing brace for the main method. Press the ENTER key twice and then type the stub of the getCost method as shown in Figure 3-31.

*The method header is declared public and static (Figure 3-31). It accepts two arguments, a double and an int, and will return a double value. The shipping variable is declared set to zero and returned to the calling method in order for this stub to work.*

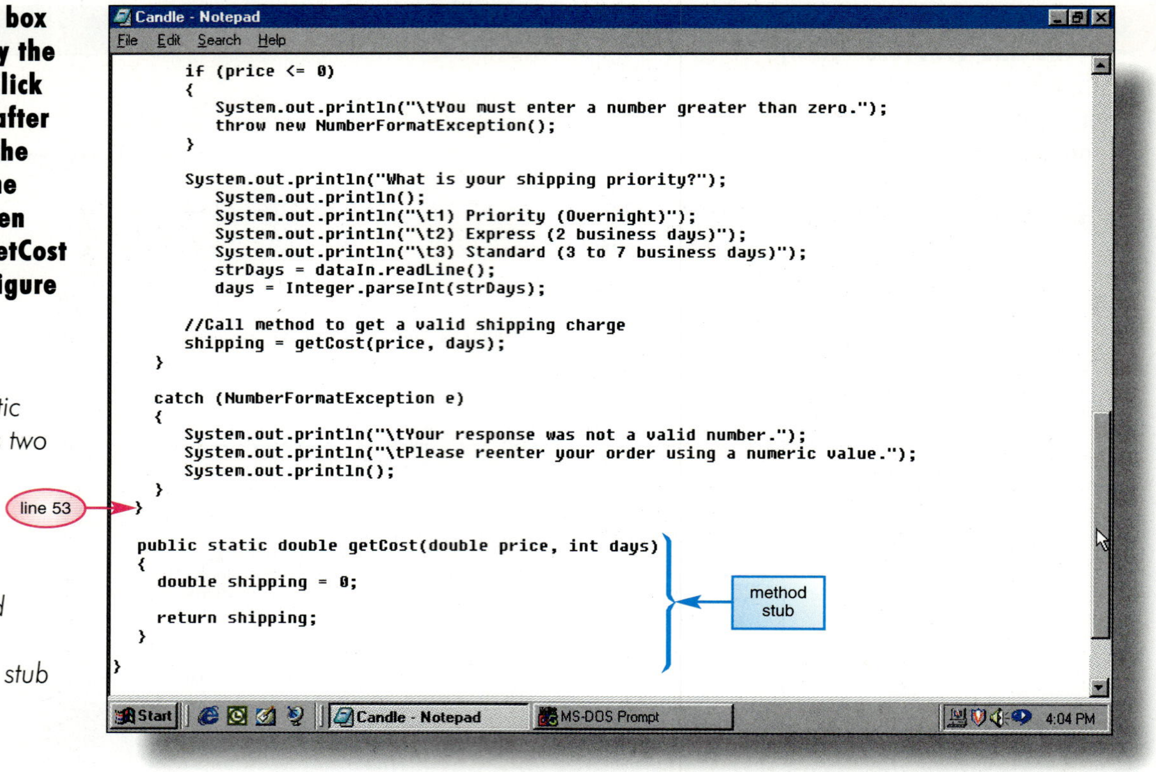

**FIGURE 3-31**

User-defined methods such as getCost must contain a method header and a set of braces. The only other requirement is that they reside inside a program or class. In this application, which does not use external methods, the getCost method is placed outside of main, but within the braces of the Candle class. So far, the Candle program has two internal methods, main and getCost.

## Coding the Output

To display the shipping cost, you must code a few lines of output to display during execution (Table 3-8).

| Table 3-8 | |
|---|---|
| *LINE* | *CODE* |
| 46 | //Display Output |
| 47 | System.out.println(); |
| 48 | System.out.println("The shipping charge is $" + (shipping)); |
| 49 | System.out.println("The total charge will be $" + (price + shipping)); |
| 50 | System.out.println(); |
| 51 | System.out.println("\t\t\tThank you for ordering from CandleLine"); |

Perform the following step to enter output code in the main method.

## TO ENTER OUTPUT CODE

**1** Click at the end of line 44. Press the ENTER key twice, indent, and then type the output code as shown in Table 3-8.

*The output code displays (Figure 3-32).*

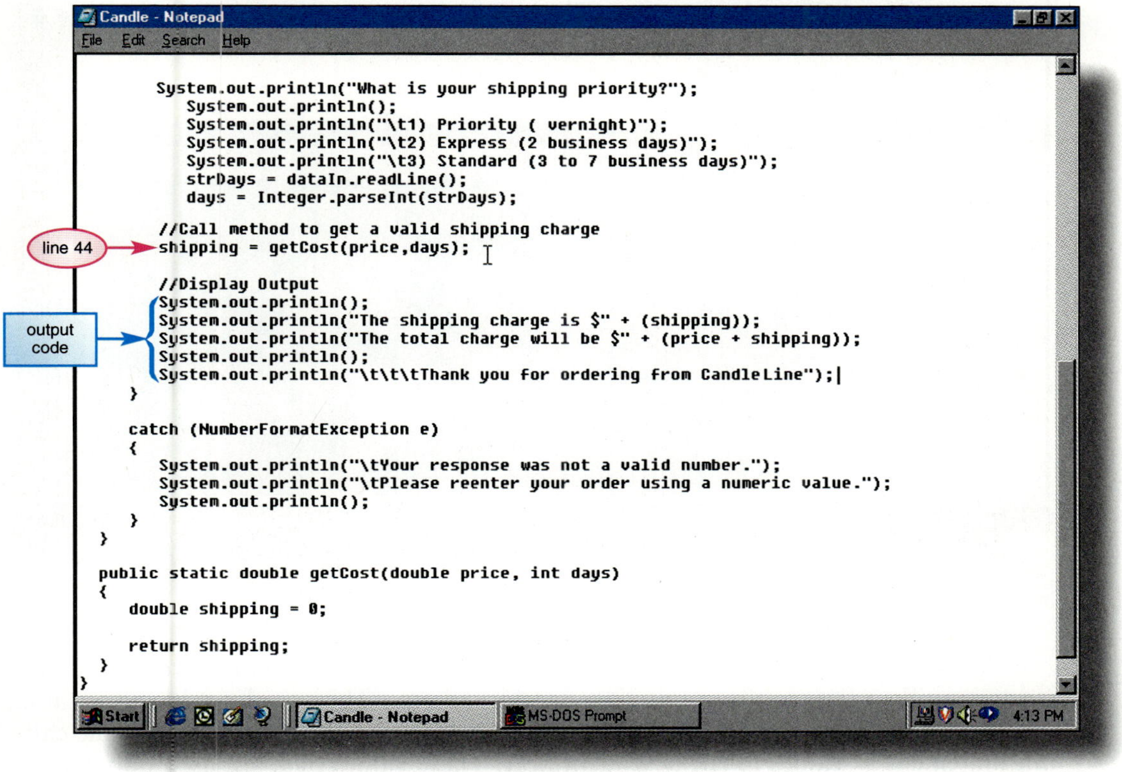

**FIGURE 3-32**

## Testing the getCost Method

Perform the following steps to save, compile, and test the getCost method stub.

## TO SAVE, COMPILE, AND TEST THE GETCOST METHOD STUB

**1** In the Notepad window, click File on the menu bar and then click Save.

**2** Click the MS-DOS Prompt button. If you previously closed the MS-DOS Prompt window, open it again, set your path, and log onto drive A.

**3** Type javac Candle.java and then press the ENTER key. If you have errors, fix them in the Notepad window, save, and then recompile.

**4** To test the program, type java Candle at the command prompt, and then press the ENTER key.

**5** When the prompt for the total dollar amount displays, type 42.75 and then press the ENTER key.

**6** When the prompt for the shipping priority displays, type 2 and then press the ENTER key.

*The shipping charge of zero ($0.0) displays (Figure 3-33 on the next page). The total charge also displays.*

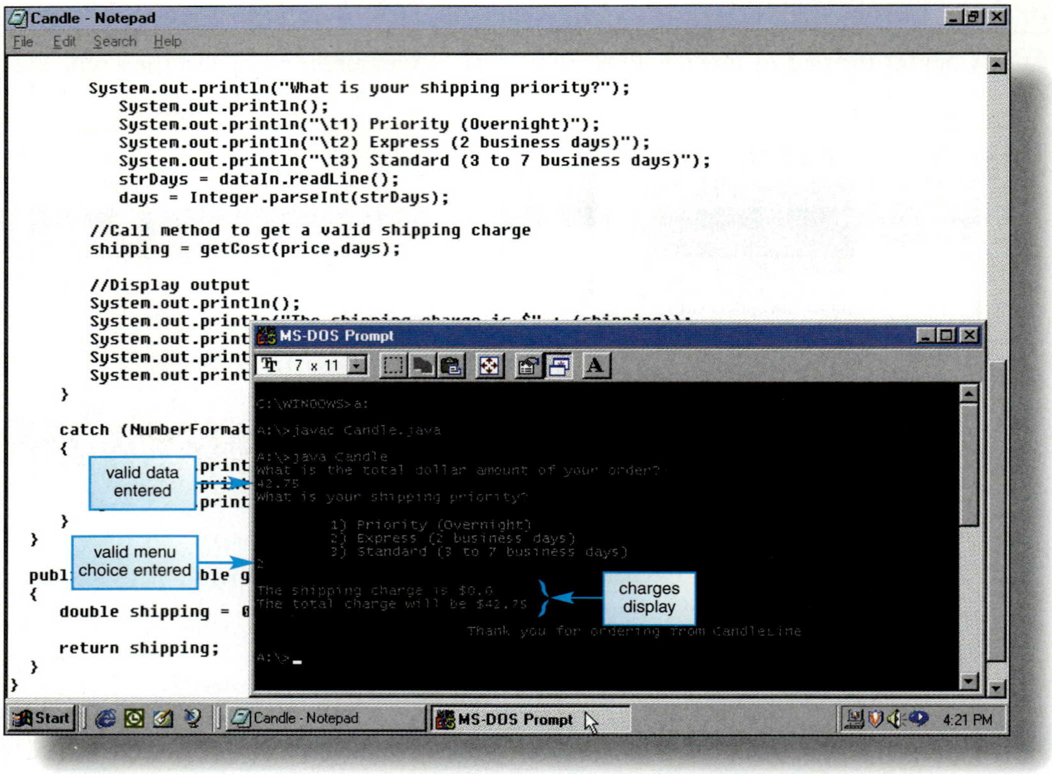

**FIGURE 3-33**

When you create a user-defined method, such as getCost, you may rename the argument identifiers in the method header parentheses. They need not have the same name as the arguments in the main method. The arguments are passed from the calling statement as values to the new identifiers. These values then are used only within the scope of the new method. **Scope** refers to the variable's visibility. In other words, if you use a new name, only the method itself will recognize that variable, thus preventing confusion or accidental overwriting of the original value. You will learn more about scope in a future project.

## The Case Structure

Sending a value to a method where it will be tested is a convenient way to make the program easy to read and to test its components. In the case of a menu selection, there might be many possible, valid choices for the user to input. When there are more than two possibilities, the logical operators become cumbersome and hard to understand, even when AND and OR are used. Most programming languages, including Java, contain a variation of the decision structure called case. In the Introduction Project, you learned that **case** is a special selection control structure that allows for more than two choices when the condition is evaluated. For example, if a user can select from several choices on a menu, the logic of the menu code evaluates the choice. If a match is found, then the appropriate action is performed. Alternatively, if no match is found, the case control structure can provide feedback to the user or store the no match result for later use in the program.

## The switch Statement

Java uses a **switch** statement to evaluate a multiple choice value. Then, depending on the value, control is transferred to a corresponding **case statement**. If the value following the case statement matches the switch value, then that case block is executed. Often, each case block contains a **break** statement at the end, which forces an exit of the structure because a match is found. After the break, no more statements within the structure are evaluated, thereby reducing processing time. Table 3-9 displays information about the switch statement.

| Table 3-9 | The switch Statement |
|---|---|
| **General form:** | ```switch (variable)
{
    case value1:
        ...statements to execute if value matches value1
        break;
    case value2:
        ...statements to execute if value matches value 2
        break;
        .
        .
        .
    default:
        ...statements to execute if no match is found
}``` |
| **Comment:** | **Switch, case, break,** and **default** are reserved words. The case value is any valid variable or constant. Switch compares the case value to the variable. If they match, the code following that case statement is executed. |
| **Example:** | ```switch (flavor)
{
    case 1:
        System.out.println("chocolate");
        break;
    case 2:
        System.out.println("vanilla");
        break;
    case 3:
        System.out.println("strawberry");
        break;
    default:
        System.out.println("Please choose one of our three flavors.");
}``` |

In the Candle program, the user will choose from three menu choices, so you will program cases for the choices, plus the possibility that the user enters an incorrect choice. Should a user enter 1, the program should assign shipping a value of $14.95. If the user enters a 2, the program should assign a shipping a value of $11.95. If a user enters a 3, then the program should evaluate the cost of the order. If the total cost of the order is more than $75.00, shipping will be assigned a value of zero; otherwise shipping will be $5.95.

If a user enters a number outside of the valid range, less than 1 or greater than 3, the program will again throw a number format exception. Java will throw its own NumberFormatException if the number is not an integer. When execution returns to the main method, the catch block then will be executed.

## Table 3-10

| LINE | CODE |
|------|------|
| 65 | `switch(days)` |
| 66 | `{` |
| 67 | `    case 1:` |
| 68 | `        shipping = 14.95;` |
| 69 | `        break;` |
| 70 | `    case 2:` |
| 71 | `        shipping = 11.95;` |
| 72 | `        break;` |
| 73 | `    case 3:` |
| 74 | `        if (price > 75)` |
| 75 | `            shipping = 0;` |
| 76 | `        else` |
| 77 | `            shipping = 5.95;` |
| 78 | `        break;` |
| 79 | `    default:` |
| 80 | `        throw new NumberFormatException();` |
| 81 | `}` |

You will use the if structure nested inside the third case structure, as shown in Table 3-10. A control structure is **nested** when it is located completely within another structure. A nested structure must end before the outer structure may end. Java programs may have multiple layers of nesting.

Perform the following step to delete the initial assignment of shipping to zero and then add a switch case structure to the getCost method.

### TO CODE THE SWITCH STRUCTURE

 Click the Notepad window to activate it. Delete =0 from line 64. Below the shipping variable declaration, enter the Java code from Table 3-10.

*The switch structure displays (Figure 3-34).*

In the default case, the program will throw a number format exception. Because the getCost method was called from within the try block, execution will pass to the corresponding catch block, if a user enters a number other than 1, 2, or 3.

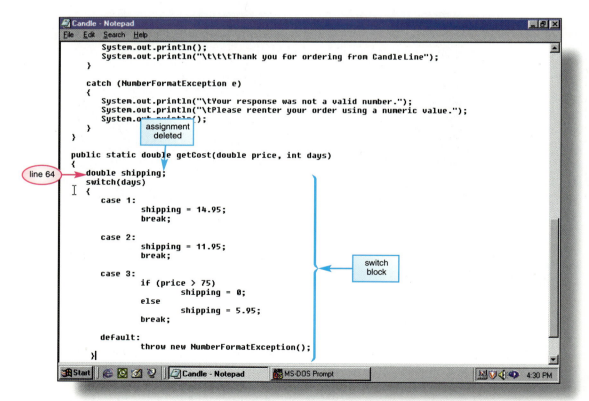

**FIGURE 3-34**

## Testing the switch Structure

Perform the following steps to save, compile, and test the switch structure.

## TO SAVE, COMPILE, AND TEST THE SWITCH STRUCTURE

**1** In the Notepad window, click File on the menu bar and then click Save.

**2** Click the MS-DOS Prompt button. If you previously closed the MS-DOS Prompt window, open it again, set the path, and log onto drive A.

**3** Type javac Candle.java and then press the ENTER key. If you have errors, fix them in the Notepad window, save, and then recompile.

**4** To test the program, type java Candle at the command prompt, and then press the ENTER key.

**5** When the prompt for the total dollar amount displays, type 150 and then press the ENTER key.

**6** When the prompt for the shipping priority displays, type 1 and then press the ENTER key.

*The shipping charge displays (Figure 3-35).*

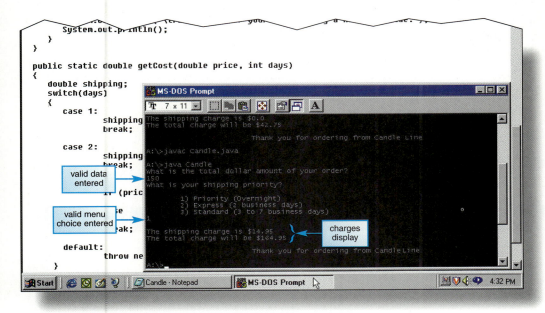

**FIGURE 3-35**

<aside>
**More** *About*

**Logos**

Variables, such as done, that are tested to see if iteration should continue sometimes are called sentinel values, or flags. Programmers design a variable that is intentionally wrong and then reset it to a correct value when some phase of the processing has been finished. Testing against that flag allows the program to continue looping until the condition is met.
</aside>

Run the program several more times and test each menu choice, as well as dollar values above, below, and exactly at 75.

# Repetition Structure

So far in this project, when the user types in an invalid or unreasonable number, the program terminates. A message displays notifying the user of the error, but it does not allow the user to reenter the information and try again without rerunning the entire program. As you may recall from the Introduction Project, computer programs are capable of repeating a set of instructions a certain number of times, or indefinitely, based on a conditional factor. The logical structure that alters the flow of sequential execution by repeating a set of code is called **looping**, **repetition**, or an **iteration control structure**. In the case of the CandleLine company, the program should repeat the instructions while the user is attempting to enter the correct information.

### The while Statement

Java uses the Do...While concept for looping when the exact number of repetitions is unknown. First you enter the keyword, **while**, and then a condition in parentheses. All code that should be repeated, based on the condition, is enclosed in braces. Table 3-11 shows the general form of the while statement.

| Table 3-11 | The while Statement |
|---|---|
| General form: | ```while (condition)`<br>`{`<br>`   ...lines of code to repeat while above condition is true;`<br>`}``` |
| Comment: | The word, **while**, is a reserved keyword. Condition must be a boolean expression that evaluates to true or false. The condition must eventually evaluate to false in order to exit the loop. |
| Examples: | ```while (!done)`<br>`{`<br>`   System.out.println("Are you done (yes or no)");`<br>`   answer = dataIn.readLine();`<br>`   if (answer == "yes") done;`<br>`}``` |

Perform the following steps to add the code for the while loop.

## To Loop Using the while Statement

**1** Click the Notepad window to activate it. Drag the scroll box to display the first part of the program. Click at the end of the declaration section on line 20.

*The first part of the program displays (Figure 3-36).*

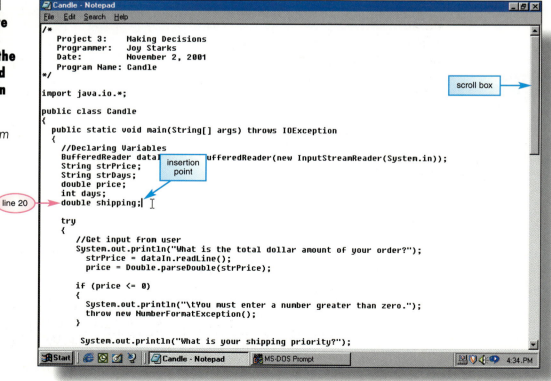

**FIGURE 3-36**

**2** Press the ENTER key. Indent and then type boolean done = false; to declare the beginning value for the while condition. Press the ENTER key twice.

The declaration for the variable, done, displays (Figure 3-37). Boolean values equate to either true or false in Java.

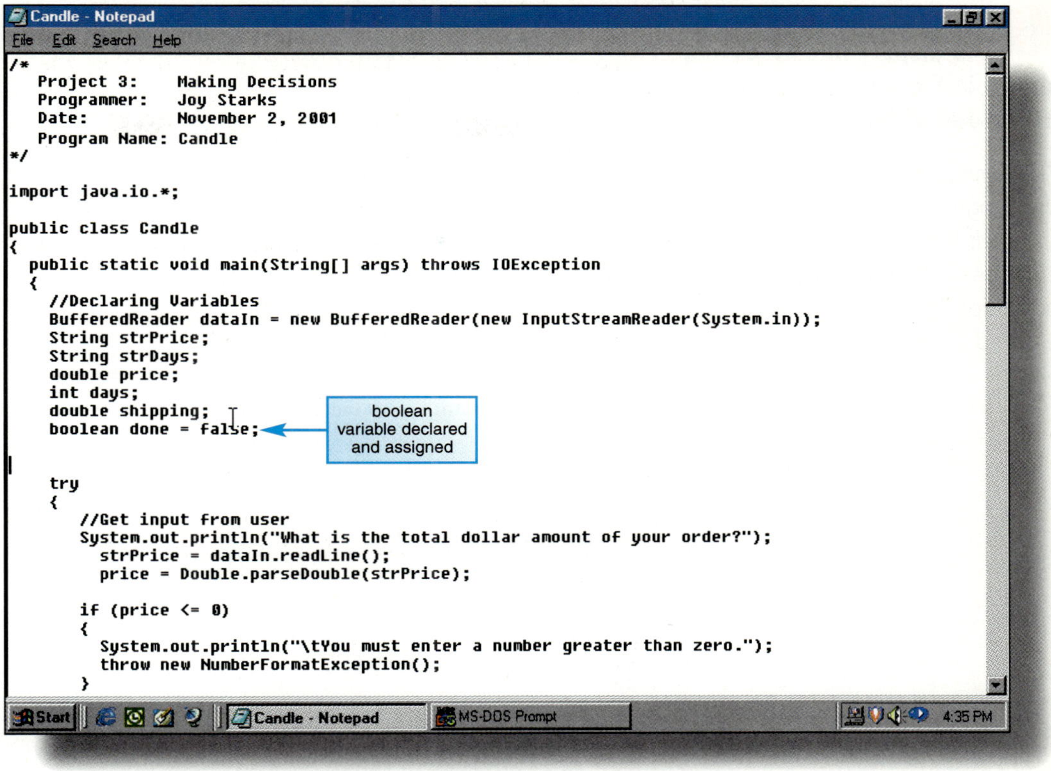

```
/*
   Project 3:     Making Decisions
   Programmer:    Joy Starks
   Date:          November 2, 2001
   Program Name: Candle
*/

import java.io.*;

public class Candle
{
  public static void main(String[] args) throws IOException
  {
     //Declaring Variables
     BufferedReader dataIn = new BufferedReader(new InputStreamReader(System.in));
     String strPrice;
     String strDays;
     double price;
     int days;
     double shipping;
     boolean done = false;       ← boolean variable declared and assigned

     try
     {
        //Get input from user
        System.out.println("What is the total dollar amount of your order?");
          strPrice = dataIn.readLine();
          price = Double.parseDouble(strPrice);

        if (price <= 0)
        {
          System.out.println("\tYou must enter a number greater than zero.");
          throw new NumberFormatException();
        }
```

**FIGURE 3-37**

**3** Indent and then type while (!done) to code the beginning line of the loop. Press the ENTER key. Indent, type an opening brace, and then press the ENTER key. Point to the scroll box on the vertical scroll bar.

The loop will test for the condition, not done, as indicated by the !, or NOT operator (Figure 3-38).

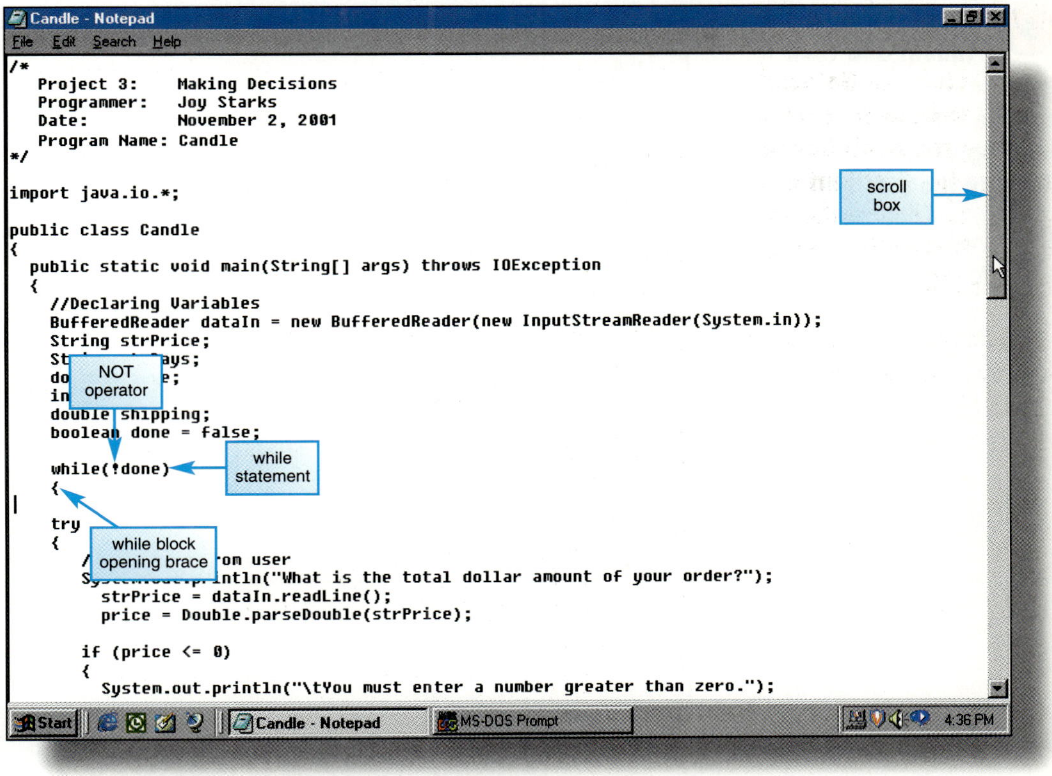

```
/*
   Project 3:     Making Decisions
   Programmer:    Joy Starks
   Date:          November 2, 2001
   Program Name: Candle
*/

import java.io.*;                                    ← scroll box

public class Candle
{
  public static void main(String[] args) throws IOException
  {
     //Declaring Variables
     BufferedReader dataIn = new BufferedReader(new InputStreamReader(System.in));
     String strPrice;
     St[NOT operator]ays;
     do[        ]e;
     in[        ]
     double shipping;
     boolean done = false;

     while(!done)         ← while statement
     {                    ← while block opening brace

     try
     {
        /[while block]om user
        Sys[opening brace]intln("What is the total dollar amount of your order?");
          strPrice = dataIn.readLine();
          price = Double.parseDouble(strPrice);

        if (price <= 0)
        {
          System.out.println("\tYou must enter a number greater than zero.");
```

**FIGURE 3-38**

**4** **Drag the scroll box to display line 47 as shown in Figure 3-39. Click at the end of line 47.**

*The Display Output portion of the program displays (Figure 3-39). If the getCost method call does not throw an exception, then the user must have entered acceptable input.*

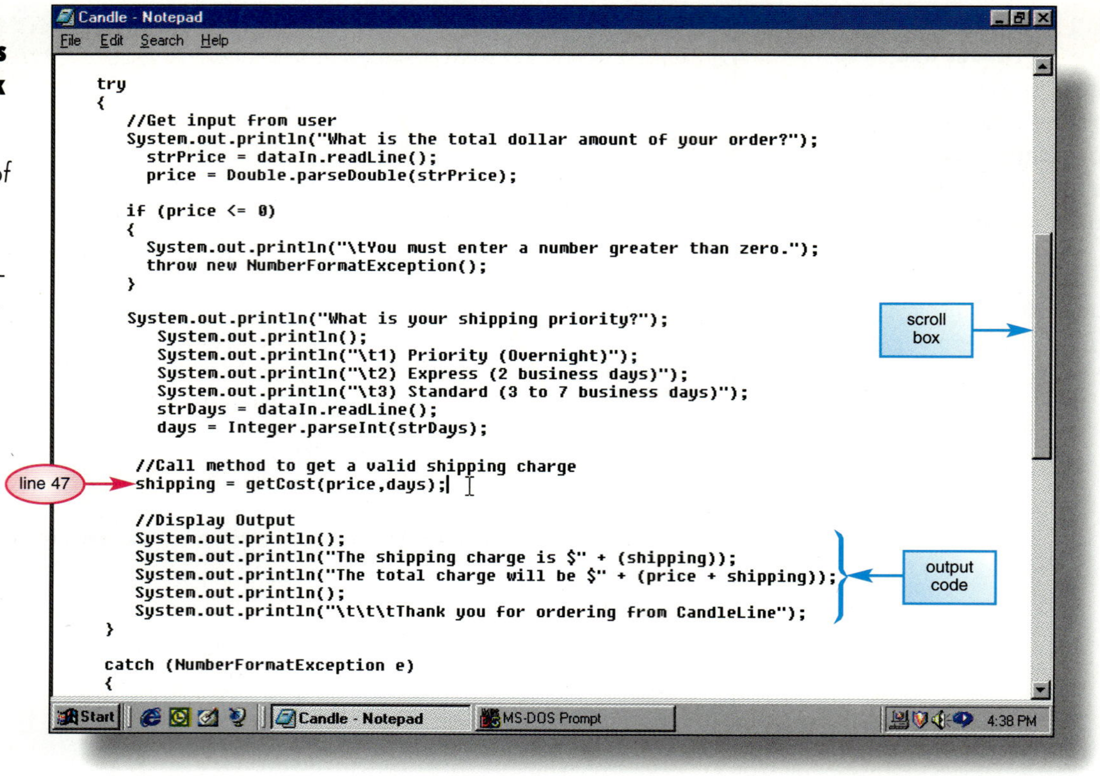

```
Candle - Notepad
File  Edit  Search  Help

    try
    {
        //Get input from user
        System.out.println("What is the total dollar amount of your order?");
            strPrice = dataIn.readLine();
            price = Double.parseDouble(strPrice);

        if (price <= 0)
        {
            System.out.println("\tYou must enter a number greater than zero.");
            throw new NumberFormatException();
        }

        System.out.println("What is your shipping priority?");
            System.out.println();
            System.out.println("\t1) Priority (Overnight)");
            System.out.println("\t2) Express (2 business days)");
            System.out.println("\t3) Standard (3 to 7 business days)");
            strDays = dataIn.readLine();
            days = Integer.parseInt(strDays);

        //Call method to get a valid shipping charge
        shipping = getCost(price,days);

        //Display Output
        System.out.println();
        System.out.println("The shipping charge is $" + (shipping));
        System.out.println("The total charge will be $" + (price + shipping));
        System.out.println();
        System.out.println("\t\t\tThank you for ordering from CandleLine");
    }

    catch (NumberFormatException e)
    {
```

scroll box

line 47

output code

Start | Candle - Notepad | MS-DOS Prompt | 4:38 PM

**FIGURE 3-39**

**5** **Press the ENTER key. Indent and then type** done = true; **to change the value of the looping condition variable. Point to the scroll box.**

*The variable, done, now is equal to true (Figure 3-40).*

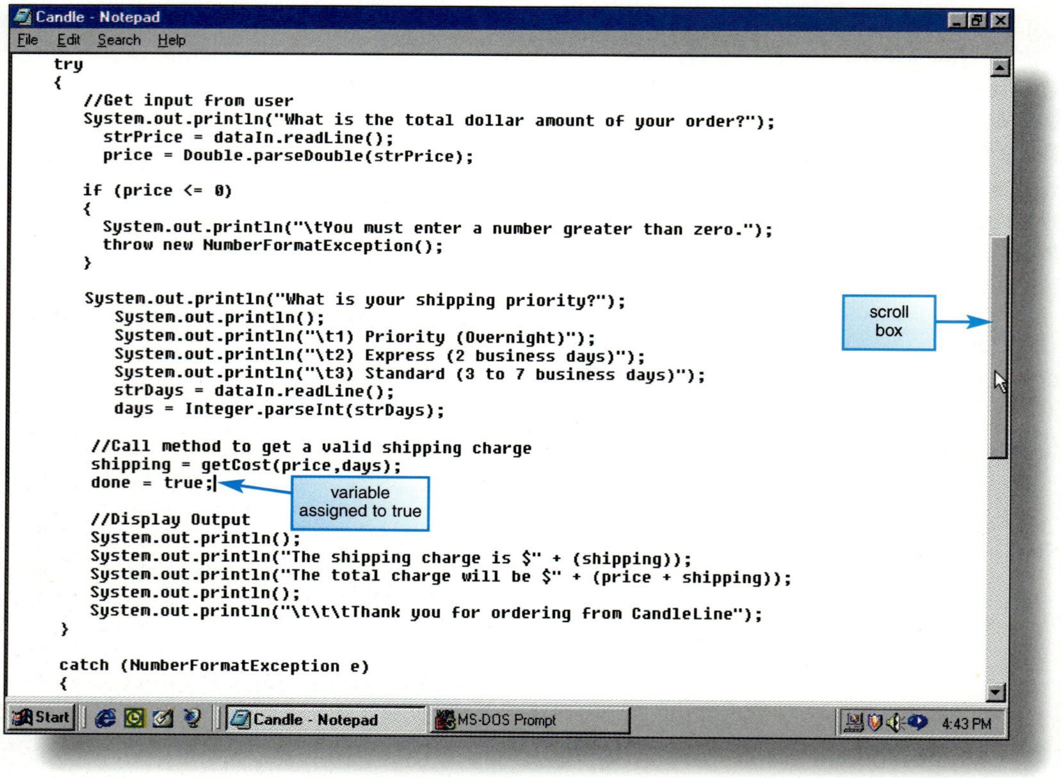

```
Candle - Notepad
File  Edit  Search  Help

    try
    {
        //Get input from user
        System.out.println("What is the total dollar amount of your order?");
            strPrice = dataIn.readLine();
            price = Double.parseDouble(strPrice);

        if (price <= 0)
        {
            System.out.println("\tYou must enter a number greater than zero.");
            throw new NumberFormatException();
        }

        System.out.println("What is your shipping priority?");
            System.out.println();
            System.out.println("\t1) Priority (Overnight)");
            System.out.println("\t2) Express (2 business days)");
            System.out.println("\t3) Standard (3 to 7 business days)");
            strDays = dataIn.readLine();
            days = Integer.parseInt(strDays);

        //Call method to get a valid shipping charge
        shipping = getCost(price,days);
        done = true;

        //Display Output
        System.out.println();
        System.out.println("The shipping charge is $" + (shipping));
        System.out.println("The total charge will be $" + (price + shipping));
        System.out.println();
        System.out.println("\t\t\tThank you for ordering from CandleLine");
    }

    catch (NumberFormatException e)
    {
```

scroll box

variable assigned to true

Start | Candle - Notepad | MS-DOS Prompt | 4:43 PM

**FIGURE 3-40**

**6** **Scroll down to the end of the catch block. Click after the closing brace on line 63. Press the ENTER key, indent, and then type a closing brace for the while loop.**

*The braces closing the catch block, the while block, and the main method display (Figure 3-41).*

```
//Call method to get a valid shipping charge
shipping = getCost(price,days);
done = true;

//Display Output
System.out.println();
System.out.println("The shipping charge is $" + (shipping));
System.out.println("The total charge will be $" + (price + shipping));
System.out.println();
System.out.println("\t\t\tThank you for ordering from CandleLine");
}

catch (NumberFormatException e)
{
    System.out.println("\tYour response was not a valid number.");
    System.out.println("\tPlease reenter your order using a numeric value.");
    System.out.println();
}
}
}

public static double getCost(double price, int days)
{
    ...ipping;
```

line 63

catch block

while loop closing brace

**FIGURE 3-41**

## Testing the while Structure

Perform the following steps to save, compile, and then test the while structure.

### TO SAVE, COMPILE, AND TEST THE WHILE STRUCTURE

**1** In the Notepad window, click File on the menu bar and then click Save.

**2** Click the MS-DOS Prompt button. If you previously closed the MS-DOS Prompt window, open it again, set your path, and log onto drive A.

**3** Type `javac Candle.java` and then press the ENTER key. If you have errors, fix them in the Notepad window, save, and then recompile.

**4** To test the program, type `java Candle` at the command prompt, and then press the ENTER key.

**5** When the prompt for the total dollar amount displays, type `-35` and then press the ENTER key.

**6** When the program notifies you of an invalid number and displays the prompt to reenter the total dollar amount, type `35` and then press the ENTER key.

**7** When the prompt for the shipping priority displays, type `3` and then press the ENTER key.

*The shipping charge displays (Figure 3-42).*

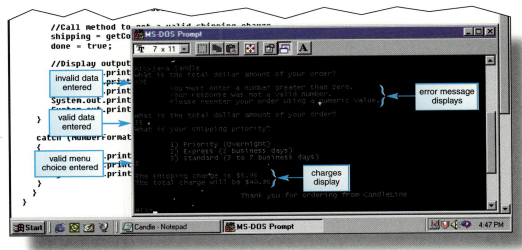

**FIGURE 3-42**

Run the program several more times and test each menu choice, 1, 2, and 3, as well as valid and invalid dollar amounts, such as zero or alphanumeric data.

The application now is complete. Figure 3-43 displays the code for the entire program with brackets matching the beginning and closing braces of each block.

```
/*
    Project 3:      Making Decisions
    Programmer:     Joy Starks
    Date:           November 2, 2001
    Program Name:   Candle
*/

import java.io.*;

public class Candle
{
    public static void main(String[] args) throws IOException
    {
        //Declaring Variables
        BufferedReader dataIn = new BufferedReader(new InputStreamReader(System.in));
        String strDays;
        double price;
        int days;
        double shipping;
        String strPrice;
        boolean done = false;

        while (!done)
        {
            try
            {
                //Get input from user
                System.out.println("What is the total dollar amount of your order?");
                strPrice = dataIn.readLine();
                price = Double.parseDouble(strPrice);

                if (price <= 0)
                {
                    System.out.println("\tYou must enter a number greater than zero.");
                    throw new NumberFormatException();
                }

                System.out.println("What is your shipping priority?");
                System.out.println();
                System.out.println("\t1) Priority (Overnight)");
                System.out.println("\t2) Express (2 business days)");
                System.out.println("\t3) Standard (3 to 7 business days)");
                strDays = dataIn.readLine();
                days = Integer.parseInt(strDays);

                //Call method to get a valid shipping charge
                shipping = getCost(price, days);

                //Display Output
                System.out.println();
                System.out.println("The shipping charge is $" + (shipping));
                System.out.println("The total charge will be $" + (price + shipping));
                System.out.println();
                System.out.println("\t\t\tThank you for ordering from CandleLine");
                done = true;
            }
            catch (NumberFormatException e)
            {
                System.out.println("\tYour response was not a valid number.");
                System.out.println("\tPlease reenter your order using a numeric value.");
                System.out.println();
            }
        }
    }

    public static double getCost(double price, int days)
    {
        double shipping;
        switch(days)
        {
            case 1:
                shipping = 14.95;
                break;

            case 2:
                shipping = 11.95;
                break;

            case 3:
                if (price > 75)
                    shipping = 0;
                else
                    shipping = 5.95;
                break;

            default:
                throw new NumberFormatException();
        }
        return shipping;
    }
}
```

**FIGURE 3-43**

# Moving to the Web

As you create the applet version of the CandleLine company's application, you will use the same techniques to build component modularity into your applet. First, you will create the HTML host document to call the applet. Then you will create the applet stub and test it by compiling. As you add components to the applet and build decision structures into the applet's code, you will create new blocks, save them, and compile them. Finally, you will run the applet and try various sample data in order to test its error and exception handling capabilities.

## Creating the Host Document

Recall from previous projects that each Java applet must be called from within another program or application. The host document usually is an HTML file with an applet tag. The code to create an HTML file to access the CandleApplet program is listed in Table 3-12.

| Table 3-12 | |
|---|---|
| LINE | CODE |
| 1 | `<HTML>` |
| 2 | `<APPLET CODE = "CandleApplet.class" WIDTH = 350 HEIGHT = 300` |
| 3 | `</APPLET>` |
| 4 | `</HTML>` |

Perform the following steps to create the HTML file and save it on your floppy disk.

### TO CREATE THE HOST DOCUMENT

**1** Start a new session of Notepad. If Notepad already is on your desktop, click File on the Notepad menu bar and then click New.

**2** Type the code from Table 3-12 in the Notepad workspace.

**3** With a floppy disk in drive A, click File on the menu bar and then click Save. When the Save As dialog box displays, type `"CandleApplet.html"` in the File name text box. If necessary, click 3½ Floppy (A:) in the Save in list. Click the Save button.

*The program saves on the floppy disk in drive A with the name, "CandleApplet.html" (Figure 3-44).*

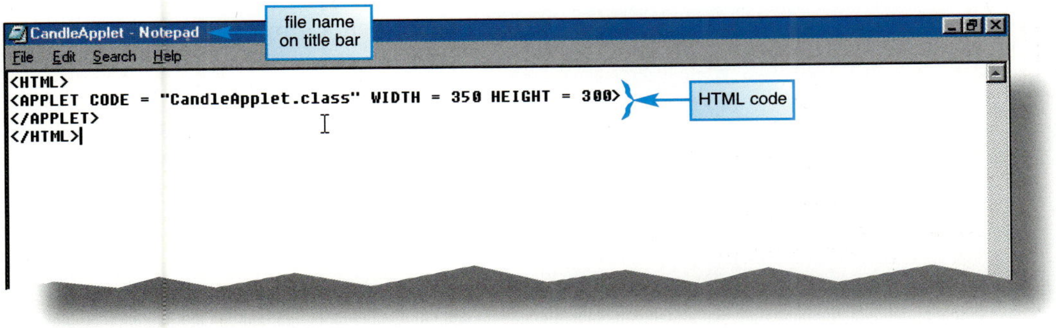

**FIGURE 3-44**

The HTML host document is complete. In the next section, you will create a stub for the applet itself.

## Creating an Applet Stub

As you may recall from previous projects, applets typically use the Abstract Windows Toolkit provided with the JDK. Programmers commonly enter the statement to import the AWT.

```
import java.awt.*;
```

The **Abstract Windows Toolkit (AWT)** consists of resources that enable you to create rich, attractive, and useful interfaces in your applets. The **java.awt** package not only contains managerial classes for complete interface layouts, but it also has the container classes to add components such as buttons, text fields, and labels. The AWT's Graphics class is very powerful, allowing you to create shapes and display images. Applets additionally must import the **java.applet** package, which lays the foundation for all applets.

The other imported package used in many applets is the java.awt.event package. The **java.awt.event** package is not a subset of java.awt package; rather, it is a separate package enabling you to implement interfaces, such as the ActionListener and the ItemListener. You may recall that ActionListener listens for events related to command buttons, such as a mouse click or ENTER key during execution of the applet. **ItemListener** can be added to listen for when the user clicks components such as check boxes. Among ItemListener's methods are addItemListener and itemStateChanged, which enable you to enliven those components and test whether or not they are selected. The java.awt, java.applet, and java.awt.event packages may be imported in any order (lines 8, 9, and 10 in Table 3-13).

Recall that applets do not have a main method. Instead, applets use the init method to **initialize** the applet from the browser or Applet Viewer (line 14). When the applet is loaded, the browser calls the init method. This method is called only once no matter how many times you might return to the Web page.

Stubbing in the program will involve typing the general block comments, importing the three classes, and entering the applet header, init method header, and the itemStateChanged method header. Perform the following steps to stub in the applet with the code from Table 3-13.

**More About**

**The ActionEvents**

An ActionEvent is the type of event that occurs when a user clicks a component, such as a button. You tell applets to expect ActionEvents with the addActionListener method. Inside the body of the corresponding ActionPerformed method, you write any statements that you want to execute when the action takes place.

### Table 3-13

| LINE | CODE |
|------|------|
| 1 | `/*` |
| 2 | `    Project 3:      Making Decision` |
| 3 | `    Programmer:     Joy Starks` |
| 4 | `    Date:          November 2, 2001` |
| 5 | `    Program Name:   CandleApplet` |
| 6 | `*/` |
| 7 | |
| 8 | `import java.awt.*;` |
| 9 | `import java.applet.*;` |
| 10 | `import java.awt.event.*;` |
| 11 | |
| 12 | `public class CandleApplet extends Applet implements ItemListener` |
| 13 | `{` |
| 14 | `    public void init()` |
| 15 | `    {` |
| 16 | |
| 17 | `    }` |
| 18 | |
| 19 | `    public void itemStateChanged(ItemEvent choice)` |
| 20 | `    {` |
| 21 | |
| 22 | `    }` |
| 23 | `}` |

## TO CODE THE APPLET STUB

**①** Start a new session of Notepad. If Notepad already is on your desktop, click File on the Notepad menu bar and then click New.

**②** Enter the code from Table 3-13 using your name and the current date in the block comment.

*The code for the program stub displays in the Notepad window (Figure 3-45).*

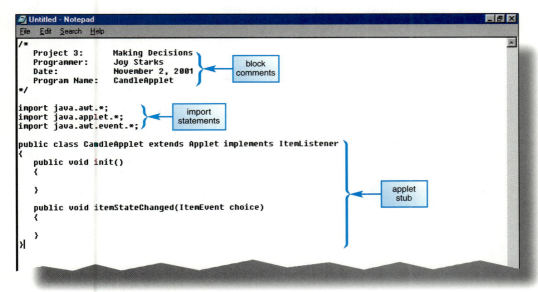

**FIGURE 3-45**

You can test the applet, even without any commands or data components. Perform the following steps to save, compile, and test the applet stub.

## TO SAVE, COMPILE, AND TEST THE APPLET STUB

**①** If necessary, click the Notepad window.

**②** With a floppy disk in drive A, click File on the menu bar and then click Save As.

**③** When the Save As dialog box displays, type "CandleApplet.java" in the File name text box. You must type the quotation marks around the file name.

**④** Click the Save in box arrow and then click 3½ Floppy (A:) in the list.

**⑤** Click the Save button.

**⑥** Click the MS-DOS Prompt button on the taskbar. If you previously closed the MS-DOS Prompt window, open it again, set your path, and log onto drive A. Type javac CandleApplet.java and then press the ENTER key to compile the program.

**⑦** If you have errors, fix them in the Notepad window, save, and then recompile the program in the MS-DOS Prompt window.

**⑧** When your program compiles successfully, execute it by typing appletviewer CandleApplet.html at the command prompt and then press the ENTER key.

*Applet Viewer displays the applet with no components (see Figure 3-46 on the next page). The program stub has no active statements or commands.*

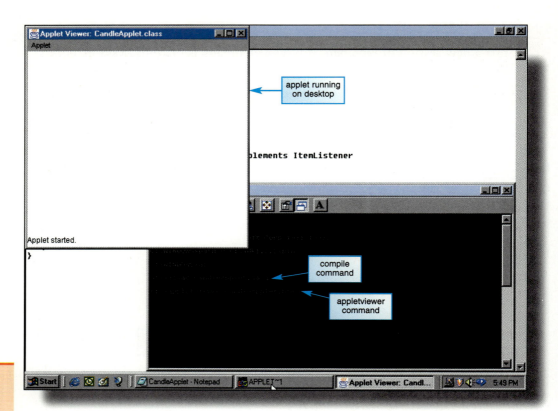

**FIGURE 3-46**

# Making Decisions in Applets

As is true in applications, a Java applet does not always perform the same series of steps. Much of the time, the path that the applet takes depends upon the actions of the user. For example, if the user enters an invalid number, the applet should display an error message and then give the user a chance to enter another number. Alternatively, if the user makes a choice from a list of options, a Java applet should branch to a certain set of code statements based on that choice.

As with the application you created in this project, applet control structures may be either object-oriented in nature or programmed to make a decision. For instance, applets may use the object-oriented try and catch blocks described on pages J 3.13 through J 3.18. In a try block, the program may throw an exception or the programmer may throw the exception to the catch block based on a condition, such as the user entering a number that is out of range.

Through the use of check boxes, Java applets may allow the user to make choices that are evaluated by the applet. For instance, a user may select a check box by clicking it. Java then allows the applet, through the ItemListener, to listen for that click, and then perform a unique set of instructions associated with that component. Thus, a multiple-choice case structure can be implemented.

Java applets also support the traditional If...Then...Else structures, as well as the switch block.

## Constructing Check Boxes

You have used constructors to create label, text field, and button components. In this project, you will create a constructor for a check box. Java has two different kinds of check boxes. The first is a traditional **check box** that displays as a small square with a caption. When selected, the check box displays a check mark (Figure 3-47). The check box has the toggled value of on or off depending on whether the check mark displays. The check box is an independent component that allows the user to select it, regardless of other choices in the interface.

The second kind of check box displays as a small circle or option button (Figure 3-47). This check box is one of a mutually exclusive group. Even though Java calls this a **grouped check box**, most people would think of it as an option button. When the user clicks one of the grouped check box components, the others automatically become deselected. Only one member of the grouped check boxes can be selected at any one time. Table 3-14 displays the code to construct the applet components.

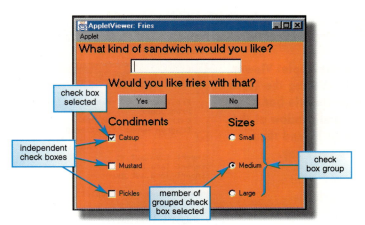

**FIGURE 3-47**

| Table 3-14 | |
| --- | --- |
| LINE | CODE |
| 14 | //Create components for applet |
| 15 | Label companyNameLabel = new Label ("CandleLine—Candles Online"); |
| 16 | |
| 17 | Label priceLabel = new Label ("Please enter the total dollar amount of your order:"); |
| 18 | TextField priceField = new TextField(35); |
| 19 | |
| 20 | Label shippingLabel = new Label ("Please choose your method of shipping:"); |
| 21 | |
| 22 | CheckboxGroup shippingGroup = new CheckboxGroup(); |
| 23 | Checkbox oneDayBox = new Checkbox("Priority (Overnight)",false,shippingGroup); |
| 24 | Checkbox twoDayBox = new Checkbox("Express (2 business days)",false,shippingGroup); |
| 25 | Checkbox moreDaysBox = new Checkbox("Standard (3 to 7 business days)",false,shippingGroup); |
| 26 | Checkbox hiddenBox = new Checkbox("",true,shippingGroup); |
| 27 | |
| 28 | Label outputLabel = new Label("We guarantee on time delivery, or your money back."); |
| 29 | |

Two methods from the AWT are employed when using a grouping of check boxes to create options. An instance of the **CheckboxGroup** is constructed first (line 22), directing the Java compiler to create a mutually exclusive grouping. You then can construct individual instances of the check boxes with unique identifiers. The **Checkbox method**, which constructs each instance (lines 23 through 26), takes three arguments: the caption, the state, and the group name. The **caption** is the string you wish to display beside the check box. The **state** is true or false, depending on whether you want the member of the grouped check box filled in for true or not filled in for false. Because it is a mutually exclusive grouping, only one member of the group may have its state value set to true at any given time. The **group name** is the identifier previously used when the CheckboxGroup was constructed. The group name assigns membership.

Perform the steps on the next page to enter the code to construct the applet components.

**Component States**

The getStateChange method can be used to test a check box for its current state. The method will return either ItemEvent.SELECTED or ItemEvent.DESELECTED. For example, if a calculate button was to test a discount check box, you could write a line of code similar to this: if (discountBox.getStateChange() = ItemEvent.SELECTED) price = price - discount.

## To Construct Components

**1** **Close Applet Viewer by clicking the Close button on its title bar. Click the Notepad window at the end of line 13 and then press the ENTER key.**

*The insertion point displays inside the CandleApplet block (Figure 3-48).*

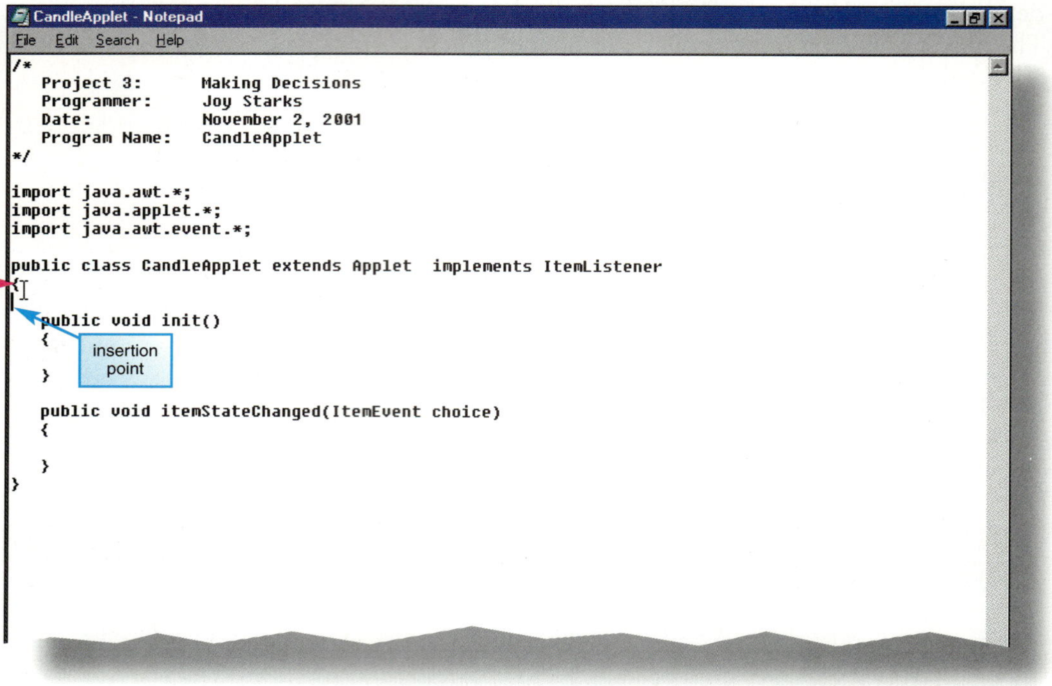

```
CandleApplet - Notepad                                          _ |8|x|
File   Edit   Search   Help
/*
    Project 3:       Making Decisions
    Programmer:      Joy Starks
    Date:            November 2, 2001
    Program Name:    CandleApplet
*/

import java.awt.*;
import java.applet.*;
import java.awt.event.*;

public class CandleApplet extends Applet   implements ItemListener
{

    public void init()
    {

    }

    public void itemStateChanged(ItemEvent choice)
    {

    }
}
```

*(callout: line 13)*
*(callout: insertion point)*

**FIGURE 3-48**

**2** **Enter the code from Table 3-14 on the previous page to create the components for the applet.**

*The code to construct the components displays (Figure 3-49). Notice the check box constructors are grouped with the name, shippingGroup.*

**3** **Click File on the Notepad menu bar and then click Save.**

*The file is saved on the floppy disk in drive A.*

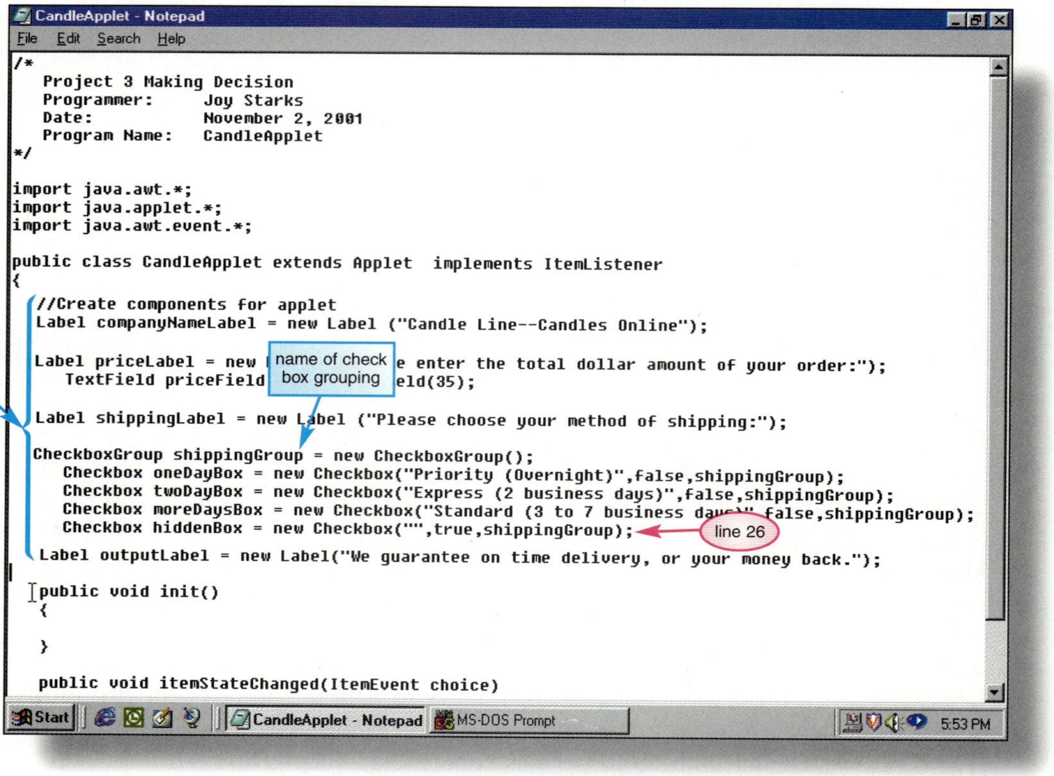

```
CandleApplet - Notepad                                          _ |8|x|
File   Edit   Search   Help
/*
    Project 3 Making Decision
    Programmer:      Joy Starks
    Date:            November 2, 2001
    Program Name:    CandleApplet
*/

import java.awt.*;
import java.applet.*;
import java.awt.event.*;

public class CandleApplet extends Applet   implements ItemListener
{
    //Create components for applet
    Label companyNameLabel = new Label ("Candle Line--Candles Online");

    Label priceLabel = new       e enter the total dollar amount of your order:");
       TextField priceField      eld(35);

    Label shippingLabel = new Label ("Please choose your method of shipping:");

    CheckboxGroup shippingGroup = new CheckboxGroup();
       Checkbox oneDayBox = new Checkbox("Priority (Overnight)",false,shippingGroup);
       Checkbox twoDayBox = new Checkbox("Express (2 business days)",false,shippingGroup);
       Checkbox moreDaysBox = new Checkbox("Standard (3 to 7 business days",false,shippingGroup);
       Checkbox hiddenBox = new Checkbox("",true,shippingGroup);
    Label outputLabel = new Label("We guarantee on time delivery, or your money back.");

    public void init()
    {

    }

    public void itemStateChanged(ItemEvent choice)
```

*(callout: component constructors)*
*(callout: name of check box grouping)*
*(callout: line 26)*

Start | CandleApplet - Notepad | MS-DOS Prompt | 5:53 PM

**FIGURE 3-49**

The hidden check box on line 26 is not added to the applet's viewing area, as you will see in the next series of steps. That way, if you want to clear all the other check boxes in the group, you can simply set the hidden check box to true, thus changing the others to false automatically.

## Adding Components, Color, and Focus to the Applet

You may recall that the **add** method takes an argument of a declared component and adds it to the Applet Viewer window when the applet is initiated. The **addItemListener** event then causes the applet to listen for clicks initiated by the user. When the click occurs, a series of associated objects and methods change, including the getState method, the itemStateChanged method, and the ItemEvent object. Table 3-15 describes the general form of the addItemListener event.

Applets and Web pages rely on the use of graphics, animation, sound, and color to entice viewing and provide entertainment. While sophisticated graphics and animation may be best served with another design tool, Java can produce colors rather simply. Two methods help you change the color of your applet: the setBackground method and the setForeground method. Each method works the same way; each takes a color argument. The **setBackground** method changes the color behind the text. The **setForeground** method changes the text color. You may want to change the foreground color to draw attention to a certain component or use a lighter color to make the text display better on darker backgrounds. The following line sets the background of the entire applet to blue.

| Table 3-15 | The addItemListener Event |
|---|---|
| General form: | component.addItemListener(ItemListener object) |
| Comment: | The component must be declared with a constructor before triggering the event. The ItemListener object may be the self-referential, **this** object or a constructor of a new object. |
| Example: | optBlue.addItemListener(this); |

```
setBackground(Color.blue);
```

If you want to set the color for a specific label or check box, you must precede the command with the name of the object.

```
myLabel.setForeground(Color.lightGray);
```

**Color** is an object that Java can reference. LightGray is an attribute. Table 3-16 lists valid attributes for the color object. The preset colors are medium gray for the background and black for the text.

Another method associated with applets that use text fields is the requestFocus method. The **requestFocus** method moves the insertion point to the control that calls it. In the case of text fields, the insertion point displays as a vertical flashing line in the text box.

| Table 3-16 | Valid Color Attributes | |
|---|---|---|
| **VIVID COLORS** | | |
| black | green | red |
| blue | lightGray | white |
| cyan | magenta | yellow |
| darkGray | orange | |
| gray | pink | |

**More About**

**requestFocus**

When a component has the focus, the insertion point will display or the button will have a dotted box around its caption. Java has no preset or default focus; you must set focus in the code. You may, however, move it from one component to the next as the user completes tasks.

```
myField.requestFocus();
```

**Table 3-17**

| LINE | CODE |
|------|------|
| 32 | //Add components to window and set colors |
| 33 | setBackground(Color.cyan); |
| 34 | add(companyNameLabel); |
| 35 | add(priceLabel); |
| 36 | add(priceField); |
| 37 | priceField.requestFocus(); |
| 38 | add(oneDayBox); |
| 39 | oneDayBox.addItemListener(this); |
| 40 | add(twoDayBox); |
| 41 | twoDayBox.addItemListener(this); |
| 42 | add(moreDaysBox); |
| 43 | moreDaysBox.addItemListener(this); |
| 44 | add(outputLabel); |

Displaying the insertion point helps users focus on the appropriate spot to enter the next item of text and commonly is used when clearing an incorrect entry, to let the user try another entry.

Table 3-17 displays the code for the init method to set the background color, add the components to the applet, and set the focus to the text field. Perform the following steps to code the init method.

### TO CODE THE INIT METHOD

**1** Click the Notepad window inside the init method at line 32.

**2** Enter the code from Table 3-17 to create the add methods, their corresponding ItemListener statements, color, and focus.

**3** Click File on the Notepad menu bar and then click Save.

*The add methods and addItemListener methods display (Figure 3-50). The file is saved on the floppy disk in drive A.*

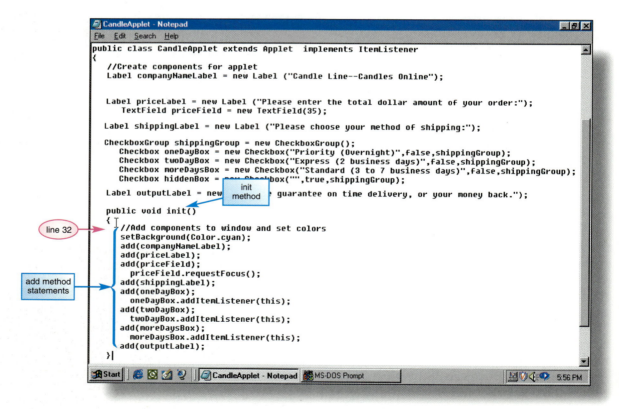

**FIGURE 3-50**

Now, during execution, the applet will display its labels, fields, and boxes, allowing the user to click one of the options created from the check box grouping. Perform the following steps to compile the applet and test the check box grouping.

**To Compile the Applet and Test the Check Box Grouping**

**1** **Click the MS-DOS Prompt button on** the taskbar. Type `javac CandleApplet.java` **and then press the ENTER key to compile the program. If there are errors, fix them in the Notepad window, save, and then recompile. Type** `appletviewer CandleApplet.html` **at the command prompt and then press the ENTER key.**

*The applet displays (Figure 3-51). Your colors may vary depending upon your system settings. Notice the insertion point in the text field. None of the options is selected, because the state value of the hidden one is set to true.*

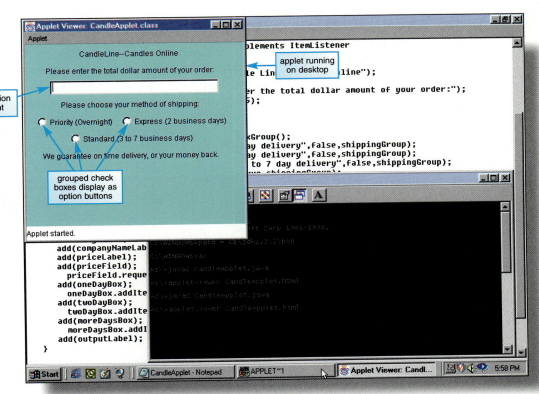

**FIGURE 3-51**

**2** **Click Priority (Overnight), and then click Express (2 business days).**

*When Express (2 business days) is selected, Priority (Overnight) automatically displays deselected (Figure 3-52).*

**3** **Close the applet by clicking the Close button on the Applet Viewer title bar.**

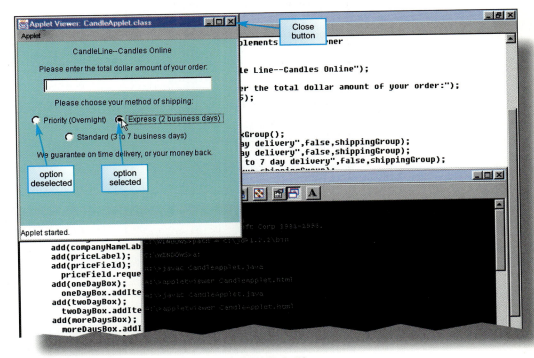

**FIGURE 3-52**

Using a hidden check box as part of the option group forces the user to make a decision, rather than letting a default selection dictate the course of the program.

## Decisions in the Applet

When one of the grouped check boxes is selected during execution, the ItemListener changes the state of the component. That means when you click a check box, the itemStateChanged event occurs automatically. The getState method then evaluates to true and can be tested with coding. In this applet, the itemStateChanged event will perform the tests necessary to check for a valid selection and assign a shipping cost. You will use Java's try and catch constant to test for errors and exceptions. The try block is shown in Table 3-18. The catch block is shown in Table 3-19.

**Table 3-18**

| LINE | CODE |
|------|------|

```
48     try
49     {
50        double shipping;
51        double price = Double.parseDouble(priceField.getText());
52
53        //Check to see if price is greater than zero
54        if (price <= 0) throw new NumberFormatException();
55
56        //Check to see which option button is selected
57        if (oneDayBox.getState())
58           shipping = 14.95;
59        else
60           if (twoDayBox.getState())
61              shipping = 11.95;
62           else
63              if (price > 75)
64                 shipping = 0;
65              else
66                 shipping = 5.95;
67
68        //Display Output
69        outputLabel.setForeground(Color.black);
70        outputLabel.setText("Your total cost is $" + (price+shipping));
71     }
```

**Table 3-19**

| LINE | CODE |
|------|------|

```
73     catch (NumberFormatException e)
74     {
75        outputLabel.setText("You must enter a dollar amount greater than zero");
76        outputLabel.setForeground(Color.red);
77        hiddenBox.setState(true);
78        priceField.setText("");
79        priceField.requestFocus();
80     }
```

Perform the following steps to code the try and catch construct for the applet.

## TO ENTER THE TRY AND CATCH BLOCKS IN THE APPLET

**1** Click the Notepad window. Click the blank line inside the braces of the itemStateChanged block.

**2** Enter the try block code from Table 3-18.

**3** Enter the catch block code from Table 3-19.

**4** Click File on the menu bar and then click Save.

*The try and catch blocks display (Figure 3-53). The file is saved on the floppy disk in drive A.*

```
CandleApplet - Notepad
File  Edit  Search  Help

        try
        {
            double shipping;
            double price = Double.parseDouble(priceField.getText());

            //Check to see if price is greater than zero
            if (price <= 0) throw new NumberFormatException();

            //Check to see which option button is selected
            if (oneDayBox.getState())
                shipping = 14.95;
            else
                if (twoDayBox.getState())
                    shipping = 11.95;
                else
                    if (price>75)
                        shipping = 0;
                    else
                        shipping = 5.95;

            //Display output
            outputLabel.setForeground(Color.black);
            outputLabel.setText("Your total cost is $" + (price+shipping));
        }

        catch (NumberFormatException e)
        {
            outputLabel.setText("You must enter a dollar amount greater than zero");
            outputLabel.setForeground(Color.red);
            hiddenBox.setState(true);
            priceField.setText("");
            priceField.requestFocus();
        }
    }
}
```

try block → (points to try block)
catch block → (points to catch block)

**FIGURE 3-53**

If the catch block is executed, a message will display in red, the visible options will be cleared, the text field will be cleared of any wrong input, and the focus will be reset to that text field.

Because the switch statement cannot test the boolean state of a check box, the nested if statements are used in the try block to determine which check box has been selected (Figure 3-53). You will learn other ways to check the state of components in a later project.

## Executing the Applet

The applet is complete. Figure 3-54 on the next page displays the code for the entire program with brackets matching the beginning and closing braces of each block. Perform the following steps to compile and execute the applet.

**More About**

**User Editing in Text Fields**

When a TextField has the capability of accepting keystrokes, which it does by default, Java considers it editable. However, if you do not wish to allow a user to go back and change their previous answers, you can use a method called setEditable. The code would be: answerField.setEditable(false).

```
/*
    Project 3:      Making Decision
    Programmer:     Joy Starks
    Date:           November 2, 2001
    Program Name:   CandleApplet
*/

import java.awt.*;
import java.applet.*;
import java.awt.event.*;

public class CandleApplet extends Applet implements ItemListener
{
    //Create components for applet
    Label companyNameLabel = new Label ("CandleLine--Candles Online");

    Label priceLabel = new Label ("Please enter the total dollar amount of your order:");
        TextField priceField = new TextField(35);

    Label shippingLabel = new Label ("Please choose your method of shipping:");

    CheckboxGroup shippingGroup = new CheckboxGroup();
        Checkbox oneDayBox = new Checkbox("Priority (Overnight)",false,shippingGroup);
        Checkbox twoDayBox = new Checkbox("Express (2 business days)",false,shippingGroup);
        Checkbox moreDaysBox = new Checkbox("Standard (3 to 7 business days)",false,shippingGroup);
        Checkbox hiddenBox = new Checkbox("",true,shippingGroup);

    Label outputLabel = new Label("We guarantee on time delivery, or your money back.");

    public void init()
    {
        //Add components to window and set colors
        setBackground(Color.cyan);
        add(companyNameLabel);
        add(priceLabel);
        add(priceField);
            priceField.requestFocus();
        add(shippingLabel);
        add(oneDayBox);
            oneDayBox.addItemListener(this);
        add(twoDayBox);
            twoDayBox.addItemListener(this);
        add(moreDaysBox);
            moreDaysBox.addItemListener(this);
        add(outputLabel);
    }

    public void itemStateChanged(ItemEvent choice)
    {
        try
        {
            double shipping;
            double price = Double.parseDouble(priceField.getText());

            //Check to see if price is greater than zero
            if (price <= 0) throw new NumberFormatException();

            //Check to see which option button is selected
            if (oneDayBox.getState())
                shipping = 14.95;
            else
            if (twoDayBox.getState())
                    shipping = 11.95;
                else
                    if (price>75)
                        shipping = 0;
                    else
                        shipping = 5.95;

            //Display Output
            outputLabel.setForeground(Color.black);
            outputLabel.setText("Your total cost is $" + (price+shipping));
        }

        catch (NumberFormatException e)
        {
            outputLabel.setText("You must enter a dollar amount greater than zero");
            outputLabel.setForeground(Color.red);
            hiddenBox.setState(true);
            priceField.setText("");
            priceField.requestFocus();
        }
    }
}
```

**FIGURE 3-54**

## Steps: To Compile and Execute the Applet

**1** **Click the MS-DOS Prompt button on the taskbar. Type** `javac CandleApplet.java` **to compile the program. If errors occur, fix them in the Notepad window, save, and then recompile. Type** `appletviewer CandleApplet.html` **and then press the ENTER key.**

*Applet Viewer displays the CandleApplet (Figure 3-55). Notice the insertion point displays in the text field due to the requestFocus method statement.*

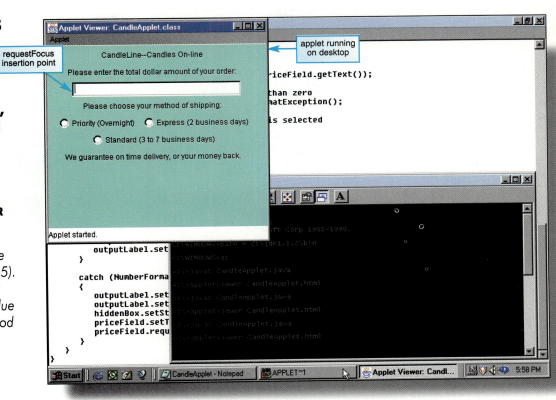

FIGURE 3-55

**2** **Type** `forty-three` **in the text field. Click any of the options.**

*The itemStateChanged event occurs (Figure 3-56). The alphabetic value created a number format exception, which then called the catch block. Notice the error message in red.*

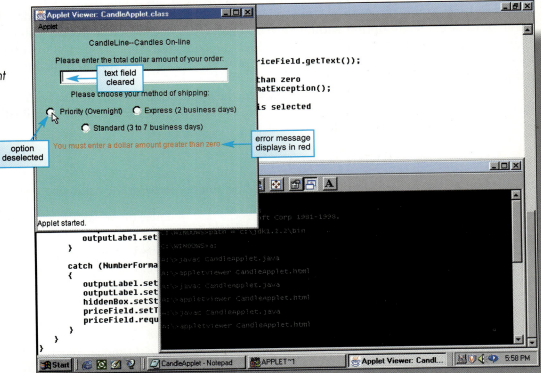

FIGURE 3-56

**3** **Type 43 in the text field and then click any option.**

The valid number caused the try block to finish without calling catch, so a total charge displays (Figure 3-57). You may test other values and shipping options.

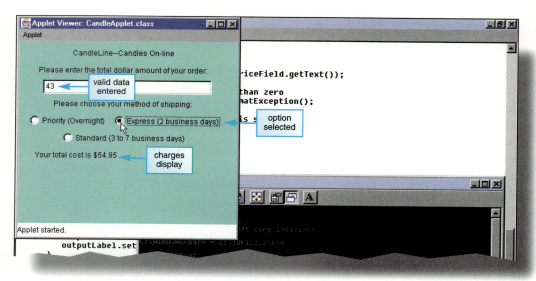

**4** **Close Applet Viewer, Notepad, and the MS-DOS Prompt window by clicking the respective Close buttons on the title bars.**

**FIGURE 3-57**

You also may run the applet using a browser. Simply type the complete path of the host document, a:\CandleApplet.html, in the Address or Location text box of the browser.

# Project Summary

This project presented a series of steps and a discussion of a Java application to calculate shipping charges for an e-commerce site. You first coded the standalone application, including the try and catch blocks to handle possible exceptions. You used an if structure to test for valid prices. You created a user-defined method, called from main, to obtain a menu option within a given range. Using the switch structure, you calculated a shipping charge based on user input. Finally, you included the code in a while loop to allow users to try again, in case they enter inaccurate data. At each step of the process, you coded a stub and then tested small sections of code before moving on to the next component.

In the last part of the project, you converted the application into an applet with check boxes. You set the focus, changed the color, and instantiated a check box grouping for a mutually exclusive choice.

# What You Should Know

Having completed this project, you now should be able to perform the following tasks:

▶ Code and Test the if Statement (J 3.24)
▶ Code the Applet Stub (J 3.45)
▶ Code the init Method (J 3.50)
▶ Code the switch Structure (J 3.36)
▶ Compile and Execute the Applet (J 3.55)
▶ Compile the Applet and Test the Check Box Grouping (J 3.51)
▶ Construct Components (J 3.48)
▶ Create the Host Document (J 3.43)
▶ Enter the Beginning Code (J 3.10)
▶ Enter Code for the getCost Method (J 3.30)
▶ Enter Output Code (J 3.33)

▶ Enter the try and catch Blocks (J 3.16)
▶ Enter the try and catch Blocks in the Applet (J 3.53)
▶ Loop Using the while Statement (J 3.38)
▶ Save, Compile, and Execute the Source Code (J 3.11)
▶ Save, Compile, and Test the Applet Stub (J 3.45)
▶ Save, Compile, and Test the getCost Method Stub (J 3.33)
▶ Save, Compile, and Test the switch Structure (J 3.37)
▶ Save, Compile, and Test the while Structure (J 3.41)
▶ Set up the Desktop (J 3.8)
▶ Test the Program for Exceptions (J 3.18)

# Test Your Knowledge

## 1 True/False

**Instructions:** Circle T if the statement is true or F is the statement is false.

T  F  1. Modularity means breaking a large program's source code down into smaller sections.
T  F  2. A stub is a program that does not accept user input.
T  F  3. Exceptions are non-primitive data types.
T  F  4. The finally block can be used to perform an end of processing routine associated with the try and catch blocks.
T  F  5. A method is the code used to perform an operation or service.
T  F  6. A user-defined method must reside within a program or class.
T  F  7. Scope is a data type.
T  F  8. An end if command must close each If...Then...Else structure.
T  F  9. Check boxes and grouped check boxes display identically in applets.
T  F  10. A set of grouped check boxes creates a mutually exclusive group.

## 2 Multiple Choice

**Instructions:** Circle the correct response.

1. A control structure is referred to as _____ when it is located completely within another structure.
   a. hidden  b. never executed  c. local in scope  d. nested

2. Statements and commands common to the beginning of interactive programs include all of the following *except*_____.
   a. import statements  b. finally block  c. class and method headers  d. comments

3. Java uses a(n) _____ statement to evaluate a value for the case structure.
   a. scope  b. case  c. switch  d. if

4. An operation that attempts to use a float value in a location declared to be integer, is an example of a(n) _____.
   a. number format exception  c. IOException
   b. memory error  d. compile-time exception

5. A(n) _____ check might be used to look for data that fits the program's specifications for a correct data type.
   a. exception  b. reasonableness  c. range  d. validity

6. Conditions in Java are _____ expressions that evaluate to true or false.
   a. untested  b. boolean  c. variable  d. iterative

7. The control structure that allows for more than two choices when a condition is evaluated is called a(n) _____.
   a. case  b. if  c. try  d. while

8. Which of the following is not a conditional operator?
   a. &&  b. >  c. ||  d. *

*(continued)*

# Test Your Knowledge

**Multiple Choice** *(continued)*

9. A hidden check box in a grouped set _____.
   a. can be used to clear others in the mutually exclusive set
   b. can receive the focus and be selected
   c. uses a constructor like other check boxes
   d. all of the above

10. When a check box is selected, the _____ method is called.
   a. itemStateChanged     b. click          c. add              d. listen

## 3 Understanding Applet Components

**Instructions:** In Figure 3-58, arrows point to components of a Java applet running on the desktop. Identify the various components of the applet in the spaces provided.

AppletViewer: Fries
Applet
What kind of sandwich would you like? — 1. _____
2. _____
3. _____
Would you like fries with that?
Yes          No          4. _____
Condiments          Sizes
☐ Catsup          ○ Small
5. _____          ☐ Mustard          ○ Medium
6. _____
☐ Pickles          ○ Large

**FIGURE 3-58**

## 4 Understanding Conditions

**Instructions:** Study the following conditions and determine whether they evaluate to true or false. In those examples that display more than one condition, tell which condition confirms the true or false state.

1. $25 == 25$ _____
2. $(18 < 19)$ && $(12 > 14)$ _____
3. $(18 < 19)$ || $(12 > 14)$ _____
4. $31 <= 31$ _____
5. $!(5 == 5)$ _____
6. $(a == a)$ || $(b == b)$ || $(c == c)$ _____
7. $!( (14 > 12)$ && $(27 => 26) )$ _____
8. $(45 < 55)$ && $(55 > 45)$ _____
9. $(100 + 5) != (40 + 65)$ _____
10. $(a == a)$ || $!(a == a)$ _____

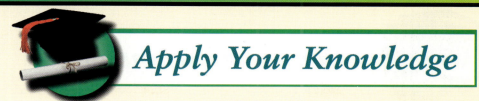

# Apply Your Knowledge

## 1 Multiplication Quiz

**Instructions:** Start Notepad and maximize the window, if necessary. Open the file Apply3.java, from the Data Disk (see the inside back cover for instructions on how to obtain a copy of the Data Disk). This Multiplication Quiz asks students to enter the multiplication table they wish to practice and then prompts them for each answer, multiplying their table value by each integer from 0 to 12. Although the program tells students whether they are right or wrong, it does not provide error checking for invalid entries such as typing errors, decimals, or strings.

Using techniques learned in this project, write the try and catch blocks to display appropriate messages if students try to enter non-integer numbers. Also write a while loop to keep repeating the prompt if the students enter invalid values. Figure 3-59 displays the completed program during execution.

**FIGURE 3-59**

1. With the Apply3.java code displayed in the Notepad window, substitute your name and date in the block comment at the beginning. Type `Multiply` as the new class name. Edit the name of the class in the class header, as well.

2. Save the file on your floppy disk with the name, "Multiply.java" as the file name. Print a copy if you wish, to reference while completing this lab.

3. Open the MS-DOS Prompt window. If you downloaded JDK from the Sun Web site, set the path to the location of your Java bin by typing `path=c:\jdk1.2.2\bin` at the command prompt and press the ENTER key. If you installed the Java compiler from the JBuilder3 CD-ROM that may accompany this text, type `path=c:\jbuilder3\java\bin` and then press the ENTER key.

4. Change to your floppy disk drive by typing `a:` and then press the ENTER key.

5. Compile your program by typing `javac Multiply.java` and then press the ENTER key.

6. Run the program by typing `java Multiply` and then press the ENTER key. As the program executes, enter an integer for the multiplication table value, such as 8. Respond to the prompts with whole numbers.

7. Now run the program again, but enter a non-integer value for the multiplication table value, such as 7.5. Java throws an exception, and you will receive a NumberFormatException message.

8. Click the Notepad window. In the main method, enclose the section of code labeled, //Calling the user-defined methods, in a try block. Remember to enter the try statement and an opening brace before the section and a closing brace after that section.

*(continued)*

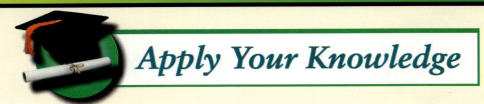

*Apply Your Knowledge*

**Multiplication Quiz** *(continued)*

9. Below the try block, enter a catch block for a NumberFormatException as follows:

```
catch(NumberFormatException e)
{
    System.out.println("I'm sorry, you may enter only whole numbers");
}
```

10. Save the file by clicking File on Notepad's menu bar and then click Save.

11. Click the MS-DOS Prompt button on the taskbar and then compile the program again with the javac command. If necessary, fix any errors in the Notepad window, save, and then recompile.

12. Run the program again, testing with both integer and non-integer values. Notice that an appropriate message now displays, but students still must run the program again to answer any additional questions.

13. Click the Notepad window and enclose both the try and catch blocks in a while loop by entering while(!done) and an opening brace before the section of code and a closing brace after that section.

14. Before the closing brace of the try block, enter a new line of code, done = true; to terminate the loop during execution. Save the file by clicking File on Notepad's menu bar and then click Save.

15. In the MS-DOS Prompt window, compile and run the program again, testing with both integer and non-integer values. Notice that students now are directed back to the beginning of the program after the message displays.

16. Click the Notepad window. In the takeQuiz method, find the statement, while (count <= 12). Click below the while block's opening brace. Enclose all the code within the while block in a try block. Include all the code statements in the try block, but not the opening or closing braces of the while block itself. The last inclusive line in the new try block will be: count = count + 1;

17. Below the try block, enter a catch block for a NumberFormatException as follows:

```
catch(NumberFormatException e)
{
    System.out.println("I'm sorry, your answer must be a whole number. Try again.");
}
```

18. Save the file by clicking File on Notepad's menu bar and then click Save.

19. In the MS-DOS Prompt window, compile and run the program again, testing with both integer and non-integer values. Students now are given a chance to answer the question again after the message displays.

20. Print a copy of your code for your instructor.

# In the Lab

## 1 Using switch and try Blocks to Validate User Input

**Problem:** You would like to write a program to help beginning Java programmers understand data types. You have noticed that students have trouble differentiating among doubles, ints, strings, and other data types. You decide to create a menu-driven program to test their knowledge. Beginning with a try block, the program should allow users to choose a data type. Then, based on a switch structure, the user should be prompted to enter a value that would fit that specific data type. If the user enters correct data — data that parses correctly — the program should display positive feedback. If the inputted data does not match the chosen data type, the parse statement will throw a NumberFormatException. In the catch block, the program should display an appropriate error message, and then allow the user to try again. A sample menu of choices displays in Figure 3-60.

**FIGURE 3-60**

**Instructions:**

1. Start Notepad.
2. Enter general documentation comments, including the name of this lab, your name, the date, and the file name, Menu.
3. Import the java.io.* package.
4. Type `public class Menu` and an opening brace to begin the class.
5. Type `public static void main(String[] args) throws IOException` and an opening brace to begin main.
6. Declare the following variables:

   ```
   BufferedReader dataIn = new BufferedReader(new InputStreamReader(System.in));
   String strChoice, strTryString, strTryInt, strTryDouble;
   int choice, tryInt;
   double tryDouble;
   boolean done = false;
   ```
7. Begin a while(!done) loop to repeat as long as the user does not enter the menu choice to quit.
8. Inside a try block, type System.out.println commands to print a menu with four choices, as shown in Figure 3-60.
9. Type `strChoice = dataIn.readLine();` to allow user input. To parse the choice, type `choice = Integer.parseInteger(strChoice);` on the next line.
10. Create a switch structure to test for each of the four choices. Type the header, `switch(choice)` and then press the ENTER key. Type an opening brace.

*(continued)*

# In the Lab

**Using switch and try Blocks to Validate User Input** *(continued)*

11. Create each case, using pages J 3.35 through J 3.37 as a guide for the switch, case and break statements.
    ▶ Case 1: Prompt the user for a string. Read the input as strTryString. Display a message that informs users they are correct, as *any* input can be saved as a string. Enter the break statement.
    ▶ Case 2: Create a try block that prompts the user for an int value. Read the input as strTryInt. Parse the value into tryInt. Display a message that informs users they are correct. Enter the break statement.
    ▶ Case 3: Create a try block that prompts the user for a double value. Read the input as strTryDouble. Parse the value into tryDouble. Display a message that informs users they are correct. Enter the break statement.
    ▶ Case 4: Set done equal to true. Display a closing message. Enter the break statement.
    ▶ Case default: Throw a new NumberFormatException
12. Close the switch block with a closing brace.
13. Create a catch block by typing, `catch(NumberFormatException e)` and then an opening brace.
14. Display an appropriate message directing the user to try again and then close the catch block with a closing brace.
15. Close the try block, the while block, and the main method with closing braces.
16. Save the file as "Menu.java" on your floppy disk.
17. Open the MS-DOS Prompt, set the path, and log onto drive A.
18. Compile the program. If necessary, fix any errors in the Notepad window, save, and then recompile.
19. Run the program. Enter various values for each menu choice. Check your answers.
20. Print a copy of the source code for your instructor.
21. As an extra credit assignment, add choices to the menu for longs, bytes, and boolean data types.

# 2 Writing User-Defined Methods

**Problem:** A small proprietary school that offers distance-learning courses would like an application that calculates total tuition and fees for their students. Users will input the number of hours and the program should calculate the total cost. Cost per credit hour for full time (greater than 15 hours) is $44.50 per credit hour; 15 hours or less costs $50.00 per credit hour.

**Instructions:**

1. Start Notepad.
2. Enter general documentation comments, including the name of this lab, your name, the date, and the file name, Tuition.
3. Import the java.io.* package.
4. Create a header for the public class, Tuition, followed by an opening brace.
5. Enter the standard main method header, which throws an IOException. Type the opening brace for the main header.
6. Declare an int identifier, hours. Declare double identifiers for fees, rates, and tuition.

# In the Lab

7. Enter the following method calls and then close the main method with a closing brace.

```
displayWelcome();
hours = getHours();
rate = getRate(hours);
tuition = calcTuition(hours, rate);
fees = calcFees(tuition);
displayTotal(tuition+fees);
```

8. Code the corresponding methods:

   ▶ Type `public static void displayWelcome()` and then, within that block, code the statements to display a welcome message.

   ▶ Type `public static int getHours() throws IOException` and then, within that block, construct an instance of the BufferedReader. Declare strHours as a String and hours as an int, setting hours to an initial value of zero. Display a prompt that allows the user to enter a string value, strHours, for the total number of hours. Parse that value into the integer value, hours. This method also should include a try and catch block for non-integer input. This method will return the int, hours to main.

   ▶ Type `public static double getRate(int hours)` and then, within that block, include an if statement for hours greater than 15, which will calculate a rate per credit hour. This method will return the double, rate to main.

   ▶ Type `public static double calcTuition(int hours, double rate)` and then, within that block, code statements to accept two values, multiply them, and return a double value, tuition to main.

   ▶ Type `public static double calcFees(double tuition)` and then, within that block, code statements to accept the double value, tuition, multiply it by .08, and then return a double value, fees to main.

   ▶ Type `public static void displayTotal(double total)` and then, within that block use the System.out.println method to display the value passed by adding tuition and fees, along with a closing message.

9. Save the file as "Tuition.java" on your floppy disk.
10. Open the MS-DOS Prompt window, set the path, and log onto drive A.
11. Compile the program. If necessary, fix any errors in the Notepad window, save, and then recompile.
12. Run the program. Enter values both less than and greater than 15. Check your answers.
13. Print a copy of the source code for your instructor.

# In the Lab

## 3 Creating an Applet with Check Boxes

**Problem:** Figure 3-58 on page J 3.58 displays an interface for an applet relating to fast food. Using the techniques you learned in Project 3, create the interface with all its components. Add enough functionality to make the selection of both grouped and individual check boxes work. The text field should receive the focus and allow data entry, but the itemStateChanged event may contain just a stub.

**Instructions:**

1. Start Notepad.
2. Enter general documentation comments, including the name of this lab, your name, the date, and the file name: FriesApplet.
3. Import the following packages: java.awt.*, java.applet.*, and java.awt.event.*. Remember to use the import statement and conclude each line with a semicolon.
4. Enter a public class header for Fries that extends Applet and implements ItemListener.
5. Create the components as shown in Figure 3-58 on page J 3.58, using a constructor for each: sandwichPromptLabel, sandwichInputField, friesPromptLabel, yesButton, noButton, condimentsLabel, sizesLabel, catsupBox, mustardBox, picklesBox, sizesGroup, smallBox, mediumBox, largeBox. Set the length of sandwichInputField to 25. The grouped check boxes represent the sizes, and the condiments are individual check boxes. Set all the condiment check boxes to false. Set the first of the grouped check boxes to true and the other sizes to false.
6. Create an init method by typing `public void init()` as the header and an opening brace.
7. Set the background color to red.
8. Enter add methods for each of the components created in Step 5. Use the requestFocus method to create an insertion point in the text field. Use an addItemListener(this) for each of the boxes and buttons. Type the closing brace for the init method.
9. Type `public void itemStateChanged(ItemEvent choice)` as the header for another method. Type an opening brace and closing brace to stub in the event.
10. Save the file as "FriesApplet.java" on your floppy disk.
11. Click New on Notepad's File menu and then enter the HTML code to display the applet. Be sure to include the beginning and ending HTML and APPLET tags. Use a width of 350 and a height of 300.
12. Save the file as "FriesApplet.html" on your floppy disk.
13. Open the MS-DOS Prompt window and set the path. Log onto drive A.
14. Compile your program by typing `javac FriesApplet.java` at the command prompt. Remember that Java is case-sensitive with respect to file names.
15. If no compilation errors occur, execute the applet by typing `appletviewer FriesApplet.html` at the command prompt. Click each of the buttons and boxes. Notice the check boxes toggle on and off, individually, while the grouped check boxes are mutually exclusive.
16. Print a copy of the source code for your instructor.
17. As an extra credit assignment, code the itemStateChanged event.

# Cases and Places

The difficulty of these case studies varies:
◗ are the least difficult; ◗◗ are more difficult; and ◗◗◗ are the most difficult.

**1** ◗ You are serving an internship with the traffic court in the city where you live. The clerks in the traffic court office want a simple application that will allow them to enter the actual speed limit, the speed at which the offender was traveling, and the number of previous tickets that person has received. The application should have a menu system to allow users to exit the application, begin again, and calculate charges. The application should calculate and display how many miles over the speed limit the offender was traveling, the cost of the speeding ticket, and court costs. Use $10.00 as the amount to be charged for each mile per hour over the speed limit. The court cost should begin at $53.20 and increase by $20.00 for each subsequent offense up to the third offense (that will represent the maximum court cost).

**2** ◗ Lions, Tigers, and Bears is a pet clinic with several locations. The office manager has asked you to create an applet that could run from a browser at all the offices. The applet should be designed with individual check boxes to select the various services such as office visits, vaccinations, hospitalization, heartworm prevention, boarding, dentistry, x-rays, laboratory work, and prescriptions. As each service is selected, the charge for the service should display . After all selections have been made, the charges should be added together to arrive at a total amount due and display when a command button is clicked. The office manager also would like to clear all the check boxes for the next customer.

**3** ◗◗ You have been asked to develop an interactive applet that will run on a kiosk at the planetarium. The applet is to display the planet names with individual check boxes, and their gravities. Then, based on a grouped check box selection, the distance of the planet to the sun or distance of the planet to the earth should display beside the checked planet.

**4** ◗◗ Reasonable Computers Corporation would like an applet to calculate the cost of adding peripherals to their basic PC system. Use at least six single check boxes for various types of peripheral devices including printers, monitors, modems, or other devices with which you are familiar. Assume a basic system price of $500 and then add appropriate prices based on user checks. Create a button to perform the calculation and display the final price.

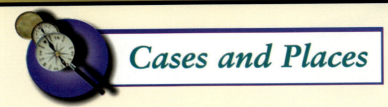

# Cases and Places

**5** ▶▶▶ Wright's Garage wants an interactive program that requires the mechanic to enter the tire pressure from four tires on any given car that comes into the garage. The program should first print out a menu for driving types: normal, hauling, and rugged. After the mechanic chooses a driving type, the program should ask for the four tire pressures with appropriate prompts. Finally, the program should tell the mechanic what adjustments to make. Assume the following:

> ▶ For normal driving, all four tires should be inflated between 33 and 43 pounds per square inch (psi).
> ▶ For hauling, the rear tires should be approximately 10% greater.
> ▶ For rugged terrain, the rear tires should be approximately 15% greater.

**6** ▶▶▶ Your city library has hired you on a consulting basis to provide them with an application for overdue charges. The charges apply to overdue books, records, tapes, CDs, and videotapes. The books can be either hardbound or paperback. The librarians want an easy way to calculate the overdue charges, keeping in mind that a borrower could be returning multiple overdue items. Some method of looping to enter the next item is necessary. The total number of overdue items and the total amount due should display.

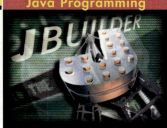

# APPENDIX A
# Installing Java

# Installing Java

Sun Microsystems calls its recent release of Java the **Java 2 Standard Development Kit** (**SDK**). The SDK includes the compiler and run-time system you will need to execute the Java projects in this textbook. You can obtain the Java 2 SDK and its documentation in one of several different ways. For more information, visit the Java Programming Web page (www.scsite.com/java/more.htm) and then click Installing Java.

## Downloading Java 2 SDK from the Sun Microsystems Web Site

If you download the free SDK from the Sun Microsystems Web site, you will get the most recent version of the Java SDK. A major drawback of downloading the SDK from the Sun Web site is the time it takes to download the necessary files. The speed is dependant upon the speed of your computer system, the speed of your modem, the connection rate, and the operation of the site itself. It may take anywhere from 20 minutes to an hour or more.

The Java 2 SDK download will save a 20-megabyte file on your hard drive. You then must run or execute that file to decompress the downloaded files and install the components on your system. The files, when installed on your system, will use approximately 44 megabytes of storage. Make sure you have a total of 64 megabytes of storage space before you begin the download process: 44 megabytes for the installed file and 20 megabytes for the download file. After the installation, you may delete the original download file because you no longer will need it.

Perform the following steps to download the SDK from the Sun Microsystems Web site.

### TO DOWNLOAD THE SDK

1. With your system connected to the Web, start your browser. Type www.scsite.com/java/more.htm in the Address or Go To textbox. Press the ENTER key. When the page displays, click the Installing Java link.

2. When the Sun Microsystems Java Web page displays, scroll to the section titled Production Releases. Click the link, Java™ 2 SDK v 1.2.2-001 Windows 95/98/NT Production Release, or the link to the most recent version of Java on the page.

3. When the Download Web page displays, scroll to the section titled, Download Java 2 SDK v 1.2.2-001 for Windows 95 / 98 / NT 4.0 (Intel Platform). Be sure that the One large bundle option button is selected and then click the continue button.

4. When the License & Export page displays, read the terms of agreement, and then click the Agree button. When the Download Java Development Kit Web page displays, click the FTP download button.

5. If a File Download dialog box displays, make sure the Save this program to disk option button is selected. At this point, some browsers automatically may begin downloading the file with the default name and the default location. If your browser begins the download, skip to Step 8.

6. If your browser displayed a File Download dialog box, click its OK button. When the Save As dialog box displays, if necessary, choose Desktop in the Save in list. Click the Save button.

7. When the download is complete, the message, Download Complete, will display in the File Download dialog box. Click the Close button.

8. Close the browser. Double-click the file, jdk1_2_2-001-win, on the desktop or in the folder to which you downloaded.

9 After a few seconds, the Welcome dialog box of the Java Development Kit Setup wizard will display. Click the Next button.

10 At each of the setup screens, after reading the screen, click the Next or Yes button to proceed. Click the Yes or OK button to accept the default folder locations for the installation when prompted. When the installation is complete, click the Finish button.

Once you have extracted the files for the Java 2 SDK, you may delete the executable file that you downloaded. Simply right-click the file and then click Delete on the shortcut menu.

An alternative to downloading is to purchase the Java 2 SDK on a CD-ROM from Sun Microsystems. Purchasing the product avoids the long download time and serves as a backup if you need to reinstall.

## Using the Java 2 SDK Documentation

Sun Microsystems also provides free documentation on the Java 2 SDK platform. Available in a wide variety of formats, including HTML and PDF files, the documentation on the Sun Microsystems Web site is updated regularly. You may browse, search, or download the documentation. For more information, visit the Java Programming Web Page (www.scsite.com/java/more.htm) and then click Documentation.

The Java 2 SDK documentation files contain a wide variety of information about Java topics including the release notes, language specifications, basic features, and the **application program interface (API)**. The Java API is the accumulation of all the specific classes and methods prescribed by Java.

Perform the following steps to browse the Java 2 SDK Documentation on the Sun Microsystems Web site.

### TO BROWSE THE JAVA 2 SDK DOCUMENTATION

1 With your system connected to the Web, start your browser. Type www.scsite.com/java/more.htm in the Address or Go To text box. Press the ENTER key. When the page displays, click Documentation.

2 When the Sun Microsystems Web page displays, click the Browse the Java 2 SDK Documentation link.

3 When the documentation page displays, read the various available documentation topics and then scroll to the section titled, Java Foundation Classes (JFC).

4 Click a topic, such as Swing Components. One at a time, click at least three different links on the page and print a copy of each page you choose for your instructor.

The Java documentation files include links to tutorials, articles about implementation, and sample programs and applets that you may run on the Web or download.

## Installing Inprise's JBuilder 3 Software

Another way to obtain the SDK and its documentation is to obtain an Integrated Development Environment (IDE) that includes the SDK. An **IDE** is a third party software tool developed to assist with the writing of Java programs. Usually, it is **GUI-based**, which means that the IDE contains buttons, menus, and Help files to support the software. A growing number of IDEs, such as JBuilder 3, have come on the market in the past few years. These IDEs provide programmers with a set of development tools, which may include color-coded editors, wizards, and pre-written Java classes. A copy of JBuilder 3 may be included on a CD-ROM with this textbook.

JBuilder 3 requires approximately 188 megabytes of storage space on your hard disk. An advantage of this software is the quick installation of the SDK compared with downloading files from the Sun Microsystems Web site. You also can use the JBuilder IDE to create Java programs and applets.

Perform the following steps to install Inprise's JBuilder 3 software that may be included with this textbook. Installing this software also will install the SDK, the compiler, and run-time environment to run applications and applets from the command prompt.

### Steps To Install Inprise's JBuilder 3 Software

**1** **Insert the Inprise JBuilder 3 CD-ROM in your CD-ROM drive. When the Install Launcher screen displays, point to JBuilder 3 University. If the installation procedure does not begin automatically, perform the steps listed in the Other Ways at the end of these steps.**

*The Install Launcher displays (Figure A-1). The installation procedure begins.*

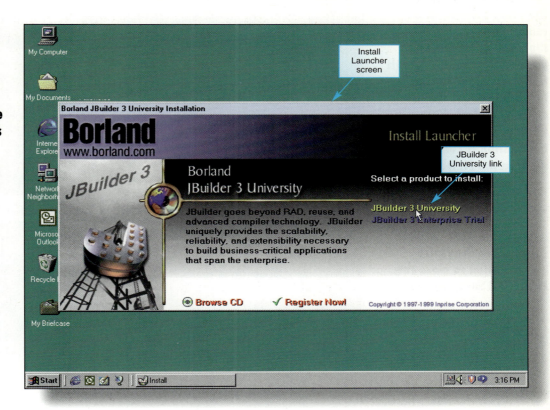

FIGURE A-1

**2** **Click JBuilder 3 University. When the Welcome dialog box of the JBuilder 3 Setup wizard displays, point to the Next button.**

*The Welcome screen is the first of several screens that display as part of the setup (Figure A-2).*

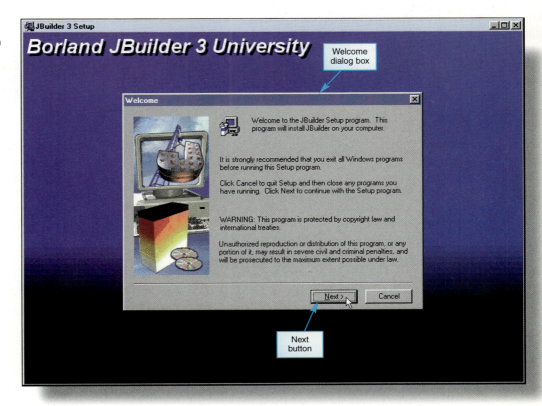

FIGURE A-2

**3** Click the Next button. At each of the setup screens, after reading the screen, click the Next or Yes button to proceed. Accept the default folder locations for the installation. Choose the default, Typical setup, when prompted. When the installation is complete, point to the Finish button.

*The JBuilder 3 software installs (Figure A-3).*

**4** Click the Finish button to close the JBuilder 3 Setup wizard.

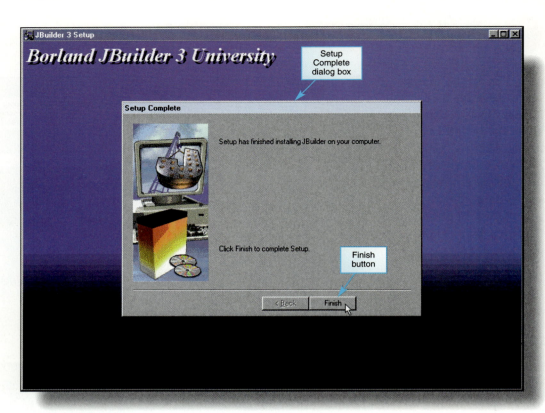

FIGURE A-3

The installation process creates a command on your Programs submenu titled, Borland JBuilder 3 University. You can use this new command to access JBuilder 3. You still can access Java from the command prompt for stand-alone applications.

*Other* **Ways**

1. Click Start button on taskbar, click Run on Start menu, click Browse button, look in CD-ROM drive, type Install.exe, click OK button

Java Programming

# APPENDIX B
# Reserved Keywords

# Reserved Keywords

The following table lists the reserved keywords in the Java programming language. Because of their reserved status, these words cannot be used as names for classes and methods or as identifiers for variables.

| | | | |
|---|---|---|---|
| abstract | else | int | static |
| boolean | extends | interface | super |
| break | false | long | switch |
| byte | final | native | synchronized |
| byvalue | finally | new | this |
| case | float | null | throw |
| cast | for | operator | throws |
| catch | future | outer | transient |
| char | generic | package | true |
| class | goto | private | try |
| const | if | protected | var |
| continue | implements | public | void |
| default | import | rest | volatile |
| do | inner | return | while |
| double | instanceof | short | |

# APPENDIX C
## Java Certification

# What Is Certification?

Certification is a process where people in the computer industry can prove they have skills in a certain computer or software related area by taking a certified exam. Software and hardware companies, government agencies, and technology consortiums offer the certified exams. For example, for application user certification, Microsoft offers several exams, including the Microsoft Office User Specialist (MOUS) exam. Another example is the A+ Certification exam, sponsored by a consortium of companies that wish to offer hardware knowledge and repair credentials. Java programmers, developers, and architects take a certified exam to demonstrate their programming skills, as well. Certification provides a standard, tangible way of measuring technical skills; it also can offer job advancement opportunities and third party validation of your skills.

Sun, IBM, and other companies offer certification exams for Java programmers. Table C-1 lists several current certification exams and their descriptions. Most of the certification exams have updated the Certified Programmer examination to the Java 2 platform.

A new Certification Initiative sponsored by companies such as Sun Microsystems, IBM, Novell, and Oracle currently is being formed which will attempt to create an industry wide standard. It will contain five exams, which will be recognized by participating companies. The goal of the initiative is to promote industry-wide standards for validating the skill of Java professionals.

Table C-1 lists some of the current certification exams. For more information on these exams and to locate an exam close to you, visit the Java Programming Web site at http://www.scsite.com/java/cert.htm.

| Table C-1 Java Certification Exams | | |
|---|---|---|
| **CERTIFICATION** | **SPONSOR** | **DESCRIPTION** |
| Sun Certified Programmer | Sun Microsystems | Beginning level. Requires the successful completion of a multiple-choice and short-answer exam covering the specifics of the Java language. It has no prerequisites. |
| Sun Certified Developer | Sun Microsystems | Requires programmer certification with any JDK release as a prerequisite. The test consists of two parts. You must download a programming assignment from the Sun Educational Services Certification Database. There is no specific time limit for the completion of the programming assignment. An essay test then is given that requires short answers regarding design decisions made in connection with the programming assignment. |
| Sun Certified Architect for Java Technology | Sun Microsystems | Requires successful completion of a multiple-choice and short-answer exam, and has no prerequisites. It is designed to test a broad scope of program design skills and object-oriented methodologies. |
| IBM Certified Specialist | IBM | Requires successful completion of a closed book, multiple-choice, computerized, knowledge-based test. It contains approximately 60 questions with a 75-minute time limit. |
| Certified Solution Developer (CSD) | IBM | Requires successful completion of 59 multiple-choice and short-answer questions, and a 120-minute time limit. |
| Certified Advanced Technical Expert (CATE) | IBM | Requires successful completion of a previous IBM/Java certification and a closed book, multiple-choice, computerized, knowledge-based test. It contains approximately 60 questions with a 120-minute time limit. |
| Certification Initiative — jCert Initiative, Inc. | Collaborative | A collaborative effort by multiple companies to bring to market a common, standard, cross-vendor, Java technology certification. |

# Why Should You Get Java Certified?

Being a Java Certified Programmer, Developer, or Architect provides a valuable industry credential – proof that you have the Java skills required by employers. By passing one or more certification exams (usually 71% is a passing grade), you demonstrate to employers your proficiency in programming or application development. Java and Internet-related technologies are among the fastest-growing areas in an ever-expanding technological society. Companies constantly are looking for employees with proven expertise and programming skills. These companies include software houses that need programmers who can get up to speed quickly, temporary employment agencies that want to prove the expertise of their workers, large corporations looking for a way to measure the skill set of potential employees, and training companies and educational institutions seeking Java programmers, teachers, and Webmasters with appropriate credentials.

# How Can You Prepare for Java Certification Exams?

Completing the projects in this textbook will give you a good start toward the certification exams. Table C-2 lists the objectives of the beginning level exam for Java Certification. Your own application and practice of Java programming is critical to your successful completion of the exam. Sun Educational Services offers a training course at various centers all over the world, as do many companies and learning centers.

### Table C-2 Objectives for Beginning Level Java Certification

**OBJECTIVES**

Demonstrate knowledge of Java programming language fundamentals by writing correctly structured Java classes for applets and applications and appropriately using all data types.

Determine the result of applying every combination of operators and assignments to any combination of types.

Declare variables and classes with appropriate use of access control, initialization, and scope.

Make correct use of all flow control constructs, including exception handling.

Make correct use of overloading, overriding, and inheritance.

Identify guaranteed garbage collection and finalization behavior.

Make correct use of Threads, Runnable, wait(), notify(), and synchronized.

Use the facility of java.lang, java.awt, java.awt.event, and java.io packages.

Recognize the benefits of encapsulation in the Object Oriented paradigm, and be able to implement tightly encapsulated classes in the Java programming language.

Use the Java Foundation Classes software to build visual applications.

Write applications that are independent of language or location, using the internationalization APIs.

Use the jar command to package together the components of a Java technology-based application.

# Shelly Cashman Series Certification Web Page

The Shelly Cashman Series Java Certification page (Figure C-1) has more than 15 Web pages you can visit to obtain additional information on Java and other certification programs. The Java Certification page (www.scsite. com/java/cert.htm) includes links to general information on certification, choosing an application for certification, preparing for the certification exam, and taking and passing the certification exam.

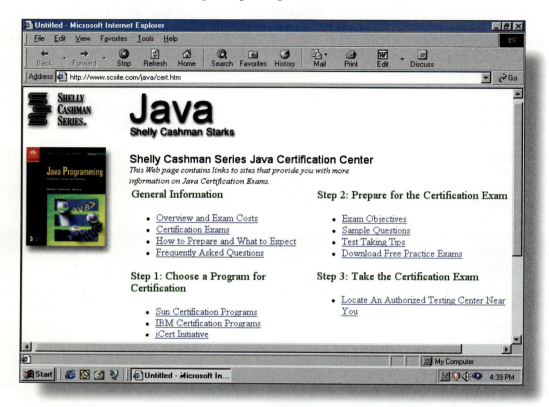

**FIGURE C-1**

Java Programming

APPENDIX D

# APPENDIX D
# Options and Exceptions

## Options and Exceptions

This appendix lists the compile and runtime options you may include at the command prompt; options that will help you manage your files, classes, and variables. This appendix also lists exceptions from the java.io package. For a complete list of exceptions from all packages, consult the Java documentation. Appendix A describes how to browse the documentation.

### Java Compiler Options

The javac compiler comes with several options to include when you compile a Java program. These options always begin with a hyphen and are typed after the word, javac. For example, if you want the compiler to display the source files that are being compiled and loaded and the total time it takes, you would type `javac -verbose Filename.java` at the command prompt. The javac compiler then would display each class that is loaded in support of the designated Filename, the creation of the new class, and the total time in milliseconds.

Table D-1 lists the options and their descriptions.

| Table D-1 | javac Options |
|---|---|
| **OPTION** | **DESCRIPTION** |
| -bootclasspath <path> | Overrides location of bootstrap class files |
| -cp <path><br>-classpath <path> | Sets search path for application classes and resources |
| -d <directory> | Specifies where to place generated class files |
| -deprecation | Output source locations where deprecated **Application Program Interfaces** (APIs) are used |
| -encoding <encoding> | Specify character encoding used by source files |
| -extdirs <dirs> | Override location of installed extensions |
| -g | Generates all debugging info |
| -g:{lines,vars,source} | Generates only some kinds of debugging information, specified by a comma-separated list of keywords: line number debugging information, local variable debugging information, or source file debugging information |
| -g:none | Generates no debugging info |
| -nowarn | Generates no warnings |
| -O | Turns on optimization, which may hinder debugging or enlarge class files (you must use an uppercase O) |
| -sourcepath <path> | Specifies where to find input source files |
| -target <release> | Generates class files for specific JVM version |
| -v<br>-verbose | Enables verbose output about what the compiler is doing and displays all the classes as they are loaded |

## Java Runtime Options

The Java interpreter comes with several options to include when you execute a Java program. After the word java, type a hyphen and then the keyword from Table D-2. For example, if you want the interpreter to display the version of the SDK that is being used, you can type java -version at the command prompt. The interpreter then would display the version of the Java virtual machine that is running on your system.

Table D-2 lists the Java runtime options and their descriptions.

| Table D-2 | Java Runtime Options |
|-----------|----------------------|
| OPTION | DESCRIPTION |
| -?<br>-help | Displays standard usage and help message |
| -cp <path><br>-classpath <path> | Sets search path for application classes and resources |
| -cs<br>-checksource | Checks to see if the source code is newer than its class file; if true, a new version is compiled |
| -D<name>=<value> | Sets a system property |
| -debug | Used with remote Java files that are to be debugged later |
| -noasyncgc | Turns off asynchronous garbage collection |
| -noclassgc | Disables class garbage collection |
| -noverify | Turns off class verification |
| -v<br>-verbose | Enables verbose output about what the compiler is doing; displays all the classes as they are loaded |
| -verbosegc | Displays a message each time garbage collection occurs |
| -verify | Verifies all class are loaded |
| -verifyremote | Verifies classes are imported or inherited (default setting) |
| -version | Displays product version |
| -X | Displays help on non-standard options (you must use an uppercase X) |

## The java.io Exceptions

The java.io package provides for system input and output through data streams, the file system, and **serialization**, which is the term used to send or receive complex objects through a stream. When you use the java.io package, you must use the words, throws IOException, in the method header to alert the compiler that input/output errors might occur. Although the compiler's thrown error messages are a clue to the encountered problem, documentation about the different exceptions is available on the Sun Microsystems Web site (see Appendix A).

Table D-3 summarizes the possible exceptions thrown by the java.io package.

## Table D-3   java.io Exceptions

| EXCEPTION | DESCRIPTION |
| --- | --- |
| CharConversionException | Throws for character conversion exceptions |
| EOFException | Throws when an end of file or end of stream has been reached unexpectedly during input |
| FileNotFoundException | Throws when an attempt to open the file at the specified pathname has failed |
| InterruptedIOException | Throws when an input/output operation has been interrupted |
| InvalidClassException | Throws when the serial version of the class does not match the class descriptor, the class contains unknown data types, or the class does not have an accessible no-arg constructor |
| InvalidObjectException | Throws when one or more deserialized objects failed validation tests |
| IOException | Throws when an unspecified input/out exception has occurred |
| NotActiveException | Throws when serialization or deserialization is not active |
| NotSerializableException | Throws when an instance is required to have a serializable interface |
| ObjectStreamException | Superclass of all exceptions specific to the object stream classes |
| OptionalDataException | Throws when unexpected data appeared in an ObjectInputStream trying to read an object |
| StreamCorruptedException | Throws when control information that was read from an object stream violates internal consistency checks |
| SyncFailedException | Constructs an SyncFailedException with a detail message |
| UnsupportedEncodingException | Character encoding is not supported |
| UTFDataFormatException | Signals that a malformed UTF-8 string, a method of storage using the least amount of space possible, has been read in a data input stream or by any class that implements the data input interface |

# Index

Abstract Window Toolkit (AWT), **J 1.34,** **J 3.44,** J 3.47
Access modifier, **J 1.15,** J 2.8
ActionEvents, J 3.44
ActionListener, **J 2.38,** J 2.40
  coding, J 2.46-48
ActionPerformed, J 2.46
Add method, J 3.49
addItemListener, **J 3.49**
Addition, precedence and, J 2.16
Algorithm, J I.8
Allocated, **J 2.8**
Analyzing problem, *see* Problem, analyzing
AND logical operator, **J 3.28**
Animation, J I.5
Answer, **J 1.16**
Applet(s), **J I.5, J 1.30**
  called from Web page, J 1.39-41
  color, J 3.49
  components, J 2.41, J 2.42-44
  converting program to, J 1.30, J 2.38-41
  displaying on desktop, J 1.4
  editing, J 1.34-35
  focus, J 3.49-50
  initializing, J 1.36, J 2.44-46, J 3.44
  interactive, J 2.51
  making decisions in, J 3.46-56
  running using Applet Viewer, J 1.41-42
  stub, J 3.44
  tags used to reference, J 1.39-41
  viewing in execution, J 1.39
Applet Viewer, **J I.6, J 1.4,** J 1.41-42
appletviewer command, **J 1.41-42**
Application, **J I.6**
  prototype, J I.19
Application program, J I.6
Application program interface (API), **J A.2**
Argument, **J 1.16,** J 1.17, J 2.18, **J 3.29**
  caption, J 2.41
  delimited, J 1.36
  graphics, J 1.36-38
  incorrect number of, J 1.23
  list, J 1.16
Arithmetic operators, J 2.14-15
Assignment statement, **J 2.13-14**
  constructor, J 2.26, J 2.41
Asterisk (*) wild card character, **J 2.41**
Attributes, **J I.16**
autoexec.bat file, path statement in, J 1.20
AWT, *see* Abstract Window Toolkit

Black box, **J I.14**
Blank lines, displaying, J 1.17
Block comment, **J 1.15**
Body of method, **J 1.17**
Boolean, **J 2.15,** J 3.22
Braces {}
  contents of class enclosed in, **J 1.16**
  lines of code enclosed in, J 1.17
Break reserved word, **J 3.35**
Break statement, **J 3.35**
Browser, **J I.5**
  calling methods, J 2.44
Buffer, **J 2.25**
BufferedReader, **J 2.26**
Buttons
  adding active, J 2.46
  clickable, J 2.44
  components, J 2.41
  option, J 3.47
Bytecode, **J I.6, J 1.19,** J 1.20, J 1.22, J 1.27
Bytecode files
  finding, J 3.11
  portable, J 1.32

Call, **J 3.29**
Call statement, matching method and, J 3.29
Calling methods, browser, J 2.44
Caption
  button, J 2.41
  check box, **J 3.47**
Careers, computer-related, J I.6, J C.1-3

Carriage return/line feed message, J 1.24
Case, **J 3.34**
Case control structure, **J I.11,** J 3.34
Case reserved word, **J 3.35**
Case statement **J 3.35**
Case-sensitive, **J 1.16,** J 1.18, J 2.10
Cast, **J 2.9**
Catch block, **J 3.13,** J 3.15-17, J 3.20, J 3.21, J 3.24, J 3.46
Catch reserved word, **J 3.13**
Catch statement, **J 3.13**
Catch the exception, J 3.12
Certification, Java, J C.1-3
Check box(es)
  grouped, J 3.47
  user choices and, J 3.46-56
Checkbox method, **J 3.47**
CheckboxGroup, **J 3.47**
Checked exceptions, J 3.14
Class(es), **J I.14**
  access modifier, J 1.15
  collections of, J 1.32
  extending, J 1.34-35
  instance, J I.14
  loading, J 1.33
  Math, J 2.16
  text field, J 2.41
  wrapper, J 2.9
Class header, changing program name in, J 1.34, J 1.35, J 2.40
Class name, **J 1.15,** J 2.8, J 2.40
  file name matching, J 1.16, J 2.35
Class providers, **J I.19**
Class users, **J I.19**
Class variables, J 2.25
Closing Notepad, J 1.29
Code
  byte-, *see* Bytecode
  debugging, *see* Debugging
  enclosing in braces, J 1.17
  ending lines of, with semicolon (;), J 1.17
  output, J 2.20-21
  source, *see* Source code
Coding convention, **J 2.42**
Coding program, J I.7, J 1.6, J 1.14-19, J 2.5, J 3.6
  ActionListener, J 2.46-48
  init method, J 2.44-46
  sample data used for, J 2.13
  user-defined methods, J 3.28-36
Color, adding to applet, **J 3.49**
Command, repeating, J 2.24
Command buttons, J 2.41
Command line, J 1.4
Command prompt, **J 1.9**
Command prompt window, J 1.7
  formatting, J 1.11-13
  opening, J 1.9-10
Commas, delimiting multiple arguments using, J 1.36
Comments, **J 1.14,** J 2.7
  block, J 1.15
  line, J 1.15
Comparative operators, J 3.23
Comparison operators, **J 2.15-16**
Compiler, **J I.6,** J 1.6, **J 1.19**
  Java 2 SDK, J A.1
  javac, J 1.6, J 1.20-22
  options, J D.1
Compile-time exception, **J 3.12**
Compiling program, J I.7, J 1.6, J 1.19-22, J 1.27, J 2.23
  after editing, J 1.27-28
  errors and, J 1.22, J 3.11
Components, **J 3.11**
  adding, J 3.49
  focus, J 3.49
  modularity, J 3.11
  states, J 3.47
Computer, programming, J I.6
Concatenation, **J 2.19**
Conditions, **J 3.22**
  If...Then...Else structure, J 3.21, J 3.46

Console mode, **J I.6, J 1.4**
Constant, **J 2.9**
Constructor, **J 2.26,** J 2.41, J 2.43
Container method, **J 2.44-46**
Control structures, **J I.10-12,** J 3.20-28, J 3.37-41, J I.11
  nested, J 3.36
Correct algorithm, **J I.8**

Data, **J 2.8**
  sample, J 2.12-13
  storing, J 2.8-12
  streams, J 2.25
  user input, J 2.24-34
  validity check, J 3.21
Data abstraction, J I.14
  implementation of, J I.18
Data manipulation, using methods, J 2.4-54
Data types, **J 1.17, J 2.9**
  concatenation, J 2.19
  constructor specifying, J 2.26, J 2.41
  correct, J 3.21
Debugging, **J 1.22-23**
Decimal results, J 2.15
  converting, J 3.18, J 3.20
Decision control structure, J 3.21, J 3.46
Decisions, making, J 3.21, J 3.46-56
Declaration, **J 2.9**
  field, J 2.10
  variable, **J 2.10,** J 2.12, J 2.30
Declaration statement, **J 2.8,** J 2.10, J 2.30
Declaration syntax, J 2.10
Declaring, **J 2.9**
  variable, **J 2.10,** J 2.12, J 2.30
Default reserved word, **J 3.35**
Delimited, **J 1.36**
Designing program, *see* Program design
Desktop
  command prompt window on, J 1.9-13
  displaying applet on, J 1.4
  setting up, J 1.7-13, J 2.6
Development tools, J 1.4
Displaying
  applet on desktop, J 1.4
  applet using HTML file, J 1.40-41
  blank lines, J 1.17
  toolbar, for command prompt window, J 1.13
Division
  integer, J 2.14
  modular, J 2.14
  precedence and, J 2.16
Do...Until loop, **J I.12**
Do...While loop, J 3.38-41, **J I.12**
Documentation, J I.7, J 1.5, **J 1.14-15**
  changing program name in, J 1.34, J 1.35
  Java 2 SDK, J A.2
DOS path, setting, J 1.20
Downloading Java 2 SDK, J A.1-2
DrawString method, **J 1.36**

Editing
  applet, J 1.34-35
  source code, J 1.7, J 1.24-26, J 1.33-36
  user, in text fields, J 3.53
Efficient algorithm, **J I.8**
Else reserved word, **J 3.22,** J 3.23
Encapsulation, **J I.18**
End tag, **J 1.39**
End user, **J I.19**
Equality operators, **J 2.16,** J 3.23
Errors
  compile, J 3.11
  run, J 3.11, J 3.12
  run-time, J 1.23
  semantic, J 1.23
  syntax, J 1.22-23
  throwing, J 3.9, J 3.12, J D.2
  user input, J 3.12-18
Escape characters, formatting output using, J 1.24-25
Event, **J I.15**
Event diagrams, **J I.15**

Event-driven, J I.15
Exams, certification, J C.1-2
Exceptions, **J 3.12**
  checked, **J** 3.14
  compile-time, J 3.12
  explicitly cause, J 3.13, J 3.14
  handling, **J 3.12**-18
  java.io, J D.2-3
  multiple, J 3.14
  number format, J 3.12, J 3.24
  run-time, J 3.12
  testing for, J 3.18-21
  unchecked, J 3.12, J 3.14
Executable files, J 1.19, J 1.20
Execute program, **J 1.9**
  exeception testing, J 3.18-21
  interactive program, J 2.35-37
  viewing applet and, J 1.39
Explicit cast, J 2.9
Explicit extension, J 2.23
Explicitly cause an exception, **J 3.13**, J 3.14
Extend the class, **J** 1.34-35

F3 (repeating commands), J 2.24
Field
  text, J 2.41
  text, user editing in, J 3.53
Field declarations, J 2.10
File(s)
  autoexec.bat, J 1.20
  default type, J 2.23
  executable, J 1.19, J 1.20
  HTML, J 1.40-41
  managing, J 2.53
  opening source code, J 1.30-32
  saving, J 1.16, J 1.18, J 1.27, J 2.35
  text, J 1.7, J 1.18
File extension, J 1.19, J 1.32
  explicit, J 2.23
File menu (Notepad)
  New command, J 1.40
  Open command, J 1.31
  Print command, J 1.28
  Save As command, J 1.18
  Save command, J 1.27
File names, J 2.23, J 2.27
  changing program name in, J 1.34, J 1.37
  class name matching, J 1.16, J 2.35
  errors, J 1.23
  saving file and, J 1.16, J 1.27
Finally reserved word, **J 3.14**
Finding
  bytecode file, J 3.11
  compiler, J 1.22
Flag, testing against, J 3.37
Flowchart, **J I.9**, J 1.6, J 2.5
  symbols, **J** I.9
Focus, adding to applet, J 3.49-50
Font, command prompt window and, J 1.12
Formalizing the solution, J I.7, J 1.6, J 2.6, J 3.6
Format, illegal number, J 3.12
Formatting
  command prompt window, J 1.11-13
  output using escape characters, J 1.24-25
Formula, **J 2.16**-17

Generalization hierarchy, **J I.14**
getText method, **J 2.46**
Graphical user interface (GUI), J I.10, **J** 1.4
  components, J 2.44
Graphics, demo applets that display, J 1.36
Graphics argument, J 1.36-38
Group name, **J 3.47**
Grouped check box, **J 3.47**
GUI-based, **J A.2**

Handler, **J 3.12**
Hierarchical input process (HIPO) chart, **J I.8**
Hierarchy chart, **J I.8**
High-level languages, J I.5
Host, **J 1.39**-42
HTML host documents, J 1.39
  creating, J 1.40-41, J 2.50-51, J 3.43
Hypertext markup language (HTML), **J I.5,**
  **J** 1.4

IDE, *see* Integrated Development Environment
Identifiers, **J 1.16**, J 2.9-10, J 2.29
  boolean variables, J 2.15
  catch block, **J 3.13**
  check box, J 3.47
  data type, J 1.17
  declaring multiple, J 2.10
  illegal, J 2.10
  legal, J 2.10
  scope of, J 2.13
  user-defined method, J 3.34
If reserved word, **J 3.22**, J 3.23
If statement, **J 3.21**-28
  reasonableness check with, J 3.24-27
If...Then...Else structure, J 3.20-28, **J I.11**
Implementation, J I.14
Implicit casting, J 2.9
Import command, **J 1.33**, J 1.34
Import statements, **J 2.41**, J 3.10
Importing packages, J 1.32-34
Indentation, J 1.18, J 2.8
Information hiding, **J I.18**
Inheritance, **J I.18**
Init method, **J 1.36**, J 3.45
  applet, **J 3.44**
  coding, J 2.44-46
Input, *see* User input
Input buffer, J 2.25
InputStreamReader (ISR), **J 2.25**
Insertion point, keeping on same line, J 1.24
Installing Java, J A.1-4
Instance, **J I.14**, **J 1.16**, J 1.36, J 2.41
Instantiation, **J 2.26**
Integer, J 2.9
  promoting, J 2.15
Integer division, **J 2.14**
Integrated Development Environment (IDE),
  **J I.6, J A.2**
Interactive programs, J I.5, **J 2.25**
  applets, J 2.51
  executing, J 2.35-37
Interactive toolbars, J I.14
Interface Development Environments (IDEs),
  **J** 1.4
Interface handler, J 2.38
Interpreter, **J I.6**, J 1.6, J 1.19, **J 1.24**
ItemListener, **J 3.44**
Iteration, **J 3.37**, **J I.12**

J++, J 1.4
Java, **J I.5**
  data types, J 2.9
  history of, J I.5
  installing, J A.1-4
java.applet package, J 2.38, **J 3.44**
java.awt package, J 2.38, J 2.46, **J 3.44**
java.awt.event package, **J 3.44**
Java 2 Runtime Environment, J I.6
Java 2 Standard Development Kit (SDK), J I.6,
  **J 1.19**-20, **J A.1**
  documentation, J A.2
  downloading, J A.1-2
  system location, J 1.22
Java certification, J C.1-3
Java Development Kit, J I.6
  downloading, J A.1-2
  packages, J 1.32-33
Java Factory, J I.19
java file extension, J 1.19, J 1.32
Java interpreter, J 1.6, J 1.19
java.io, J 3.9, J D.2-3
java.lang package, J 1.33, J 2.16
Java program, creating, J 1.4-43
Java programming, introduction to, J I.4-20
Java Virtual Machine (JVM), **J I.6**, J 1.19
Javac compiler, J 1.6, **J 1.20**-22
  finding, J 1.22
  options, J D.1
JavaScript, **J I.5**
JBuilder 3 program, J I.6, J 1.4, J 1.20-21
  installing, J A.2-4

Keyboard input, J 2.25
Keywords, reserved, J B.1

Label, **J 2.41**, J 2.42-44
Label components, J 2.41, J 2.44
Libraries, J 1.32
Line comment, **J 1.15**
Lines, displaying blank, J 1.17
List, **J 1.9**
Literal, **J 1.17**
Loading classes, J 1.33
Logic, debugging, J 1.22
Logical operators, J 3.23, J 3.28
Looping, **J 3.37-41**, **J I.12**

Main method, **J 1.16**, J 1.36
  header, J 2.8
Maintaining program, J I.7, J 1.6, J 2.6, J 3.6
Math class, **J 2.16**
Mathematical operators , J 2.14-15
  incorrect use of, J 1.23
Menu bar, J I.14
Menu selection, testing user input, J 3.28-36
Message, **J I.15**
Method, **J I.15**, **J 3.28**
  ActionListener, J 2.38, J 2.40, J 2.46-48
  ActionPerformed, J 2.46
  add, J 3.49
  body of, J 1.17
  Checkbox, J 3.47
  container, J 2.44-46
  creating user-defined, J 3.28-36
  data manipulation using, J 2.4-54
  default, J 1.36
  drawString, J 1.36
  getText, J 2.46
  init, J 1.36, J 2.44-46, J 3.45
  invoking, J 2.18
  main, *see* Main method
  Math class, J 2.16
  paint, J 1.36
  parse, J 2.9, J 2.29, J 2.32, J 3.30
  parts, J 1.16
  print, J 1.24
  println, J 1.17, J 1.24
  readLine, J 2.29
  requestFocus, J 3.49
  scope of, J 3.34
  setBackground, J 3.49
  setForeground, J 3.49
  setText, J 2.46
  using in output, J 2.19-20
Method header, **J 1.16**, J 2.8, J 3.32
Method modifiers, **J 1.16**
Method name, J 1.16
Methodology, **J I.7**
Microsoft Word, writing code using, J 1.7
Modular division, **J 2.14**
Modularity, J I.8, J I.10, **J 3.11**
Modules, J I.8, J I.10, J 3.11
Modulus operator, J 2.14
MS-DOS Prompt window, J 1.7, J 1.9-13
  closing, J 1.29
Multiplication, precedence and, J 2.16

Name
  class, J 1.15
  file, *see* File name
  identifier, J 2.9
  method, J 1.16
Naming convention, **J 2.41**-42
Nested control structure, **J I.12**, **J 3.36**
Netscape, J I.5
New command (Notepad File menu), J 1.40
New keyword, J 3.24
NOT logical operator, **J 3.28**
Notepad
  closing, J 1.29
  starting, J 1.7-8, J 1.30, J 2.6, J 2.7
  wordwrap in, J 2.49
Number, storing, J 2.12
Number format exception, J 3.12, J 3.24

Object, J I.12, **J I.14**
  attributes, *see* Attributes
  component, J 2.41, J 2.42-44
  declaration, J 2.8, J 2.10
  instance, J I.14

message, *see* Message
pre-built, J I.19
Object exception, **J 3.12**
Object-oriented, **J I.12-19**
Object-Oriented Analysis and Design (OOAD),
  **J I.12**
Object-oriented language, J I.4, J I.5, J I.12-19
Object-Oriented Programming (OOP), **J I.12**
  benefits of, J I.19
  philosophy of, J I.17
  terminology, J I.14-17
Object structure diagram, **J I.16**
Open command (Notepad File menu), J 1.31
Opening
  command prompt window, J 1.9-10
  source code files, J 1.30-32
Operation, **J I.15**
Operators
  arithmetic, J 2.14-15
  comparative, J 3.23
  comparison, J 2.15-16
  equality, J 2.16, J 3.23
  logical, J 3.23, J 3.28
  mathematical, J 1.23, J 2.14-15
  overloading, J 2.16
  relational, J 2.16, J 3.23
  types of, J 2.15
Option button, J 3.47
Options
  compiler, J D.1
  runtime, J D.2
OR logical operator, **J 3.28**
Out object, J 1.17
Output, J 2.18-21
  formatting using es cape characters, J 1.24-25
  to Web window, J 1.32-34
  using methods in, J 2.19-20
  using variables in, J 2.19
Output device, J 1.17
Overloading operator, J 2.16

Packages, **J 1.32**
  importing, J 1.32-34
Paint method, **J 1.36**
Parentheses, operation precedence and, J 2.16
Parse method, J 2.9, **J 2.29**, J 2.32, J 3.30
Parsimonious, **J I.5**
Path command, **J 1.20**
Pixel, **J 1.41**
Platform-independent, J I.4, **J I.6**
Polymorphism, **J I.18-19**
Portability, **J I.6**
Precedence, **J 2.16**
Precision, storing number and, **J 2.12**
Primitive data types, **J 2.9**
Print command (Notepad File menu), J 1.28
Print method, **J 1.24**
Printing source code, J 1.28-29
Println, J 1.17
  escape characters added to, J 1.24-25
  identifier inside, J 2.19
Problem, analyzing, J I.7, J 1.5, J 2.4
Procedures, **J I.10**
Program, **J I.5, J 1.14**
  coding, *see* Coding program
  compiling, *see* Compiling program
  interactive, **J 2.25**
  maintaining, *see* Maintaining program
  moving to Web, J 1.30-39, J 2.38-50, J 3.43-46
  stand-alone, **J I.6**
  starting new, J 2.6-8
  stubs, J 3.9, J 3.10, J 3.11
  testing, *see* Testing program
Program design, J I.7, J 1.5-6, J 2.5, 6
Program development life cycle (PDLC), **J I.7,**
  **J 1.5-6**
Program name, changing, J 1.34
Programming
  conventions, J 2.41-42
  structured, J I.8-12
Programming languages, **J I.5**
  object-oriented, J I.12-19
  structured, J I.8
Promotes the integers, **J 2.15**

Properties command (shortcut menu), command
  prompt window, J 1.12
Prototype, **J I.19**
Pseudocode, **J I.8**
Punctuation errors, J 1.22, J 1.23

Range check, **J 3.28**
Rapid application development (RAD), **J I.19**
readLine method, **J 2.29**
Reasonableness check, **J 3.24-27**
Reference variables, J 2.10
Relational operators, **J 2.16**, J 3.23
Remainder operator, J 2.14
Repeating commands, J 2.24
Repetition control structure, **J 3.37-41, J I.11**
RequestFocus method, **J 3.49**
Reserved keywords, J B.1
Return statement, **J 3.29**
Return value, J 1.16
Robust, **J I.5**
Run command (Windows Start menu), J 1.9
Running applet, using Applet Viewer, J 1.41-42
Running program, **J 1.9**, J 1.24, J 1.27-28,
  J 2.23-24
  errors, J 1.23, J 3.11
  interactive applets, J 2.51
  interactive program, J 2.35-36
Run-time errors, **J 1.23**
Run-time exception, **J 3.12**
Run-time options, J D.2
Run-time system, **J I.6**
  Java 2 SDK, J A.1

Sample data, testing program using, **J 2.12-13**
Save As command (Notepad File menu), J 1.18
Save command (Notepad File menu), J 1.27
Saving
  file, J 1.16, J 1.18, J 1.27, J 2.35
  source code, J 1.18-19, J 1.27
  text file, J 1.7, J 1.18
Scope, **J 3.34**
Screen
  output on, J 2.18
  printing literal text on, J 1.17
  resolution, J 1.41
Screen tab, command prompt window, J 1.12-13
Scripting tool, J I.5
Secure, **J I.5**
Selection control structure, **J I.11**
Semantic errors, **J 1.23**
Semicolon (;)
  lines of code ending with, J 1.17
  missing, J 1.23
Sequence control structure, **J I.10-11**
Serialization, **J D.2**
SetBackground method, **J 3.49**
SetForeground method, **J 3.49**
setText method, **J 2.46**
Simula, **J I.13**
Single-entry, single-exit, **J I.10**
Solution, formalizing, *see* Formalizing the
  solution
Source code, J 1.6, **J 1.14**
  editing, J 1.7, J 1.24-26, J 1.33-36
  entering, J 1.17-18
  opening files, J 1.30-32
  printing, J 1.28-29
  saving, J 1.18-19, J 1.27
Spacing, in syntax, J 3.23
Spelling errors, J 1.23
Stand-alone mode, **J 1.4**
Stand-alone programs, **J I.6**
Start menu (Windows), Run command, J 1.9
Start tag, **J 1.39**
Starting
  new program, J 2.6-8
  Notepad, J 1.7-8, J 1.30, J 2.6, J 2.7
State, check box, J 3.47
Storage location, data, J 2.8-12
Storyboard, **J I.10**
Streams, **J 2.25**
String of characters, method's argument as,
  J 1.17
Strongly typed language, J I.5, **J 2.9**
Structured programming, J I.8-12

Stubs, **J 3.9.** J 3.10, J 3.11
  applet, J 3.44
  getCost method, J 3.32
Subclasses, **J I.14,** J I.18
Subclassing, **J I.18**
Subtraction, precedence and, J 2.16
Sun Microsystems, J I.5, J I.6, J I.19, J A.1
Superclasses, **J I.14**
Switch reserved word, **J 3.35**
Switch statement, **J 3.35-36**
Syntax, **J I.5, J 1.4**
  declaration, J 2.10
  spacing in, J 3.23
Syntax errors, **J 1.22-23**
System.err, J 2.25
System.in, J 2.25
System.out device, J 1.17, J 2.19, J 2.25

Tags, **J 1.39-41**
  end, J 1.39
  start, J 1.39
  width and height attributes, J 1.41
Test data, J 2.12-13
Testing program, J I.7, J 1.6, J 1.19-22, J 2.5,
  J 2.5, J 3.6
  against flag, J 3.37
  check box grouping, J 3.51
  for exceptions, J 3.18-21
  getCost method, J 3.33
  partial programs, J 3.18-21
  sample data used for, J 2.12-13
  switch structure, J 3.36-37
  user input, J 3.28-36
  while structure, J 3.41
Text boxes, J 2.44
Text editor, J 1.4, J 1.7
Text field, **J 2.41**
  user editing in, J 3.53
Text files, J 1.7, J 1.18
Throw new, **J 3.13, J 3.14**
Throw statement, J 3.24
Thrown error messages, J 3.9, J D.2
Throws error, **J 3.12**
Throws exception, **J 3.12-18**
Throws IOException, **J 2.29**, J 3.9, J 3.12
Toolbar
  command prompt window, J 1.13
  creating, J I.14
Top-down chart, **J I.8**
Transparent, **J I.18**
Trigger, **J I.15**
Try and catch construct, **J 3.13**
Try block, **J 3.13**, J 3.15-17, J 3.46
Try reserved word, **J 3.13**
Try statement, **J 3.13**
txt file extension, J 1.19, J 1.32, J 2.23

Unchecked exceptions, **J 3.12**, J 3.14
User choices, check boxes for, J 3.46-56
User-defined methods, J 3.28-36
User editing, in text fields, J 3.53
User input, J 2.24-34, J 3.9-10
  errors, J 3.12-18
  testing, J 3.28-36
User interface, **J 1.4**
  creating, J 1.5

Validity checks, data, J 3.21
Variables, **J 2.9**
  boolean, J 2.15
  declaring, J 2.10, J 2.12
  reference, J 2.10
  streams, J 2.25
  using in output, J 2.19
Viewing applet, in execution, J 1.39

Web, J I.4, J I.6
  moving program to, J 1.30-39, J 2.38-50,
  J 3.43-46
Web browser, *see* Browser
Web page, applet called from, J 1.39-41
Wordwrap, in Notepad, J 2.49
Wrap, **J 2.25**
Wrapper class, J 2.9

# INTERNATIONAL LICENSE AGREEMENT FOR EVALUATION OF PROGRAMS

## Part 1 - General Terms

PLEASE READ THIS AGREEMENT CAREFULLY BEFORE USING THE PROGRAM. IBM WILL LICENSE THE PROGRAM TO YOU ONLY IF YOU FIRST ACCEPT THE TERMS OF THIS AGREEMENT. BY USING THE PROGRAM YOU AGREE TO THESE TERMS. IF YOU DO NOT AGREE TO THE TERMS OF THIS AGREEMENT, PROMPTLY RETURN THE UNUSED PROGRAM TO IBM.

The Program is owned by International Business Machines Corporation or one of its subsidiaries (IBM) or an IBM supplier, and is copyrighted and licensed, not sold.

The term "Program" means the original program and all whole or partial copies of it. A Program consists of machine-readable instructions, its components, data, audio-visual content (such as images, text, recordings, or pictures), and related licensed materials.

**This Agreement includes Part 1 - General Terms and Part 2 - Country-unique Terms and is the complete agreement regarding the use of this Program, and replaces any prior oral or written communications between you and IBM. The terms of Part 2 may replace or modify those of Part 1.**

## 1. License

## Use of the Program

IBM grants you a nonexclusive, nontransferable license to use the Program.

You may 1) use the Program only for internal evaluation, testing or demonstration purposes, on a trial or "try-and-buy" basis and 2) make and install a reasonable number of copies of the Program in support of such use, unless IBM identifies a specific number of copies in the documentation accompanying the Program. The terms of this license apply to each copy you make. You will reproduce the copyright notice and any other legends of ownership on each copy, or partial copy, of the Program.

You will 1) maintain a record of all copies of the Program and 2) ensure that anyone who uses the Program does so only for your authorized use and in compliance with the terms of this Agreement.

You may not 1) use, copy, modify or distribute the Program except as provided in this Agreement; 2) reverse assemble, reverse compile, or otherwise translate the Program except as specifically permitted by law without the possibility of contractual waiver; or 3) sublicense, rent, or lease the Program.

This license begins with your first use of the Program and ends on the termination of this license in accordance with the terms of this Agreement. You will destroy the Program and all copies made of it within ten days of when this license ends.

## 2. No Warranty

SUBJECT TO ANY STATUTORY WARRANTIES WHICH CANNOT BE EXCLUDED, IBM MAKES NO WARRANTIES OR CONDITIONS EITHER EXPRESS OR IMPLIED, INCLUDING WITHOUT LIMITATION, THE WARRANTY OF NON-INFRINGEMENT AND THE IMPLIED WARRANTIES OF MERCHANTABILITY AND FITNESS FOR A PARTICULAR PUR-POSE, REGARDING THE PROGRAM OR TECHNICAL SUPPORT, IF ANY. IBM MAKES NO WARRANTY REGARDING THE CAPABILITY OF THE PROGRAM TO CORRECTLY PROCESS, PROVIDE AND/OR RECEIVE DATE DATA WITHIN AND BETWEEN THE 20TH AND 21ST CENTURIES.

This exclusion also applies to any of IBM's subcontractors, suppliers or program developers (collectively called "Suppliers").

Manufacturers, suppliers, or publishers of non-IBM Programs may provide their own warranties.

## 3. Limitation of Liability

NEITHER IBM NOR ITS SUPPLIERS ARE LIABLE FOR ANY DIRECT OR INDIRECT DAMAGES, INCLUDING WITHOUT LIMITATION, LOST PROFITS, LOST SAVINGS, OR ANY INCIDENTAL, SPECIAL, OR OTHER ECONOMIC CONSE-QUENTIAL DAMAGES, EVEN IF IBM IS INFORMED OF THEIR POSSIBILITY. SOME JURISDICTIONS DO NOT ALLOW THE EXCLUSION OR LIMITATION OF INCIDENTAL OR CONSEQUENTIAL DAMAGES, SO THE ABOVE EXCLUSION OR LIMITATION MAY NOT APPLY TO YOU.

## 4. General

Nothing in this Agreement affects any statutory rights of consumers that cannot be waived or limited by contract.

IBM may terminate your license if you fail to comply with the terms of this Agreement. If IBM does so, you must immediately destroy the Program and all copies you made of it.

You may not export the Program.

Neither you nor IBM will bring a legal action under this Agreement more than two years after the cause of action arose unless otherwise provided by local law without the possibility of contractual waiver or limitation.

Neither you nor IBM is responsible for failure to fulfill any obligations due to causes beyond its control.

There is no additional charge for use of the Program for the duration of this license.

IBM does not provide program services or technical support, unless IBM specifies otherwise.

The laws of the country in which you acquire the Program govern this Agreement, except 1) in Australia, the laws of the State or Territory in which the transaction is performed govern this Agreement; 2) in Albania, Armenia, Belarus, Bosnia/Herzegovina, Bulgaria, Croatia, Czech Republic, Georgia, Hungary, Kazakhstan, Kirghizia, Former Yugoslav Republic of Macedonia (FYROM), Moldova, Poland, Romania, Russia, Slovak Republic, Slovenia, Ukraine, and Federal Republic of Yugoslavia, the laws of Austria govern this Agreement; 3) in the United Kingdom, all disputes relating to this Agreement will be governed by English Law and

will be submitted to the exclusive jurisdiction of the English courts; 4) in Canada, the laws in the Province of Ontario govern this Agreement; and 5) in the United States and Puerto Rico, and People's Republic of China, the laws of the State of New York govern this Agreement.

## Part 2 - Country-unique Terms

### AUSTRALIA:

No Warranty (Section 2): The following paragraph is added to this Section: Although IBM specifies that there are no warranties, you may have certain rights under the Trade Practices Act 1974 or other legislation and are only limited to the extent permitted by the applicable legislation.

Limitation of Liability (Section 3): The following paragraph is added to this Section: Where IBM is in breach of a condition or warranty implied by the Trade Practices Act 1974, IBM's liability is limited to the repair or replacement of the goods, or the supply of equivalent goods. Where that condition or warranty relates to right to sell, quiet possession or clear title, or the goods are of a kind ordinarily acquired for personal, domestic or household use or consumption, then none of the limitations in this paragraph apply.

### GERMANY:

No Warranty (Section 2): The following paragraphs are added to this Section: The minimum warranty period for Programs is six months.

In case a Program is delivered without Specifications, we will only warrant that the Program information correctly describes the Program and that the Program can be used according to the Program information. You have to check the usability according to the Program information within the "money-back guaranty" period. Limitation of Liability (Section 3): The following paragraph is added to this Section: The limitations and exclusions specified in the Agreement will not apply to damages caused by IBM with fraud or gross negligence, and for express warranty.

### INDIA:

General (Section 4): The following replaces the fourth paragraph of this Section: If no suit or other legal action is brought, within two years after the cause of action arose, in respect of any claim that either party may have against the other, the rights of the concerned party in respect of such claim will be forfeited and the other party will stand released from its obligations in respect of such claim.

### IRELAND:

No Warranty (Section 2): The following paragraph is added to this Section: Except as expressly provided in these terms and conditions, all statutory conditions, including all warranties implied, but without prejudice to the generality of the foregoing, all warranties implied by the Sale of Goods Act 1893 or the Sale of Goods and Supply of Services Act 1980 are hereby excluded.

### ITALY:

Limitation of Liability (Section 3): This Section is replaced by the following: Unless otherwise provided by mandatory law, IBM is not liable for any damages which might arise.

### NEW ZEALAND:

No Warranty (Section 2): The following paragraph is added to this Section: Although IBM specifies that there are no warranties, you may have certain rights under the Consumer Guarantees Act 1993 or other legislation which cannot be excluded or limited. The Consumer Guarantees Act 1993 will not apply in respect of any goods or services which IBM provides, if you require the goods and services for the purposes of a business as defined in that Act. Limitation of Liability (Section 3): The following paragraph is added to this Section: Where Programs are not acquired for the purposes of a business as defined in the Consumer Guarantees Act 1993, the limitations in this Section are subject to the limitations in that Act.

### UNITED KINGDOM:

Limitation of Liability (Section 3): The following paragraph is added to this Section at the end of the first paragraph: The limitation of liability will not apply to any breach of IBM's obligations implied by Section 12 of the Sales of Goods Act 1979 or Section 2 of the Supply of Goods and Services Act 1982.